PROCEEDINGS OF TH

1ST

EUROPEAN CONFERENCE

ON

RAPID PROTOTYPING

EDITED BY DR P M DICKENS

THE UNIVERSITY OF NOTTINGHAM

6TH - 7TH JULY 1992

Organising Committee :-

Dr. P.M. Dickens (Conference Chairman)
Dr. R.C. Cobb
Dr. I. Gibson
Prof. U. Menon
Dr. M.S. Pridham

ISBN 0 9519759 0 0
Printed and bound by Quorn Litho, Loughborough, Leicestershire.

Contents

Stereolithography Resins and Systems Accuracy

Rapid Prototyping Benchmarking and Accuracy

CAD for Rapid Prototyping and User Experiences

FOREWORD

Dr. Philip M. Dickens
Conference Chairman

(Leader of the Rapid Prototyping Research Group)

Department of Manufacturing Engineering
and
Operations Management

UNIVERSITY OF NOTTINGHAM

Rapid Prototying is a relatively new subject which has already shown great potential for reducing lead times for new products and reducing design manufacturing and tooling costs.

The majority of Rapid Prototyping systems have originated in the U.S.A. and so companies across the Atlantic have gained a head start in this subject. This is highlighted by the number of papers from the U.S.A. in these proceedings. However, European companies are catching up quickly (see the paper from Rover) and are determined to extract maximum benefit from this new and exciting technology. The potential yet to be tapped is vast!

In editing these proceedings I have raced against the clock to try and make all papers conform to a common format. However, because of the mix of papers from the U.S.A and Europe some papers are in metric while others use imperial units, the most likely cause of confusion may arise from the term 'mils'. This word is used in the U.S.A. to denote thousands of an inch, whereas here in the U.K. it is used for millimetres! I have tried to eliminate 'mils' where possible but I beg your forgiveness for those I have missed.

It will all be easier when the U.S.A. goes 'metric'. We may also be able to get them to drive on the correct side of the road!

Dr. P.M. Dickens.

FUNDAMENTALS OF STEREOLITHOGRAPHY

Dr Paul F Jacobs
Director of Research & Development

3D Systems, Inc.
Valencia, California

1   Introduction

It has only been a little over four years since the introduction of the first Stereolithography systems, the SLA-1. From early 1988 until June 1992 over 300 SLA-1, SLA-250, SLA-190 and SLA-500 units have been sold by 3D Systems. These machines, currently operating in 20 countries on five continents, amount to about 90 percent of all the rapid prototyping systems now in use.

Notwithstanding these figures, the field of rapid prototyping is still quite young. The author has been surprised to note that even among existing users, knowledge of the most basic relationships of this new technology is at best uncertain. For newcomers, even less is known.

It is therefore appropriate, on the occasion of the First European Conference on Rapid Prototyping, for us to develop those fundamental relationships which form the foundation of this technology. In the transition of StereoLithography from an art to a science, it is natural that we should attempt to develop a model of the process. Although the mathematics may seem formidable to some readers, the physical model is actually quite simple. While requiring only <u>three</u> key assumptions, we shall derive <u>seven</u> fundamental relationships, leading to <u>nineteen</u> important conclusions.

The interaction of actinic photons with reactive photopolymer involves some very complex physics and chemistry. Nonetheless, the theoretical predications of the model described herein are in good agreement with numerous experimental measurements, at least to first order. The primary benefit of this analysis is the development of a good physical understanding of the basic phenomena. This description avoids the extreme complexity and inevitable loss of generality that would likely result from either analytical or numerical attempts at an even more accurate model. While advanced studies continue, it was felt that the material presented is certainly appropriate at the operational level.

2   Gaussian Laser Scanning

Consider an actinic laser beam being scanned in a straight line, at constant velocity, over the free surface of a vat of liquid photopolymer. We shall make three key assumptions:

1. The photopolymer resin obeys the Beer-Lambert law of exponential absorption.

2. The laser irradiance distribution is Gaussian.

3. The resin transitions from the liquid phase to the solid phase at the so-called "gel point".

Let us now define a coordinate system as shown in Figure 1. Here the laser is scanned directly along the x axis, in the direction of increasing x. The y coordinate is laterally orthogonal to the laser scan axis, with positive y defined by the right hand rule. Thus, y = 0 directly under the centerline of the laser scan axis. Finally, the positive z coordinate extends downward into the resin, and is measured normal to the x-y plane of the free resin surface, where z = 0. To define the origin, consider some arbitrary point Q(x,y,z) within the resin. Let Q'(0,y,0) be the project of Q onto the resin surface. We shall arbitrarily select the origin such that both the x and z coordinates of Q' are zero.

From the Beer-Lambert law (Reference 1),

$$H(x,y,z) = H(x,y,0) \exp[-z/Dp] \qquad (1)$$

Where H (x,y,z) is the irradiance at any arbitrary point, H (x,y,0) is the surface irradiance at any point x,y,0, and Dp is the "Penetration Depth" of the resin at the laser wavelength. Dp is defined as that depth of resin which will reduce the irradiance to 1/e (about 37%) of the surface irradiance.

Further, if we assume that the laser irradiance distribution is Gaussian (as seen in Figure 2, this is generally a reasonably good approximation), then from Reference 2,

$$H(x,y,0) = H(r,0) = Ho \exp[-2 r^2/Wo^2] \qquad (2)$$

Where Wo is the radius of the Gaussian beam, defined per Reference 2 at the $1/e^2$ point (i.e. at that location where irradiance equals about 13.5 percent of the peak irradiance, Ho). Note that since the Gaussian function is circulatory symmetric, it is also convenient to perform some of the calculations in cylindrical coordinates.

3   Total Laser Power

To determine Ho, we recognize that the total laser power incident on the resin surface, P_L, must equal the integral for the laser irradiance distribution over the entire resin surface (i.e. from r = 0 to r = ∞). Thus,

$$P = \int_0^\infty H(r,0) \, 2\pi \, r dr$$

$$\qquad (3)$$

$$= 2\pi \, Ho \int_0^\infty \exp[-2r^2/Wo^2] \, r dr$$

Define $u = 2r^2/Wo^2$ or $rdr = (Wo^2/4) \, du$ (4)

3

Substituting equation (4) into equation (3),

$$P_L = \frac{\pi}{2} Wo^2 Ho \int_o^\infty \exp [-u] \, du = \frac{\pi}{2} Wo^2 Ho$$

(5)

Solving for the peak irradiance at the free resin surface, Ho, we obtain the result,

$$Ho = 2 P_L \pi Wo^2$$

(6)

Substituting this result into equation (2), and then into equation (1), we obtain the Gaussian laser irradiance distribution function in cylindrical coordinates,

$$H (r,z) = (2 P_L / \pi Wo^2) \exp [- z / Dp - 2r^2 / Wo^2]$$

(7)

4   The Exposure Function

For Stereolithography photopolymers, the extent of reaction depends upon the number of actinic photons absorbed per unit volume. This quantity can be shown to be directly proportional to the actinic exposure, E, which has the units of energy per unit area (e.g. millijoules per square centimetre). By definition, the actinic exposure is the time integral of the actinic irradiance. Hence,

$$E = \int H \, dt$$

(8)

Since the laser is being scanned at constant velocity, Vs, along the x axis, with x increasing, then

$$Vs = dx/dt \qquad \text{or} \qquad dt = dx/Vs \qquad (9)$$

Substituting equations (7) and (9) into equation (8),

$$E (r,z) = (2 P_L / \pi Wo^2 Vs) \exp -z / Dp \int_{-\infty}^\infty \exp [-2r^2 / Wo^2] \, dx$$

(10)

where the factor exp [-z/Dp] can be moved outside the integral sign since z is not a function of x. From the Pythagorean theorem,

4

$$r^2 = x^2 + y \qquad (11)$$

thus,

$$\exp[-2r/Wo^2] = \exp[-2x^2/Wo^2] * \exp[-2y^2/Wo^2]$$

$$(12)$$

Substituting equation (12) into equation (10), moving the factor exp [-$2y^2/Wo^2$] outside the integral, as it is also not a function of x, and further recognizing that since the integral of equation (10) is symmetric about x = 0 (viz. the contribution from - ∞ to 0 is exactly equal to that from 0 to ∞) then the total integral must be twice the value from 0 to infinity. Therefore,

$$E\ (y,z) = (4P_L\ /\ \pi\ Wo^2 Vs)\ \exp\ [-z\ /\ Dp - 2y^2\ /\ Wo^2]\ \int_0^\infty\ \exp\ [-2x^2/Wo^2]dx$$

$$(13)$$

Define

$$Define \quad v \ \equiv \sqrt{2}\ x\ /\ Wo$$

$$(14)$$

Taking differentials of equation (14),

$$(15)$$

$$dv = (\sqrt{2}\ /\ Wo)\ dx\ or\ dx = (Wo\ /\ \sqrt{2})\ dv$$

Thus, evaluating the integral in equation (13), by substituting from equations (14) and (15), we obtain,

$$\int_0^\infty\ \exp\ [-2x^2\ /\ Wo^2]\ dx = (Wo\ /\ \sqrt{2})\ \int_0^\infty\ \exp\ [-v^2]\ dv$$

$$(16)$$

This integral is related to the error function. From Reference 3 we find that

$$\int_0^\infty\ \exp\ [-v^2]\ dv\ =\ \sqrt{\pi}\ /\ 2$$

$$(17)$$

Substituting equations (16) and (17) into equation (13), we obtain after some algebra,

5

$$E\ (y,z)\ =\ (2/\pi)^{1/2}\ (P_L)\ Wo\ Vs)\ \exp\ -\ [z\ /\ Dp\ +\ 2y^2\ /\ Wo^2]$$

(18)

From equation (18) it is evident that the exposure reaches its maximum value E = Emax when y = 0 (i.e. on the laser scan axis) and z = 0 (i.e. on the free resin surface). This <u>maximum laser exposure</u> value is given by the wonderfully simple expression;

$$Emax\ \ =\ \ (\ 2\ /\ \pi)^{1/2}\ P_L\ /\ Wo\ Vs$$

(19)

Equation (19) is our <u>first</u> important result. It shows that the maximum actinic laser exposure is:

* <u>Directly proportional to the laser power.</u>

* <u>Inversely proportional to the product of the beam radius and the scan velocity.</u>

* The proportionality constant is simply $\underline{(2\ /-\pi)^{1/2}\ =\ 0.7979..}$, a pure number involving no empirical quantities whatever.

5   The Parabolic Cylinder

For photopolymer resins, when the exposure is less than a critical value, Ec, the resin remains liquid. When E > Ec, the resin undergoes at least partial polymerization. However, if E = Ec, the resin is at the so called "gel-point", corresponding to the transition from the liquid phase to the solid phase. Hence, we may solve for the locus of points y = y*, and z = z*, which are just at the gel point. All points <u>inside</u> this locus will be at least partially solidified while all points <u>outside</u> this boundary will still be liquid. Clearly, the resulting boundary will then define the cross-sectional shape of a single laser cured photopolymer "string".

Thus, setting y = y* and z = z* when E = Ec in equation (18), after some algebra we find,

$$\exp\ [\ 2y*^2/Wo^2\ +\ z*\ /\ Dp]\ =\ (\ 2\ /\ \pi\ )^{1/2}\ (P_L\ /\ Wo\ Vs\ Ec\ )$$

(20)

Taking natural logarithms of equation (20), and substituting from equation (19), we obtain the result,

6

$$2 y*^2 \,/\, Wo^2 + z* \,/\, Dp = \ln \,[\, Emax \,/\, Ec \,]$$

(21)

This is our <u>second</u> important result. We may write equation (21) in the form

$$A \, y*^2 + B \, z* \, = C$$

Where A, B, and C are all positive constants. From Reference 4, this is the equation, in three dimensions, of a <u>parabolic cylinder</u> whose axis is the x axis, which, by definition of our coordinate system is precisely the laser scan axis.

Figure 3 shows a parabolic cylinder which results from simply scanning an actinic laser in a straight line at constant velocity over the surface of a vat of liquid photopolymer, provided that Emax > Ec. Thus, the <u>fundamental building elements of Stereolithography are actually parabolic cylinders</u>, often referred to as "strings".

6   The Working Curve

We may now define the <u>maximum cure depth</u> of a single laser cured string by the symbol Cd. From either Figure 3, or equation (21), it is evident that Z* = z(max) = Cd when y* = 0. Or, simply stated, the maximum cure depth will occur directly under the laser scan axis. Thus, setting z* = Cd when y* = 0 in equation (21), we finally obtain the fundamental "Working Curve" equation of StereoLithography, as discussed in Reference 5;

$$Cd = Dp \, \ln \,[\, Emax \,/\, Ec \,]$$

(22)

This is our <u>third</u> important result, and is <u>absolutely fundamental</u> to an understanding of this technology. Equation (22) shows that:

*   <u>The cure depth should scale as the natural logarithm of the maximum actinic laser exposure</u>.

*   <u>A semi-logarithmic plot of Cd vs ln Emax should result in a straight line relationship</u>, known as the Working Curve.

*   The <u>slope</u> of the Working Curve is exactly the <u>penetration depth</u>, Dp, of the resin, at the laser wavelength.

*   Since ln(1) = 0, the <u>intercept</u> of the Working Curve (i.e. the value of Emax where Cd = 0) is precisely the <u>critical exposure</u>, Ec, of the resin, at the laser wavelength.

*   Since Dp and Ec are purely resin parameters, then within the limits of this model, both the slope and the intercept of the Working Curve should be <u>independent</u> of either the laser power, P_L, the laser spot size, Wo, or the laser scan velocity, Vs.

Figure 4 shows an actual Working Curve for Ciba-Geigy resin XB 5149. Note the excellent linearity of this semi-logarithmic plot. The resulting values of DP and Ec are indicated.

7   The Cured Linewidth

Returning to equation (21) and Figure 3, it is also clear that the maximum cured linewidth, Lw, will occur at the resin surface, where the parabolic cylinder has its greatest width. Therefore, setting y* = y(max) = Lw /2, when z* = 0, we obtain after some algebra,

$$Lw = \sqrt{2}\ Wo\ \{\ \ln\ [\ Emax\ /\ Ec\ ]\ \}^{1/2}$$

(23)

Substituting for ln [Emax / Ec] from equation (22), we obtain the basic "Cured Linewidth" equation,

$$Lw = Wo\ \sqrt{2\ Cd\ /\ Dp}$$

(24)

This is our <u>fourth</u> important result. It shows that:

*   <u>The cured linewidth of a string is directly proportional to the laser spot size at the plane of the resin surface.</u> In calculating numerical values, remember that Wo is the <u>radius</u> of the laser spot, not the diameter.

*   The cured linewidth is also proportional to the <u>square root of the ratio of the cure depth to the resin penetration depth</u>. Thus strings of greater cure depth will also be wider, but their width will <u>not</u> increase linearly with Cd.

*   Even if Wo and Cd are held constant, the cured linewidth will depend upon the <u>resin penetration depth</u>. This is important to remember whenever one changes resins.

8

8   Laser Scan Velocity

A modified form of equation (22) may be written as follows:

$$Emax = Ec \exp [Cd / Dp] \qquad (25)$$

Substituting for Emax from equation (19) we find,

$$Emax = (2 / \pi)^{1/2} [P_L / Wo \; Vs] = Ec \exp [Cd / Dp]$$

$$(26)$$

Solving for the laser scan velocity, Vs, we obtain the result

$$Vs = (2 / \pi)^{1/2} \{ P_L / Wo \; Ec \} \exp [-Cd / Dp]$$

$$(27)$$

This is our <u>fifth</u> important result. It illustrates the following:

* <u>The laser scan velocity is directly proportional to the laser power</u>. Thus, subject to system servo limits, the higher the laser power the faster the scan speed for a given resin, laser spot size, and cure depth.

* The laser scan velocity is <u>inversely proportional to the laser spot size</u>. Thus, increasing the spot size decreases the laser scan velocity for a given laser power, resin and cure depth.

* The laser scan velocity decreases in an <u>exponential</u> manner with an increase in the ratio Cd / Dp. For a given resin, this is the reason why increased cure depths draw much more slowly than shallow cure depths.

* Again, the <u>constant of proportionality</u> predicted by this model is the same pure number, $(2/\pi)^{1/2} = 0.7979......$

Equation (27) is currently incorporated into 3D Systems software. It is the basis for all automatic laser scan velocity calculations on the SLA-190, the SLA-250, and the SLA-500. Experimentally measured cure depths, generated using the automatic laser scan velocity algorithm, are typically within a few percent of the desired values. Further, the residual errors are approaching the limits of the experimental technique (viz. standard deviations of +/- 0.00015 inches or about +/- 4 microns).

9   Drawing Time Per Unit Area

In StereoLithography, the great majority of the laser drawing time is spent "hatching" to solidify the regions of parts interior to their borders. Except for very tiny parts, the time required to draw the borders is generally a small fraction of the time required to complete the hatching process. For complete generality we could analyze any arbitrary cross section. However, to simplify the calculations, let us consider a rectangle of length L, in the scan direction, and width w, perpendicular to the scan direction. Figure 5 shows this rectangle, whose area is simply A = Lw.

Now, let us perform the hatching operation by drawing straight parallel vectors with a hatch spacing, hs, as occurs with the advanced building techniques WEAVE™ and STAR-WAVE™. Neglecting finite acceleration and deceleration effects at the ends of each hatch vector, the time required to draw a single string of length L is simply:

$$t = L / Vs \tag{28}$$

Within integer round-off, the number of such vectors, N, is given by

$$N = w / hs \tag{29}$$

Thus, to close approximation the laser drawing time, t_d , is given by the following:

$$t_d = N t = (w / hs) (L / Vs) = A / hs\, Vs \tag{30}$$

Finally, in the advanced build methods WEAVE™ and STAR-WEAVE™ the hatch spacing is taken proportional to the laser spot size Wo. Thus,

$$hs = k\, Wo \tag{31}$$

Where k is a constant, generally near 2, so that the optimum hatch spacing is of the order of the beam diameter. Substituting equations (27) and (31) into equation (30) we obtain after some algebra:

$$\boxed{t_d / A = (1/k)\, (\pi / 2)^{1/2}\, \{ Ec / P_L \}\, \exp [Cd / Dp] \tag{32}}$$

This is our <u>sixth</u> important result. Equation (32) indicates that within the accuracy of the approximations we have made;

* The drawing time per unit cross-section area is <u>directly proportional to the resin critical exposure</u>, Ec. Resins with higher values of Ec will draw more slowly.

* The drawing time per unit area is <u>inversely proportional to the laser power</u>, P_L. As one might expect, higher power lasers will reduce draw time, provided one has not reached the system servo limit.

* The drawing time per unit area <u>increases exponentially with the increased cure depth to penetration depth ratio</u>. For a given resin with a specific value of D_p, increased cure depths draw <u>much more slowly</u>. Thus, in addition to improved part accuracy, because the advanced techniques WEAVE™ and STAR-WEAVE™ utilize reduced cure depths relative to the former Tri-Hatch method, they actually draw faster even though many more individual vectors are required.

* Finally, and especially significant, is the observation that at least to first order, the laser drawing time per unit area is independent of the laser spot size. This result, which is probably not intuitively obvious, has been substantiated experimentally for all the approved StereoLithography resins.

The latter point leads to the seventh important result. Since laser drawing time is independent of laser spot size to first order, then dynamic optical zoom is of limited utility in such a system, unless one is always operating at the servo limit. Dynamic zoom (viz. the ability to vary the laser spot size over a wide dynamic range) would increase system cost, increase system complexity, reduce reliability, and as the above analysis shows, provide productivity gain only for those laser power levels which exceed the system servo limit.

10   Summary

We have derived some of the most fundamental relationships of StereoLithography. Each of these results has been experimentally confirmed to varying levels of accuracy. Higher order effects such as optical self-focusing, resin "bleaching", radiation scattering, non-Gaussian laser modes, finite acceleration and deceleration intervals, and system servo limitations will alter the trends somewhat. Nonetheless, the mathematical results discussed in this paper are predominantly valid, and should be considered fundamental to a solid understanding of this technology.

References

1. Kauzmann, W., "An Introduction to Quantum Chemistry", Academic Press, New York, 1957, pp. 578-579.

2. Siegman, A.E., "An Introduction to Lasers and Masers", McGraw-Hill, New York, 1971, Chapter 8, pp. 312-314.

3. Sneddon, I.N., "Special Functions of Mathematical Physics and Chemistry", Oliver and Boyd, London, 1961, pp. 13-14.

4. Sherwood, G.E.F. and Taylor, A.E., "Calculus", Prentice-Hall, Inc., Englewood Cliffs, New Jersey, Third Edition, 1958, p. 310.

5. Richter, J., and Jacobs, P.F., "The Present State of Accuracy in StereoLithography", Conference Proceedings, Second International Conference on Rapid Prototyping, University of Dayton, Dayton, Ohio, June 23-26, 1991, pp. 269-294.

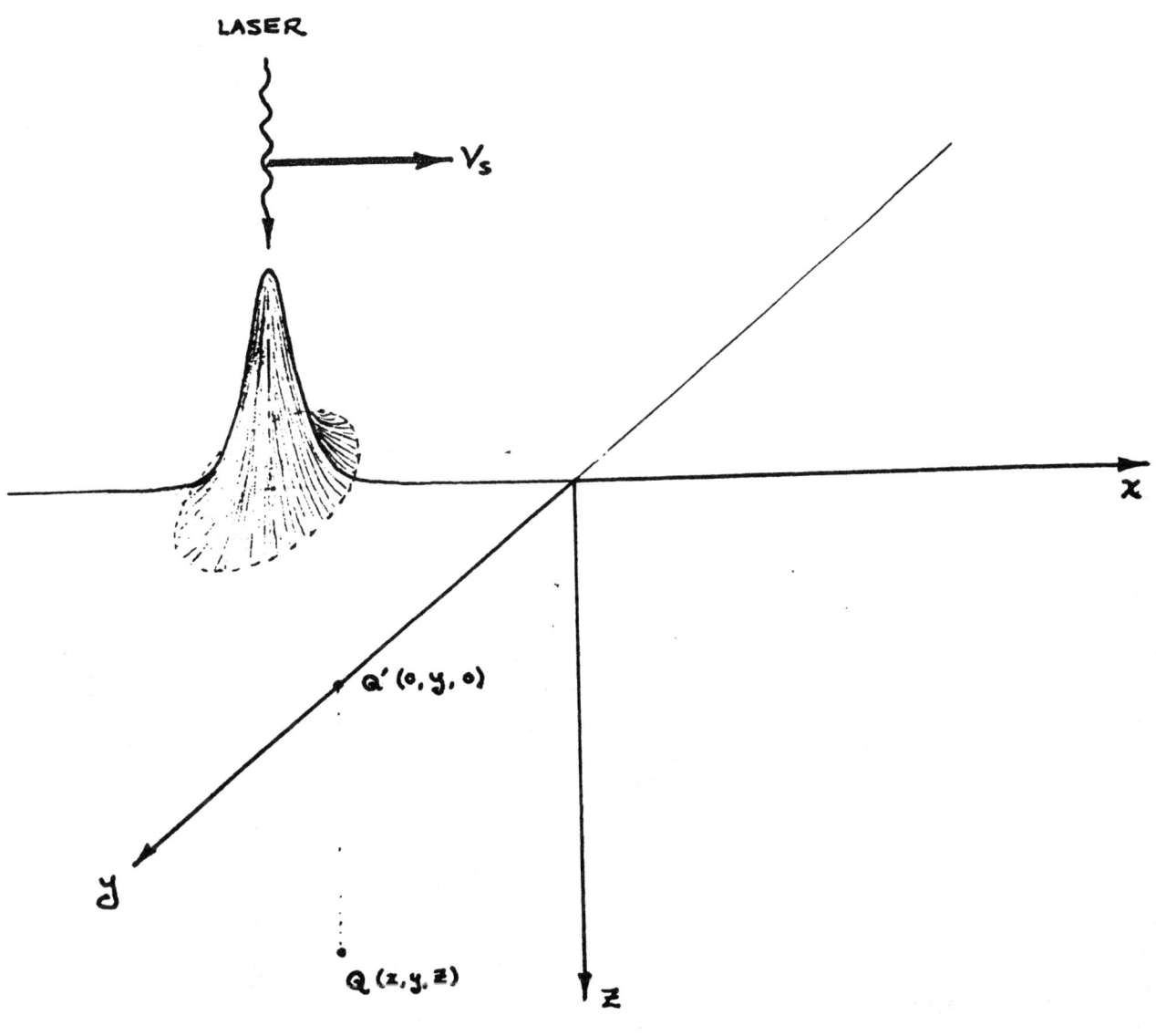

Figure 1 Laser Coordinate System

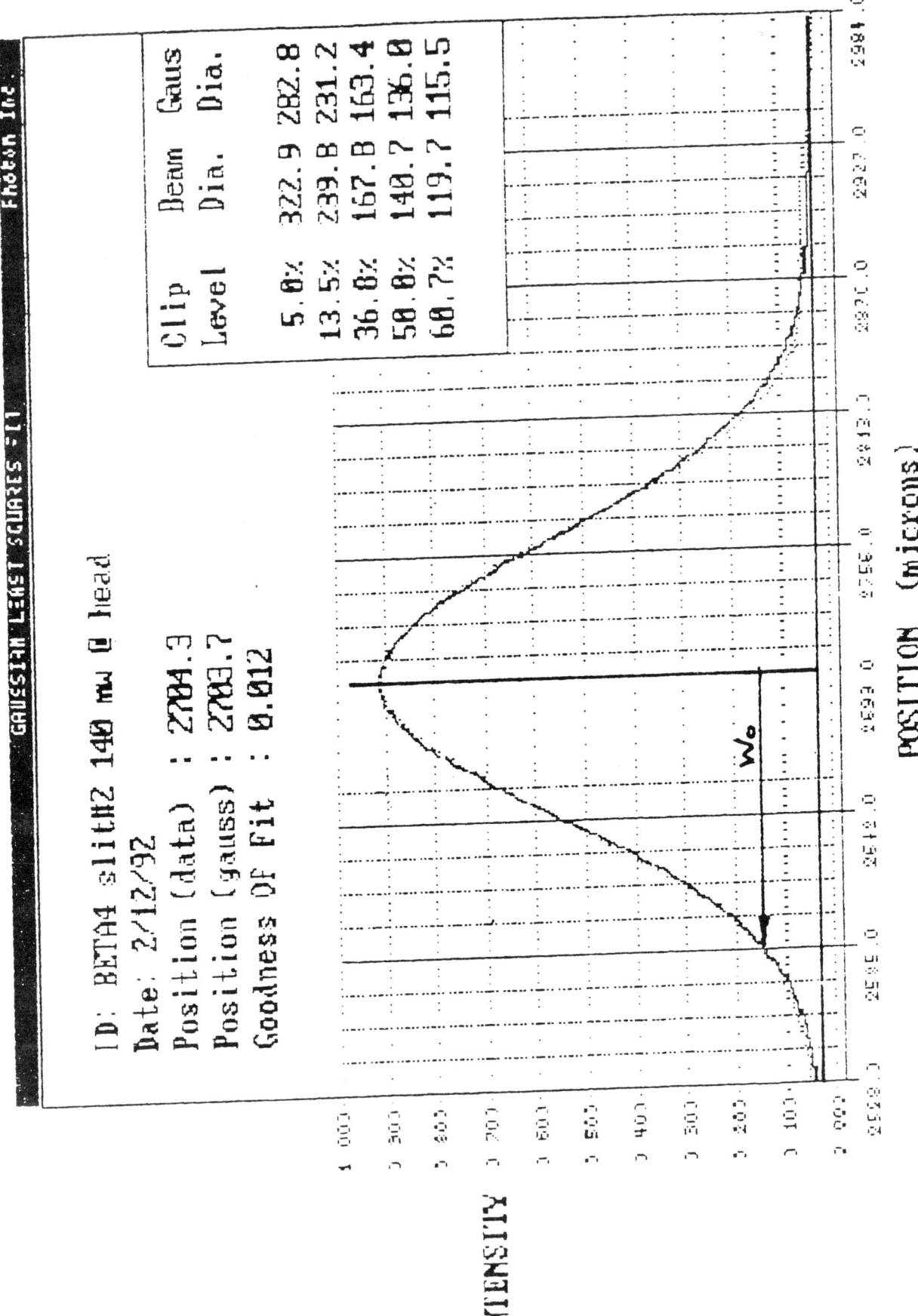

Figure 2 Gaussian Beam Distribution

14

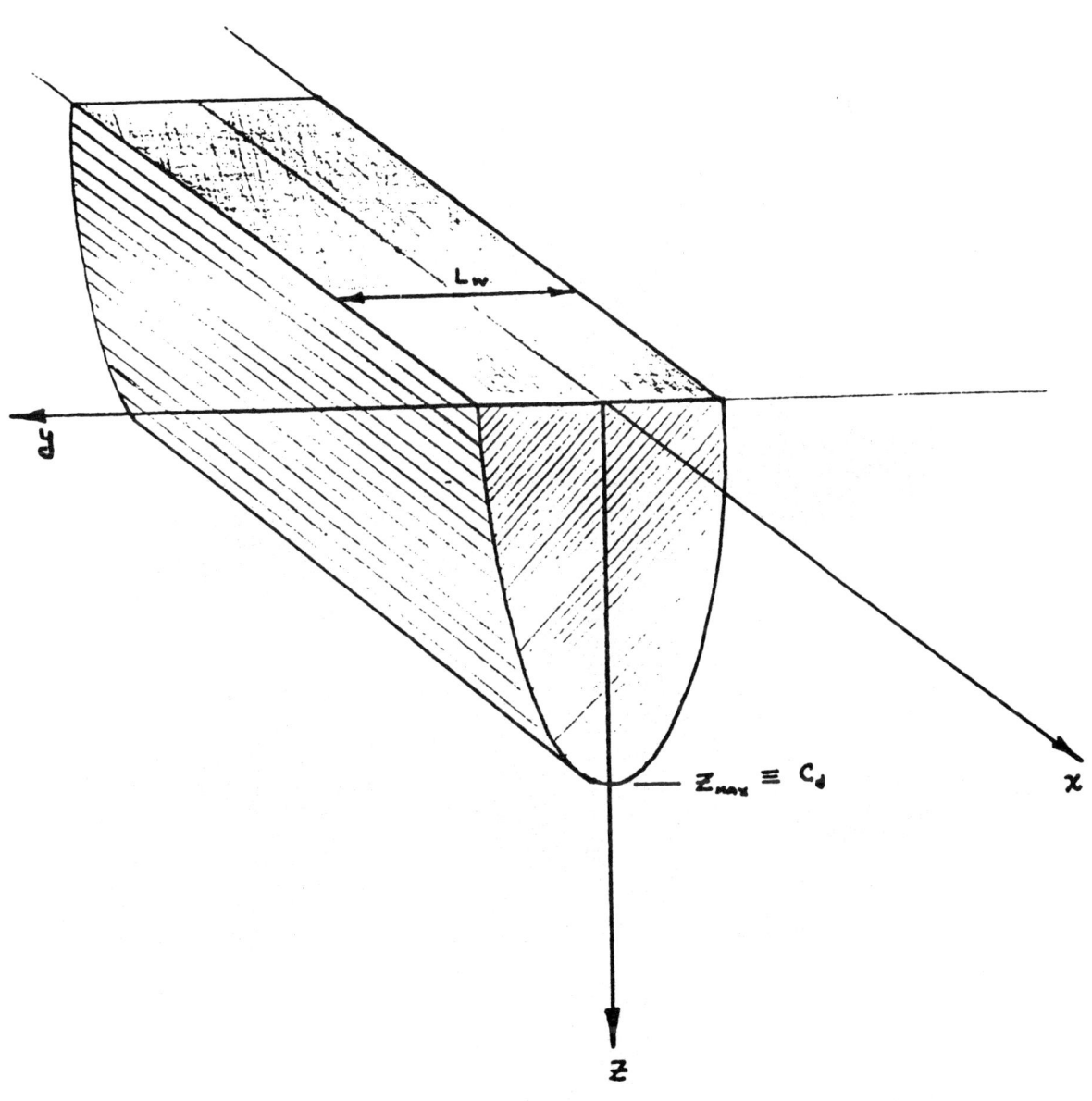

Figure 3 Parabolic Cylinder

15

Figure 4 Working Curve

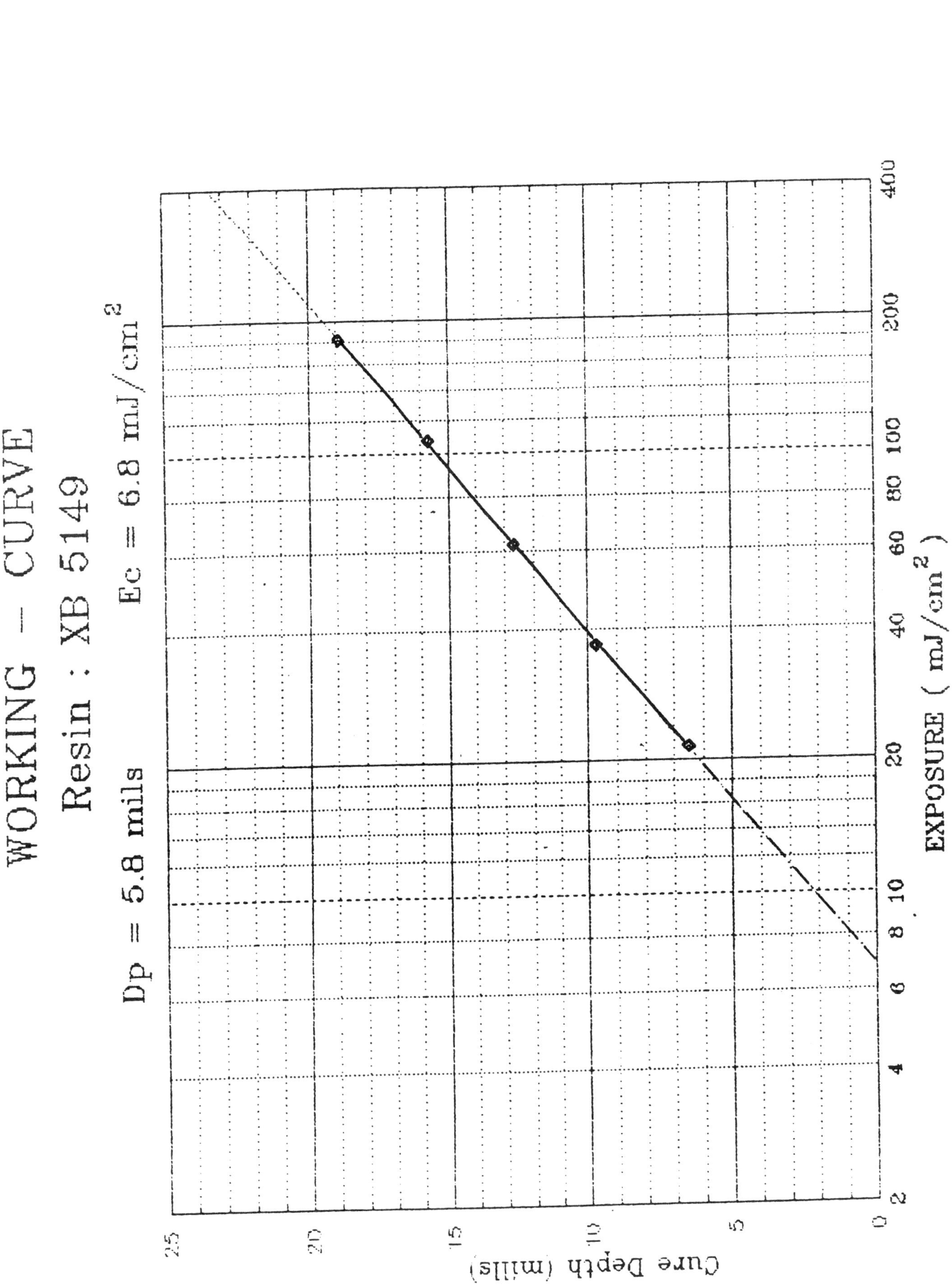

16

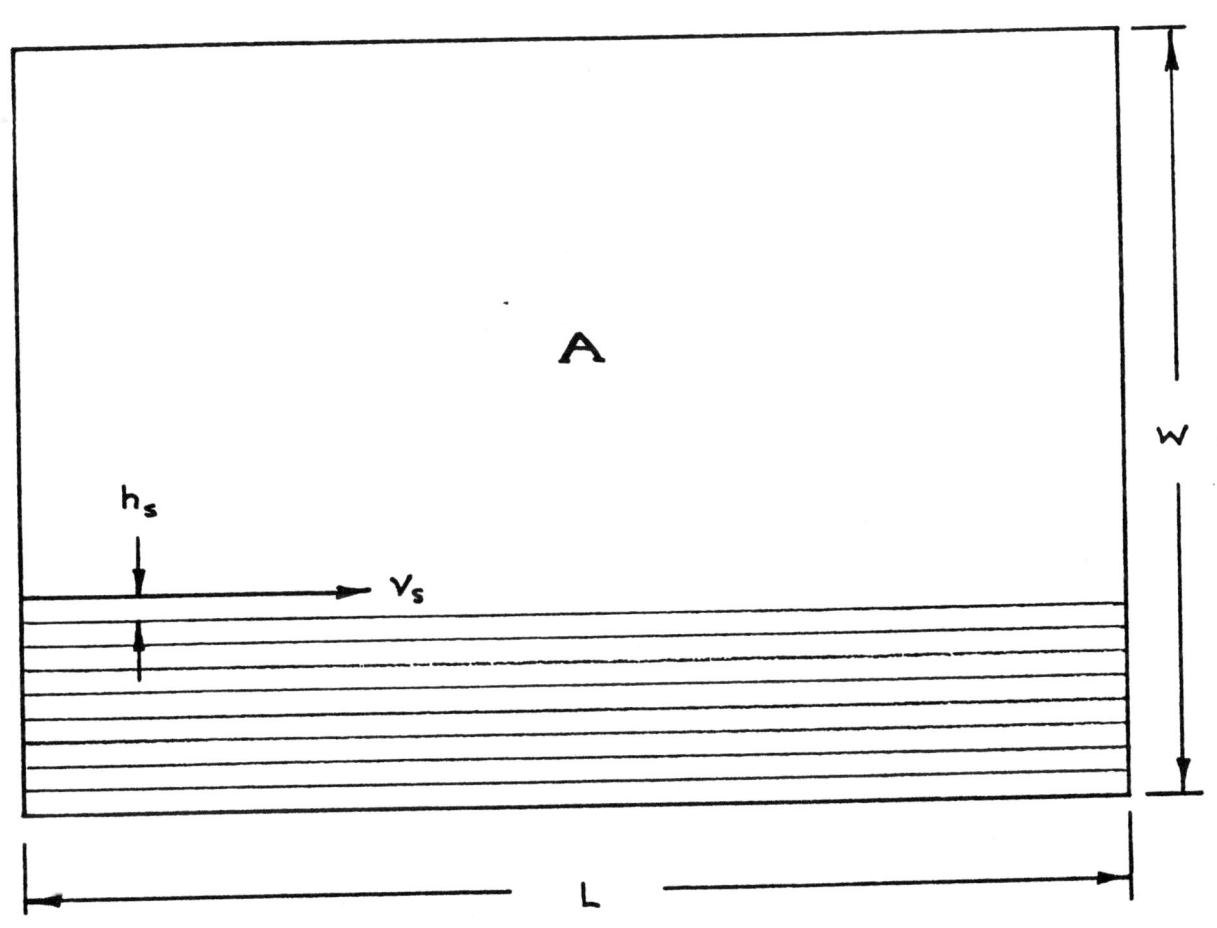

Figure 5 Scanning Rectangle

THE EOS RAPID PROTOTYPING SYSTEM

M C Shellabear, H J Langer
and M Cabrera

EOS GmbH Electro Optical Systems
Pasinger Str. 2, W-8033
Planegg/München, Germany

Abstract

EOS is currently the only European manufacturer of rapid prototyping machines with the STEREOS laser modelling system. This paper explains the company's concept of Rapid Prototyping as a complete process in which the various elements (CAD design, prototype manufacture, quality control and data transfer) need to be carefully integrated. Significant advances have been made in each of these individual areas which can lead to greatly improved overall efficiency. Descriptions and photographs of the company's rapid prototyping and rapid measurement systems are presented, together with comparative results to demonstrate the present performance in terms of speed and accuracy.

1.   Introduction - the Rapid Prototyping Concept

Rapid Prototyping is an old dream of mankind that has come to reality only recently with the last developments in lasers, optics, photopolymers and Computed Aided Design. This explains why the early attempts to establish this technology were unsuccessful (Munz , 1951; Beckerle, 1954; Pollak , 1978), until the works of Kodama (1981), Herbert (1982), and Hull (1984) in the USA and also independently André (1984) in Europe.

Over the past few years a variety of new Rapid Manufacturing technologies have been introduced with two important common features.

First, the prototype part can be automatically produced from a CAD description under computer control.

Second, the part is produced by creating or adding solid material, rather than removing existing material (as is the case for milling and other conventional prototype production techniques) with a two dimensional process controlled by the energy of light which is usually a laser beam (photohardening of liquid resin, photocuring of solid resin, or laser melting of powder for example).

As there is no possibility of collision between the laser beam and the part and as the laser beam movements are only plane drawings, we can consider a Rapid Prototyping machine as an infinite axis device. In other words, parts or moulds are produced directly without tools.

The combination of these factors has enabled the manufacturing time for many prototype parts to be drastically reduced, and has generated considerable interest in the concept of Rapid Prototyping.

One effect of introducing Rapid Manufacturing technology has been, in many cases, to shift the scheduling bottlenecks to other operations in the prototyping process. For example, the time taken to convert the CAD model to the required format may take longer than actually producing the part. This has highlighted the potential for time-saving in these other areas, and also demonstrated some shortcomings in the way that the new technology fits into the existing system.

It is clear that maximising the efficiency of the entire production process requires not only improving the individual technologies involved, but also creating an integrated system which can operate without bottlenecks. This is the concept which has been adopted by EOS for developing our rapid prototyping systems.

This concept is summarized in Figure 1 which shows the essential elements for introducing a rapid prototyping system into a company.

At the top is the CAD system which is used to design and modify parts, and may also be used to generate tool paths for conventional manufacturing equipment (CAM).

Many different types of CAD system are in use worldwide, therefore it is important that any rapid prototyping machine which is introduced can communicate with the existing system. Standard data-transfer formats (STL, VDA-FS or IGES) are available, but problems can occur when trying to convert model files between different formats.

A software interface is required to handle these different data inputs and enable the different parts of the system to communicate - this is labelled as the 'EOS Processor' in Figure 1. This processor also has to perform checks on the input data and optimise the process parameters (including part orientation, support structures etc.)

The output from the processor controls the rapid manufacturing machine, called STEREOS, which actually produces the part.

The final element in the diagram is a coordinate measurement machine (CMM), generically called EOSCAN.

As with any production process, a quality control check is required to ensure that the product is as it should be. Because rapid prototyping processes typically involve creation of solid material from liquid or powder, effects such as shrinkage can occur. Any such distortions need to be compensated during manufacture, therefore dimensional checking of finished parts is particularly important. In some cases the distortion can be defined by a few critical dimensions which can easily be measured by conventional techniques, but if a large number of points need to be checked then the measurement can itself become a long process.In these cases a Rapid Measurement system is required to compliment the rapid manufacture.

This is also the case when the initial design is created as a solid model rather than in a CAD system, as occurs for example with the clay models which are sculpted in styling studios. Having arrived at the desired shape, a CAD description is usually required in order to replicate the shape as a prototype. The process of digitizing the actual model into the computer is known as Reverse Engineering, and can again require considerable time and resources for the necessary measurement.

The rapid manufacture (STEREOS) and rapid measurement (EOSCAN) components of the EOS concept will be described in more detail in the following sections.

2. The STEREOS Laser Modelling system

The STEREOS rapid manufacturing system uses the process known as stereolithography, in which liquid photopolymer resin is cured using ultra-violet light from a laser. The laser beam is focused onto the surface of a vat of resin, and scanned under computer control to solidify a thin layer corresponding to one slice of the CAD model. This layer is then submerged by one layer thickness, and the laser scans the next layer which bonds to it. In this way the entire model is built up slice by slice.

A number of special features have been designed into the STEREOS system to improve the performance and functionality, as compared to previous systems. These are summarised below:

2.1. Model size

Two machines (STEREOS 400 and 600) are available, which can build models of up to 400x400x250 mm and 600x600x400 mm respectively.The STEREOS 400 is shown in Figure 2. A STEREOS 1200 with a capacity of 1200x600x600 mm is also planned for 1993. Each machine can be supplied with interchangeable vats of 2 to 280kg capacity, enabling small models to be built without requiring large quantities of resin. This is particularly useful when testing new resins, and can lead to significant cost savings.

2.2. Laser

The machines can be operated with various ultra-violet emitting lasers (typically Argon Ion) depending on power requirements. This gives the possibility of exchanging lasers or upgrading the system as required. The laser output is controlled from the computer, and for the lower power option (100mW Argon) no external cooling water is required.

2.3. Optics and Scanner

The laser beam is focused using a flat field lens, which enables a laser spot size of 0.1-0.15mm to be maintained across the entire vat. This produces a significant improvement over conventional focusing optics, as indicated in Figure 3.The two-dimensional galvanometer scanning system is also state-of-the-art, offering a vector speed of up to 10m/s at the liquid surface with a positioning accuracy of ±0.05mm. The laser beam position is automatically calibrated within the machine to ±50μm.

2.4. Recoating method

A novel recoating method has been developed to improve performance. The new procedure reduces recoating time by eliminating dip delay, minimises bubble formation, and greatly improves the quality of parts containing closed volumes.

2.5. Materials

A range of different resins can be used, including all UV-sensitive resins compatible with argon ion lasers. Standard resins are SOMOS™ 3100, which is rigid but tough and machinable, and SOMOS™ 2100, which offers high flexibility.The interchangeable vats enable the resin to be changed rapidly without the need to clean the machine.

2.6. Computer hardware and software

CAD models are prepared in the 'EOS Processor' described in the introduction. This uses a workstation with 32-bit RISC processor operating under OSF Motif environment. The existing and planned functions of the processor are shown in Figure 4 as solid and broken boxes respectively.

Software features include: interfacing with STL and CATIA for data input (VDA and IGES interfaces are planned, which can also be used for measurement data from a CMM); checking and repair of model descriptions; and automatic support generation.

The CATIA interface is not based like the STL interface on a design of the surface of the part. In fact this interface is based on the description of the part by its sections and the STEREOS software is able to fill all sections with the hatch pattern of the part. This interface is a new way to make an efficient and automatic direct connection from the CAD system to the STEREOS. Similar interfaces from other CADs are also planned.

Process control in the STEREOS machine is performed by an IBM-compatible PC with 486 processor, operating under MS-Windows environment. This generates filling patterns on-line. Exposure vector control is controlled by a second PC-386 computer operating in parallel. The software is menu-driven and user-friendly, and process parameters are continuously monitored and displayed during part building.

3. Part Building with the STEREOS

The performance of the STEREOS system can be assessed by considering some actual models. Three examples are given below which have been used for testing stereolithography systems. These give a good indication of the improvements which have been achieved in recent years.

3.1 Exhaust Manifold

The exhaust manifold is a classic example of a complex part containing curved surfaces and internal features, for which dramatic savings in time and cost can be achieved by using Rapid Prototyping. Producing such a prototype manifold by conventional methods takes typically several weeks or more, whereas with the STEREOS the complete part can be produced in 15 hours.

Figure 5 shows how the completed part looks before being removed from the STEREOS machine.The support structure which can be seen under the tubes is removed during the post-cure cleaning process. Figure 6 charts how the manufacturing time has decreased over the last three years.

3.2 Stereolithography User Group Test Part

For testing the in-plane accuracy of stereolithography machines, a special test part was adopted by the 3D Systems User Group (Gargiulo, 1991).This part has also been manufactured using a STEREOS 400 machine and measured using a conventional CMM, as shown in Figure 7. The part is 240 mm (9.5") square.

108 individual points were measured, and the resulting x and y dimensions

compared with the nominal values in the CAD model. Regression analysis of the deviations yields a 'residual error', which is the RMS error after removing a linear best-fit. This value indicates the machine accuracy when a material shrinkage compensation factor is correctly applied. Calculating the residual errors separately for points probed in opposite directions (i.e. internal or external dimensions) yields a second value which indicates the accuracy when the laser beam diameter is also correctly compensated. These values and the build time are plotted in Figure 8, and are compared with data published in Gargiulo (1992) (beam-compensated residual error was not available in this data).

3.3 Winglet

The third part is an aircraft winglet, designed in a CAD system by British Aerospace. A graphic display of the CAD model is shown in Figure 9. A scaled-down prototype was required for aerodynamic wind-tunnel testing, and rapid prototyping was chosen to make it. Accuracy and quality of the surfaces was very important for the aerodynamic tests, so parts were obtained from different manufacturers (using the same CAD description) for comparison by British Aerospace.

The STEREOS model was found to be the most accurate, with a mean error of 0.01 mm and an RMS error of 0.24 mm on a critical section (British Aerospace: private communication). Actually measuring the shape of free-form surfaces such as this is itself a time-consuming procedure, and is well-suited to rapid measurement systems as discussed in the next section.

4. The EOSCAN Optical Measurement System

Coordinate measurement is conventionally performed using a touch-probe positioned by a 3- or 5-axis mechanical system. The necessity for the probe to be repositioned for each individual measurement point inevitably makes this a slow procedure when large numbers of data points are required. This is especially the case for free-form surfaces which cannot be defined in terms of simple geometrical parameters. These types of surfaces are also ideally suited to rapid manufacturing techniques, as they would otherwise typically require 5-axis machine tools with complicated tool paths. In this type of application the combination of rapid manufacture with rapid measurement can yield enormous benefits.

The EOSCAN is a video-based optical measurement system which can digitize up to 250,000 surface coordinate points simultaneously.

It works on the principle of projection moiré, which is shown in Figure 10. A fine grating of parallel lines is projected onto the object surface, and is observed at an oblique angle through a similar reference grating. The reference grating acts as a filter for the projected grating, which appears distorted due to the shape of the object surface and the oblique viewing, and creates a form of interference pattern known as 'moiré fringes'. Under certain geometrical conditions these fringes correspond to surface height contours. Figure 11 shows the moiré fringe pattern as seen by the video camera on the surface of the winglet shown in Figure 9.

The moiré fringes describe the shape of the surface, but further processing is required to calculate the actual height information.

This can be achieved using the method of phase stepping (Shellabear, 1991), in which three or more images are recorded while the phase of the projected grating is varied. In the EOSCAN the phase is varied by translating the projected grating using a computer-controlled piezocrystal.

The video camera is also linked to the computer via an image-processing board, which performs the calculations to determine the surface height. Video images containing all the necessary information can be acquired in less than one second, and the PC486 computer currently requires approximately 30 seconds to calculate the 3-dimensional coordinates for up to 512x512 data points in the image. This time is also being steadily reduced as the system is improved.

Figure 12 shows the result of the phase-stepping calculation, while Figure 13 and Figure 14 show examples of how the data can be displayed on the monitor. These are a pseudo-3D plot of the entire image, and a profile section selected by mouse from the screen display.

The digitized coordinates can also be exported to a CAD system as a data file, or further processed within the computer to perform other functions, such as automatic detection of feature lines.

Just as STEREOS is designed to integrate with an existing CAD system, so EOSCAN is intended to integrate with existing measurement systems. A prototype measuring head has been constructed which weighs less than a kilogram and can be mounted to a mechanical CMM via a 2-axis rotation head. In this configuration the optical head can be considered an accessory to the standard machine to be used for rapid digitization of free-form surfaces.

The EOSCAN head incorporates a laser triangulation sensor for measuring the absolute range to the object surface, and it is planned to integrate the software and control hardware with that of the CMM so that tactile point measurements and optical surface measurements can be output in the same coordinate system.

5. Summary

EOS is actively working to improve the efficiency of prototype and product development through the concept of Rapid Prototyping. The STEREOS laser modelling system has introduced a number of features which improve the speed and accuracy of solid part building from CAD descriptions, and the performance is continuing to improve with further development. The interface between this machine and the CAD systems has also been improved to remove the need for interactive conversion between different file formats. Dimensional checking of finished parts is being used to further improve the process accuracy, and the EOSCAN rapid measurement system is being developed to quickly digitize free-form surfaces for quality control and reverse engineering applications.

References

André J.C., Le Mehauté A., de Witte O. (1984) Dispositif pour réaliser un modèle de pièce industrielle, french Patent 84 11 241.

Beckerle L.D.(1954) Three-dimensional Reproduction Method, US Patent 3 428 503.

Gargiulo E.P. et al. (1991) Stereolithography Process Acuracy: User Experience in Second International Conference on Rapid Prototyping, Dayton (Ohio), pp 311-326.

Herbert A.J. (1982) Solid object generation, J. Appl. Phot Eng., vol 8, pp185-188.

Hull H.W.(1984) Apparatus for production of three dimensional objects by stereolithography, US Patent 4575330.

Kodama H. (1981), Automatic method for fabricating a three-dimensional plastic model with photo-hardening polymer, Rev. Sci. Instrum, 51(11).

Munz O.J. Photo-glyph recording (1951), US Patent 2 775 758.

Pollak J.A. (1978) Forming three dimensional objects from two dimensional designs using photolymerizable compositions, UK Patent 2 035 602.

Shellabear M.C. et ali. (1991) Electro_optic shape measurement of free-form surfaces in Laser '91 Congress, Munich.

SOMOS™ is a trademark of E.I. DuPont de Nemours & Co., Inc.

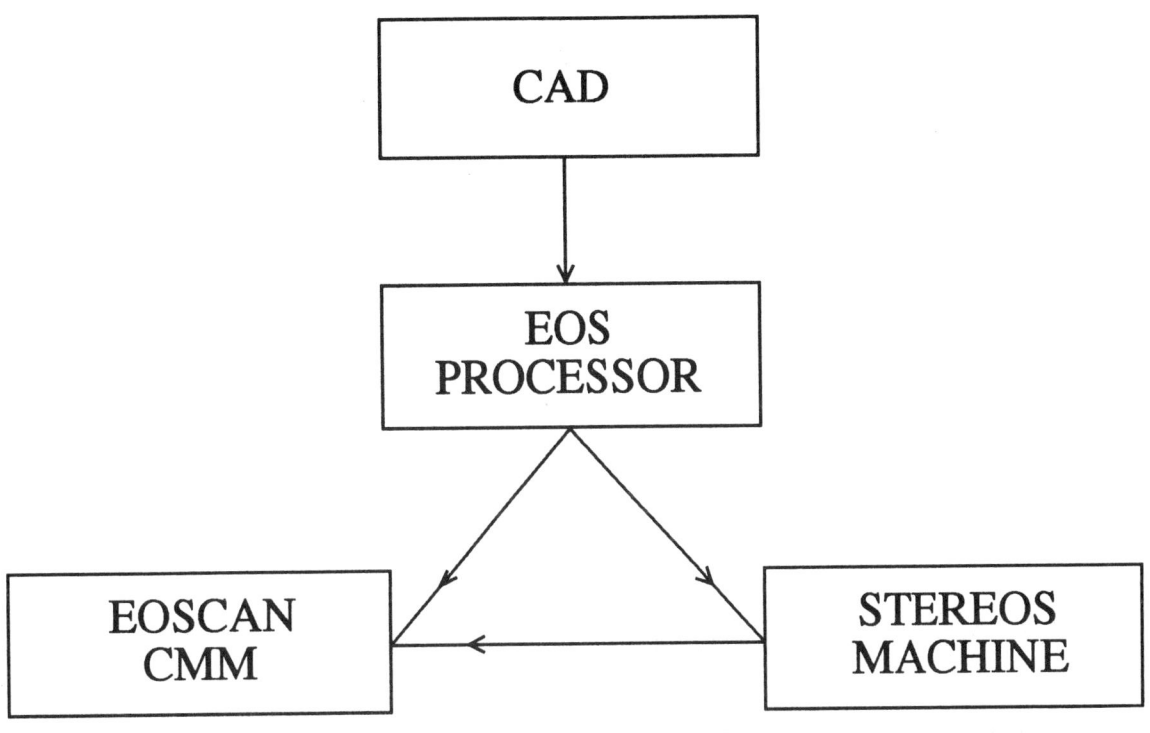

Figure 1: Elements of a Rapid Prototyping System

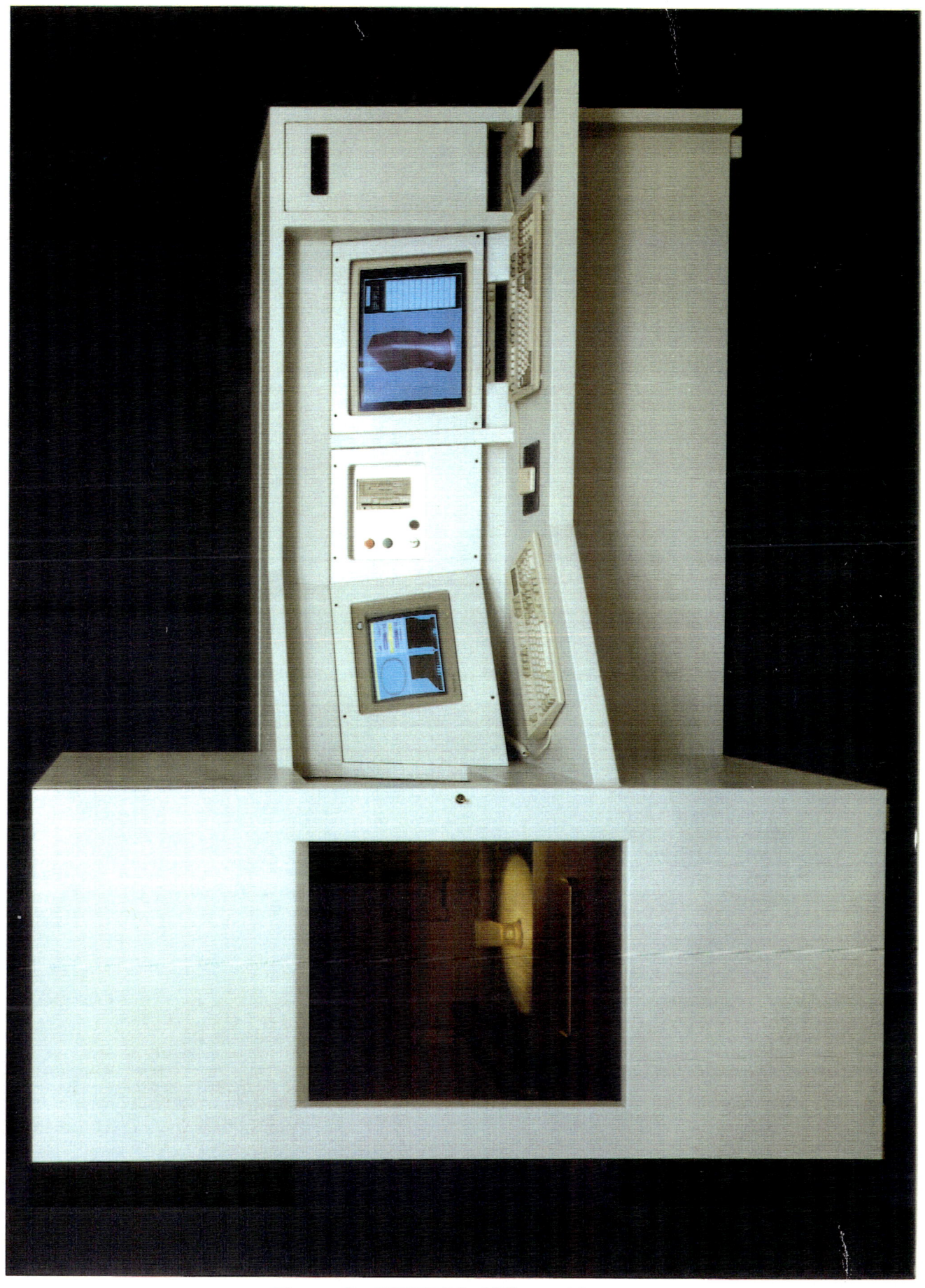

Figure 2: STEREOS 400 machine

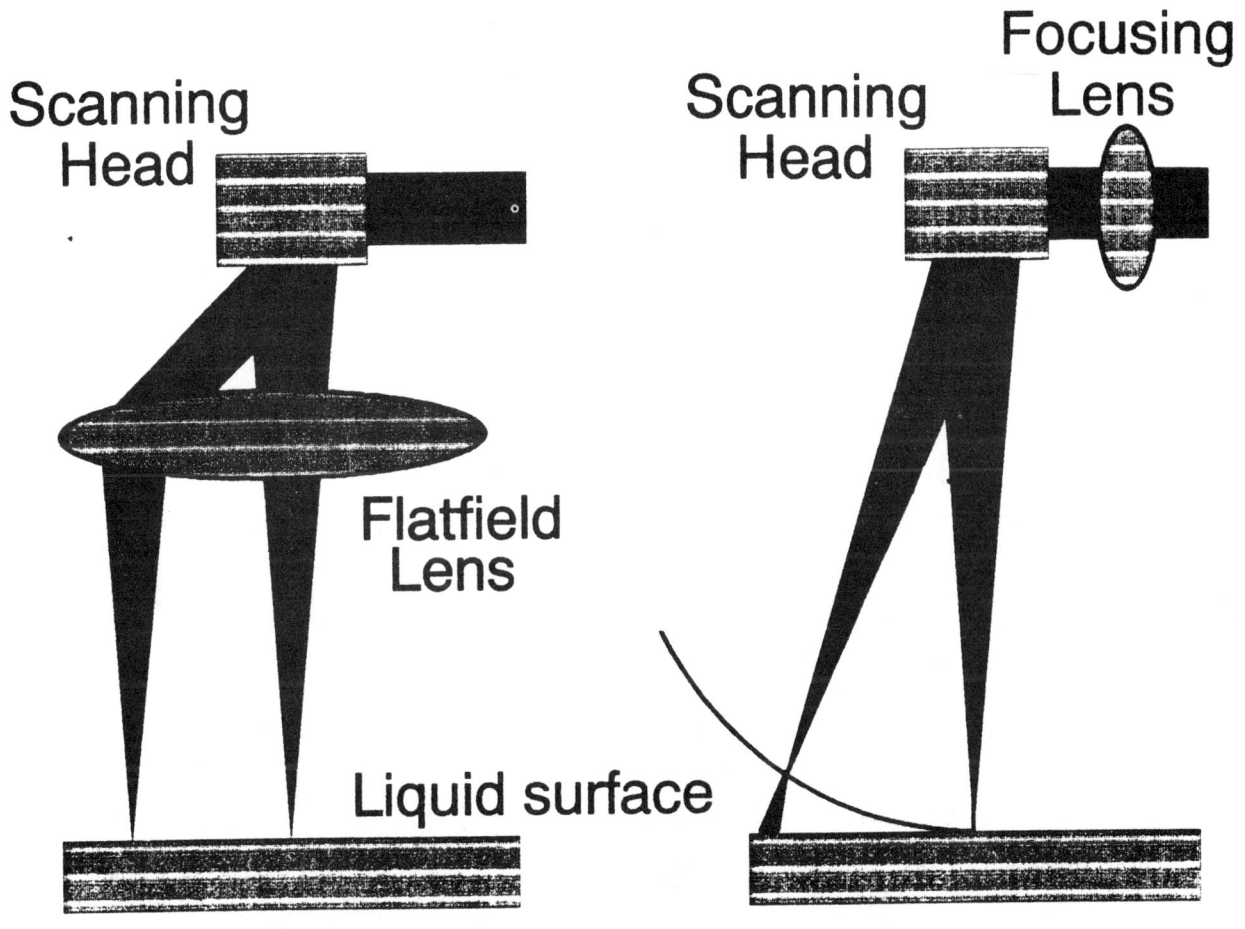

Flatfield vs. conventional focusing lens

Figure 3: Flat-field vs. conventional lens

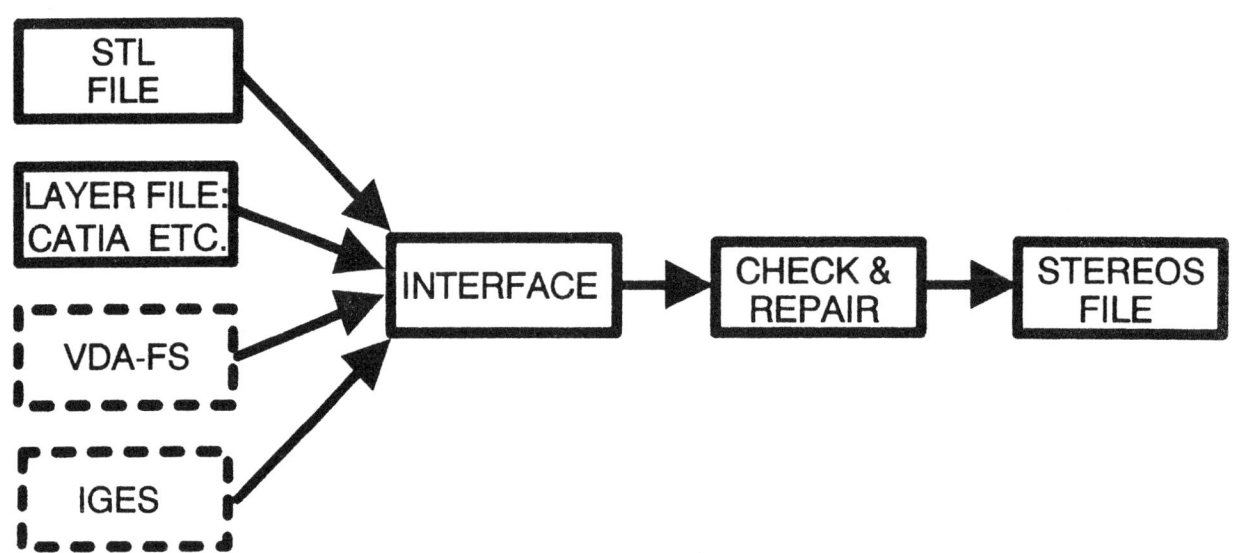

EOS Data Processor

Figure 4: EOS Processor functions

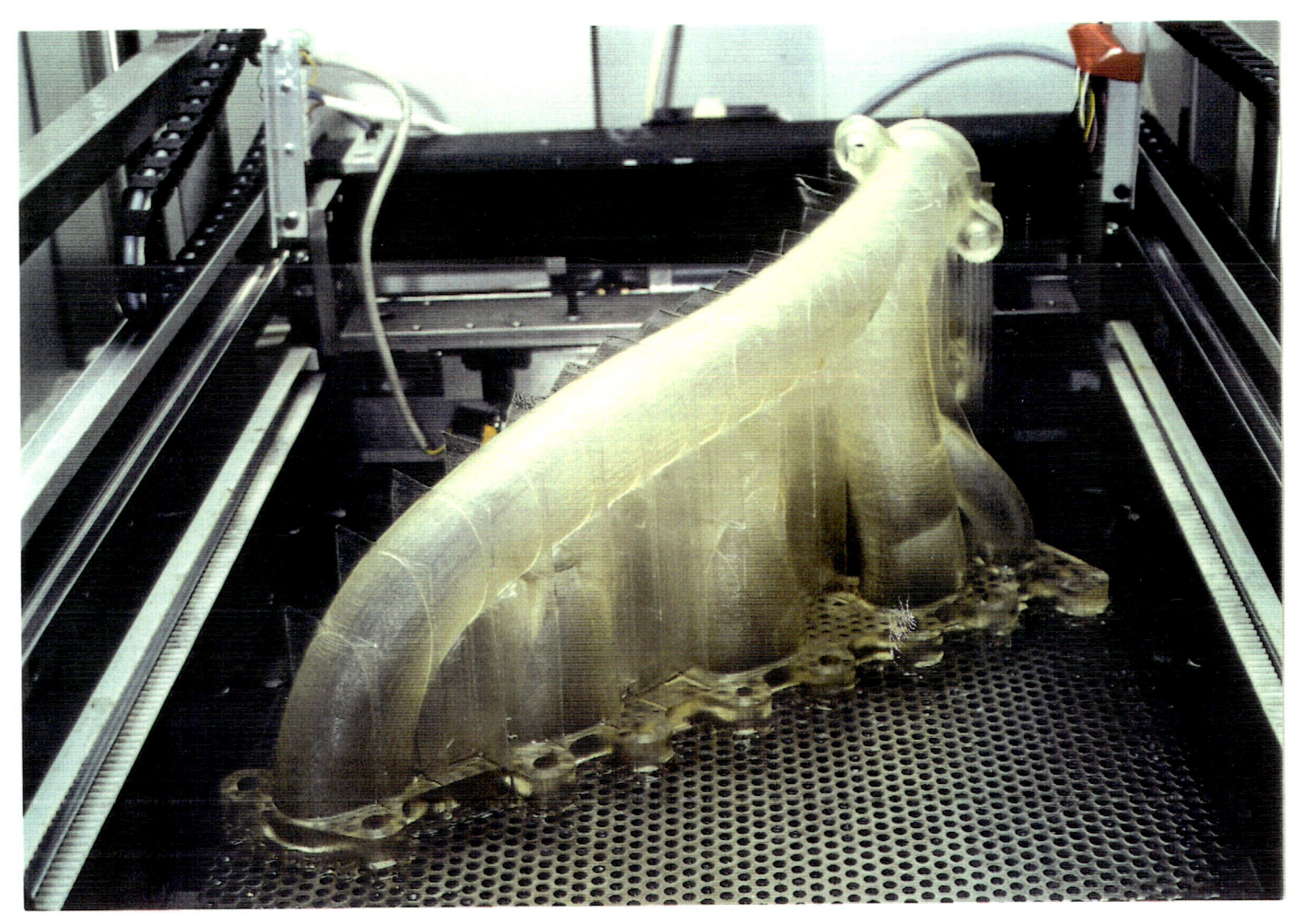

Figure 5: Completed exhaust manifold in the STEREOS 400 machine

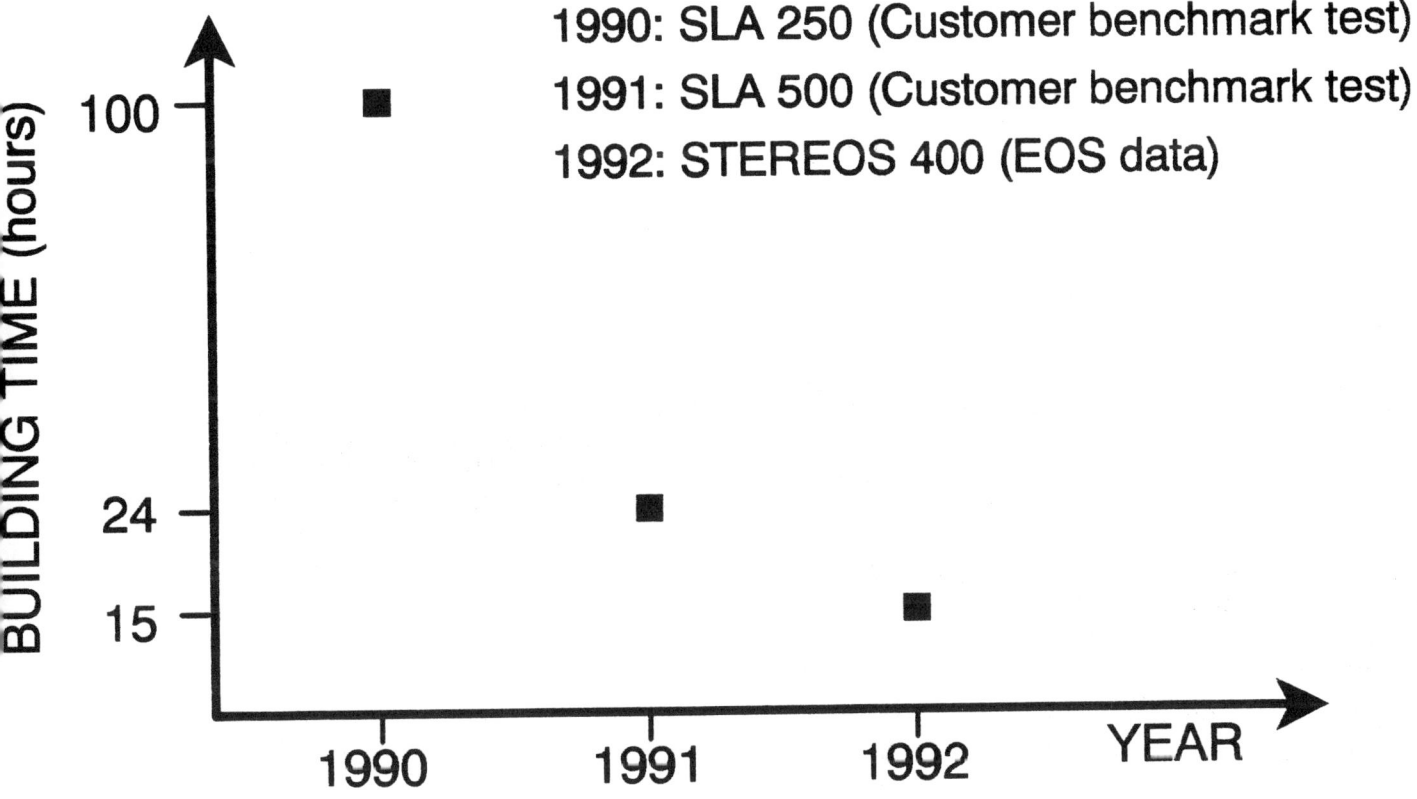

Building time for exhaust manifold

Figure 6: Building time for exhaust manifold

Figure 7: User Group test part in CMM

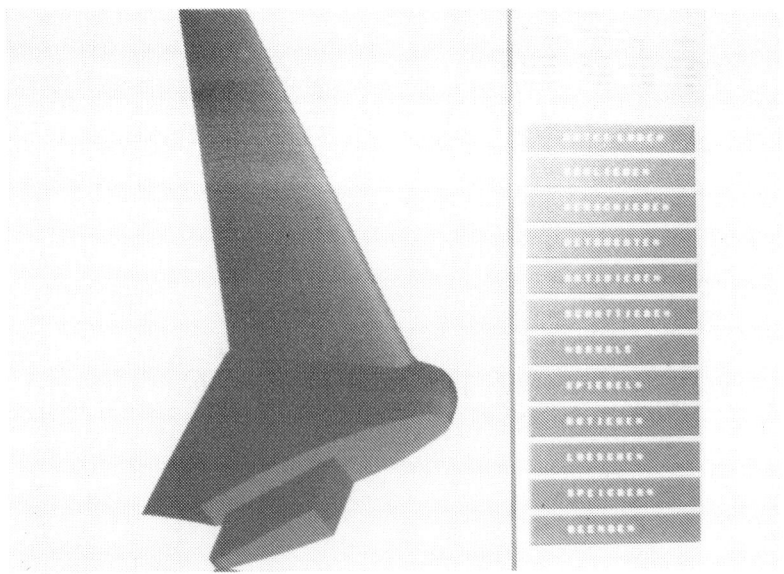

Figure 9: CAD display of British Aerospace winglet

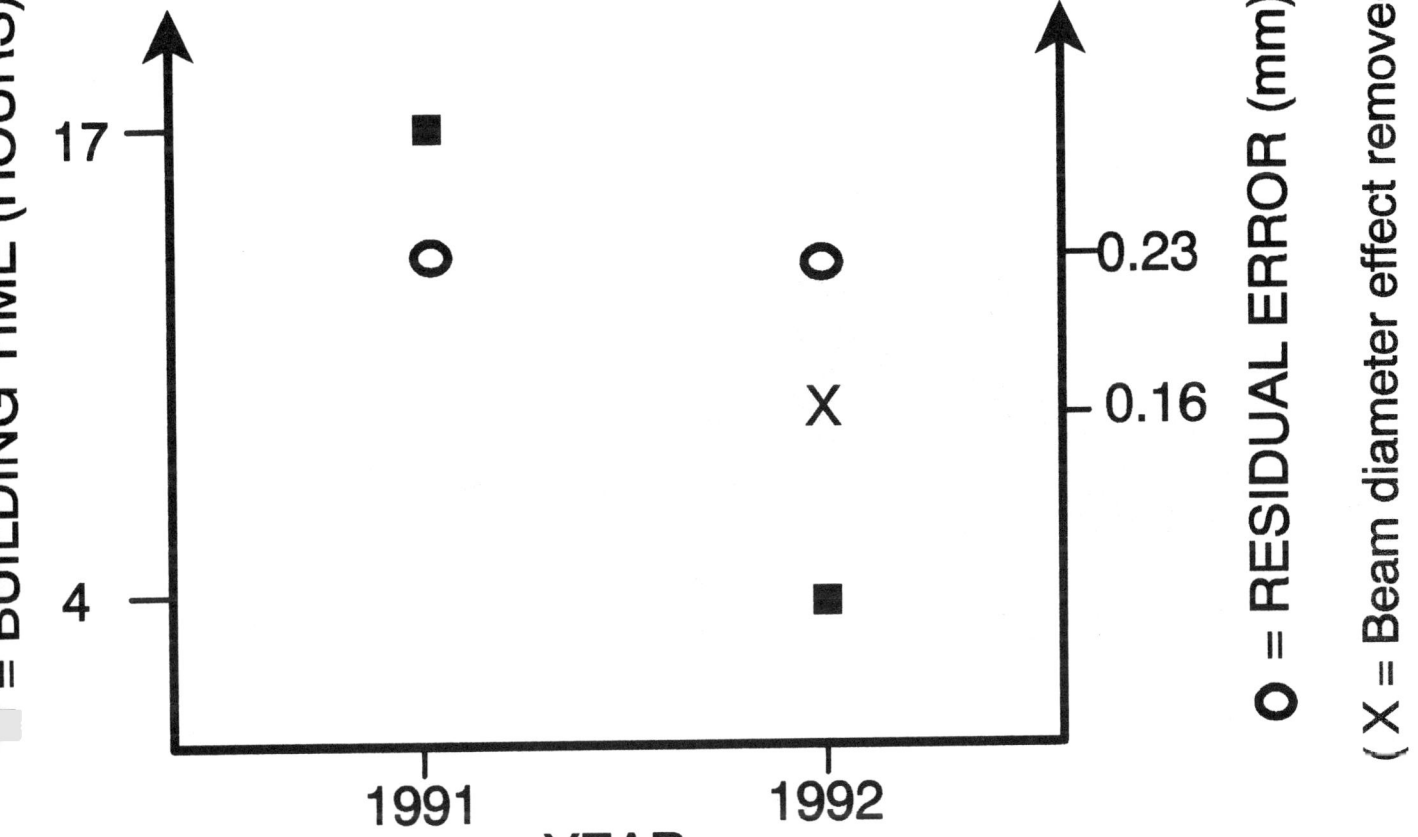

User Group Test Part

Build time and Accuracy

Figure 8: Build time and In-plane accuracy (residual error)
of User Group test part

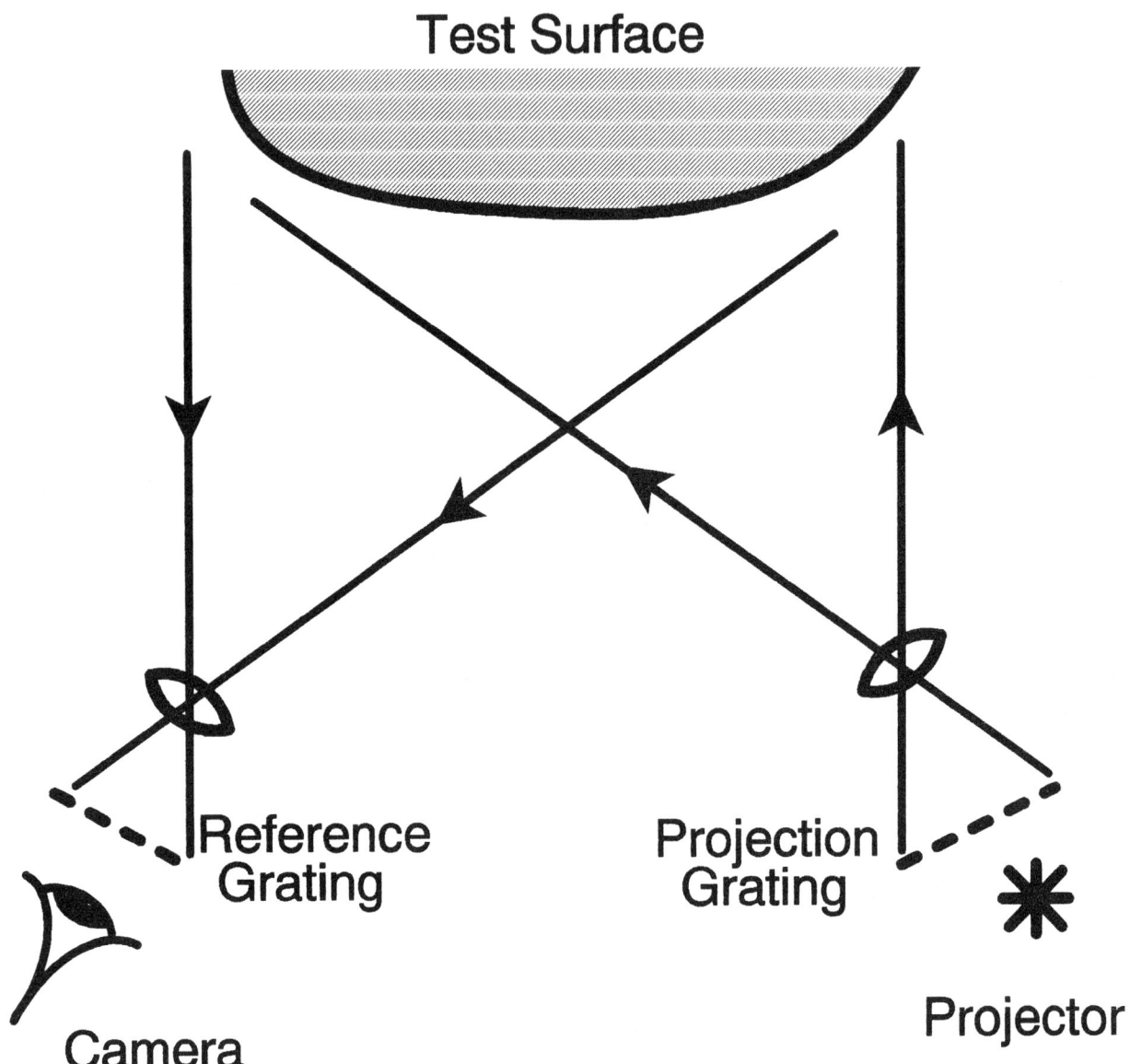

Principle of projection moire

Figure 10: Principle of projection moiré

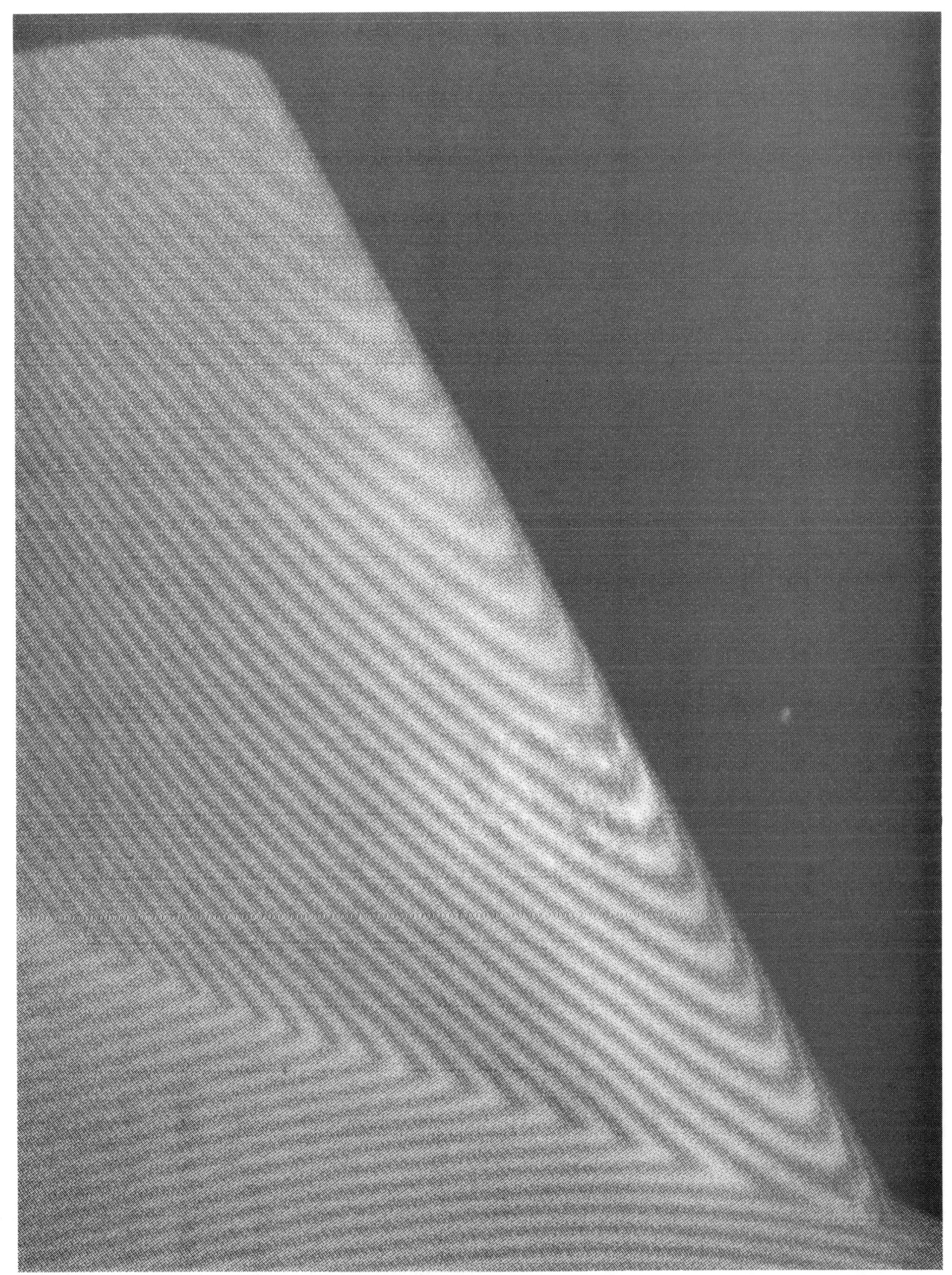

Figure 11: Moiré fringe pattern on the winglet

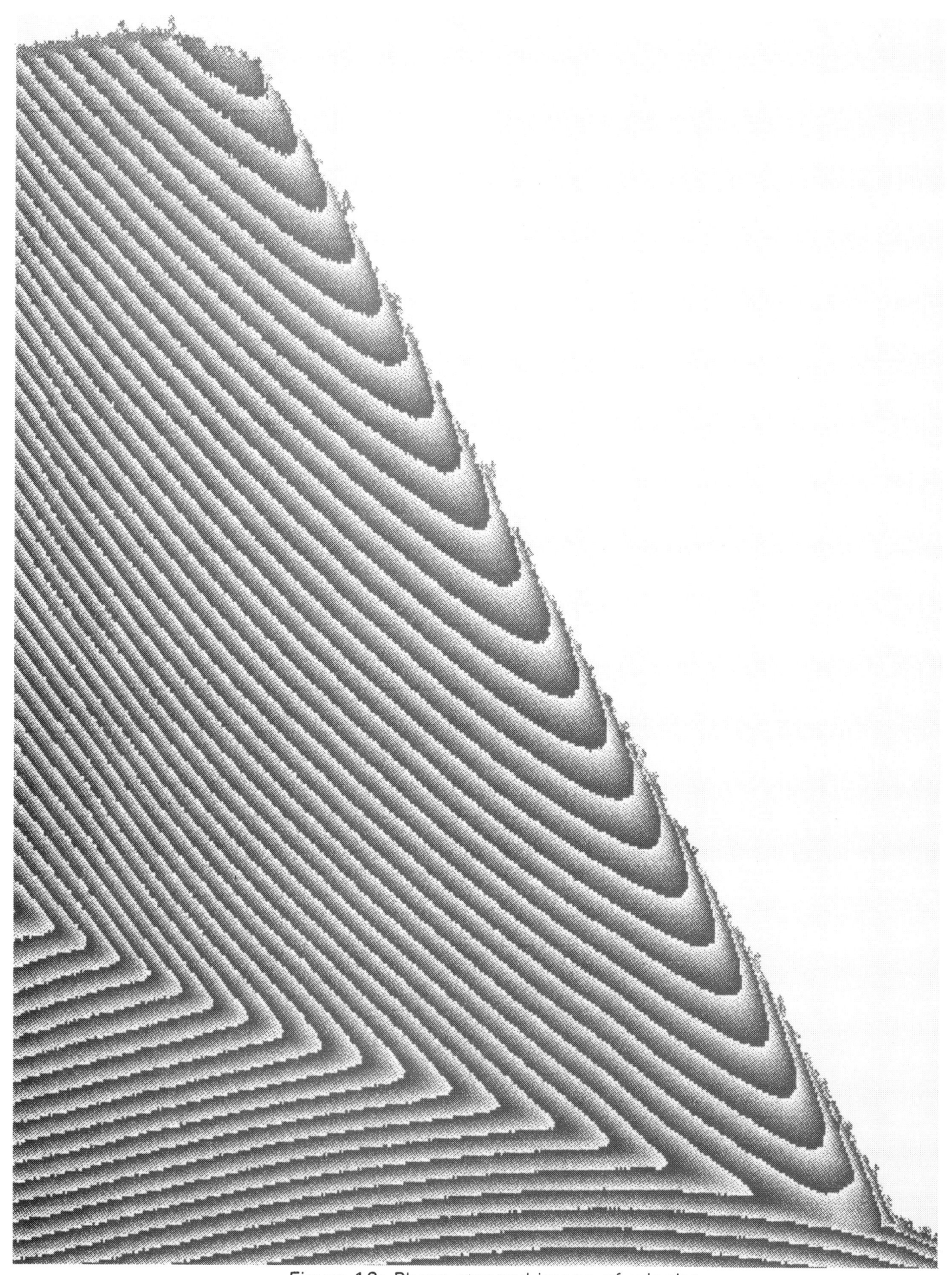

Figure 12: Phase-stepped image of winglet

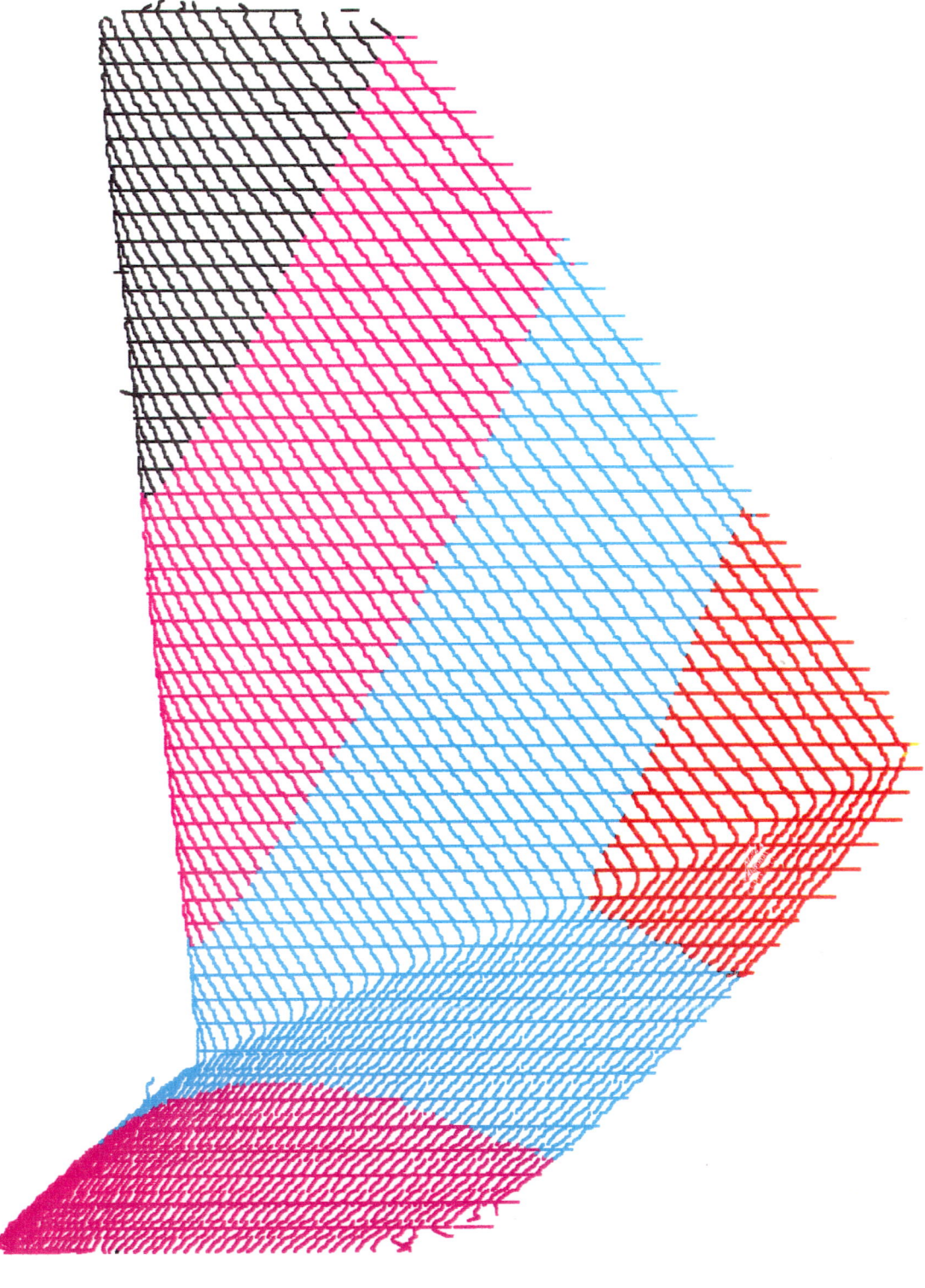

Figure 13: Pseudo-3D plot of winglet surface shape

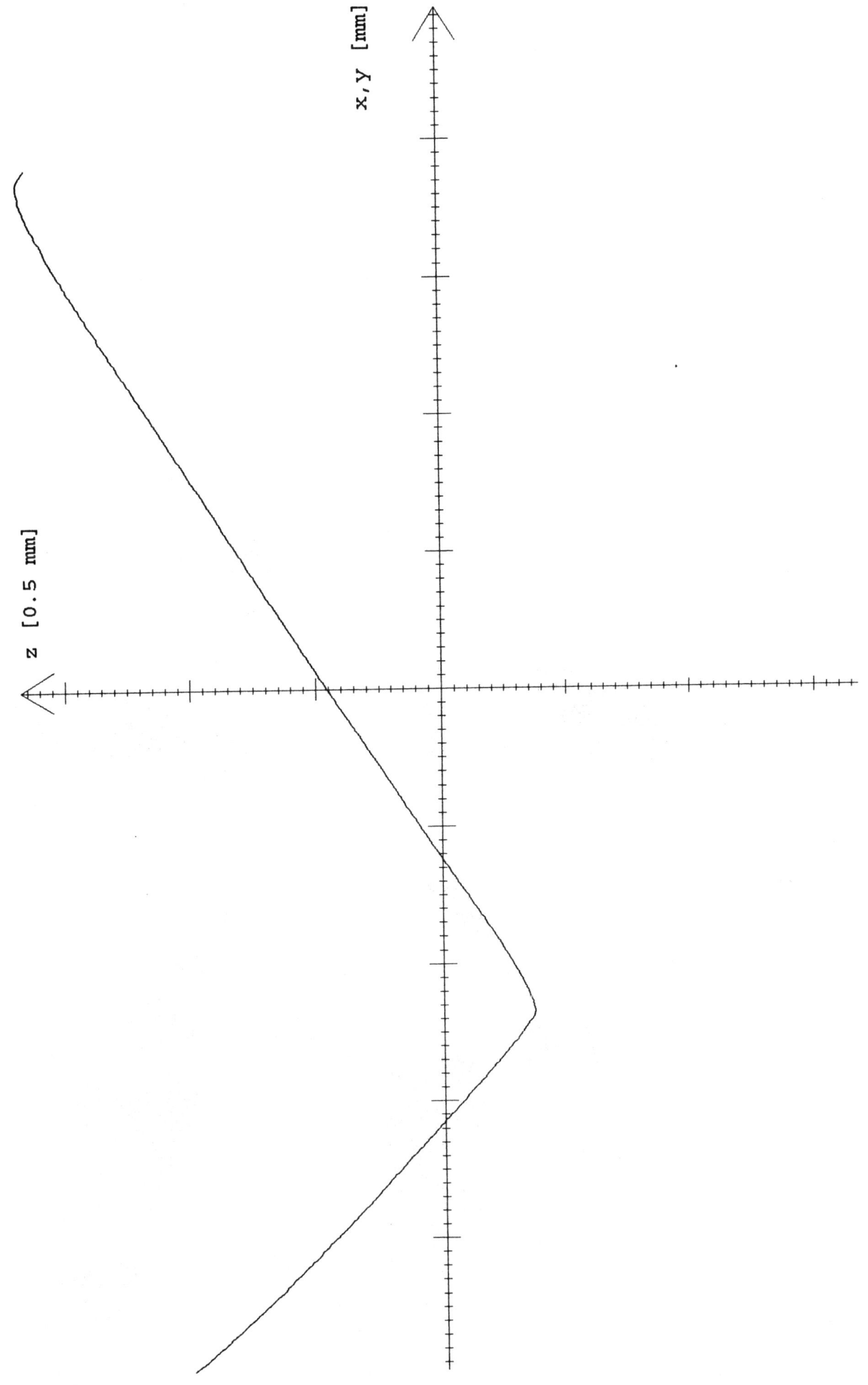

Figure 14: Profile section of winglet surface

CUBITAL'S SOLIDER 5600 SYSTEM: A SECOND GENERATION, ACCURATE RAPID PROTOTYPING SYSTEM

Mr Haim Levi

Cubital, Israel.

1   Introduction

A few years ago, a new technology of rapid prototyping entered the market place to create a huge impression on industry, offering the opportunity to greatly reduce the lead times from conception to market of new products. This first generation system, using liquid baths of photopolymer and laser curing techniques, produced models directly from CAD files. After a couple of years, as new vendors introduced their products in this field, and customers have gained much experience and understanding of this new technology, a much more serious and demanding approach has been required. This is reflected in the thorough evaluations of the different systems and technologies available today by customers looking for a technology that will best fit their needs.

A survey of the market requirements of industry today, highlights the following requirements:-

1.1   Model Size

Most customers require models that fall with cubic dimensions of 480mm x 330mm x 480mm. Where models exceed these dimensions, a method is required of producing accurate locations whereby the model is split, so that subsequently the individual parts of the model can accurately be joined together by these registers. Cubital's software enables this to be accomplished.

1.2   Resolution

The model is built up layer by layer. The maximum steps of each layer for complex geometrical shapes should be no more than 0.1mm although deeper steps may be acceptable for less complicated components. The Cubital system allows a variation between 0.05mm to 0.15mm for the thickness of each layer, thus enabling the operator the choice of the most economic build-up, consistent with the model requirements.

1.3   Accuracy

The most commonest problems experienced by many rapid prototyping technologies are shrinkage and distortion, thus considerably limiting the accuracy of the finished model. Although the precision and repeatability of these systems is considerable, accuracy should, in this context, have only one meaning; the lack of deviation from the CAD model. The responsibility for model accuracy in many systems is left to the user, relying on the experience and ability of the operator. Cubital's 'Solider 5600' system, fully curing each layer as it is built, and fully supporting it with wax, provides an accuracy of 0.1% of any dimension and does not rely on the know-how of the operator. This also provides a level of safety that cannot be achieved by liquid bath systems.

1.4 Geometry

There should be no limit to the geometric complexity of any model requirement. In many systems, it is necessary to manipulate the software to cater for undercuts and concave features and to provide supports for overhanging areas of the model, relying heavily on the experience and ability of the operator. The system itself should be capable of handling all these problems without reliance on the operator. The Solider 5600 system, utilising existing technology in a novel way, provides this capability, and provides a greater freedom in the types and makes of photopolymer resins that can be used.

1.5 Capacity

To ensure the greatest speed and production capability, it should be possible to nest a number of models within the working envelope. By supporting each model in wax, it is possible to multiplex each machine run, and by fully curing each layer of the model simultaneously, thus not needing post machine curing operations, the Cubital system provides the highest productivity. When allied to the simplicity of the implementation of the software, without the need for manipulation and building of supports, a real benefit in the basic requirement - a reduced lead time - is apparent.

2 Description of the Cubital Solider 5600 System

The process starts with the creation of the three dimensional composition of the set of nested models that are to be produced in the next run, and a definition of the layer thickness of each slice. The Solider computer then slices the whole composition into the required layers and generates a precise raster image of each layer.

The lowest slice image is sent to the mask plotting unit of the machine, where a high resolution, precise optical image is generated on to a flat plate glass. This latent image is then treated with black toner powder to form the mask.

While the mask is being generated, the working platform is spread with a thin layer of liquid photopolymer, and positioned under the exposure station. The optical mask is positioned precisely over the platform, a shutter opened, and the workpiece exposed for about 3 seconds through the mask, to a high power (2,000 W) UV lamp. Light, passing through the mask fully cures the cross section of the pattern of that slice. Unexposed areas of the layer surface remain in a liquid state.

The workpiece now passes under an aerodynamic wiper that sucks away all the residual liquid polymer, leaving behind only the cured pattern.

The mask plate is now returned to the mask plotter, discharging and erasing the first layer mask, and preparing the mask for the next layer.

The workpiece now travels to the next station, where a thin layer of melted wax is spread over the surface, filling all the voids and cavities left after removal of the untreated liquid. A cold plate is then lowered onto the surface, cooling and solidifying it. The results is a fully solid layer that is composed partly of cured polymer and partly of wax.

The workpiece now passes under a milling cutter that trims the layer's thickness down to the predetermined thickness, creating a flat smooth surface ready for the next layer. The process is repeated until the run has been completed, building up a block on the work platform of 480mm x 330mm up to a height of 480mm.

When the last layer has been completed, we are left with a block of wax, within which the model or models are embedded. The wax can be melted away in a microwave oven, by the use of a hot air gun or even by using warm water (60°C), and the finished models are ready for use.

Accuracy of the resulting models is achieved by the full curing and supporting of each layer as it is built, by the high resolution and accuracy of the mask in the x and y planes and by the precise milling of each layer to it's required thickness in the z plane.

Benefits that this technology offers are:-

-   Shrinkage and distortion minimised, even for thin sections.
-   No final curing process required.
-   No manipulation of software to generate supports etc. required.
-   Model structural strength and stability are higher, and models less brittle. This is because internal stresses are minimised and as a result of the ability to use better polymers.
-   No limitation on geometrical shapes.
-   High output by instant curing of full slice and 3D nesting of models in wax.
-   No hazardous vapours are generated. The operational resin is in a liquid form for a very short time, uncured resin is removed immediately. Thus safety factors are much higher.
-   By modifying the process slightly, wax models can be made for use in the lost wax casting process.

3   Cubital Interfacing Capabilities

Director solider interfaces exist for the following input formats:

1)   CPL (Cubital's own format; was submitted to the NCGA as a proposal for a new industry standard for Rapid Prototyping data transfer.
2)   STL (sometimes referred to as SLA) - both binary and ASCII formats from 3D-systems/Spectra-Physics SLA systems.
3)   VDA-FS 1.0.
4)   VDA-FS 2.0 - without trimmed/composite surfaces.
5)   I-DEAS (CAD software from SDRC) universal file format.
6)   Unipax (from Unigraphics CAD software) 7 Robface.

The following input formats can also be processed, but at this time require specific handling and cannot be referred to as interfaces:

1)   Postscript.
2)   Hpgl.
3)   Raster images from CT/MRI scanners.

CAD data files in the native format of the following systems can be interfaced through subcontractors (subject to former approval, restrictions, longer handling times, and at extra cost).

1)   ComputerVision CADDS 4/4x.
2)   ComputerVision Personal Designer.
3)   Catia solids.
4)   Catia surfaces.
5)   Autocad dxf.
6)   pdges (Ford Motor Company graphics system).
7)   GM DES (General Motors Company graphics system).
8)   IGES.

The following media may be used for file transfer:

1)   TK50 tape cartridge, (VMS/ULTRIX/unix).
2)   1600 CPI magnetic tape (standards or VMS).
3)   5-¼" DOS diskettes (DD or HD).
4)   3-½" diskettes, DOS or Unix (DD or HD).
5)   DAT (digital audio tape, 4mm, 1300 Mbyte - unix).
6)   ¼" tape cartridge 60 - 525 Mbyte (unix).

THE SLS™ SELECTIVE LASER SINTERING PROCESS: AN UPDATE ON THE TECHNOLOGY, MATERIALS, AND APPLICATIONS

Mr Kent L Nutt

DTM Corporation
USA

1   Introduction

Since its introduction in 1989, the SLS™ Selective Laser Sintering Process, offered by DTM Corporation, has been continually improved and refined to meet the current and future requirements of rapid prototyping and manufacturing applications for the creation of models, patterns and prototypes. Initially created and patented at the University of Texas, the SLS process was commercialized by DTM Corporation through company-operated Service Bureaus. During early 1992, 5 SLS Beta Systems were installed in major corporations in key industry segments including Aerospace, Automotive, Imaging/Health/Chemical, Department of Energy, and Service Bureau.

SLS technology is a free form fabrication process that allows for the creation of engineered components by the precise thermal fusing of powdered materials. Complex part geometries are built in successive layers that define cross sections of the component features. As with most currently available rapid prototyping systems, the SLS process requires solid three-dimensional CAD files in .STL file format.

2   An Update on The SLS Process

The SLS process has evolved through two commercial system versions beginning with the SLS Model 125 first introduced in 1989 and operated today in DTM Service Centers. This earlier SLS platform, while a proven performer in daily operation, did not contain the level of integarated process control required for customer installations. Operation of the SLS Model 125 Systems in DTM's Service Centers allowed the identification and incorporation of a number of design improvements now included within the production SLS System - The Sinterstation™ 2000 System. Significant improvements were made in three basic areas: system software, hardware, and the basic underlying SLS process. Specific improvements include the following:

2.1   Sinterstation 2000 Software Improvements

The Sinterstation 2000 employs an X Window, Motif-based graphical user interface (GUI) for advanced person-machine interface. The earlier SLS Model 125 used a conventional menu approach to user interface and did not include many of the process parameter controls included within the Sinterstation 2000 System such as laser energy output, process chamber temperature, and scanning speed. In addition, specific material processing parameters acquired through computer simulations developed at the University of Texas were incorporated in the Sinterstation 2000 System. The parameters are now accessed through the system user-interface and are integrated with the system's programmable Logic Controller (PLC) in a closed-loop configuration that allows the system to operate in a self-correcting, unattended mode.

Other software enhancements in the Sinterstation 2000 include beam compensation, or software-based laser control that results in greater dimensional accuracy in the sintering of part geometries. Also, part previewing and build status are graphically displayed through the system's user interface. These features allow users to view and orient multiple parts within the part-building cylinder prior to beginning the build process, and to view a graphic representation of the build status parts undergoing the sintering process. Finally, the System's operating software is UNIX, a platform gaining widespread acceptance for industrial engineering multi-tasking applications.

2.2   Sinterstation 2000 Hardware Improvements

There are a number of hardware improvements incorporated in the Sinterstation 2000 including a new powder feeding mechanism that uses two cartridges flanking the part-build cylinder. This allows for bi-directional powder feeding to the roller that lays powder across the part-build cylinder and results in faster overall build times. This new system design also provides an integrated powder handling capability in which unsintered powder can be returned to the powder feeding cartridges for recycling and extending the use of materials in the SLS process.

The CO_2 laser has been increased to 50 watts from the 25 watts used on the SLS Model 125 System.

Another hardware improvement is the integration of the atmospheric control unit (ACU) within the system cabinet as a modular component. This unit provides the nitrogen flow for inerting the Sinterstation 2000 process chamber with nitrogen to ensure safe material sintering operations. The earlier, SLS Model 125 required additional, peripheral equipment to provide this inerting capability. All that is required for system emissions is a single external vent for exhausting very low levels of nitrogen.

As discussed in software improvements, a closed-loop PLC provides the Sinterstation 2000 System with advanced operational control that allows the system to operate in an unattended mode, an important capability for users building large, complex part geometries.

Finally, the system CPU has been upgraded to a 486 personal computer. This computer provides the interface to the applications software and performance the slicing functions of the STL file concurrent with system processing.

2.3   Sinterstation 2000 Process Improvements

DTM has improved the basic SLS process through the implementation of a statistical process control program (SPC). This ongoing SPC program has allowed DTM's Development Engineers to better understand the basic process parameters such as material particle size and distribution, thermal dynamics, scanning speed, and geometry-specific variables, all of which vary by each material used in the SLS process. This SPC program includes the analysis of material coupons and tensile bars produced on the SLS Model 125 and Sinterstation 2000 Systems within DTM's and BF Goodrich's Process Development groups, the DTM Service Bureau, and Beta Systems installed at customer facilities as part of the Sinterstation 2000 Beta Program.

Substantial material property improvements have been obtained as a result of SLS process development during the past two years. In particular, parts fabricated from polycarbonate and nylon materials have been measured within ranges of 75% to 92% for polycarbonate and 87% to 93% for nylon of the density these materials would yield through standard injection molding processes.

Table 1 indicates specific material properties of processed SLS materials.

MATERIAL CHARACTERISTICS			
Specifications	**Nylon**	**Polycarbonate**	**Wax**
Color	White	White	Green
Particle Size	95% < 105 Micron	95% < 105 Micron	95% < 180 Micron
% Moisture	< 0.1	< 0.1	< 0.5
Performance			
Density (g/cc)	0.91	0.82	0.80
Flex Strength (psi)	8,300	4,800	N/A
Flex Modulus (psi)	160,000	122,000	N/A
% Ash	N/A	N/A	<0.015%

2.4 Accuracy of the SLS Process

Recent data from SLS Model 125 Systems operating in the DTM Service Bureau indicate accuracy on the order of +/- 0.05 inches across the part cylinder in the X, Y and Z axis in the building of small parts. This level of accuracy meets the design target set by DTM for SLS Systems. Accuracy data for the Beta Sinterstation 2000 Systems is being obtained through the Beta Program and was not available as of the date of this manuscript.

2.5 The Sinterstation 2000 System Beta Program

Five customers in key industry segments received Sinterstation 2000 Beta Systems during the first quarter of 1992. These installations include: Eastman Kodak Corporation, General Motors Corporation, Sandia National Laboratories, United Technologies Pratt & Whitney, and Plynetics Corporation. The Beta Program will have a duration of one year and is intended to provide these customers with early access to SLS technology in exchange for providing feedback on system operation and functions that may be incorporated in the production version of the Sinterstation 2000 System.

3   SLS Materials and Applications - Current Status and Future Directions

A primary advantage of SLS technology is the ability to achieve functional prototypes and patterns through the use of a growing number of non-toxic, conventional engineering materials. Currently available materials include polycarbonate, nylon, and investment casting wax. New thermoplastic materials that meet specific performance criteria and ceramic and metal materials are under development.

3.1   SLS Material Development

DTM has adopted a materials development strategy that addresses four basic goals designed to meet customer requirements. These include the following:

1)   The necessity of providing customers with a broad materials portfolio for selection of materials best suited to specific application requirements. Included here are materials that contain properties of improved strength, rigidity, imact resistance and other desired attributes.

2)   DTM will develop materials within the product portfolio with properties that are predictable and repeatable.

3)   DTM will develop the capability for customers to develop their own proprietary materials for use in the SLS process.

4)   DTM and the BF Goodrich Company will develop relationships with a number of suppliers of SLS materials to ensure a wide variety of competitive material sourcing.

The SLS material selection process is currently focused on the functional prototyping applications in a variety of industries that require material performance that closely approximate the mechanical properties found in injection molding applications. Specifically, new materials considered for use in the SLS process are measured for their abilities to meet the following material properties: tensile strength, flexural modulus, flexural strength, impact, elongation, HDT and specific gravity.

Polyurethane is an example of a new thermoplastic material under development for applications requiring material flexibility for the production of gaskets, prototyping rubber-based products and other flexible thermoplastic parts.

Reinforced nylon is an example of a new thermoplastic material intended for functional prototyping applications. These types of materials produce prototypes with material property characteristics that include low coefficients of gravity, excellent impact resistance, and improved overall strength.

Table 1 indicates the material properties for the currently available materials used in the SLS process.

Once a new material is selected, an extensive material characterization process is undertaken to ensure the material is both safe and optimized for use in the SLS process. This includes powdering the material in a manner consistent with the known requirements for specific particle sizes, particle size distributions and particle shapes. The new material is then tested against rigorous quality control standards set by the DTM material characterization program managed by the BF Goodrich Company.

4   SLS Metal and Ceramics Development

The use of thermoplastic models and prototypes are an important part of the industrial product design and manufacturing process, however market research has indicated that as much as 80% of all industrial prototyping is comprised of metal materials of various types. Additionally, the potential for technologies that can produce tooling, molds and fixturing using different metals and ceramics are advanced capabilities that many leading companies are exploring with RP Manufacturers.

4.1   Indirect Ceramics and Metals

In response to these market requirements, DTM Corporation has instituted a two-tiered approach to the development of sintered ceramic and metal materials. First, an indirect approach to the fabrication of ceramics and metals involves the use of proprietary polymer binders to act as adhesive agents for the sintering of both ceramics and metal materials.

Already verified in practice on the existing Sinterstation 2000 product platform, materials such as copper mixed with binders have been fabricated to produce EDM electrodes. Alumina ceramic molds for investment casting applications have been been produced in the same low-temperature process using a relatively low-powered laser. A silica ceramic material is under development for the fabrication of ceramic cores also used within the invstment casting process.

4.2   Direct Ceramics and Metals

DTM Corporation is sponsoring a development program at the University of Texas known as the High Temperature Workstation (HTW) program for the direct sintering of metals and ceramics. The HTW uses a 1000 watt CO_2 laser to sinter high temperature materials. Metal materials under development at the University of Texas include aluminium, bronze, copper, stainless steel, nickel and tungsten carbide. Ceramics in development include alumina and glass powders.

The HTW Research Program is funded by DTM Corporation for the advanced development of the SLS process. Among the goals of this research program is the determination of the optimum process parameters for materials used in the next generation of SLS systems that will sinter metals and ceramics for future applications that include prototype and production molding and tooling applications.

5   Summary

Significant improvements in SLS technology have been made since its introduction in 1989. The new commercial platform, the Sinterstation 2000 System, has incorporated a number of design improvements in the following areas: System Software, hardware and the underlying SLS process itself.

Major software improvements include a graphical user interface, a UNIX operating system, and beam compensation software for greater dimensional accuracy.

Major hardware improvements include a new bi-directional, integrated powder feeding mechanism, a closed-loop PLC for unattended operation, a 486-based personal computer and a 50 watt CO_2 laser.

SLS Process improvements have resulted from a Statistical Process Control Program (SPC) that has produced parts with greater densities and overall material properties.

Accuracy in the SLS process is now on the order +/- 0.05 for the SLS Model 125 with data not yet available for the Sinterstation 2000 System.

The University of Texas is developing processes for both indirect (uses proprietary binders) and the direct sintering of ceramic and metal materials. This technology is one and two years away from commercialization, respectively. This advanced SLS materials develop program will address applications such as the fabrication of prototype and production molds and tooling.

HELISYS LAMINATED OBJECT MANUFACTURING

Mr Leon Bowman

UMAK Limited, Armoury Road,
Birmingham B11 2RQ

1   Introduction

Many companies engaged in production processes have a requirement for a model or prototype component to be manufactured before commencing full scale volume production. Such models can be used for "fit and function" trials or indeed for secondary manufacturing processes such as casting and moulding.

The requirement for accurate prototypes that can be used for the purposes described has traditionally been served by producing models using skilled craftsmen or alternatively machining from the solid using a conventional CNC Machining Programme.

The Helisys Laminated Object Manufacturing systems distributed by UMAK offers designers the capability of producing accurate low cost models and patterns in a fraction of the time employed by traditional methods.

The Laminated Object Manufacturing process from Helisys enables accurate prototypes to be constructed directly from a computer model with no special tooling or fixturing being needed and with the designer having the ability to make modifications almost instantaneously.

The system utilises the industry standard "STL" data format which can be processed without alteration. Additionally the system software within the Helisys machine control automatically checks the incoming data for closing of the surface geometry triangles and if any open parts are found, those identified are closed. This system allows models to be produced even from corrupted files giving a degree of latitude found only in the Helisys LOM process.

Additionally, scaling and the facility to include compensation for shrinkage factors, needed for moulding, is included. Furthermore objects can be oriented into the optimum attitude for component strength or minimum time to manufacture. The flexibility of the system also allows several objects to be produced at the same time.

These can be multiples or handed variants of the same design or a mixture of completely different parts.

2   Machine Description

The LOM 1015 machine is a free-standing self contained unit operating from a normal 240 volt supply and requiring no special environmental considerations. This facility enables the unit to be installed either on the shop floor or in an office. Within the machine base is a mechanism to feed the laminating material from a roll into the working position where it is cut by an x-y positioned laser beam. It is also in this position where each laminate is bonded to the previously laminated stack. Models can be produced from a variety of materials which only have to reach the criteria that they can be bonded by heat and are capable of being cut by a CO_2

laser beam. Typical materials include paper coated with heat sensitive adhesive, polyester film or other laminates to suit the characteristics of the object that is required.

3   Process Sequence

Reference to the schematic arrangement will show that the material is fed into a working position to be bonded to the previous layer, it is then simultaneously compressed and raised in temperature by means of a heated roller which passes over the laminated area and then retracts into a standby position. This is followed by a CO_2 laser traversing over the bonded laminate to cut the external and internal profiles for any given cross section which has been generated by the CAD system. Upon completion of the cutting action the "Z" axis table lowers slightly, the material is fed forward, the "Z" axis returns to the working position and the process repeated.

4   Lamination Control

By utilising this bonding and cutting technique it is possible to construct a model of virtually any complexity from a large number of thin laminations which can be varied in thickness to give a higher or lower degree of resolution as required.

Since solid materials are utilised, the speed of cutting depends on the peripheral length of each cross section rather than on the total surface area as is the case with some alternative technologies. Therefore, parts with thick walls are produced just as fast as those with thin walls.

Each successive laminate has it's nominal thickness calculated each time a layer is placed onto the object. This is to ensure that despite variations in thickness of successive layers the profile that is cut is appropriate to the height of the model at that stage of build. This is achieved by a feed back system on the z axis ensuring absolute accuracy regardless of the height of the object being constructed or tolerance variations in the laminate material.

5   Model Support Structure

During the process of cutting there is a certain amount of waste material which is within the cutting area but not required in the finished model. This material is sliced into cubes by the laser beam to ensure it's easy removal once the model has been finished. This process is quite deliberate. The cubes can be removed during the manufacturing process in order to expose completely enclosed cavities but is normally left in position to provide support and stability to the model during the manufacturing process. The technique ensures that the roller only passes over a complete sheet of laminate and that thin sections are adequately supported during the cutting operation. The size of the cubes can be varied to suit the detail required.

Upon completion the model is removed from the machine as a complete unit and the small cubes subsequently separated to expose the stable and finished model.

6   Applications

The models produced by the process fall basically into two different categories.

1.   Models which are to be used for verification of a design to ensure that a correct fit is obtained with mating parts.

Additionally it enables a designer to obtain a 3 dimensional appreciation of the aesthetics in the event that it is a consumer product where the overall design can be as important as the function.

2.   Models can be used as parts of a further production process such as casting in it's various forms. Indeed models are being used as masters for sand castings and also as forms which can be burnt out in investment casting. Being paper the model will burn at 1,400° F making the process ideally suited to the investment casting industry. Other applications involve manufacturing a silicone mould from the paper from which can be produced plastic, urethane and epoxy parts, or wax parts for the more traditional investment process for multiple components.

7   Accuracy and Finish

With an overall accuracy of approximately +/- 0.005" (0.13mm) a high degree of detail can be incorporated into the models and of course the possibility always exists for hand finishing if the design calls for an extremely high surface finish. The models when completed exhibit similar characteristics to that of plywood, including strength and machinability.

As the models are constructed from laminates of solid material, there are no phase changes which occur during the transition of a liquid to a solid and no shrinkage. This ensures that the model has a predictable accuracy level.

A by-product of the simplicity of the system is the relatively low capital cost and greatly reduced maintenance and running charges due to the use of a CO_2 laser and readily available low cost production materials.

8   The Future

As the main criteria required for the production of a model on the LOM System are simply those of being able to be cut by laser and fused by heat it follows that a large number of laminate materials can be used.

In addition to the Model 1015 a model LOM 2030 is currently available which has a working volume in excess of 9 cubic feet. Examples of this machine are in production and open up a further market for the production of very large models. The free working ability of the material also allows models to be joined together either by moulding in a dovetail on 2 parts or by simply using readily available instant adhesives.

Under investigation at the present time are metallic foils and composite materials which clearly will have an impact in the direct manufacture of component parts.

9   Summary

The Helisys Laminated Object Manufacturing System distributed and supported by UMAK offers designers the capability of producing accurate low cost models in a fraction of the time employed by traditional methods.

Typical models are being produced within a 24 hour period and since the process is automated, the machine can be left running overnight unattended.

For the first time a technology is available which is capable of producing component parts in materials having the appearance and characteristics of a hard wood, or of a polyester based plastic.

Now there is a realistic way to reduce the "time to market" without inhibiting the development of the product with unacceptable process lead times.

RAPID PROTOTYPING USING FDM: A FAST, PRECISE, SAFE TECHNOLOGY

Lisa H Crump

Stratasys, Inc
Minneapolis, USA

1   Introduction

This paper outlines the use of FDM to speed product design and to streamline the manufacturing process.

Time compression, the ability to quickly reduce the time it takes to get new products to market, has increased the pressure on all phases of the manufacturing process. Manufacturers must find and implement time saving systems without sacrificing quality.

Fused Deposition Modelling (FDM) provides a synergistic solution for design and manufacturing engineering: visualization models and part concept designs become accurate physical models leading to final working parts right within the normal engineering office environment (see figure 1).

This clean running, single step operation uses non-toxic, thermoplastic wire-like filaments eliminating liquid photopolymers, powders or lasers from the process.

The current technological quest has been to create a true desktop system suitable for use in an office environment. The FDM process has moved the state of the art beyond lasers, beyond systems that require messy materials and beyond large, cumbersome units to allow for true 3D desktop prototyping.

FDM quickly and safely produces non-toxic physical prototypes from 3D CAD data reducing the time to market, reducing product development costs and allowing verification of production tooling.

2   Background

In 1988 Scott Crump invented the FDM process (patent pending), an automatic, non-laser based technology using non-toxic materials for rapid part creation. The process builds on early professional experiences with thermofusion control mechanisms and low temperature thermoplastics.

FDM is unique technology to empower design and manufacturing engineers to be able to quickly produce precise, multi-material models in an engineering environment, right at the CAD workstation.

3   The Need for Rapid Prototyping

Stratasys, Inc. is a privately held company with partial funding provided by Battery Ventures in Boston. Stratasys, Inc. began shipping 3D MODELERS in the second quarter of 1991.

In today's business environment, manufacturers need every competitive advantage to get a quality product to market as quickly as possible. The ability to rapidly produce 3D models of the images created on CAD workstations has become an additional tool to positively impact both quality and speed (Marks, 1990).

By allowing design and manufacturing engineers to quickly, accurately and efficiently create prototypes, the design process will improve. When an accurate physical model is generated in less than an hour, the designer can economically create multiple iterations prior to final design.

Rapid prototyping gives shape, form and feel to the image on the computer screen by producing 3D models of complex, sculptured-surfaced parts within minutes or a few hours. Rapid prototyping will increase experimentation and allow improvements to be quickly incorporated (Wohlers, 1990).

4   3D Modeler

The FDM process uses the Stratasys 3D MODELER® in conjunction with a CAD workstation. Stratasys' 3D MODELER is a single step, self-contained modelling system that offers the user several advantages. Speed is an important benefit of this technology; typical models can be produced in minutes rather than hours or days. As no post curing is required, the FDM technique enables the designer to create multiple versions of a part design within a short time frame.

5   Elements of the FDM Process

In this process a conceptual geometric model is created on the CAD workstation. It is then imported into a UNIX-based workstation where it is sliced into horizontal layers that are down-loaded to the 3D MODELLER (see figure 2).

Liquid thermoplastic material is extruded and then deposited into ultra thin layers from the lightweight FDM head one layer at a time. This builds the model upward off a fixtureless base. The plastic or wax material then solidifies in 1/10 of a second as it is directed into place with an X-Y controlled extrusion head orifice that creates a precision laminate.

A spool of .050 inch diameter modelling filament feeds the FDM head and can be changed to a different material in 1 minute.

Maintaining the liquid modelling material just above the solidification point is fundamental to the FDM process. The thermoplastic melt temperature is controlled to 1 degree Fahrenheit above solidification. The material then solidifies as it is directed into place with an X-Y controlled extruding head nozzle that creates a precision laminate.

Successive laminations, within the 0.001 to 0.050 inch thickness range and a wall thickness of .009 to .250 inch range, adhere to one another through thermal fusion to form the model. Our overall tolerance is + or - .005 inches in the X,Y,Z axis over a 12 inch cubed working envelope.

6   Safety Benefits

The Stratasys 3D MODELER is a stand-alone modelling system that is located next to the CAD workstation. It stands 6 feet tall with a 3' by 2.5' footprint. The system requires no exhaust hood or special facilities, providing a natural extension to the engineering workstation and easily fitting into an office environment.

The process operates at a temperature of 180 degrees fahrenheit, about the temperature of a cup of coffee, making it safe for office use. There is no worry of possible exposure to toxic chemicals, lasers, or liquid polymer baths. The Stratasys process uses no powders and there is no messy cleanup. Concern over disposal of hazardous materials is eliminated.

7   Materials

The Stratasys technology allows a variety of modelling materials and colours. All are inert, non-toxic thermoplastics which closely resemble actual production materials. The system uses a wax-filled plastic adhesive material, a tough nylon-like material or investment casting wax. There thermoplastics soften and liquefy when heat is applied.

The Stratasys investment casting wax material is excellent for lost wax investment casting and does not have to be specially burnt out. Using this material streamlines the model making process and helps bring products to market faster.

The machinable wax is primarily used for conceptual modelling and spray metal moulding (see figure 3). For instance, the accuracy of the model allows its use in the spray metal process for injection mould prototyping. Both the investment casting wax and the machinable wax can streamline the manufacturing process by allowing the user to go directly to soft tooling using the model as the pattern for investment casting or spray metal injection moulding.

The plastic filament is a tough material producing sturdy models suitable for concept models or fit, form and some function applications.

In the three years the FDM technology was in development several obstacles were overcome. A major breakthrough was the decision to settle on a filament system of material media as opposed to a "hopper" system. The spool based filament system has proven to be a significant strength of the 3D MODELER.

The spools give the user the ability to change material in about one minute by threading the desired material into the prototyping unit. There is virtually no waste and no vat to clean.

The materials to produce a part are cost effective, usually under twenty dollars. For example the material for one golf club head costs approximately $9.00 and one spool of material can produce roughly 20 club heads.

The FDM process is not limited by the UV polymers required by many other rapid prototyping systems and new materials are continuously under development.

8   Supports

The FDM process does not need elaborate supports to produce a part as do some other systems. The 3D MODELER has the ability to create a support in mid-air rather than building the support up from the base in some applications. The system is also capable of extruding plastic into free space depending on the part geometry. When supports are not used, the FDM head forms a precision horizontal support in mid-air as it solidifies.

9   Open Systems

The 3D MODELER imports geometry through standard RS 232 serial ports. Either wireframe, surface or solid CAD data from all standard CAD software packages can be imported through IGES running on UNIX workstations.

There are three methods of driving the modeller:

1.   Through IGES

A file is brought into the CAD software program in an IGES format (see the Table of Stratasys Supported IGES entitles). This file can be edited, scaled, oriented and even surfaced if required. Supports, if needed, can be added graphically.

2.   Direct through NC code

NC code taken directly from other CAM programs can drive the Stratasys 3D MODELLER. CAM systems than can compute multiple continuous surfaces with an every increasing positive Z Axis are supported.

3.   Through .STL format

It is possible to import an .STL file and post out NC code to drive the modeller.

TABLE OF STRATASYS SUPPORTED IGES ENTITIES	
Geometric	**Annotation Entities**
100 Circular Arc	106 Crosshatching (limited support)
102 Composit Curve	202 Angular Dimension
104 Conic Arc	206 Diameter Dimension
106 Copious Data	210 General Label
108 Plane	212 General Note (limited support)
110 Line	214 Leader Arrow
112 Parametric Spline Curve	216 Linear Dimension
114 Parametric Spline Surface	218 Ordinate Dimension
116 Point	220 Point Dimension
118 Rule Surface	222 Radius Dimension
120 Surface of Revolution	228 General Symbol
122 Tabulated Cylinder	
124 Transformation Matrix	
126 Rational B-Spline Surface	**Structure Entities**
128 Rational B-Spline Surface	
140 Offset Surface (limited support)	308 Subfigure Definition
141 Boundary Surface	314 Colour Definition (limited support)
142 Curve on a Parametric Surface (limited support)	402 Associate Instance
143 Bounded Surface	404 Drawing (limited support)
144 Trimmed Surface	406 Property
	408 Singular Subfigure Instance
	410 View (limited support)
	412 Rectangular Array Subfigure Instance
	414 Circular Array Subfigure Instance

10   Applications

Applications cross a wide spectrum of industries. Any industry that manufactures a tangible product and can benefit from reducing design and manufacturing errors, increasing manufacturing speed or compressing the time to manufacturing has a potential for this technology.

Companies using rapid prototyping are finding the benefits of the technology go beyond the ability to produce more models faster. Once the model has been completed and approved, the prototype may be used in the next step in the manufacturing process.

Both injection moulding and investment casting can use the Stratasys prototype as a direct input master to the manufacturing process.

10.1 Investment Casting

Manufacturing complex metal components requires a multi-step investment casting process. As the name implies, the Stratasys investment casting wax is excellent for lost wax investment castings.

The time consuming step of producing a wax replica of the part to be manufactured can be eliminated. The desired part created in Stratasys' investment casting wax can be dipped or invested directly into the ceramic slurry. The wax quickly dewaxes from the ceramic shell (see figure 4).

A report published in INCAST states this about the Stratasys investment casting wax, "for investment casters, these models are an ideal pattern material. They are gated, dewaxed and fired in shell or solid moulds exactly as normal wax patterns are processed." (March, 1991)

10.1.1 Investment Casting Examples

The investment casting process is used by a manufacturer of products for the orthopaedic surgeon. These products include reconstructive parts such as hip and knee replacement implants as well as shoulder, ankle and other less frequently replaced joints (see figure 5).

Typically the parts are machined from solid blocks of titanium. The need for high quality is apparent when considering the part will be a component of someone's leg or knee for life. From a financial aspect the need for quality is apparent when considering the expense of the titanium. Precision, quality parts with complex surfaces are an ideal match for the FDM process.

The ability to rapidly produce models allows evaluation by the consulting orthopaedic physicians, along with the team members for marketing, design, engineering and manufacturing.

Once a design has been analyzed and consensus is reached the company benefits from the advantages of Stratasys' investment casting wax. By saving steps in the manufacturing process, the company can speed its products into this competitive market.

The jewellery industry is another example where investment casting is used extensively (see figure 6). Although it lacks the emotional impact of a life changing knee implant, other parallels exist. Certainly the high cost of raw material makes the use of a prototype in a less expensive material desirable.

10.2 Injection Moulding

The accuracy of the Stratasys model allows the use of the model in the spray metal process for injection moulding. The filament materials used by Stratasys have high durability and stability required for a master for spray metal moulding.

Using a 3D model produced in the Stratasys machinable wax, allows manufacturers to go directly to the spray metal moulding process. Customers create spray metal tooling by spraying the metal onto the model in thin coats.

This technique has been applied across industries from the simple casting of urethane in the shoe industry to injection moulding of glass filled resins. These glass filled resins are used for high strength, heat resistant, wear resistant parts such as photo equipment, small power tools and appliances.

Saving steps in the manufacturing process translates into time savings for manufacturers using investment casting or injection moulding techniques. These savings allow manufacturers to speed products to market.

10.3 Fit, Form and Function Applications

A common frustration in assembled products occurs when interior components are built that will not fit together or do not fit the housing. The ability to rapidly produce prototypes reduces this sources of manufacturing error or decreases the time it takes to hand produce prototypes of all components.

The aerospace industry is just one example where fit, form and function are a concern.

10.4 Conceptual Modelling

The prototype or model itself can be a marketing tool for the manufacturer (see figure 7). To be able to hand a client a prototype of the proposed part at the final presentation or to include a prototype with the proposal package has strong emotional appeal in the sales process.

Conceptual modelling also enables engineers to quickly produce multiple iterations of a sample part to streamline the design process.

Concept models are important in the shoe industry. One major shoe manufacturer creates hundreds of new shoe heel designs each year. Each heel style is normally produced in one size based on the designer's drawing. After this initial prototype design is verified, models are created for sizes 3 through 12, with the heel dimensions graded for the size.

The ability to quickly and accurately produce the concept model allows this manufacturer to improve quality and productivity in the manufacturing process.

11   Summary

FDM provides a combination of attractive features to provide true desktop 3D modelling. It is a non-laser based system providing a cost effective, accurate and environmentally safe way to produce 3D models and prototypes.

Reducing time to market by accommodating engineering changes quickly and improving product quality demands state-of-the-art prototyping tools.

References

Kennerknecht, S. and Sifford, D., "New Dimensions in Rapid Prototyping Explored for Aluminium Investment Castings", INCAST, March 1990, Vol. IV, Numbers 3, pp. 5-10.

Marks, P., 1990, "The Rapid Prototyping Revolution ...Better Products Sooner," Proceedings, The First International Conference on Desktop Manufacturing Cambridge, Massachusetts, October, 1990.

Wohlers, Terry, "Plastic Models in Minutes," Cadence, July, 1990.

Figure 1   The Stratasys 3D MODELER is suitable for an office environment, measuring 30" x 36" x 68" and weighing 250 lbs.

FDM — FUSED DEPOSITION MODELING

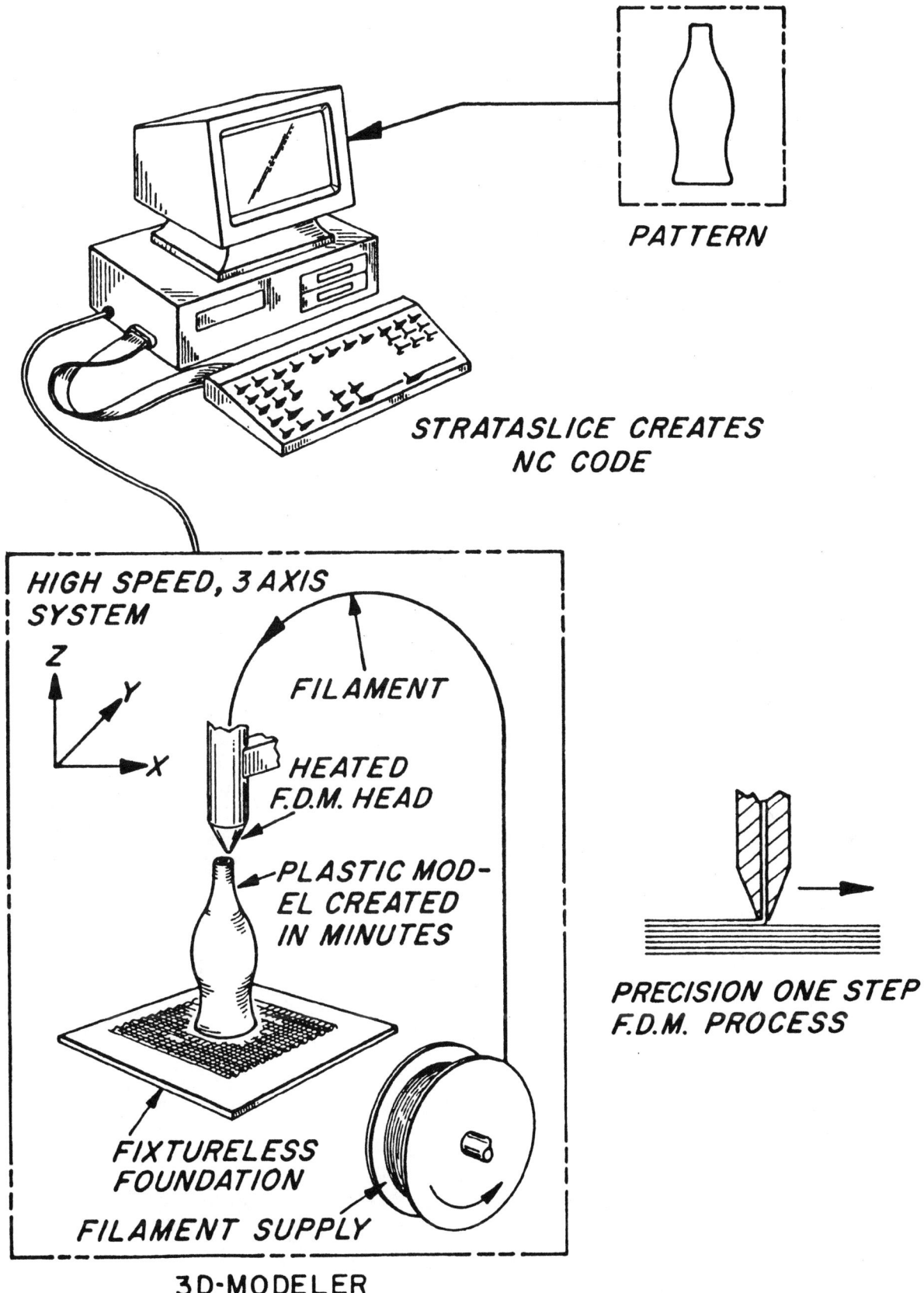

PATTERN

STRATASLICE CREATES
NC CODE

HIGH SPEED, 3 AXIS
SYSTEM

Z
Y
X

FILAMENT

HEATED
F.D.M. HEAD

PLASTIC MOD-
EL CREATED
IN MINUTES

FIXTURELESS
FOUNDATION

FILAMENT SUPPLY

3D-MODELER

PRECISION ONE STEP
F.D.M. PROCESS

Figure 2   The Fused Deposition Modeling (FDM) process produces safe,
accurate 3D models in minutes.

Figure 3   Airfoil part produced in Stratasys machinable wax. Model creation
time: 5 hours, 45 minutes. Resolution .010 inches.

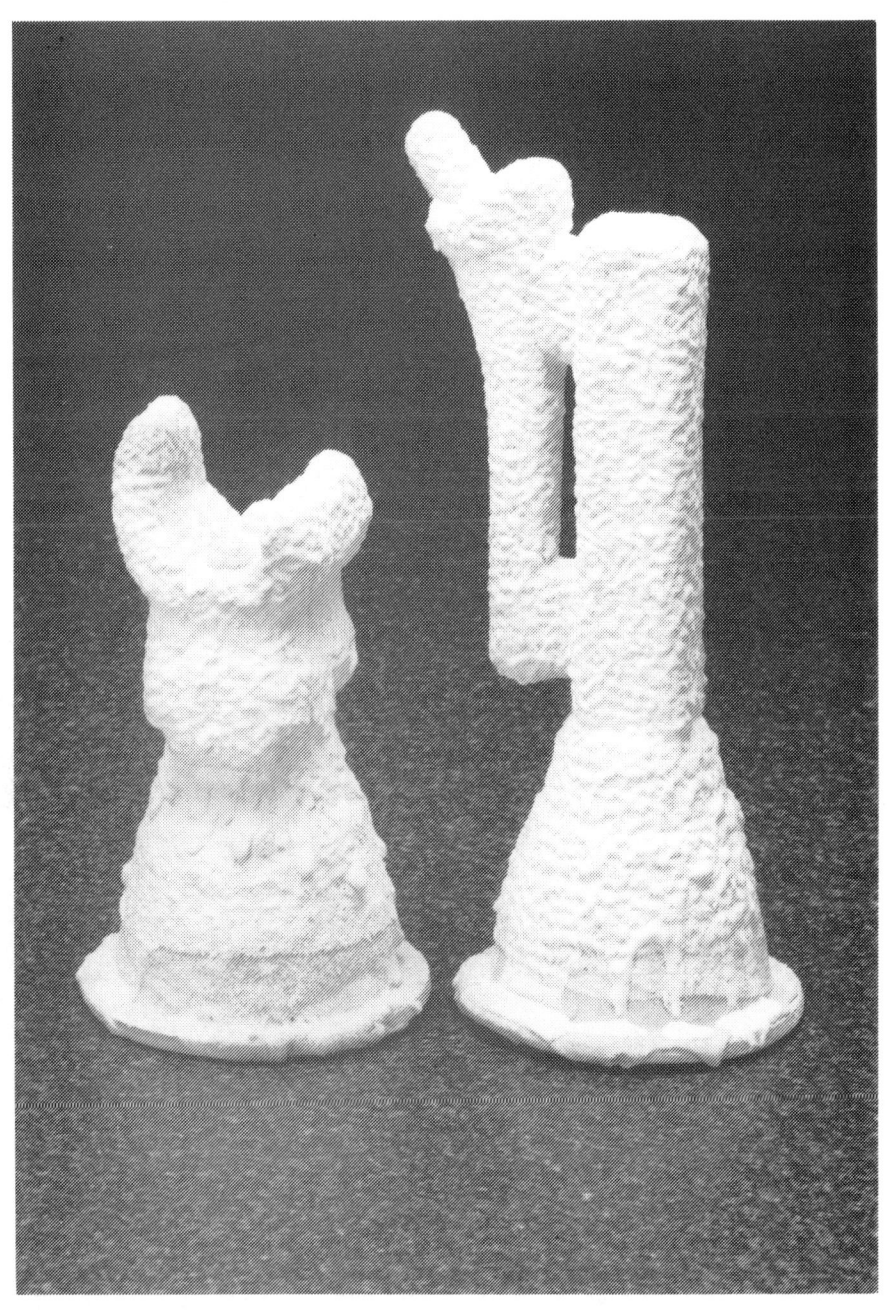

Figure 4   Investment casting shells created from parts made of Stratasys
investment casting wax.   Left: knee implant shell.   Right: hip
replacement shell.

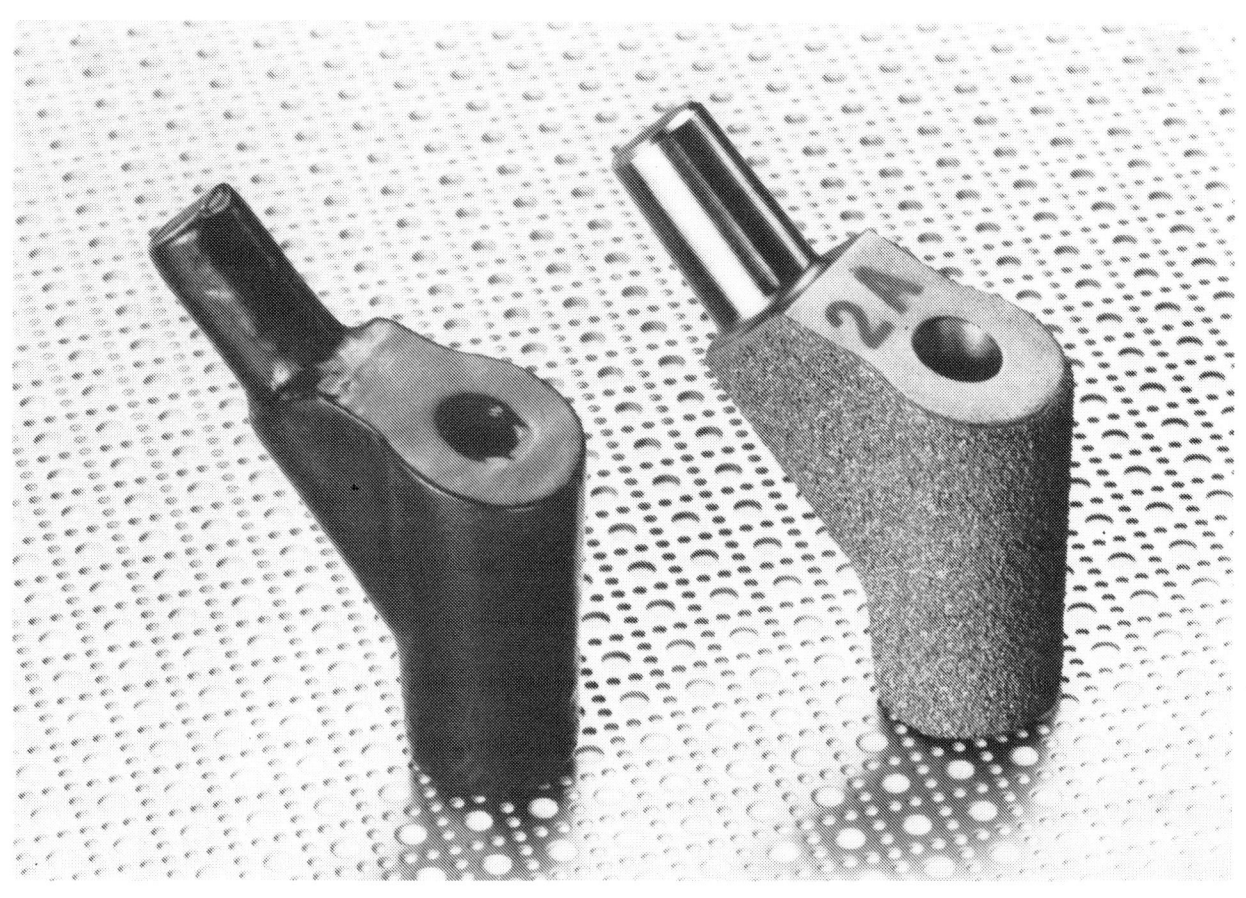

Figure 5   Biomet hip replacement joint produced by the Stratasys 3D
            MODELER. Left part was made in the Stratasys investment casting
            wax. Right part was investment cast directly from the wax. Model
            creation time: 58 minutes.

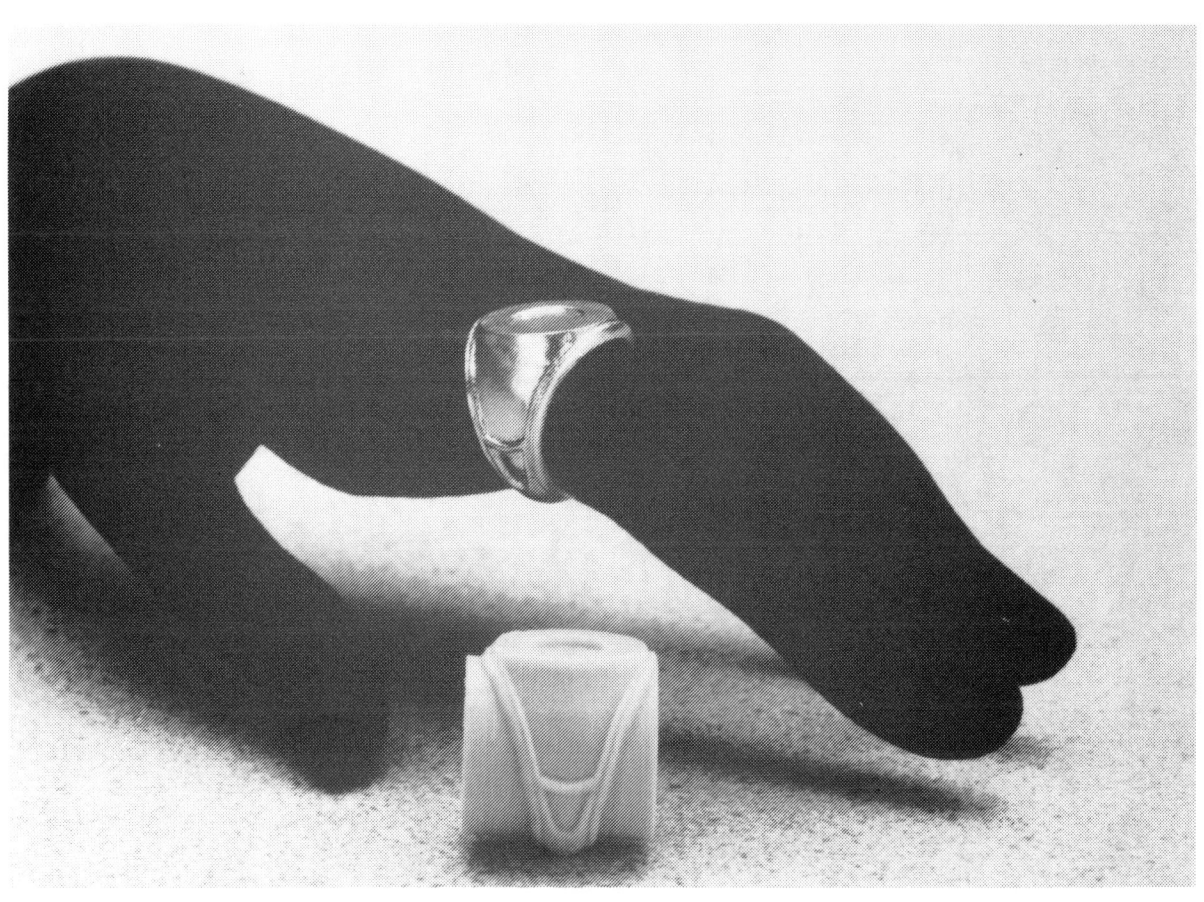

Figure 6   Ring produced by the Stratasys 3D MODELER in investment casting wax and actual ring investment cast directly from the wax. Model creation time: 35 minutes. Resolution: .002 inches.

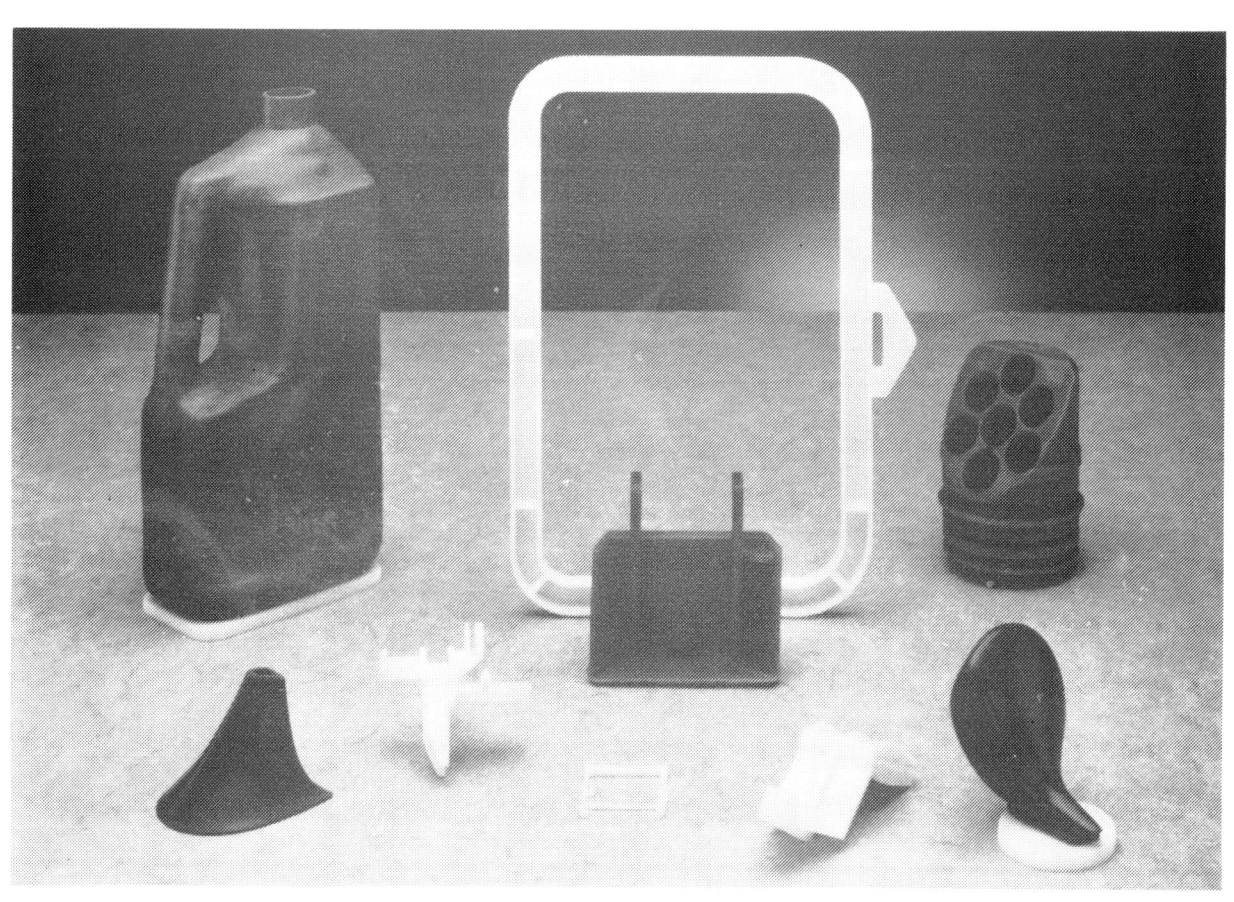

Figure 7   An assortment of concept models created on the Stratasys 3D
MODELER showing a variety of geometries, complexities, and
materials.

3-D WELDING

Dr P M Dickens, Dr M S Pridham, Dr R C Cobb,Dr I Gibson
and Mr. G Dixon
Department of Manufacturing Engineering
and Operations Management,
University of Nottingham, UK.

1   Introduction

Rapid Prototyping has taken on a great importance with the rise in interest of concepts such as 'Concurrent Engineering' and the fact that many product life cycles have been significantly reduced. Time to market has become critical to the success of new products with the rapid advance of technology leading to, perhaps almost premature, obsolescence. Many manufacturers now recognise the potential of Rapid Prototyping systems to combat these problems.

A common feature of all Rapid Prototyping systems is that they are based, almost exclusively on polymer, or paper materials. The dimensions of the parts produced are necessarily limited by the volume of the processing area within the machine, and many parts have the tendency to warp or distort as a result of shrinkage and lack of support. Also the mechanical properties of the part produced are restricted to those of the processable materials and thus in many cases required 'engineering properties' cannot be obtained.

At Nottingham University work on Rapid Prototyping systems based on a 3-D welding system has been undertaken to try to combat some of the weaknesses of the other processes. There is some history of the use of welding as a means of building up components and parts for salvage and reclamation; thicknesses up to 50mm being typical (1). The basis for using welding for creating free standing shapes was established in Germany in the 1960's when limited steel supplies and economic pressures led to the search for new production processes (2). This led to companies such as Krupp, Thyssen and Sulzer developing welding techniques for the fabrication of large components of simple geometry, such as pressure vessels which could weigh up to 500 tonnes (3). The technique was to become known as 'shape welding'.

Other work in this area has been undertaken by Babcock & Wilcox (4) who have been working mainly on large components produced in austenitic material. Also, work by Rolls-Royce (5) has centred on investigating the technique as a means of reducing the wastage levels of expensive high performance alloys which can occur in conventional processing.

As a production technique 3-D welding offers significant advantages over conventional processing, these include:

-       The potential for robot control of the welding torch allowing large variation in part dimensions and geometry.

-       A highly automated system.

-       Parts with, consistent properties.

-       Rapid processing times, hence vastly reduced development times

-       Efficient use of materials

-       Direct production of a metal part - unique amongst current Rapid Prototyping systems.

2　3-D Welding Trials

The initial work on 3-D welding was aimed at verifying the potential of the welding technique as a Rapid Prototyping system. The first parts produced by robot welding were simple unsupported vertical walls in a square box formation (figure 1). The successful completion of these parts led to trials involving the production of sloping walls in the form of a truncated pyramid (figure 2).

Once it was established that more complicated structures were possible a thermostat housing from a Ford Fiesta automobile was obtained and the robot programmed to manufacture this shape. This part was manufactured in two main stages. Firstly the base and body of the housing was produced. This was then rotated through 90° and the outlet pipe welded. The thermostat housing, as shown in figure 3, required 22 minutes of welding. This part proved the ability to manufacture parts that would normally be produced by casting. A sheet metal part was chosen as the next prototype shape for experimentation. Figure 4 illustrates the original part with the welded version alongside. As there was more material in this part the welding time was much longer at approximately 3 hours.

The welding system used with the robot was a Murex Transmig 400, MIG welding torch with a Transmatic 162 wire feed controller. Welding took place using ArgoShield 5, an Argon/CO_2 mix, with a welding current of approximately 100A. With a 0.8mm gauge wire, the feed rate was fixed at 6.5m/min. This lays down a bead of weld that is approximately 4.5mm wide and 1.4mm thick. Using this equipment, these dimensions represent the resolution of the system.

The robot used is a Cincinnati T3-276 machine, running Acramatic software for robot control V.4 release 8 (1985). Using signal control lines, the robot has only the ability to switch the welding system on and off with an automatic gas purge at the beginning and end of each welding sequence. There is no direct feed control of the wire by the robot. The robot itself has a nominal repeatability of 0.1mm throughout its working volume. Although it is quite old technology, the working conditions of the robot are fairly moderate with a light payload, working speeds of approximately 8mm/s, and very little wrist movement. All movement is close to the column, providing optimum accuracy within the robots working volume. Most robot welding system inaccuracies do not result directly from the robot itself.

3　Effect of Welding Parameters on Weld Bead Characteristics

The shape and dimensions of the weld bead are very important in the use of 3-D welding as a Rapid Prototyping system since these will determine the limits to the wall thickness which may be produced, and will also influence the quality of the surface finish.

Numerous trials were undertaken to produce single weld beads for a range of welding conditions. The parameters which were varied included voltage, wire feed rate, wire stickout, wire diameter and welding velocity. The technique employed was to vary one parameter at a time, whilst holding the rest constant. The arc voltage and welding current under each condition was monitored and the dimensions of the bead produced (height and width) were subsequently measured using a shadowgraph technique. A vast amount of data was generated in this way but the general trends are presented in Table 1.

Increasing Variable	Effect on Measured Variable			
	Arc Voltage	Current	Bead Width	Bead Height
Voltage	↑	= / ↑	↑	↓
Wire feed	↓	↑	↑	↑
Stickout	↑	↓	↓	↑
Wire Dia.	↓	↑	↑	↑
Velocity	=	=	↓	↓

Table 1 - Effect of Variables on Measured Parameters

This initial work has produced very useful information to go towards constructing a welding parameter database but the potential for further work is enormous and areas such as the effect of multiple layers on weld bead dimensions require further investigation, even though wall smoothness has been improved (see figure 5).

4   Materials

Since one of the main potential advantages of robot welding as a Rapid Prototyping technique is the direct production of a metal part, which is often more suited to in situ testing, it is very important to confirm the mechanical and structural properties of parts produced in this way. In order to do this a programme of mechanical and microstructural examination was undertaken. Using typical operating parameters, and mild steel welding wire based on Fe-C(0.08%) - Si:(0.9%) Mn(1.5%), square box section walls were produced and test-pieces were cut at different positions and orientations within the walls.

Vickers hardness measurements (10kg load) made in a range of positions over the wall surface showed little variation along the wall length, but a definite increase in hardness from 146.3 VHN at the base to 172.6 VHN at the top of the wall was noted (the height of the wall being approximately 100mm and corresponding to around 70 welding passes).

Tensile tests were carried out on test-pieces cut from various orientations in the wall, with samples being taken (i) with the tensile axis corresponding to the vertical direction and (ii) with the tensile axis corresponding to the horizontal direction both from the upper, and lower part, of the wall. The tensile strength results were very consistent regardless of orientation, with typical values of 490 MPa measured.

The good strength values obtained from the vertical specimens indicated there are few areas of weakness between adjacent weld layers. The elongation to failure values however, did show a marked difference between horizontal test-pieces cut from the bottom and the top of the wall. Typical values for the base of the wall are in excess of 30% whilst those at the top average 22.5%. The measured mechanical properties are summarised in Table 2.

Specimen Orientation	Ultimate Tensile Strength MPa	Elongation to Failure %
Vertical	489	35.0
Horizontal (Top)	484	22.5
Horizontal (Bottom)	499	33.1

Table 2 - Average Tensile Test Data

Optical microscopy revealed the microstructure of the material in the wall to be largely equiaxed ferrite (a) and pearlite (a + Fe_3C) with a grain size of approximately 60 μm, see figure 6. It was discovered that there are local regions where the structure is much less equiaxed and more columnar in nature (grain size approximately 600 μm x 100μm) as would be expected in an as-cast material, seen in figure 7. These regions however are restricted to the very top layers of the wall where the weld layers have not been subjected to the effects of reheating, from the deposition of subsequent weld layers. This structure accounts for the lower levels of ductility measured in specimens cut from the top of the wall in the horizontal direction. Due to the localisation of this structure a simple heat treatment procedure could be used to produce a more uniform microstructure throughout the wall.

The microscopy work revealed no evidence of voids or cavities in the structure and the measured density of the welded material was found to be approximately 99.5% of the equivalent wrought material. No indication was found of any oxidation between adjacent weld layers and again this is supported by the strength measurements obtained for the vertical test pieces.

The material test results indicate that parts produced by the 3-D welding process have good structural integrity and property levels which would allow them to be exploited in service conditions.

5   Off-Line Robot Programming

The parts which have been produced and described so far have been produced using a cumbersome and highly time consuming on line robot programming technique. It is evident that to be a viable process for producing prototype parts in the desired timescale an efficient off-line programming system is required.

To test the robot welding system for more complex and representative shapes, a CAD system was used to generate welding trajectories. The following procedure was adopted:-

1)   A CAD image of the part to be manufactured was created using the PEPS2 CAD machining package (6). This package does not have a robot post processor but the instructions are similar to those used for milling. The milling process could be considered to be the negative of the welding process.

2)   Once the part has been designed and a simulation of the process has been successfully presented, the post processor generates the spatial positions required for the welding torch along with commands to signify the tool status (torch/gas on/off).

3)   The file of positions is not fully understandable to the robot. A further post processing (written on a PC in the C programming language) is required to include robot command words. This file is then concatenated with an initialisation program which provides start positions, velocity profiles, and signal levels. This concatenated file is then capable of being directly down-loaded to the robot for part fabrication.

A number of limitations to the system can be identified and some modifications need to be made.

As has already been mentioned, there is no feedback loop between the robot controller and the welding system. It is not possible, therefore, to dynamically control the welding quality through the robot system. Sensory feedback would be a requirement for improvement of the system quality through process monitoring and for post inspection purposes. Some of this information could be used to direct any further machining of the part that may be required. Attention must also be given to the use of sensors to prevent possible collapse of the part through temperature build up. The CAD/CAM link and post processor is only of limited value, allowing only sequential machine operations with no facility for sensory update. The PEPS2 system will only provide code using a cartesian coordinate system for 3 axis machines which is only of limited use for robot systems. The technique used required a substructure that is directly below the current welding path. Part manipulation is therefore required to build up complex shapes (like the thermostat housing in figure 3) by combining simpler ones. The need for extra degrees of freedom and integration of robots with part manipulators (rotary XY tables), requires a software simulation and post processing system beyond the capabilities of PEPS2.

6   Future Developments

The 3D robot welding system relies as much on CAD/CAM technology as welding and robotic technology. Further development will be linked very strongly with the CAD system used and the manipulator post processor. The fabrication procedure involves the building up of complex geometric shapes from more simple constituent shapes. It has been found that cylinders (for instance) are best built in the form of rings laid on top of each other. It can be seen therefore that the layer formation used by conventional rapid prototyping is not appropriate for this technique. Since the constituent shapes can be placed in an infinite number of ways with respect to each other, it is obvious that some form of part manipulation will be required in conjunction with the robot welder. A future system must therefore incorporate both a robot and a 3-axis part manipulator.

The formulation of the geometry will require the development of a new CAD package, or the adaptation of an existing one. This package will be used to design the part and then determine the best geometric procedures required to fabricate it. This information will then be passed on to a robot simulation package (e.g. GRASP (7)) which will calculate the robot and part manipulator instructions. The post processor within this system will be used to program the robot once simulation has been shown to adequately construct the part. This whole procedure of design and simulation may require an iterative process with some human intervention. Some ergonomic considerations may therefore be required to develop a man machine interface.

Initial experiments have already shown that although complex shapes can be formed, the results are not perfect. There are a number of basic reasons for such imperfections:-

-       Heat build up due to the welding process can cause earlier welding passes to remelt and cause part distortion or collapse of the structure.

-       Inaccuracies in the welding and robot parameters can cause cumulative errors, resulting in the torch being too close or too far away from the surface.

-       Solid layers (i.e. filling in of outline shapes) cannot be performed sufficiently accurately to form a smooth surface. This means that gaps can occur inside solid objects.

It is evident from these problems that some form of sensing is required to control the process. Real time weld monitoring systems do exist but it is unlikely that such systems can be used to overcome all of these difficulties. However, it will be necessary to stop welding at intermittent stages to leave the part to cool down and avoid collapse due to heat build up, or to implement forced cooling. Sensors can be used at this time to determine how much cooling is required and to perform post inspection of the welding process. This inspection information can be used to update the robot position to avoid cumulative errors, plot new robot trajectories to avoid gaps, and generally control the weld parameters.

7   Conclusions

The object of this work has been to expand the use of 3-Dimensional Welding from large simple pressure vessels to a wide range of part sizes having much greater geometrical complexity.

There are several targets to aim for in the future:-

- Part Complexity: Parts will be produced such as engine casings, cylinder heads, and inlet and exhaust manifolds, in order to demonstrate the capability of the system.

- Part accuracy: At present the part accuracy is about ± 0.5mm but it is expected that eventually this will be reduced to ± 0.1mm.

- Surface Roughness: The present poor surface roughness is unacceptable for many situations but better weld control and appropriate cooling techniques will improve this considerably.

The applications for this technique can be characterised by two main groups:-

- Parts: Prototype parts or small batches can be rapidly produced without any specific tooling. In addition small modifications could be made to existing components, such as different brackets or lugs on a car chassis.

- Tooling: If it is possible to build a part without tooling then it should also be possible to produce prototype tools such as press or forge tools, plastic moulds, and dies.

Further investigation of the welding technology will also be required. As yet, other welding techniques that may result in smoother, more predictable finishes have not been tried. Investigation into this branch of technology may result in the development of new welding based processes. In the past it has usually been more important to develop new welding systems that can lay down as much weld as possible in a short time. The 3D welding system relies on precision methods and may require development of robotic welding system with very small diameter filler wires.

References

1. American Society for Metals,1983, "Metals Handbook, 9th Edition, Vol 6: Welding,Brazing, and Soldering", prepared under the direction of the ASM Handbook Committee, Ohio,pp 771-803.

2. Kussmaul, K.; Schoch, F.W. and Lucknow, H., September 1983, "High Quality Large Components "Shape Welded" by a SAW process", Welding Journal.

3. Piehl, K-H., January 1989, "Formgebendes Schweißen von Schwekomponenten", Company report: Thyssen Aktiengesellschaft, Duisburg.

4. Doyle, T.E. (Babcock & Wilcox), October 1991, "Shape Melting Technology", The Third International Conference on Desktop Manufacturing: Making Rapid Prototyping Pay Back, The Management Round Table.

5. Private communication with the Manufacturing Technology Section, Rolls-Royce Aerospace Group, Bristol, U.K.

6. Camtek, March 1990, "PEPS2 NC Part Programming System, Version 2.3", Camtek Ltd.

7. Sorenti, P. and Bennaton, J., December 1989, "Off-line programming moves into practice", The Industrial Robot, vol 16(4), pp 205-207.

Figure 1 - Square Box Formation

Figure 2 - Truncated Hollow Pyramid

Figure 3 - Welded Thermostat Housing

Figure 4 - Sheet Metal Part and Welded Version

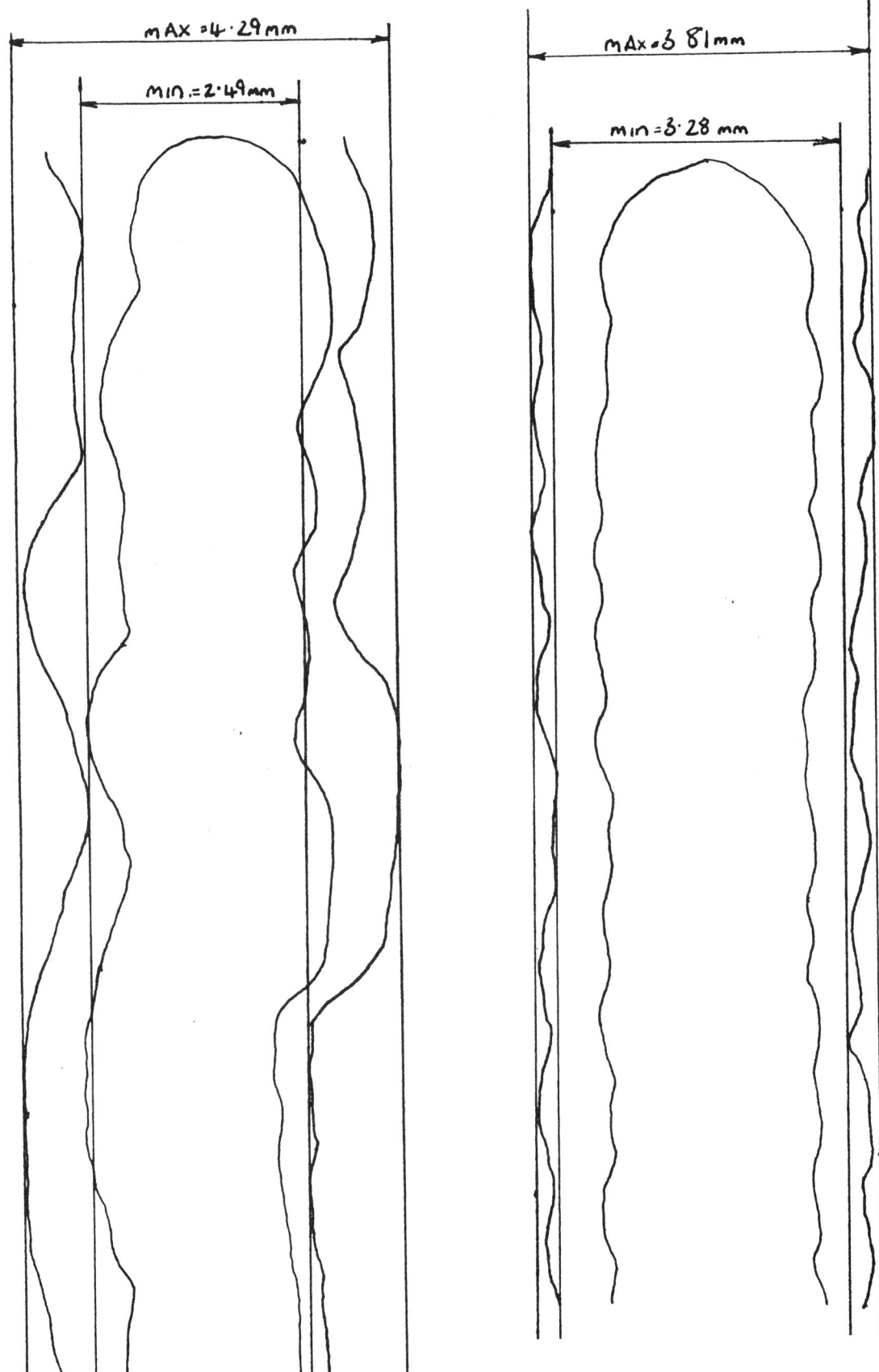

Figure 5 - Cross-section of welded walls before and after investigating the effect of weld bead parameters

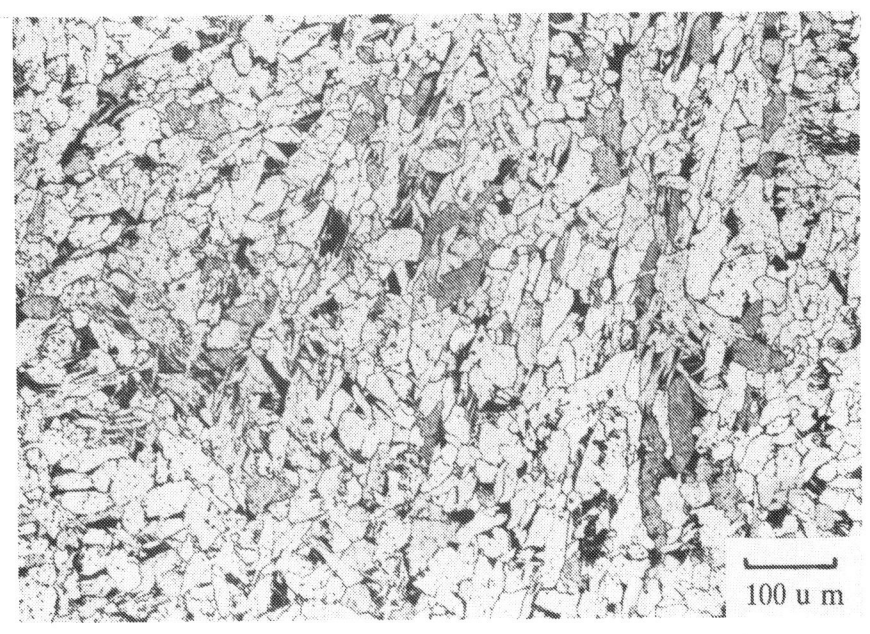

Figure 6 - Large equiaxed Ferrite and Pearlite structure

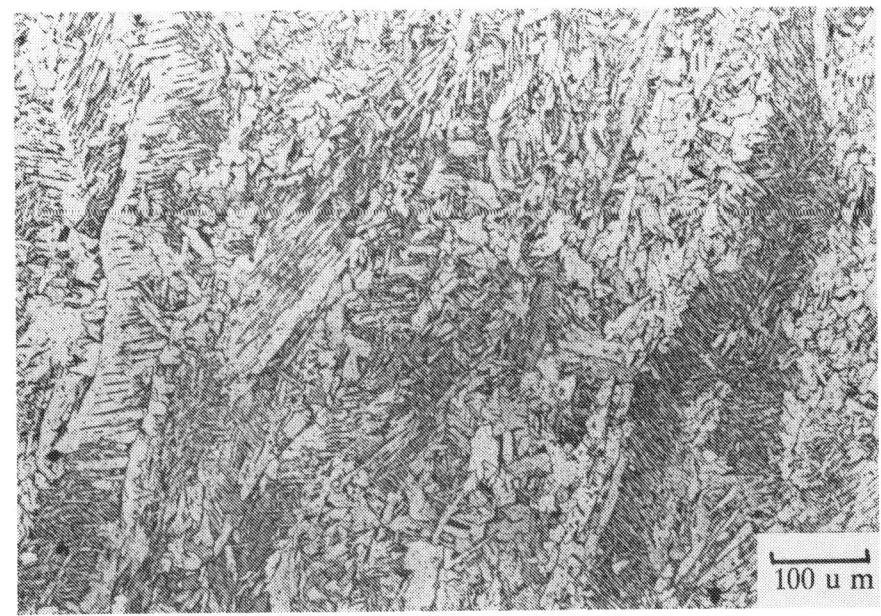

Figure 7 - As-cast type structure

PROTOTYPING OF PRINTED CIRCUIT BOARDS USING SELECTIVE JET ELECTRODEPOSITION

MR C BOCKING

The GEC-Marconi Hirst Research Centre
East Lane, Wembley, Middlesex HA9 7PP

Abstract

High speed selective electrodeposition (HSSJE) is a selective electrodeposition process that requires no masking. A non-submerged, high velocity jet of a suitable plating electrolyte is directed from a small diameter nozzle to impinge on the area to be plated. By the passage of an electric current, metal can be deposited within the impingement region in a controlled and defined fashion. By moving the nozzle under computer control, patterns may be directly written from CAD designs. This paper briefly describes the principles of HSSJE and examines its use for the rapid prototyping of Printed Circuit Boards.

1   Introduction

Printed circuit boards (PCB's) are an integral part of virtually all electronic equipment. They function as both the support for electronic components and devices as well as providing a means of interconnecting them. A printed circuit board is usually a composite structure consisting of a laminate of interwoven glass fibre reinforced with epoxy resin. The top and bottom surfaces are additionally coated with resin in order to confer a smooth surface. The board, when manufactured, is clad on one or both sides with a thin copper foil forming a continuous adherent conducting layer. In order to produce the appropriate interconnection patterns to suit the required circuitry, a number of specialised techniques are used to remove the unwanted copper. The most widely used method involves etching away the copper in predetermined areas with the aid of photolithographic masking. During the design and production of a new board, prototype test boards are often built. However, the cost of producing a complex interconnect pattern can be expensive and time consuming. This paper describes a novel approach to the production of prototype and small production batches of PCB's by means of selective jet plating. Selective jet plating is an electrodeposition technique that has not been widely exploited commercially. A number of papers have been published on the subject (NASA Patent, 1974, Bocking, 1988, 1991, 1992) which describe in detail the fundamentals of the process and the nature of the deposits produced. The operating principle of the process is that a non-submersed jet of a suitable plating electrolyte impinges on a substrate at a high velocity and an electric current is passed. Due to both electrochemical and hydrodynamic properties of the jet, metal is deposited only within the impingement region and the immediate surroundings. In this way, the spread of the deposit is limited. By use of suitable control engineering, the jet can be moved under computer control allowing the direct writing of tracks. If an appropriate metal is deposited, the unplated copper cladding may be removed selectively by conventional etching methods leaving the plated tracks intact. In this fashion, a PCB may be produced directly from a computer aided design (CAD) very rapidly without the need for the more complex and costly photo-masking methods.

2 Outline of Conventional PCB Production Processes

There are a number of ways in which a prototype PCB may be produced. The simplest method is one in which the tracks are defined by the designer drawing the tracks on the copper clad surface with a pen using a special etch resistant ink. The unwanted copper is then removed by conventional etching, usually in a solution of ferric chloride. This is only used for the simplest of boards where track width and feature density is not critical. It is only as accurate as the designer's skill allows. Another technique which is used for prototyping is more sophisticated. This makes use of photoresist. A photoresist is a polymeric organic material that is sensitive to ultra-violet (UV) light. The photoresist is applied to the copper, dissolved in a solvent, by means of spraying or spinning. The solvent is then evaporated leaving a continuous layer of resist on the surface. More modern non-solvent systems make use of a thin sheet of the polymer that is hot rolled onto the surface. There are two kinds of photoresist. The first type reacts with the UV to create additional cross linking of the polymer chains, which makes it more chemically resistant to solvents. This is known as a negative resist. The other type reacts with the UV by breaking down cross links and rendering it susceptible to chemical attack. This is known as positive resist. There are advantages and disadvantages to both types and the choice of the resist is largely determined by the subsequent manufacturing route.

The PCB design is either drawn by hand or printed from a CAD computer onto a transparent plastic film. For simple boards, where very high precision is not required, this film may be used directly as the mask. The positive resist is most commonly used for this method. The film is placed directly onto the coated board and exposed to UV light . Where the tracks mask the light, no chemical changes occur to the resist. The coating is then "developed" like a photograph by immersion in a dilute alkaline solution. This removes the resist from the areas unprotected from the UV and leaves the track regions coated. The board is then etched, usually in ferric chloride or an ammoniacal oxidising solution. After the excess copper has been etched away, the resist on the tracks which remain can be removed using a solvent. By using two masks and suitably aligning them, both sides of the PCB may be prepared at the same time.

Where fine line widths, greater track densities and maximum precision are required, the mask has to be prepared differently. In this case, the mask is usually produced three or four times as large as the final pattern. The artwork is then photographed and the negative reduced to the correct size using specialised (and very expensive) cameras. The resulting film is then used as the mask.

Modern PCB's frequently require both sides of the board for interconnections and often require connections through the board. For prototype boards, these interconnects are frequently made by hand after etching and drilling using special tubular rivets or rods. However, for high volume production, this method would be extremely slow. Such boards are produced by a technique known as through hole plating. It is beyond the scope of this paper to describe this process in detail and the reader can refer to a suitable work on the subject (eg. Coombes 1988).

The method of through hole plating can be fairly time consuming and expensive for a one off board such as prototype with turn-round times being in the order of several days. Many PCB manufacturers will offer a 24 hour turn-round but at an extra cost premium.

There is another type of PCB that is used specifically for microwave applications. Conventional glass/epoxy boards are unsuitable for use with microwaves for electrical reasons associated with high frequencies. For these applications, sintered alumina, single crystal quartz or PTFE composite materials are used, depending on the microwave frequency. Alumina and quartz require special preparation techniques. The material is cut into thin wafers and polished. The surfaces are then metallised with a very thin layer of nickel/chromium alloy about 40 nm thick followed by 150 nm of gold using magnetron or radio frequency sputtering. Gold is the preferred metal to use in these applications and the gold tracks can be built up using either an additive or a subtractive method. In the additive method, a layer of positive photoresist is applied, exposed through a negative mask and developed. The gold tracks are then built up to the required thickness onto the exposed metallisation by conventional electroplating. After removal of the resist, the metallisation is removed by etching. The subtractive method requires that the gold be plated all over. A layer of negative photoresist is then applied, exposed through a negative mask and developed. The unwanted gold is then etched off, together with the underlying metallised layers leaving the required tracks. Producing prototypes by either method is expensive and time consuming. PTFE boards are produced by similar techniques to those used for conventional PCB boards.

Many of the cost and time disadvantages of these conventional methods can be reduced by eliminating the need to create masks or use photoresists. The selective jet plating method has been developed in order to achieve this by directly writing either the etch resist in the case of copper clad boards or directly writing the tracks themselves onto the pre-metallised substrates for microwave applications.

3   High Speed Selective Jet Electrodeposition

3.1   Principles of electrodeposition.

Electrodeposition, otherwise known as electroplating, is a process involving the coating of a material with a layer of metal. It is a widely used method of modifying the surface characteristics of a material in order to confer specific surface properties. These properties include corrosion or wear resistance, electrical conductivity or simply an improved appearance. The technology is applied throughout the engineering and electronics industries as well as for decorative purposes. The principle of electrodeposition is simple. The workpiece is made the cathodic electrode in an electrolyte containing, amongst other things, ions of the metal to be deposited. This is achieved by connecting it to the "negative" terminal of a low voltage DC supply. The circuit is completed by means of a second electrode, the anode, connected to the "positive" terminal of the supply. The anode is usually made of the same metal as that to be deposited although an inert material can be used. By the application of a suitable voltage from the supply, the metal ions adjacent to the cathode surface are electrochemically reduced to the metal thereby producing an electrodeposit. Oxidation reactions occur at the anode.

The thickness of the deposit is controlled by both the magnitude of current per unit area, or the current density (C.D.) and the time of deposition. However, there is a limit to the rate of deposition, as it is a function of both the electrochemical characteristics of the electrolyte and the prevailing hydrodynamic conditions during electrodeposition. The upper limit is set by the maximum rate of mass transfer of metal ions to the surface of the cathode. In the region of this limit, the deposit becomes powdery and poorly adherent. Generally, high rates of deposition can only be realised under conditions of vigourous agitation or high flow rates of the electrolyte. This assists in the transport of the metal ions to the surface. For many processes, the maximum rate of deposition for acceptable quality coatings is around 0.5 to 1.0 μm/minute. However, by the use of high rates of electrolyte flow this can be increased to about 0.5 μm/second. Generally, gold for example, is deposited at a rate of about 0.25 μm/minute.

3.2   Principles of high speed selective jet electrodeposition

In HSSJE, a free standing, non-submersed jet of electrolyte flowing at a high velocity impinges onto a substrate. The application of a suitable voltage between the substrate (cathode) and the nozzle (anode) causes metal to be deposited within the impingement region and the immediately surrounding region. Figure 1 shows a schematic view of the electrolyte flow. The properties of the hydrodynamic flow surrounding the impingement region are such that the electrolyte forms an extremely thin radial layer as it flows away. Because this layer, termed the wall jet region, is so thin, the electrical resistance of the electrolyte is comparatively high. This means that under certain conditions, deposition is limited to the impingement region, with little or no deposition occurring within the highly resistive wall jet region. In this way, the desired selectivity is achieved.

Because the electrolyte is flowing at high velocities, the metal ions that are removed by deposition are rapidly replaced and this allows very high deposition rates to be achieved. Most of the development work on this process has been carried out using a gold plating electrolyte and deposition rates as high as 3.5 μm per second have been attained. The width of the deposit produced is dependent on the chemistry of the electrolyte used and the diameter of the jet. Using an optimised gold electrolyte for the jet system, a 0.4 mm diameter jet will produce a deposit track width of 1.2 mm. However, because the deposit profile is gaussian, subsequent etching of the copper cladding results in a loss of 0.1 mm of gold at each edge, leaving final track width of 1.0 mm $\pm$ 2%. Gold has been used for this purpose as it provides not only good etch resist properties but is solderable and imparts a tarnish free finish to the track. However, its high cost may preclude it from general use for conventional PCB's. In addition, gold can cause problems with solder joints due to the formation of brittle inter-metallic compounds. This can lead to joint failure if subjected to mechanical stresses. Whilst this may not cause difficulties for a prototype, it could present a problem if the process was used for small batch production.

As a consequence, work is underway to develop a suitable tin electrolyte to replace gold. This would also have the advantage of being considerably less toxic than the gold electrolyte which contains cyanide.

4   PCB Prototyping using the Jet System

By means of a computer control system, a PCB design produced on any of the standard CAD packages could be used to control the movement of the jet, mounted on an X-Y table, allowing tracks to be written directly onto the board. Figure 2 schematically represents the jet plating system. The computer was a standard 286 PC. The rest of the control system consisted of;

1.   A stepper motor translator card to provide control signals to the motor driver.

2.   A stepper motor driver to operate the stepper motors.

3.   A power supply for the DC plating current. This was a controlled current type capable of providing up to 100mA at up to 60 volts with a resolution of 0.01mA. The current was controlled by means of a reference voltage obtained from a computer generated signal.

4.   An analogue to digital card to deliver appropriate control signals to the Dc power supply setting the current and switching it on and off.

5.   An X-Y-Z table operated by stepper motors to move the jet and maintain the required substrate to nozzle distance. The X-Y table was designed to give a motion of 2.5 μm per step with a repeatability of 2.5 μm. Z direction control could be provided either manually or by means of a feedback system controlled by the voltage drop between the nozzle and the workpiece during deposition.

The master program was capable of taking an HPGL file generated from a CAD PCB design program and converting it to the appropriate control signals to operate the X-Y-Z table and the plating power supply. The thickness of the deposit produced was a function of both the applied current density and the speed of the nozzle across the board. Figure 3 shows an example of a PCB produced using a 0.4 mm diameter nozzle. Because the gold electrolyte can produce an immersion deposit (through a chemical replacement reaction) on the copper, it was necessary to plate a 0.05 μm of gold all over the board prior to writing the tracks. The circuit was written using a current density of 6.0 A/cm^2 and a nozzle speed of 0.8 mm/second. The thickness of gold was 3.5 μm. After writing, which took approximately 40 minutes, the thin protective gold layer was removed using a gold etch. Virtually none of the gold track was affected during this operation. The copper was then etched in ferric chloride, although commercially available ammoniacal oxidising etches could also be used.

Figure 4 shows a circuit produced in the same way except that a 0.1 mm nozzle was used. This board took just 15 minutes to write. Whilst these boards shown here are single sided, double sided circuits can be produced as the computer controls the registration signals that allow precision alignment between the two sides. However, the system cannot provide plated through holes for connection between the two sides. This would still have to be carried out manually. There are plans to provide a facility utilising automatic placement technology but this would depend on the consumer demand.

An additional benefit of the direct write method of prototyping PCB's is that by the use of more than one nozzle, several boards can be written at the same time. This would be useful for small batch production of boards for a comparatively low cost.

Microwave printed circuits can be produced in a similar fashion. After the initial metallisation, the gold tracks can be written as described previously. However, in this case, much greater thicknesses are required. Figures 5 and 6 show examples of such circuits. The example in figure 5 was written at a current density of 5.0 A/cm^2 and a nozzle speed of 0.3 mm/second. As the track width was greater than that which could be produced using the 0.4 mm nozzle, a double pass was used with a small lateral displacement of the nozzle during the second pass. Microsections of a deposit produced in this way have revealed complete deposit integrity. The resultant track thickness was 10.6 μm at its centre. The example in figure 6 was produced using a single pass of a 0.1 mm diameter nozzle. The circuits produced by this method are currently not as good as those produced conventionally due to greater signal losses. This has been found to be due to the gaussian profile of the deposit. Work is currently being carried out in order to produce a more rectangular profile by modification of the electrolyte and some improvements have been achieved. An alternative approach is to modify the design of the circuit to accommodate these small losses. Whilst this would not be appropriate for single prototypes, small batch production could benefit from this approach. The circuits could be produced at a significantly lower cost and faster than by conventional routes especially if a multiple nozzle system was used.

5   Summary

It has been shown that the high speed selective jet electrodeposition process can be used to produce prototype PCB's for both low frequency and microwave electronics systems. By the use of the direct write process, the processing steps associated with artwork production and photolithography are eliminated. This can lead to a significant reduction in prototyping costs. Although the process is still in its early stages of development, the factors that control such parameters as deposition rate, line width and writing speed are well understood. this process has the potential for a wide range of applications within the electronics industry and although it cannot replace conventional PCB production methods, it can certainly augment or replace the more expensive and time consuming processes of prototyping boards. It could also be used for small batch production "in house" because following a short training period, the equipment could be used by any competent person.

References

Bocking, C. (1988) Laser Enhanced and High Speed Jet Selective Plating. Trans. IMF, 66, pp 50-54

Bocking, C. (1991) High Speed Selective Jet Electrodeposition. Trans. IMF, 69, (4),

pp 119-127

Bocking, C (1991) High Speed Selective Jet Electrodeposition of Gold. Proc. European Academy of Surface Technology Conference 1991, Schwabisch Gmund W. Germany, 27-30 November 1991

Bocking, C. (1992) High Speed Selective Jet Electrodeposition of Gold and Copper. GEC Journ. Res. (To be published June 1992)

Coombs, C.F. (Ed.) (1988) Printed Circuits Handbook, McGraw-Hill

NASA, J.C. Fletcher (1974) US Patent No. 3,810,829

ZONE I   Free jet
ZONE II   Impingement zone
ZONE III Wall jet

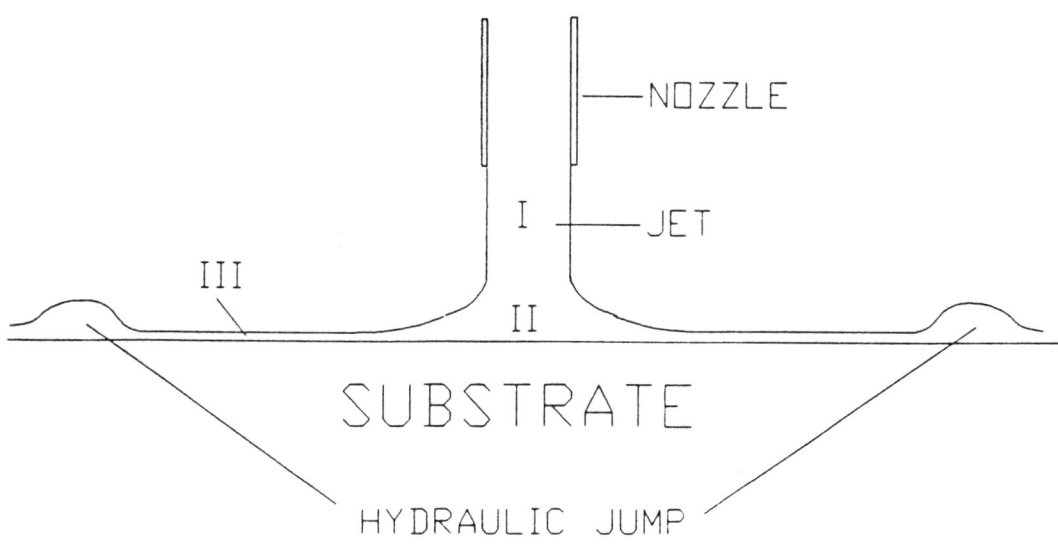

Figure 1. A schematic diagram of the flow regime of the non-submerged jet. Reproduced with permission, GEC Journal of Research.

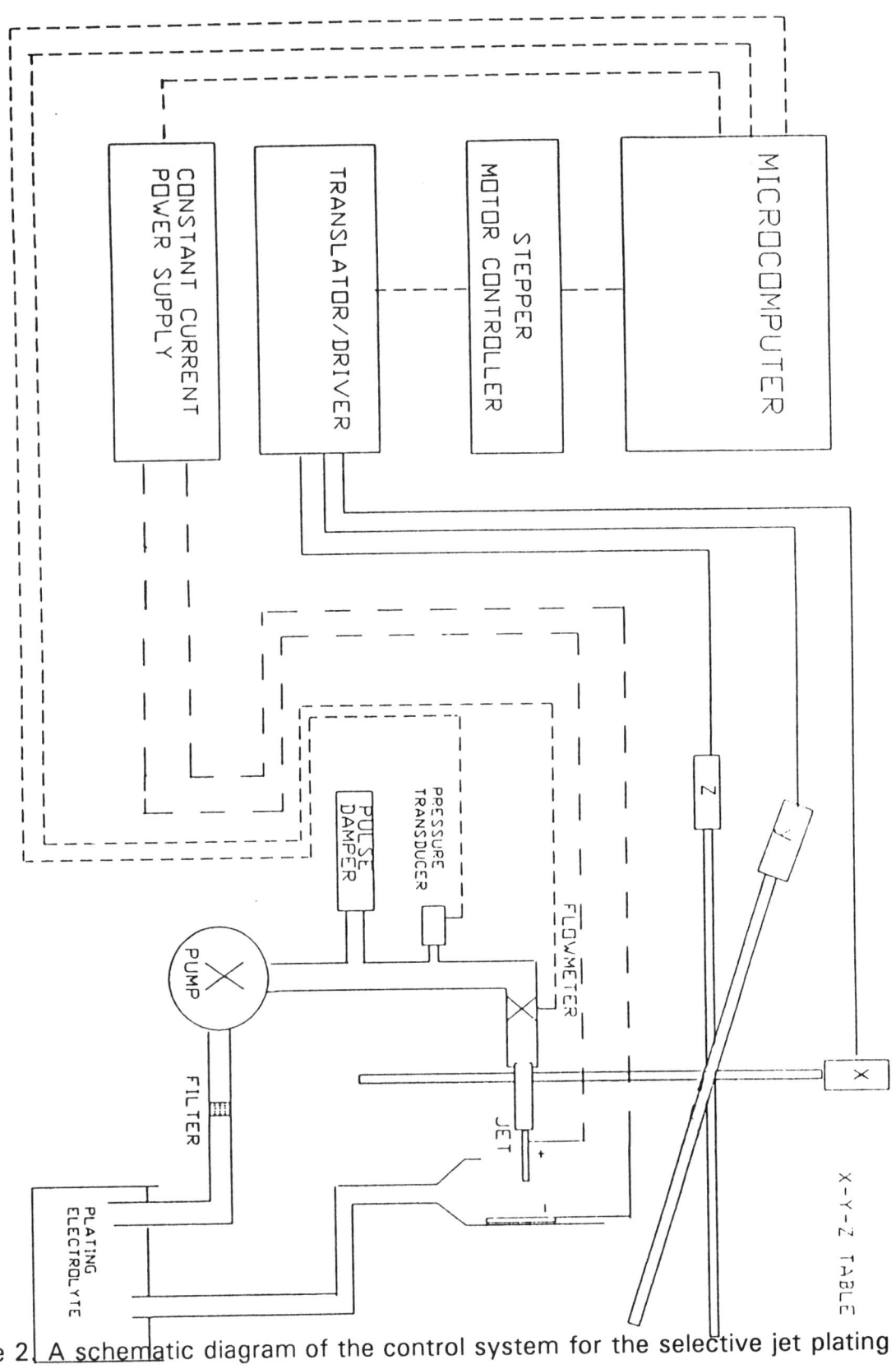

Figure 2. A schematic diagram of the control system for the selective jet plating unit.

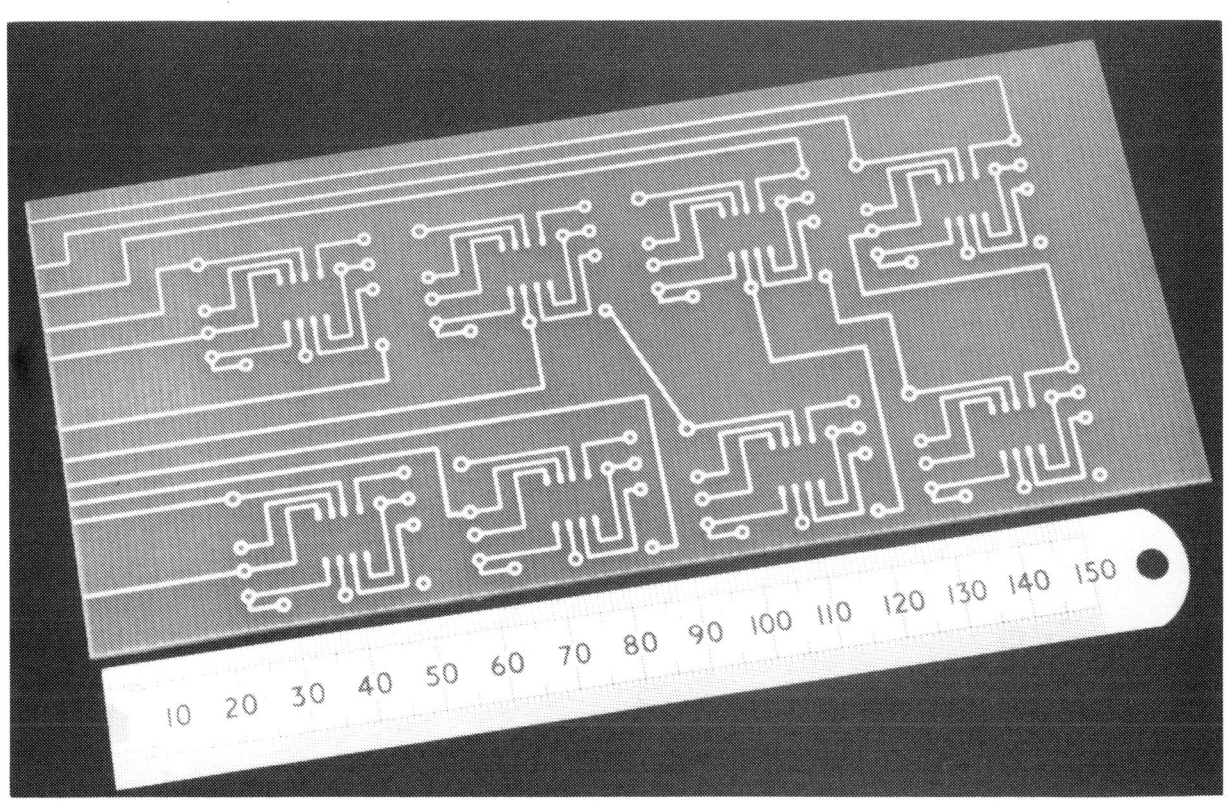

Figure 3. A printed circuit board produced using a 0.4 mm jet to "write" a gold etch resist pattern. Reproduced with permission, The Institute of Metal Finishing.

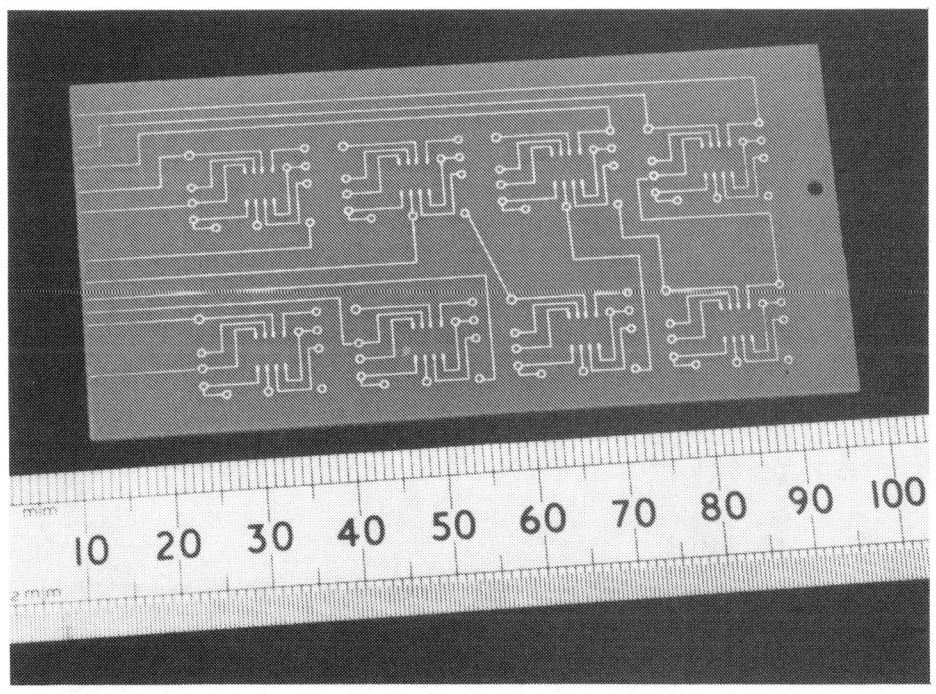

Figure 4. A printed circuit board produced using a 0.1 mm jet to "write" a gold etch resist pattern. Reproduced with permission, The Institute of Metal Finishing.

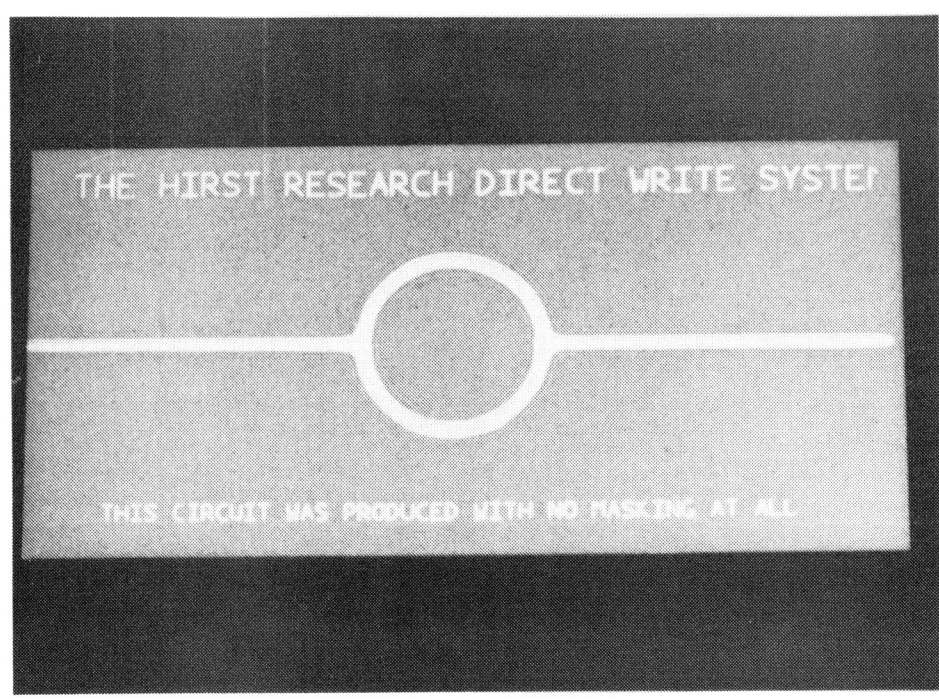

Figure 5. An example of a directly written microwave ring resonator circuit produced on a pre-metallised alumina substrate using a 0.4 mm jet with a gold electrolyte. Shown after the removal of the initial metallisation layers outside the tracks. Reproduced with permission, The Institute of Metal Finishing.

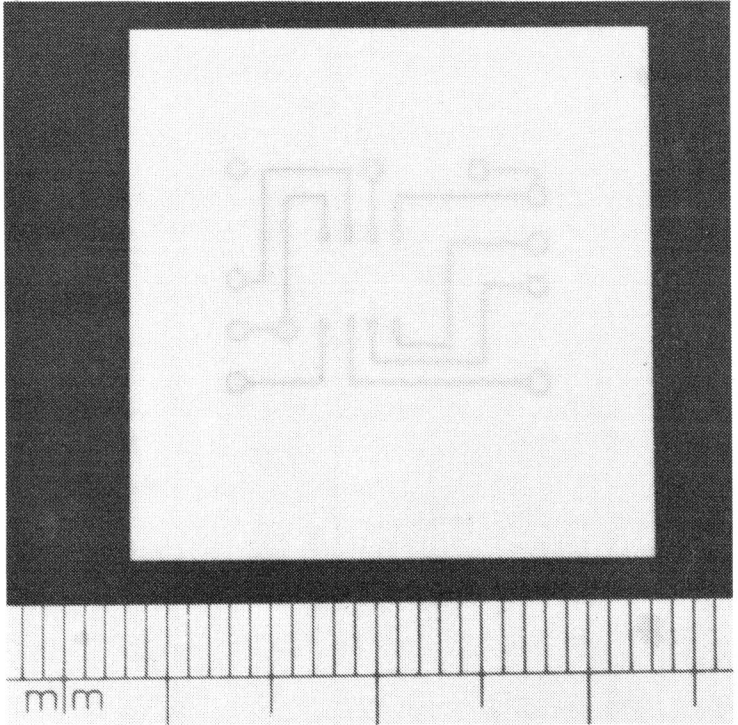

Figure 6. A gold test pattern directly written onto a pre-metallised alumina substrate using a 0.1 mm jet. Shown after the removal of the initial metallisation outside the tracks.

CURE MONITORING IN STEREOLITHOGRAPHY RESIN DEVELOPMENT

Dr. Paul Bernhard, Dr. Manfred Hofmann,
Dr. Max Hunziker

Ciba-Geigy AG, Switzerland

Summary

Experimental tests have been developed aiming at the characterization of photopolymers for StereoLithography (SL) under SL - like conditions, i.e. a scanning focussed laser beam and realistic liquid formulations.

Holographic cure monitoring (HCM) gives access to the kinetic behaviour of a formulation. Effects of additives or special monomers in formulations can easily be investigated.

Shrinkage measurements by a buoyancy method show that after short exposures with a laser beam the density of the partially cured material keeps changing for a considerable length of time (> 1 min), indicating that shrinkage may lag behind the chemical reaction.

A newly developed interferometric method to measure shrinkage in conjunction with strong CW or pulsed lasers has the potential of giving access to the true shrinkage behaviour in the millisecond time domain.

1 Introduction

The development of resins for StereoLithography needs its own formulation strategy, although some of the components may be identical to those in other photopolymer applications such as resists or coatings. In addition to the final material properties, arising from an intended application of the SL part, the process of 3 dimensional laser polymerization itself imposes stringent requirements such as a finetuned penetration depth of the laser light, an appropriate fast rate of polymerization, sufficient stability of the partially cured part (green strength), etc.

A thorough understanding of the laser cure process in a layered structure together with computer modelling of the local (laser spot) process might be a tool to design and evaluate a resin from basic physical properties. Shrinkage, thermal effects, buildup of mechanical strength all have a strong influence on the performance of a material in the build process.

Once a successful product is developed and should become commercially available, some safety criteria and stability minima have to be established, too. All the major components have to be listed (TSCA or EINECS) and an appropriate Safety Data Sheet must be ready with the product. Accelerated stability tests for shelf life evaluation are common practice, but for SL the extended usage time in the vat, at elevated temperature, must be considered, even if fresh resin is replenished at certain intervals.

Knowing all these constraints, every new resin under development has to go through an extensive set of standardized and some specially developed tests which assure a minimal suitability for the SL process. Depending on the intended special application, tighter limits are set on certain parameters, e.g. viscosity or photo sensitivity.

Successful candidates are subject to further testing, such as impact resistance or burnout behaviour in an investment casting shell.

The tests should be quick, efficient, and reveal directly physical or application relevant information. Due to the typically small (monochromatic) light penetration depth of StereoLithography resins (0.13 - 0.18 mm) quantitative measurements on partially, but homogeneously cured samples, be it the extent of cure, shrinkage, kinetics or mechanical properties, are best done on thin layers (a small fraction of the penetration depth).

One of the current problems is the inevitable cure shrinkage of fast photopolymer materials, and its influence on deformation of multilayer parts and internal stress. For resin evaluation it can be quantified (currently named 'curl') with a cantilever test part, built on the SLA with well defined cure parameters and build style.

Previous experiments have shown that neither gross shrinkage of a formulation alone, nor a 'static' model which accounts for progressive shrinkage with increasing exposure in a profile, can fully explain the observed curl factors of different resins. Therefore new methods for real time observation of the cure degree, during and after short laser exposure, have been developed and adapted for thin layer samples.

In this paper we would like to present some of the advanced test methods and results from our ongoing studies aiming at a more complete understanding of the 3D laser polymerization in order to counteract the problems mentioned above.

2   Formulations

As characteristic examples, four experimental or commercial formulations, developed in our laboratories, were chosen to illustrate the test procedures and results:

- XB5081-1, a commercial resin, widely used in StereoLithography, based on (meth)acrylic components; fully cured, it exhibits a high Young's modulus (> 3000 N/mm2), but is rather brittle (strain: ca. 3%).

- PBIII, an experimental resin, based on acrylic components, and exhibiting very high cure speed and high modulus in the fully cured state.

- #1133, an experimental resin, based mainly on acrylic and methacrylic components, some of which are urethane acrylates, leading in the cured state to more flexibility (strain ca. 20 %) and higher toughness.

- #1367-3, an experimental resin, containing acrylic and epoxy components for both radical and cationic cure, with corresponding initiators.

3   Holographic Cure Monitoring

This very sensitive method is based on the creation of a refractive index (or absorption) grating in a photopolymer induced by two interfering UV laser beams as proposed by Bräuchle (1983) or Fouassier (1989). The grating will deflect a probe laser beam, which then produces a corresponding signal on a photodetector; it is related to cure degree and well suited to monitor the polymerization in real time under SL like conditions (Hunziker (1990)).

The sample is a thin film of resin between two UV transparent glass plates, which are separated by precision spacers. The film thickness is 20 - 40 μm, i.e. much less than typical penetration depths of SL resins (0.13 - 0.18 mm). The exposure can thus be considered homogeneous.

According to theory by Tomlinson (1980) the diffraction efficiency (h), i.e. the relative intensity of the diffracted analyzing HeNe laser beam (I_{diff}/I_o), is related to the change in refractive index by eq. 1

$$\eta \ = \ I_{diff}/I_o \ = \ \sin^2 (K \ \Delta n) \qquad (1)$$

$$K \ = \ \pi \ d_o \ / \ (\lambda \ \cos \theta)$$

where Δn, d_o, λ, and θ are the amplitude of the refractive index variation in the sample, the film thickness, the wavelength of observation, and the Bragg diffraction angle, respectively. The change in refractive index is primarily determined by (a) the change in polarizability of the material associated with the chemical conversion and (b) the shrinkage which results from this conversion.

Figure 1 shows that the hologram growth curves for the four fomulations differ greatly, with PBIII being by far the most reactive material on that timescale. The inhibition period is mainly determined by the oxygen content of the resin, and the rising slope of the curve can be used as a characteristic parameter for the rate of polymerization. It appears that the kinetic behaviour of a formulation influences its performance in part building considerably, and this technique can therefore be used to optimize the cure rate in a screening procedure. Furthermore, efficiencies of photoinitiators, influence of additives or particular monomers can be studied: Figure 2 shows the effect of styrene on the kinetic behaviour of formulation PBIII: There is a dramatic decrease in cure rate even with only a small amount of styrene, due to the relative stability of the styrene radical.

4   Shrinkage Monitoring

4.1. Buoyancy method

It is needless to say that excessive shrinkage of SL resin upon curing can lead to serious problems in part building such as distortions and stress in parts. Moreover, the inhomogeneous cure within a polymer will be reflected in inhomogeneous shrinkage accordingly, which, in turn, manifests itself as curl on certain structural features such as the cantilevered beam test parts. Methods to quantify shrinkage as a function of exposure and of time after exposure are therefore a clear necessity as tools to study their influence on part building.

From the literature, e.g. Kloosterboer (1984), it is known that there is a lag between the chemical reaction as monitored by real time DSC and shrinkage measurements, resulting in a certain amount of free volume which relaxes on a slower timescale. These measurements were done at rather low intensities (< 1 W/cm^2) but at higher intensities this phenomenon may be even more pronounced.

One test method which allows for quantifying the relation between exposure and shrinkage is based on the buoyancy change in water of a deformable cell (containing a thin layer of photopolymer of known weight, ca. 20 mg) upon UV irradiation by a focussed scanning laser beam. The results for a series of measurements on XB5081-1 are given in Figure 3. The onset of shrinkage (5.8 mJ/cm^2) is lower than the critical (gel point) energy (7.0 mJ/cm^2, obtained by extrapolating the measured cure depth as a function of surface exposure to zero depth (the so-called "working curve" in StereoLithography)) implying that shrinkage sets in before the gel point is reached. The other resins exhibit the same trend. This pre-gel shrinkage is an important parameter since it should not cause any distortions in the final part.

Whereas this method is not suited to follow shrinkage on the very short timescale because the entire layer has to be scanned, the changes that occur after exposure on the timescale of 10 - 100 seconds, i.e. typical layer building times, are also of interest. Figure 4 shows that after an exposure of 20 mJ/cm^2, well above the threshold energy, XB5081-1 shrinks rapidly and stabilizes after ca. 1 min, whereas for #1367-3 it is evident that the reaction goes on for much longer, presumably due to the greater stability of the cationic species compared to radicals. Evidence of a relatively slow relaxation after exposure was also obtained by Valdez-Aguilera (1990) using fluorescence cure monitoring.

4.2 Interferometric method

A second method to follow shrinkage in real time uses a similar deformable cell for liquid resin (thickness ca.40 μm), but with a reflective coating on the upper cover slide.

This cover slide is used as the 'moving mirror' in a Michelson interferometer, built up with a 50/50 beam splitter, three fixed mirrors and a HeNe laser with beam expander. As the resin in the sample cell shrinks due to polymerization, the fringe pattern of the interfering beams moves accordingly and can be captured as an intensity modulation by a stationary photodiode. Each wave of this beat signal on the detector corresponds to a linear displacement of half a laser wavelength, and the beat frequency is proportional to the linear shrinkage velocity (see fig. 5).

A high power CW laser with beam expander, or a pulsed UV laser is needed to expose the whole area of the sample in a short time, if SL-like conditions and actual reaction rates shall be obtained. For initial experiments we have used a high power UV Argon laser and exposure times of a few seconds.

In fig. 6 we can clearly see the dramatic difference in shrinkage rate for the standard formulation XB 5081 and the slow #1367_3, where the reaction proceeds for more than 20 s after the laser pulse. Comparison with the HCM curves also shows that the holographic deflection is influenced by two parameters (of opposite sign), probably a fast chemical reaction (steep rising slope) and a slower relaxation, with a time constant of several seconds.

Using the information of such experiments has helped us to correlate curl and part deformations of different resins in a more consistent way than the gross cure shrinkage.

References

Bräuchle, C.; Burland, D. M.; Angew. Chem. Int. Ed. 1983, 22, 582;

Carre, C.; Lugnot, D. J.; Fouassier, J. P.; Macromolecules, 1989, 22, 791

Hunziker, M.; Bernhard, P. Proc. 1st Nat. Conf. Rapid Prototyping, Dayton, Ohio, June 4-5, 1990, pp.79-85.

Tomlinson, W. J.; Chandross, E. A. Adv. Photochem. 1980, 12, 201.

Kloosterboer, J. G.; van der Hei, G. M. M.; Gossink, R. G.; Dortant, G. C. M.; Polymer Commun. 1984, 25, 322

Valdez-Aguilera, O.; Pathak, C. P.; Neckers, D. C. Macromolecules, 1990, 23, 689.

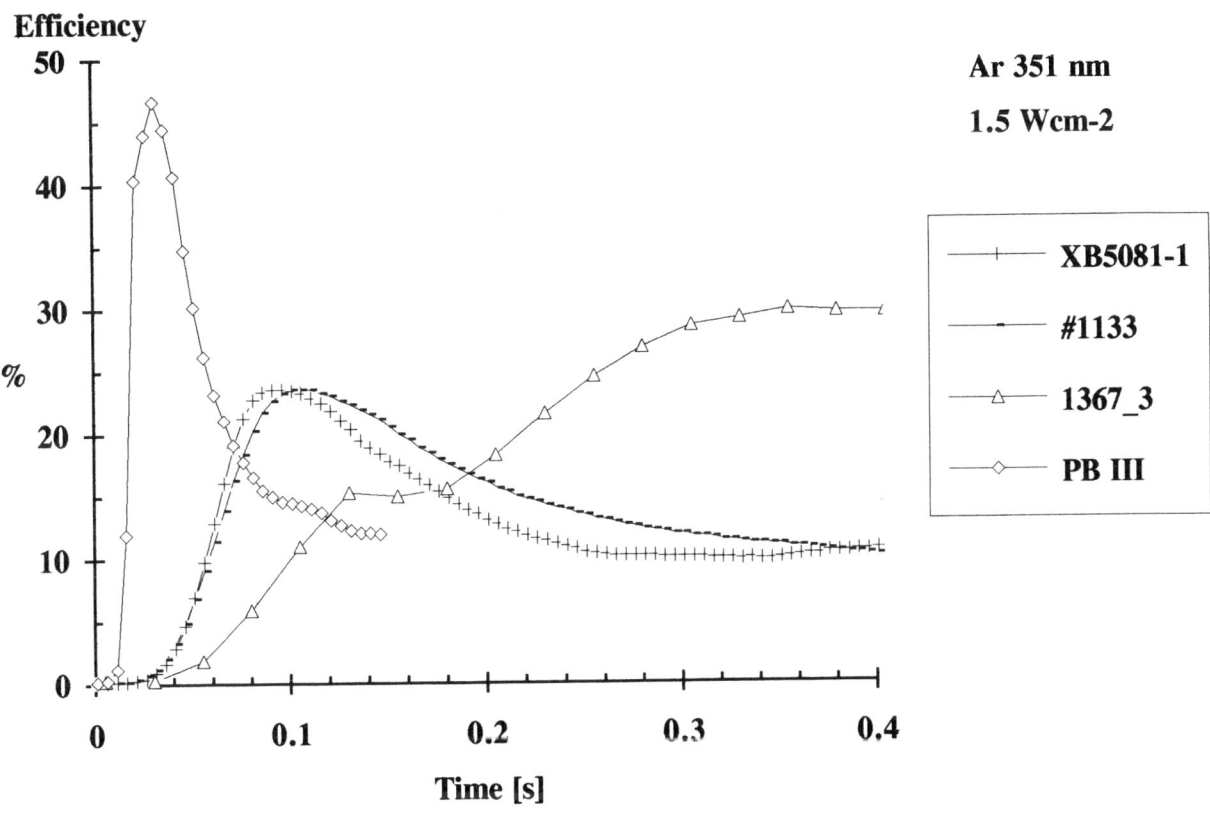

Figure 1.   Holographic cure monitoring (HCM) of 4 different formulations at continuous irradiation with the filtered line (351 nm) of the Ar-laser; power density is 1.5 W/cm²

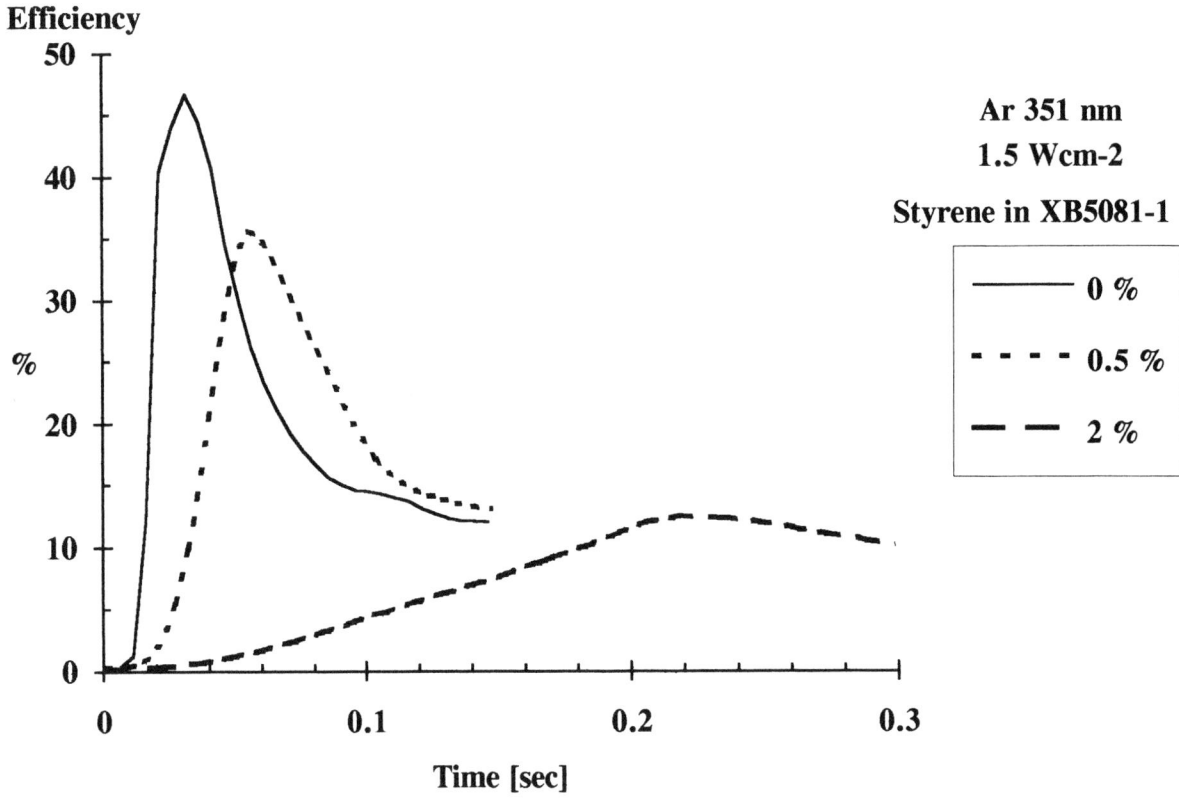

Figure 2.   Holographic cure monitoring of a fast formulation slowed down by adding small amounts of styrene; laser conditions are as in fig. 1

XB5081-1

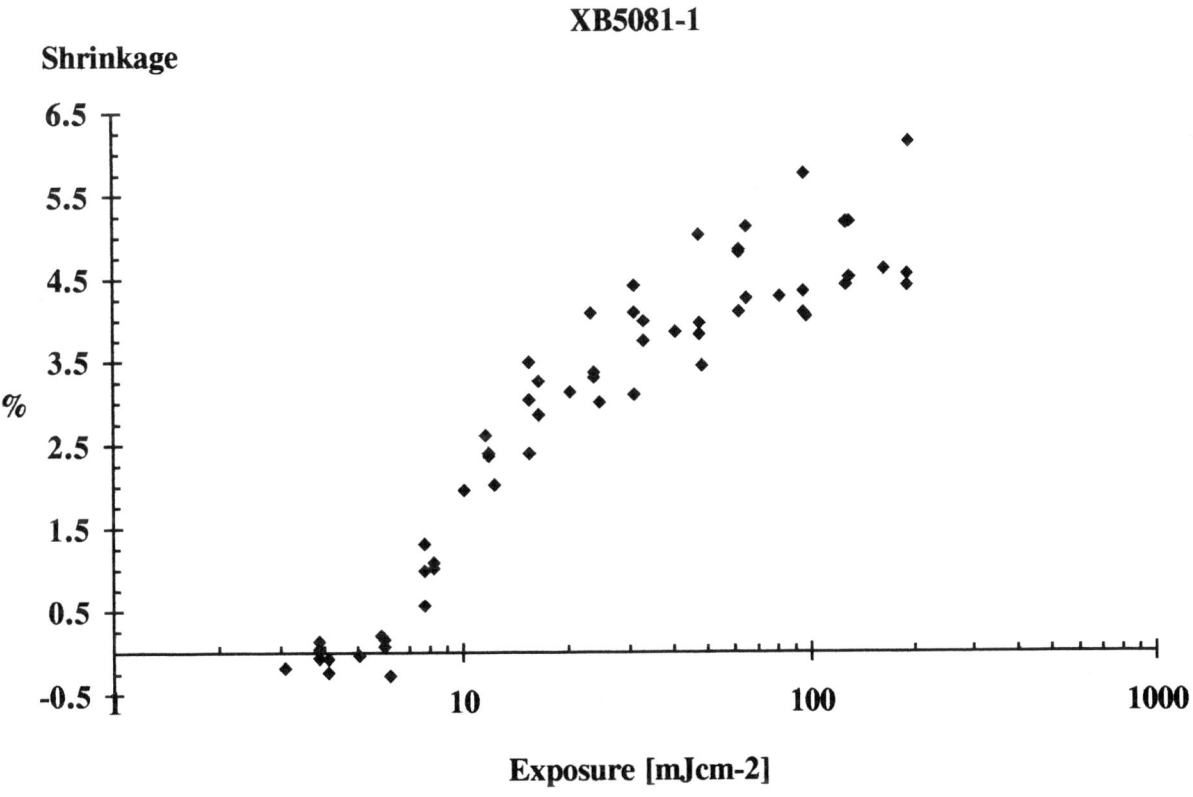

Figure 3.   Buoyancy method to measure density increase (shrinkage) of a resin film for a range of exposures; note the minimum energy required to start the reaction after O_2 inhibition

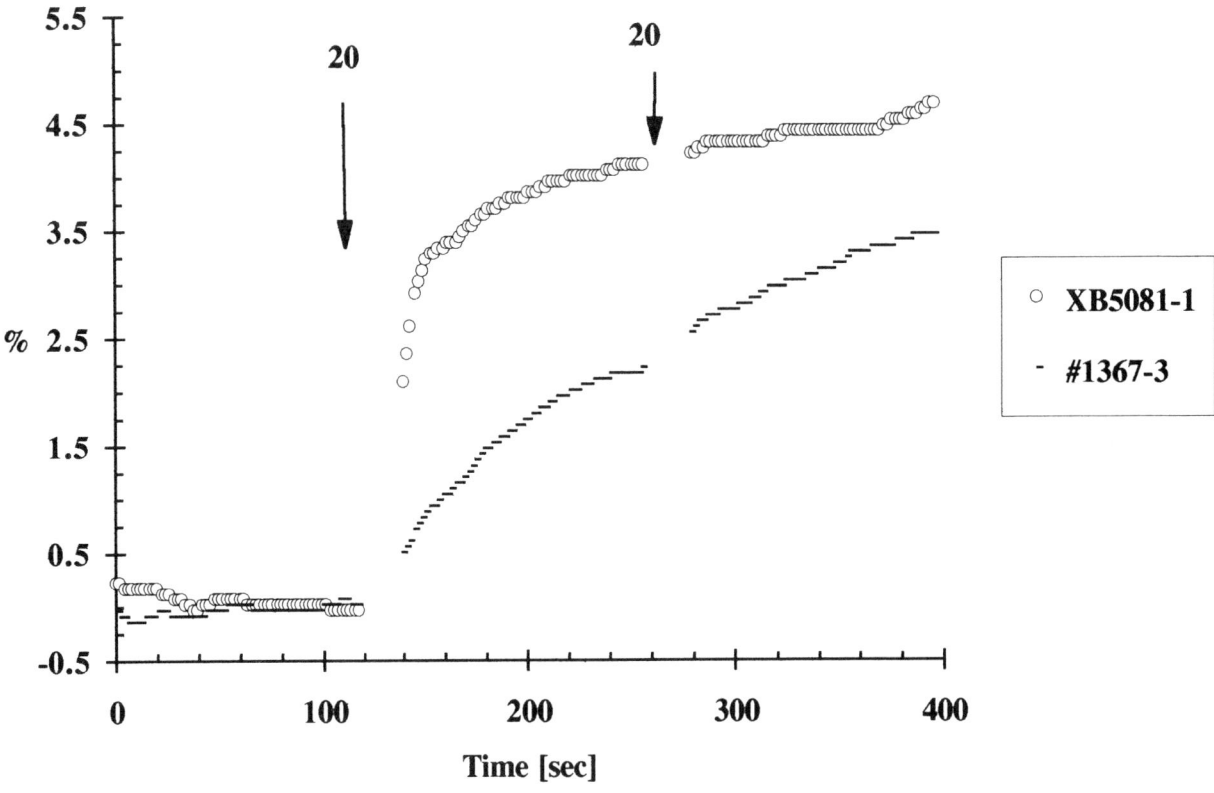

Figure 4.   Time dependance of shrinkage by buoyancy method, for a fast and a slow formulation, following two laser scans (at 120 and 260 s) with 20 mJ/cm² each

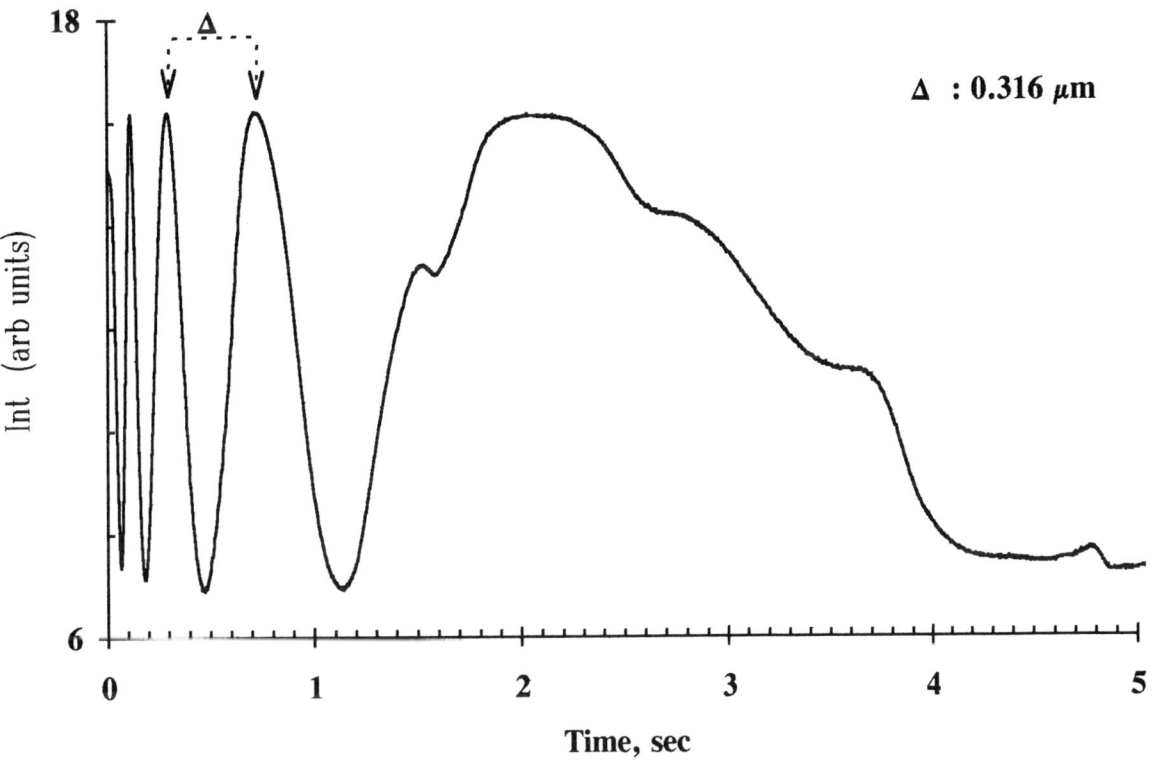

Figure 5.   Interferometric fringe signal of an XB5081-1 sample irradiated with pulse of the Ar laser (UV, 1 W/cm^2, 0.1s duration)

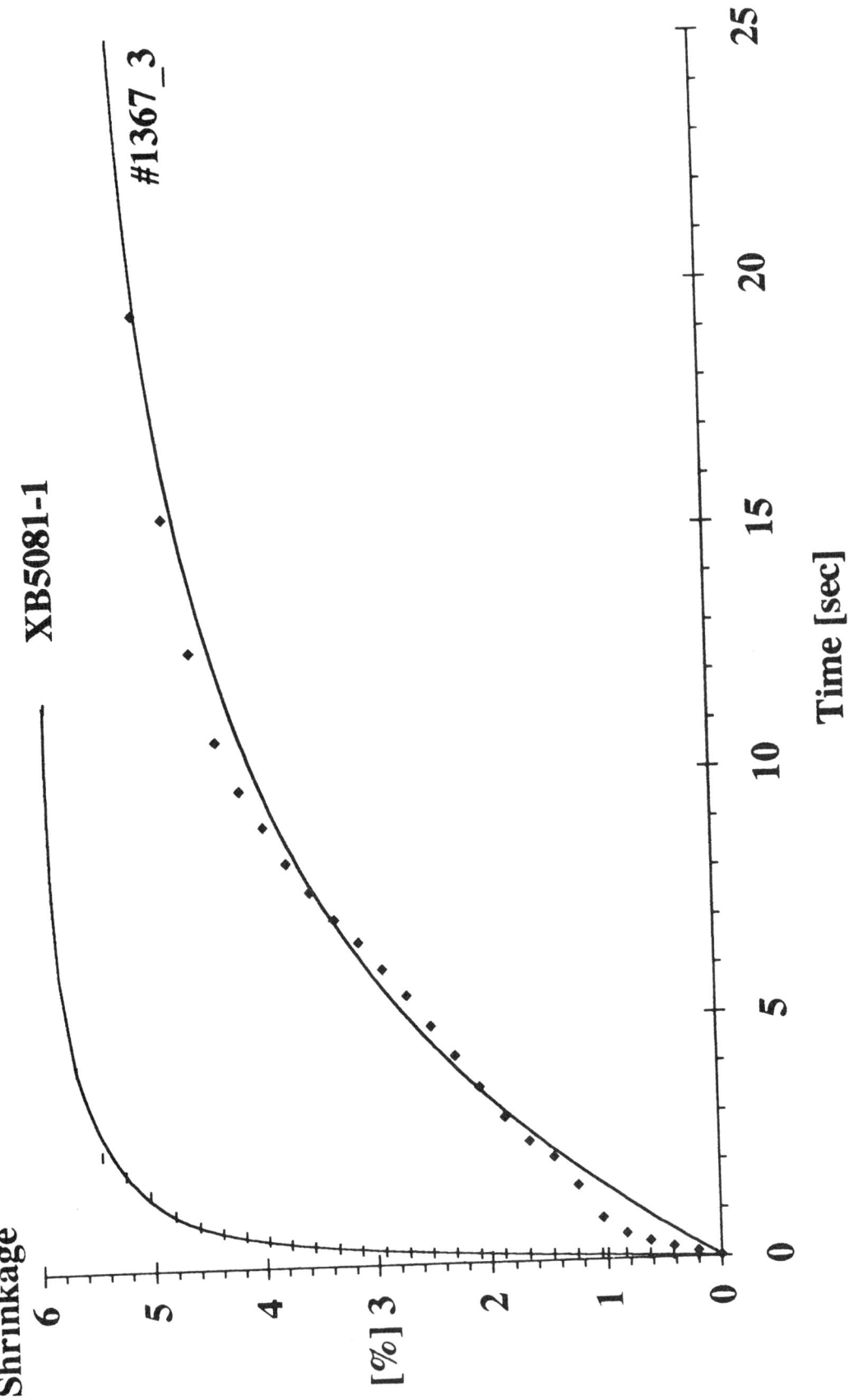

Figure 6.   Interferometric shrinkage measurement of the standard formulation and a hybrid cationic system, measured under constant UV laser illumination; each data point corresponds to a zero crossing or turning point in the interferogram, reproduced here as a relative shrinkage

STEREOLITHOGRAPHY ACCURACY: INFLUENCE OF PHOTOSENSITIVE MATERIALS

Dr Robert W. Peiffer

The Du Pont Company, Du Pont Imaging Systems
Wilmington, USA.

1   Introduction

Since the initial demonstration and commercialization of equipment for the formation of prototype models and parts by the stereolithography process, interest in the users community has focussed on system repeatability and utility. During the past two years significant progress has been made in:

* Developing more reliable stereolithography equipment,

* Improving photosensitive materials (photopolymers),

* Identifying and controlling the process-of-use, and

* Developing a greater understanding of the entire stereolithography process.

With the rapid evolution of stereolithography to a more "user friendly" system, increased emphasis has been placed on understanding and improving those factors which control total system accuracy. This paper will discuss the elements of system accuracy that are dependent upon the photosensitive materials used to make prototype models and parts (Peiffer, 1991, 1992).

2   Elements of Accuracy

When total system accuracy is considered, the process of making solid images with stereolithography can be best understood by examining the five major elements which control the process. These general factors are shown in Figure 1.

All five of these factors are interrelated and changes in one will, in general, influence the others. One of the elements, however, has a strong interaction with all of the other four variables. This dominant system element is related to the characteristics of the photosensitive materials used in the stereolithography process.

The CAD design and desired physical properties of the part to be manufactured determines the type of photopolymer material to be used. If hard, tough, non-brittle characteristics are desired, then a material which will provide these properties must be selected. Similarly, if a flexible material is desired, then an appropriate photopolymer composition must be used to prepare the part.

In addition to the design and the desired physical properties of the part, the nature of the equipment used to manufacture the solid image influences the selection of the photosensitive material. If a SLA-250 system, with a HeCd laser, is used, then a photosensitive material should be selected that will provide optimum performance with this laser. Other materials should be selected if an Argon-ion laser (SLA-500) is to be used.

With the identification of the design, equipment and photosensitive material completed, the process-of-use for imaging the desired part can be identified. As for the previously identified variables, the process-of-use employed to prepare the part is directly dependent upon the nature of the photosensitive material. In particular, the exposure parameters (E_c, D_p, shrinkage and line width compensation factors) are, in part, determined by the characteristics of the selected photopolymer.

Once the desired part has been imaged, the process of completing the model, cleaning and post-treatment, are related to the characteristics of the selected photosensitive material. A solvent and process must be selected that will not damage or destroy the imaged part and the post-treatment process, whether it be light and/or heat, must not induce distortions in the model.

Only through careful control of the entire stereolithography process can a high and reproducible degree of accuracy be obtained. In addition, the characteristics of the photosensitive material can have a significant impact on all the individual system elements that control accuracy of the entire process.

3   Photopolymer Compositions for Stereolithography

The vendors of photosensitive resins for stereolithography have devoted a large amount of effort and expense during the past several years to develop improved and unique photosensitive materials. In general, these companies have strived to develop formulations with the following properties:

*   High reactivity to actinic light (e.g. high degree of cure with a HeCd or Argon-ion laser)

*   Stable and controlled viscosity

*   Good aging characteristics

*   Wide process-of-use latitude

*   Low volatility

*   Low Toxicity

*   Low shrinkage

*   High degree of cure in both the "green" and fully "cured" states

*   High strength of both "green" and "cured" parts

A large degree of technical expertise has been required to develop the photosensitive materials that are currently available for users of the stereolithography process. Considering the multiplicity of compounds that could be used for these formulations, most commercially available materials can be described by the following generalized composition:

* Low molecular weight monomers - used to control viscosity and, to a lesser extent, physical properties

* Higher molecular weight monomers - primarily determines the ultimate physical properties of the model or part

* Photoinitiator - absorbs laser light energy and initiates the polymerization process

* Additives - used to stabilize, modify and impart unique properties depending upon the intended application

When the photosensitive mixture is exposed, crosslinking of the monomers occurs (normally by either a free-radical or cationic process) to obtain higher molecular weight materials. With low levels of irradiation, crosslinking leads to only an increase in molecular weight (i.e. molecular size) while not significantly changing the solubility of the imaged material in the photosensitive composition. As the exposure process continues, the "super molecules" that are formed continue to grow until the imaged material passes through the "gel state" and, with additional exposure, eventually to a clearly defined physical form (Reiser, 1981). The "characteristic curve" for this photopolymer imaging process is shown in Figure 2.

The exposure corresponding to the "gel point", E_g, is a measure of the "photographic speed" of the system. The practical exposure that leads to the formation of solid images is higher than E_g and is identified as the "working point" in Figure 2 (Reiser, 1981).

In all photosensitive materials there are a number of potential "reactive sites". Some of these have a "reactive functionally" of one, two, three or more. Following the light induced photopolymerization process, some active sites remain trapped in the solid matrix. It is these reactive groups that are responsible for additional crosslinking that occurs during the post-treatment process. It is these same trapped "reactive sites" that can lead to a small amount of additional reaction during the first week after the part has been completed. This additional curing can lead to what is termed "creep distortion".

During the polymerization (crosslinking) process there is a reduction in the volume in the photopolymer. This volumetric shrinkage is a consequence of the reacted, crosslinked, "active sites" occupying less volume than the corresponding unreactive "active sites". It has been shown that the amount of shrinkage is related to:

*   The density of the potential "reactive sites" (i.e. "equivalent reactive column" of the monomer - see section on Viscosity), (Nichols, 1950),

*   The rate of reaction (Kloosterboer, 1984), and

*   The amount of conversion during imaging (Kloosterboer, 1984)

In general, resin compositions which contain a low concentration of small size monomers, which have a high reaction rate, and which exhibit high conversion during the imaging process will show the lowest level of shrinkage.

In this section, I have attempted to briefly identify the important characteristics of the photopolymer formulation and the basis process for the conversion of these reactive materials into solid objects. In the balance of this paper, I will discuss how the properties of stereolithography resins can influence the accuracy of the process.

4   Influence of Photopolymer Materials on Accuracy

When discussing how photosensitive materials can influence the accuracy of the stereolithography process, we can consider four main sets of characteristics.

*   Basic Material Characteristics

*   Material Handling Procedures

*   Imaging Properties

*   Post-Treatment Processes

The impact of each of these four main groups on accuracy will be addressed in this section.

4.1   Basic Material Characteristics

There are at least four different general characteristics of photopolymers that can have an influence on the final accuracy in stereolithography. Remember from the introduction (see Figure 1) that all the processes in this rapid prototyping method are interrelated and often we can not clearly separate the impact of material properties from the other process variables. Such is the case for many of the following material characteristics.

4.1.1 Viscosity

The viscosity, or the ability to flow, of stereolithographic resin mixtures influences mainly the uniformity, and thus the accuracy, of the "recoating process" and, to a lesser extent, the ultimate shrinkage in the part. In general, these two factors are opposite in their impact on the imaged model. With some machine design, the most accurate application of photopolymer layers is obtained at lower viscosities; viscosity < 750 cP. To achieve these low viscosities, the resin vendors have incorporated into the compositions a large amount of low molecular weight monomers. Since the amount of shrinkage in a photopolymer is directly related to the density of potentially "reactive sites" in the formulation (more are present in a formulation with a higher concentration of low molecular weight monomers), more shrinkage, and its accompanying distortion, are usually present in lower viscosity resin mixtures (Nichols, 1950). In contract, at solution viscosities > 8,000 cP the amount of time required to achieve uniform layer thickness can be unacceptably long. Photosensitive materials at these higher viscosities, however, usually exhibit fewer accuracy errors induced by shrinkage. New "recoater" designs have been proposed in patents and patent applications that offer the ability to obtain improved layer accuracy that take advantage of reduced shrinkage usually associated with the high viscosity resin mixtures.

4.1.2 Surface Tension

The surface tension, or the ability of the liquid resin mixture to uniformly recoat an imaged layer, can have an influence on the reproducibility of the stereolithography process. If the resin mixture does not sufficiently "wet" the previously imaged layer, then an irregular thickness will result during the recoating process. In addition, if the surface tension of the liquid resin is too high, it is possible that when recoated, the resin mixture will tend to exhibit increasing thickness from the edge to the interior of previously imaged layer (i.e., a meniscus effect). Most photosensitive compositions used in stereolithography do not show these potential defects.

4.1.3 Volatility

The volatility of components in the resin mixture can have a detrimental impact on system accuracy and operator safety. It has been reported that volatile reactive ingredients can vaporize and condense on some of the interior components of the stereolithography machine. This is especially critical if these reactive materials coat the optical system and disrupt the imaging process. High volatility of ingredients can also lead to increased odour and greater potential for operator contact.

4.1.4 Material Uniformity and Stability

The uniformity and stability of the photopolymer mixture in the vat can influence the accuracy and the physical properties of the imaged part. If separation of the mixture occurs during the process of making a part, it is possible that the photosensitive material can show different light sensitivity, and hence different accuracy, during the process. Most commercial resins are stable and do not exhibit separation.

4.2   Material Handling Procedures

In addition to some basic characteristics of photopolymer mixtures, the methods by which these materials are handled or controlled during the stereolithography process can also impact part accuracy.

4.2.1 Material Vat Temperature

Control of the photopolymer temperature during the stereolithography process is important for the production of accurate models. The impact of resin viscosity on system accuracy has been previously discussed and one of the process variables that can influence viscosity is the temperature of the resin. As the temperature is increased, the solution viscosity usually decreases as shown in Figure 3. If the temperature of the resin in the vat varies during the part manufacturing process, it is possible to introduce some inaccuracy in the individual layer thickness. Most stereolithography systems control the temperature of the photosensitive resin in the imaging vat.

4.2.2 Bubble Formation/Entertainment/Release

With some part designs, resin mixtures, and process-of-use conditions it is possible to generate small bubbles in the vat. If these bubbles are trapped in the resin during the imaging process, non-uniformity and inaccuracy can result. It is also desirable for the surface tension and viscosity of the photosensitive mixture to be low enough to permit bubbles, if formed, to move to the surface and break. The formation of bubbles is also dependent upon the recoating method.

4.2.3 Addition of New Material to the Vat

During the stereolithography process fresh material is added to the vat to compensate for that consumed during the part making process. It is important for the resin to be a robust formulation so that small changes that might occur with the material in the vat are insignificant relative to the fresh material added as make-up. Most commercial materials are sufficiently uniform and robust when used according to the recommended process-of-use conditions.

4.2.4 Contamination

Contamination of the photosensitive mixture should be avoided to maintain desired performance. Small amounts of added materials, such as machine oil, dirt, etc., can influence the imaging performance of most resin mixtures. If the characteristic imaging parameters (E_c, D_p) change as a result of contamination, inaccuracy can result due to incorrect exposures being used to image the individual layers.

4.3   Imaging Properties

Probably the largest source of error in the stereolithography process is the use of incorrect exposure conditions. The imaging process and the characteristics of the photosensitive resin are strongly dependent upon each other. Uncontrolled changes in either can have a large influence on ultimate system accuracy.

4.3.1 Material "Working Curve"

The accurate determination of the variables that define the "working curve" for the resin mixture is probably the most important factor in controlling the accuracy of the stereolithographic process. Earlier in this report the relationship between material conversion and the amount of applied light energy was presented (Figure 2). In the practical case of stereolithography, the relationship between the thickness of the exposed layer and the applied energy is called the "working curve".

A generalized plot of the "working curve" is shown in Figure 4 where the critical exposure parameters, E_c, and D_p, are used to define the position and slope of the line.

The equation representing the "working curve" relationship is

$$C_d = D_p \ln (E/E_c)$$

here C_d is the cure depth or thickness of the solidified layer, D_p is the "penetration depth" or the slope $[\Delta C_d/\Delta \ln(E)]$ of the working curve, E is the exposure energy used to solidify the resin mixture and E_c is the "critical exposure" at which solidification starts to occur. This relationship has been shown to be applicable to the stereolithographic process since the early 1980's (Yamada, 1983).

If the critical parameters (E_c, D_p) that control this curve are not accurately determined and controlled, substantial errors in the cure depth are likely. This effect is graphically shown in figure 5.

In addition to the determination of E_c and D_p, it is important to accurately determine the line width compensation factor for the photosensitive material being used. The line width in the stereolithography process is, in part, influenced by the amount of light scattering present in the resin mixture. Light scattering is a consequence of certain additives that can be added to the photopolymer to achieve the desired balance of imaging and/or physical properties. The effect of material induced light scattering on line width for two resin mixtures is shown in Figure 6. It can be seen from this figure that an accurate knowledge of the line width characteristics of the resin are needed so that the appropriate line width compensation factor may be used in the exposure process to achieve the desired layer thickness and part accuracy.

4.3.2 Shrinkage

The source of shrinkage inherent with photopolymer compositions was discussed in two separate sections. It is the control of the shrinkage that occurs during the imaging process that influences the accuracy of the desired model. The effect of material shrinkage can usually be minimized if a reproducible set of shrinkage compensation factors can be determined. In addition to the properties of the resin mixture, the "build style" can influence the shrinkage that occurs during the imaging and post-treatment process. "Build styles" that provide close to solid fill imaging and materials that exhibit rapid, and a high, degree of cure will generally show the lowest amount of shrinkage.

4.3.3 Extent of Cure

The amount of cure that is obtained in the resin mixture during the imaging process can have an influence on the resultant accuracy of the part. In general, if high conversion is obtained during the imaging process, less reaction is needed during subsequent post-treatment to obtain the desired physical properties. Less post-treatment is usually associated with lower residual stress and distortion. The extent of cure obtainable during imaging is dependent upon both the process-of-use and the characteristics of the resin mixture. The latest 3D Systems "build styles" are designed to give greater resin conversion with enhanced part accuracy. In addition, some resins have been formulated to give higher levels of conversion with the same amount of light energy. The combination of improved "build styles" and high conversion resins can lead to improved accuracy.

4.3.4 Delayed Cure

As was discussed earlier in this report, most resin mixtures are rapidly solidified at energies above E_c. As this solidification processes proceeds it eventually reaches a point where no further crosslinking can occur because the "reactive centers" have been trapped in a matrix of rigid polymer. During post-treatment, it is possible to achieve additional reaction of some with these trapped active centers. Depending upon the formulation of the resin, some of the centers will still be active after post-treatment. During the week after the part has been completed, these active sites can migrate and further crosslink. This additional crosslinking can lead to delayed cure, or what has been termed "creep". The extent of this post-cure creep is dependent upon the imaging style, the characteristics of the photopolymer and the post-treatment process used to obtain final cure. New process-of-use procedures and improved materials have reduced the observed level of creep.

4.3.5 Heat of Polymerization

During the process of crosslinking to produce a solid image, heat is evolved from the reaction of the monomeric materials. If a large amount of unreacted monomers are still present in the part, it is possible that excessive heat generation will occur during the post-treatment process. This heat can lead to distortion and warpage of the part with accompanying inaccuracies.

4.3.6 Swelling

In the early days of stereolithography, swelling of imaged parts in the resin mixture was quite common. The swelling process originates from the diffusion of mobile components from non-imaged photopolymer into the interior of the imaged part. Swelling can lead to significant accuracy errors depending upon the design and height of the part. In addition, swelling can be a consequence of low conversion in the photosensitive material during imaging. With the newer "build styles" tending towards solid fill imaging and materials which are capable of higher degrees of conversion, the problem of part swelling in the vat has been minimized.

4.3.7 Green Strength

"Green strength" is a term which describes the mechanical properties of the imaged part before post-treatment. If the photosensitive resin mixture produces parts with low green strength, there is a good possibility that the part will be damaged or distorted upon removal from the imaging platform. Some new resin mixtures exhibit high green strength reducing the possibility of damage during removal of the imaged part from the platform.

4.4   Post-Treatment Processes

Many of the accuracy issues related to the post-treatment of imaged materials have already been discussed; shrinkage, extent of cure, delayed cure (creep), heat of polymerization and green strength. Only one topic specifically associated with post-treatment will be reviewed in this section.

4.4.1 Swelling With Cleaning Solvent

Following imaging, parts are typically cleaned with solvent to remove unreacted photosensitive resin. Depending upon the "build style" and the extent of crosslinking in the resin, the imaged part may be distorted during the cleaning process. This effect was particularly pronounced with the more open "build styles" and aggressive solvents. With the "build styles" approaching a solid fill and more solvent-resistant materials, damage with the cleaning solvent has been minimized. Recent work by 3D Systems with procedures using TPM (tripropylene glycol monomethyl ether) has shown promise in eliminating part damage due to the cleaning solvent.

5   Summary

In this report I have attempted to show that total system accuracy is dependent upon many different variables including such things as the design of the part, the stereolithography equipment, the process-of-use, the characteristics of the photopolymer resin mixture, and the post-treatment process. In addition, I have discussed many of the known properties of photosensitive materials and how these characteristics interact with other system variables to influence part accuracy.

Significant progress in understanding and controlling the stereolithographic process has been made during the past several years and the method has reached a point of increasing sophistication where accurate prototype models and parts can now be reproducibly prepared. Equally rapid progress is anticipated in the next several years in improving the materials and equipment used in this evolving rapid prototyping process.

Acknowledgements

The help and encouragement of those associated with the Du Pont SOMOS™ Solid Imaging Materials Group is gratefully acknowledged.

References

Kloosterboer, J.G., et al., **Polym. Commum.** (1984), 25, 322-325.

Nichols, F.S., Flowers, R.G., **Ind. Eng. Chem.** (1950), 42(2), 292-295.

Peiffer, R.W., previously presented in part; "Improving Stereolithography Accuracy Workshop", **Second International Conference of Rapid Prototyping** (June 23-26, 1991), Dayton, OH; "Solid Imaging - New Opportunities for Photopolymers", **Redtech Europe '91 Conference** (September 29 - October 2, 1991), Edinburgh, **UK; U.S. SLA Users Group Meeting,** (March 30 - April 1, 1992).

Reiser, A. and Pitts, E, **J. Photogr. Sci.** (1981), 29, 187-191.

Yamada, T., et al., **Japanese J.Appl.Phys.** (1983), 22(10), L636-L638

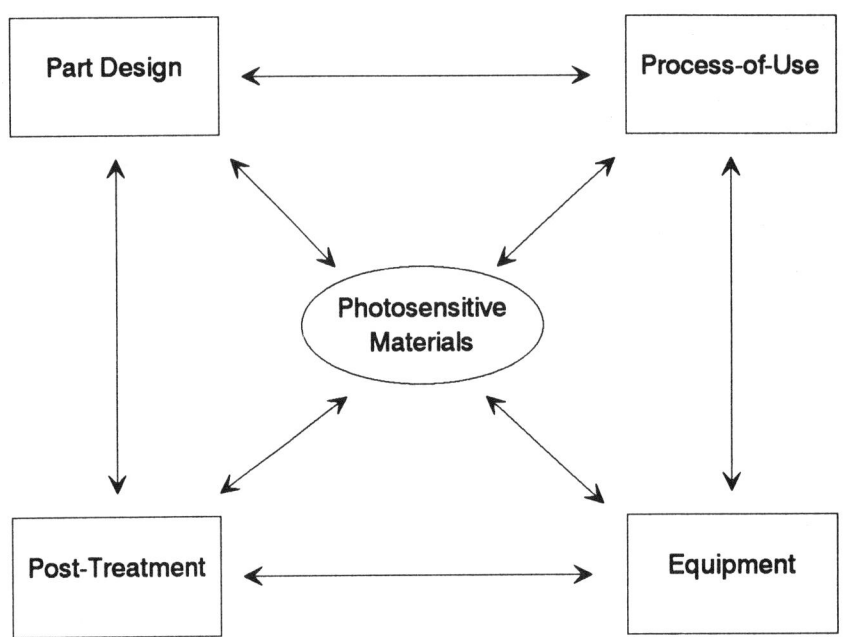

Figure 1   Elements of Accuracy in the Stereolithography Process

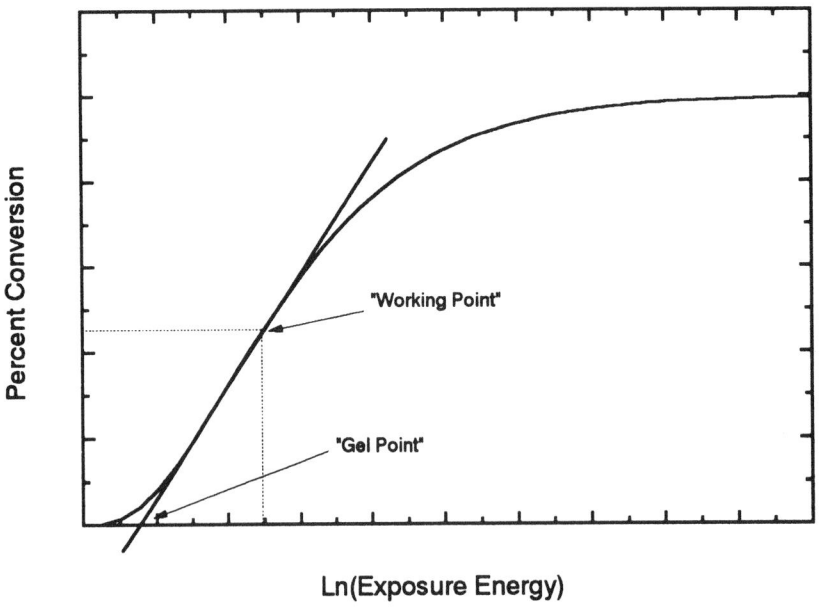

Figure 2   Characteristics Curve for Photopolymer Imaging

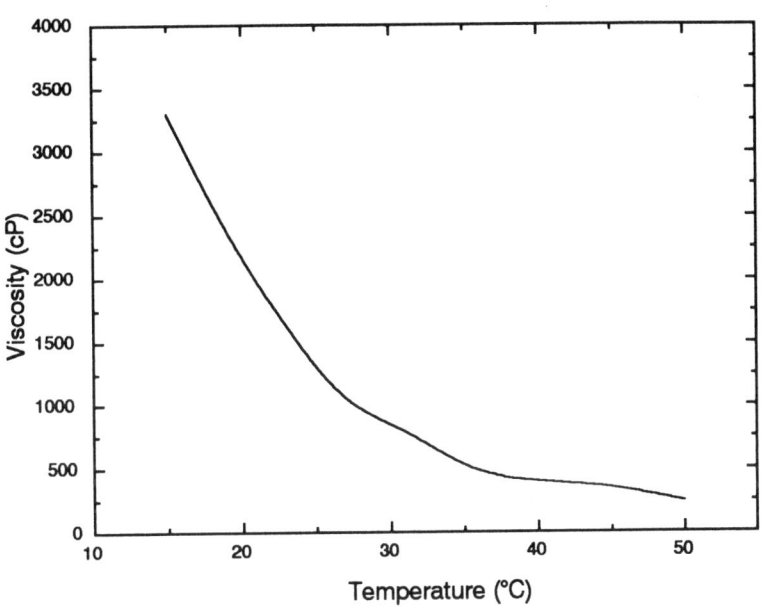

Figure 3   Resin Viscosity as a Function of temperature

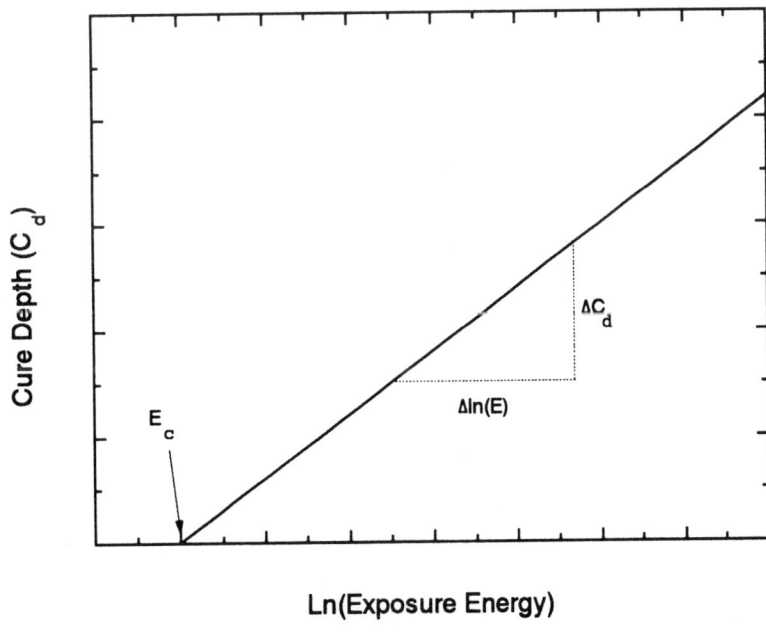

Figure 4   "Working Curve" for the Stereolithographic Imaging Process

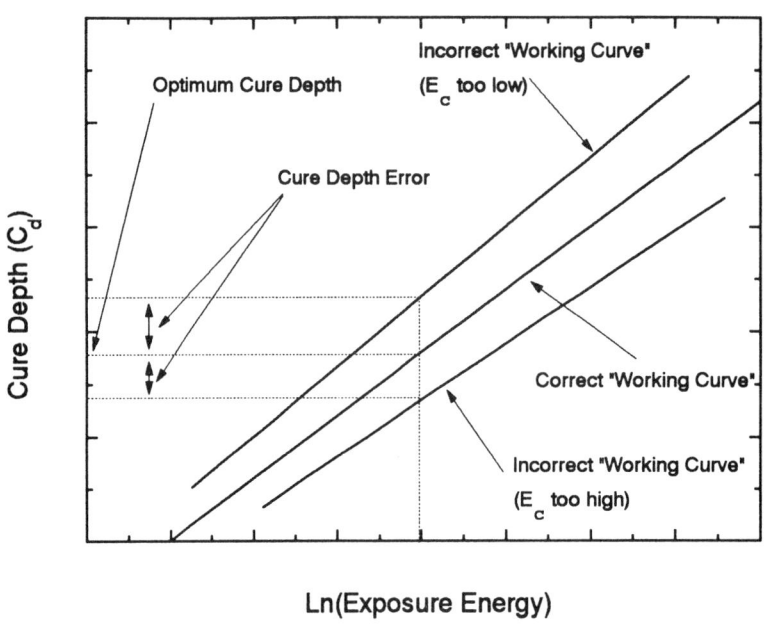

Figure 5   Influence of Working Curve Errors on Cure Depth

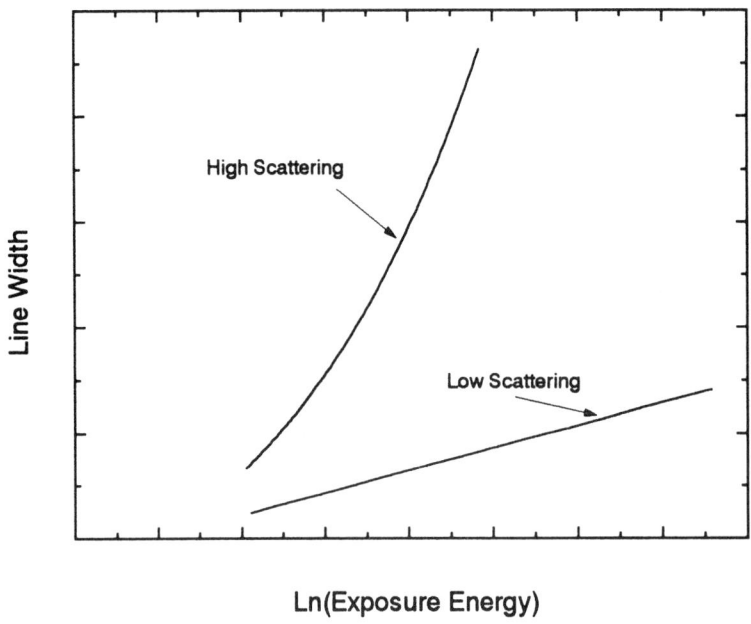

Figure 6   Effect of Light Scattering on Line Width

ON WINDOWPANES™ and CHRISTMAS-TREES™: Diagnostic Techniques for Improved Part Accuracy

Mr. Hop Nguyen
Senior Research Scientist

Mr. Jan Richter
Senior Research Engineer

Dr. Paul F. Jacobs
Director of Research and Development

3D Systems, Inc.
Valencia, California

1   Introduction

To build StereoLithography parts with the highest levels of accuracy, the system should be properly calibrated, the resin parameters precisely determined, and the build parameters optimized. To date, all of these quantities are established when the SLA is acceptance tested and installed. 3D Systems, Inc. performs the complete set of initial calibration procedures prior to final acceptance test, and then field service personnel subsequently calibrate the system again at the user site.

Further, detailed quality control procedures are currently employed for all "Supported" SL resins. These involve the measurement of the resin "Penetration Depth", Dp, in addition to the "Critical Exposure", Ec. Finally, 3D Systems also performs extensive testing to determine relevant linewidth compensation and shrinkage factors for each part building method, using all the Supported resins.

Notwithstanding these efforts, two trends became evident. First, at the 1991 StereoLithography User Group meeting in Orlando, Florida, 3D Systems was specifically requested to provide a practical means for the system operators to determine some of these parameters themselves. Second, it also became clear that due to numerous small perturbations, even if "perfect" parameters were established initially, they would not always remain constant over time.

For example, the laser beam diameter may change slightly as the tube ages, optical alignment may shift imperceptibly due to small temperature variations, the mode structure of the laser may alter as the result of tiny internal mirror misalignments resulting from low level vibrations, and the laser power reading of the SLA may drift away from absolute calibration.

Also, in the normal course of part building the resin parameters Dp and Ec may vary ever so slightly as the "pedigree" of the photopolymer is inevitably altered upon refilling the vat with resin from different lots. However, the linewidth compensation value, as an example, depends upon the laser beam diameter, the cure depth and Dp. Thus tiny variations among these parameters can result in small changes to the cured linewidth. Similar effects may also lead to small shifts in the cure depth, or the system shrinkage factors.

While all these changes may indeed be quite small, when one is trying to produce parts accurate to within a few thousands of an inch, tiny errors become significant. It does not take much variation in any of these quantities to undermine our overall goal of improved part accuracy. The remainder of this paper describes three specific diagnostic test methods that are capable of providing a practical means to account for such changes. Occasional use of these techniques should enable users to produce more accurate parts.

2 Background

During the early days of StereoLithography, measurements of cure depth were made as a function of exposure by generating individual "strings" at a given laser power, spot size and scan velocity. The exposure, and hence the cure depth, would then be varied by drawing a number of strings at different velocities. The maximum cure depth of each string would then be measured with a micrometer. Unfortunately, three problems occurred.

1. The strings were often quite fragile and were therefore easily destroyed. This was especially true for those strings having smaller cure depths. Unfortunately, it is the data from these shallow strings which is especially important in establishing the lower end of the Working Curve, and hence the determination of Ec.

2. The dependence of the results upon experimental technique was problematic even for those strings that survived. Some examples were: variations in the amount of pressure exerted on the sample when using the micrometer, differences in technique between individuals performing the test, and the tendency of the strings to "roll over" slightly during measurement. All of these effects increased experimental error.

3. The standard deviation of the data was typically about 0.0005". While this may seem adequate, one must recognize that in an ensemble of 100 data points, errors as large as +/- three standard deviations are probable. Current depths either 0.0015" too deep or too shallow were not previously a significant problem when building parts using the Tri-Hatch style with 0.02" layer thickness. However, such errors become very significant when building parts with 0.005" layer thickness using STAR-WEAVE™.

The net results was that the values of Dp and Ec, as determined from "strings", were not sufficiently accurate for use with the newer advanced part building methods. Also, the test results showed a significant lack of repeatability from operator to operator. As a result, a better method was needed to determine Dp and Ec.

After considerable design, development, test, evaluation, iteration, and optimization, the final result is the so-called WINDOWPANE™ diagnostic technique, currently employed and trademarked by 3D Systems, Inc.

3 Superposition of Gaussian Scans

When an actinic Gaussian laser beam is scanned in a straight line at constant velocity along the x direction, over the surface of a vat of liquid photopolymer, it can be shown that the exposure in the y direction (i.e. laterally orthogonal to the scan axis) will also be Gaussian. Therefore, if the laser is scanned in a "raster" fashion, with hatch spacing, hs, the surface exposure at any point P(x,y) will be equal to the sum of the exposure contributions from all the various scan lines.

A detailed WINDOWPANE™ laser distribution/superposition computer program was then written by H. Nguyen of 3D Systems (References 1 and 2). This code analyzed the exposure contributions due to a series of parallel laser raster scanned "lines". Each of these "lines" was assumed to have resulted from scanning an actinic Gaussian laser beam having a radius, Wo, defined in the conventional manner at $1/e^2$, (about 13.5 percent) of the maximum value of the irradiance distribution.

Figure 1 illustrates an actual SLA-500 Argon Ion laser intensity distribution, as measured using a Photon, Inc., Model 1280 - XY, "BeamScan" apparatus. A best-fit Gaussian distribution is also superimposed upon the experimental data, with Wo shown graphically. Note that for this case, the assumption of a Gaussian laser irradiance distribution is quite good.

Furthermore, in this analysis the independent variable is the dimensionless ratio, hs / Wo, where hs is the centerline to centerline separation of adjacent raster scanned lines and Wo the beam radius as defined above. The results of this analysis led to the following conclusions:

3.1 Separate Lines

The laser cured lines on the resin surface are completely separated from one another when either of the following conditions obtain:

A. hs / Wo > >2 Thus, whenever the line spacing is much greater than one full beam diameter, neighbouring lines will not be laterally attached to one another. This condition is shown in Figure 2.

B. Whenever E < Ec at various intermediate points in the overlapped area between any two adjacent lines. As a result, midway between the scan lines the exposure is below Ec and the resin has not solidified. This condition, involving residual uncured liquid resin between the scan lines, is shown in Figure 3.

3.2 Uneven Cure Depths

When the line spacing is in the range between the beam radius and the beam diameter (i.e. 1 < hs / Wo < 2) the total exposure at all intermediate points will exceed Ec, and the whole region between the scan lines is at least partially solidified. Thus, the "lines" are now laterally attached; forming a "skin".

However, while the top surface of this skin may be very flat, owing to the planar nature of the original free resin surface, the bottom surface will still be quite bumpy. This is so because the exposure distribution is still sufficiently nonuniform that the resulting variation in cure depth is significant. Figure 4 illustrates the superposition of Gaussian beams for hs / Wo = 1.5. In this case the variation in exposure, from the "peaks" directly under the laser scan centerlines, to the "valleys" halfway between the scan centerlines, is about 35 percent of the maximum exposure.

3.3   Planar Curing

When the line spacing is such that hs / Wo < 1, the difference between the exposure values at the "peaks" and those at the "valleys" becomes quite small. As a direct consequence, the variation in cure depth also becomes quite small.

Figure 5 shows the resulting exposure distribution for the case where hs / Wo = 0.8. Note that the curve representing the total exposure distribution for nine raster lines is very flat over the central five. Almost all of the variation in exposure occurs within the region of the outermost two scan lines on each edge. Thus, one might expect that the cure depth of a raster scanned region of this type would be quite uniform except near the edges. These conclusions regarding planar curing formed much of the conceptual basis for the WINDOWPANE™ diagnostic test part.

4   The Condition for Planar Curing

Given the current state of accuracy of StereoLithography, an area may be considered to be essentially planar cured when the difference between the cure depth at the "peak" and that at the "valley" is less than or equal to 0.0002" or about 0.005mm. Using this criteria, we may now calculate the maximum allowable line spacing. The basic "Working Curve Equation" of StereoLithography (Reference 3) is as follows:

$$Cd = Dp \ln [Emax / Ec]$$

(1)

Where   Cd   = the maximum cure depth on the scan axis, (thousands of an inch).

Dp   = the "Penetration Depth" of the resin, defined as that path length of resin which results in a reduction of the actinic exposure to a value equal to 1/e of the surface exposure, (thousands of an inch).

Emax   = the maximum exposure on the resin surface and on the centerline   of the scan axis, (mJ/cm^2).

Ec   = the "Critical Exposure" for that resin, defined as the actinic exposure at which the resin transitions from the liquid phase to the solid phase, also know as the "Gel" point, (mJ/cm^2).

For simplicity and ease of notation, let us define the surface exposure corresponding to the "peaks" in Figure 4, as Ep, and that corresponding to the "valleys" as Ev. Also, let the respective cure depths be Cd(p) and Cd(v). From equation (1),

137

$$Cd(p) = Dp \ln [Ep / Ec] \tag{2}$$

$$\text{and} \quad Cd(v) = Dp \ln [Ev / Ec] \tag{3}$$

Subtracting equation (3) from equation (2) we find

$$Cd(p) - Cd(v) = Dp \ln [Ep / Ec] - Dp \ln [Ev / Ec]$$
$$= Dp \ln [Ep / Ev] \tag{4}$$

Now, applying our "planar curing criteria",

$$Cd(p) - Cd(v) <= 0.0002" \tag{5}$$

This criteria requires that the right side of equation (4) must also be less than or equal to 0.0002". Equivalently,

$$[Ep / Ev] <= \exp \{0.20 / Dp \} \tag{6}$$

The penetration depths of SL resins are generally in the range from about 0.005-0.007". Since Dp appears in the denominator of the exponent in equation (6), then the largest value of Dp will correspond to the most demanding requirement on the exposure ratio. Hence, using the value Dp = 0.0071", for resin XB 5081-1, we find that the worst case planar cure criteria is equivalent to requiring that the ration Ep / Ev <= 1.029. Consequently, in order to assure that the area in question will have a cure depth that is uniform within 0.0002", the variation in exposure over this area must be less than 3 percent!

A detailed computer analysis was then performed to determine the quantity Ep / Ev as a function of the ratio hs / Wo, (Reference 2). Figure 6 shows the result of this analysis when hs / Wo = 1. For this particular case we discover that indeed Ep / Ec = 1.029. The coincidence that our criteria for planar curing happens to be exactly satisfied when hs = Wo, is really more a matter of our arbitrary choice of 0.0002" as the dividing point between uneven curing and planar curing. Nonetheless, this result shows that in order to maintain "peak" to "valley" cure depth variations less than 0.0002", the line spacing must be less than the beam radius.

Thus, to achieve planar curing per our specific criteria, three laser raster scanning conditions must be satisfied.

I. The line spacing, hs, must be less than the beam radius Wo.

II. The scanned dimensions must be large compared to Wo in order to minimize nonuniform thickness effects near the edges, as noted earlier.

III. Conversely, the scanned dimensions must not be too large, or "curl" effects which are proportional to the square of any unsupported lengths, can lead to distortions that will increase measurement errors and reduce repeatability.

It is important to note that although the analysis was performed for the case of a purely Gaussian laser beam, numerous detailed experiments at 3D Systems have confirmed that the three laser raster scanning conditions listed above are appropriate for both the Helium-Cadmium and Argon Ion lasers currently used in StereoLithography. While the Argon Ion lasers are generally very close to Gaussian as seen earlier in Figure 1, the Helium-Cadmium lasers typically exhibit considerable higher order mode structure. Nonetheless, the test results confirm that the rules noted above apply regardless of which laser type is employed.

5   Average Exposure

Provided the laser raster scanning is performed in accord with the above conditions, then the exposure will be extremely uniform over the sample area. Thus, since so little variation exists, to close approximation we may take the exposure everywhere to be equal to the "average" exposure, Eav, which is simply the total actinic laser energy delivered per unit area, or

$$Eav = P_L t_d / As \qquad (7)$$

where   Eav   = average actinic laser exposure on the resin surface due to raster scanning (mJ / cm^2)

P_L = laser power at the resin surface (mw)

t_d = total drawing time required to complete a laser raster scan of the sample (sec).

As   = surface area of the sample (cm^2).

While the sample area could be of any arbitrary shape, it is convenient to pick a simple rectangle. Let L be the length of the rectangle in the scan direction (e.g. the x axis), and w be the width of the rectangle (e.g. in the y axis). The area of our sample rectangle is simply As = wL. Assuming that the laser is moving at a constant scan velocity, Vs, then the time to draw a single line is simply t = L/Vs. the number of lines to be drawn, within integer round-off, is simply N = w/hs. Therefore, neglecting acceleration and deceleration effects, which are normally extremely small provided that w and L have been properly selected; we may now calculate the total laser drawing time from the expression:

$$t_d = N t = (w/hs)(L/Vs) = As / hs \ Vs \qquad (8)$$

Substituting equation (8) into equation (7), we obtain the deceptively simple, but very important result:

$$Eav = P_L / hs \, Vs$$

(9)

Equation (9) is the basic equation used to calculation the exposure for the WINDOWPANE™ method described below.

6   The WINDOWPANE™ Method

Figure 7 is a schematic showing both a top view as well as a projection view of the WINDOWPANE™ diagnostic test part used for evaluation resins on an SLA-250. A photograph of an actual WINDOWPANE™ generated for an SLA-250 resin is shown in Figure 8. Note the small size of this diagnostic part, as evident from the adjacent penny. The corresponding part for the SLA-500, shown in Figure 9, is slightly different, and will be discussed shortly.

The name "WINDOWPANE™" stems from the observation that, when completed, this diagnostic test part looks very much like a series of tiny windowpanes held together by a frame.

In fact, a single WINDOWPANE™ test part consists of two supports, one frame and five side by side "double-panes" labelled Cd1 through Cd5, for a total of ten individual panes. Each double-pane (e.g. Cd1...Cd5) will be formed with a different cure depth. The choice of five cure depths insures that the resulting Working Curve will be based on enough points to establish good linearity, without requiring so many points as to significantly increase build, measurement and data input time. Experience has demonstrated that five sets of double-panes per diagnostic test part represent a good compromise between obtaining accurate and repeatable results on the one hand, while not demanding an unreasonable amount of time to complete the test on the other.

For the SLA-250 version, each double-pane consists of a single layer part, 0.150" by 0.400". This size is small enough that curl is not a problem per laser raster scan condition III, and large enough that each pane can still be conveniently measured per condition II. Nonetheless, in order to assure that the part will be sufficiently rugged to withstand physical handling, the minimum cure depth must be greater than Dp. However, the maximum cure depth must not exceed 4Dp or such phenomena as optical self-focusing, optical "bleaching", and optical scattering can lead to nonlinear behaviour in the Working Curve which may result in an erroneous determination of either Dp or Ec, or both.

At this point, the user will hopefully appreciate that the choices for virtually all the parameters associated with the design, development, test and evaluation of the WINDOWPANE™ diagnostic test part were far from arbitrary. This was a classic "Lions on the left, Tigers on the right" exercise. A detailed discussion of all the test results obtained over almost one year of R&D, and how they influenced the final choice of each of the parameters, would extend well beyond the scope of this paper.

We shall soon describe in detail the extraordinary precision and repeatability of the WINDOWPANE™ results achieved by the members of the Research and Development Department at 3D Systems. Indeed, standard deviations of a large ensemble of cure depth measurements in the range of 0.0015" or about 0.04mm are certainly quite outstanding.

However, even more impressive is the fact that similar levels of precision have also been accomplished by over twenty of 3D Systems Application Engineers and Field Service personnel from the U.S., Europe, and Asia. We believe that these results, achieved by a wide range of people, are the proper criteria for determining if the parameters have been correctly selected. The WINDOWPANE™ geometry, the number of individual panes, as well as the range of cure depth values for those panes, have been very carefully optimized.

Therefore, to enhance the probability of achieving accurate results we strongly recommend that each of these parameters not be altered in any way whatsoever without first contacting 3D Systems.

Furthermore, consider the acceleration and deceleration of the laser beam. In order to achieve highly uniform exposure, the laser spot must be moving at constant velocity, Vs, for a minimum length of about 0.05" at the middle of a drawn vector. This span occurs after the acceleration period, and before the deceleration period. The 0.150" by 0.400" dimensions for a double-pane are appropriate for the SLA-250 system. However, for the SLA-500 system, test data has shown that optimum results are obtained when the two thinnest pairs of double-panes have dimensions 0.250" by 0.400". This minor difference between the WINDOWPANE™ diagnostic test parts for the two systems is evident in Figures 8 and 9.

Finally, each double-pane is separated by a gap of 0.125" from its nearest neighbours. This distance is small enough to keep the part at a very convenient size, while being large enough to insure that as one pane is being drawn, this action will not effect the others in any manner. The supports and the frame are designed and built to keep the panes from moving on the resin surface. They are removed prior to performing the measurements.

7   Required Equipment

The equipment, instruments, tools and materials required to perform the WINDOWPANE™ diagnostic test procedure are as follows:

1.   An SLA system to generate a precise actinic laser raster scan over the free surface of the photopolymer.

2.   A calibrated UV laser power sensor accurate to 5 percent is recommended. If an SLA-500 is being used, the recently installed "Full Area Detector", should satisfy this requirement. If an SLA-250 is used, the self-consistency

of the power reading should be checked by building the so-called "Reverse WINDOWPANE™" diagnostic test part to be described shortly. Otherwise errors in determining laser power may result in errors in the resulting cure depths.

3.	Absorbing material. Scott C-Fold paper towels are fine.

4.	A thermal chamber or oven capable of reaching and maintaining a temperature. of 80 degrees C or 176 degrees F.

5.	A custom ground digital point micrometer with 0.00005" (1.3 micron) resolution. 3D Systems has obtained excellent results with the Mitutoyo Corp. model 342-741 "Digimatic" ratchet clutch digital micrometer. The points are then precision ground to produce flat circular measuring tips each having a diameter between 0.025 and 0.030 inch.

These dimensions are absolutely critical. If the diameter of the tip is too small, it will pierce the cured resin surface leading to systematically low readings. If the diameter is too large, finite acceleration and deceleration effects near the ends of each pane may cause systematically high readings.

Further, the micrometer measuring force is regulated by an internal clutch. This is essential to avoid variations among operators. The contact force must be weak enough so that the tips will not significantly deform the test parts, and yet strong enough to yield reproducible results. 3D Systems has found it necessary to modify the clutch spring to produce a lower spring constant than that supplied with the micrometer. With all current approved resins, the optimum force at clutch release is roughly 3 Newtons or about 10 Oz. This force results in a compression stress of about 8 Newtons per square millimetre, producing a sample deformation in the fully post cured resin of less than 1 micrometer. This is less than the instrument resolution.

6.	A flat glass plate, approximately 6" by 6" by 0.25" thick.

7.	A safety razor blade, or Exacto knife.

8.	A pair of tweezers.

9.	An actinic fluorescent Post Curing Apparatus, or PCA.

10.	And, of course, a vat full of the resin to be tested.

NOTE: To achieve accurate results with the WINDOWPANE™ method, ALL of the above equipment is required. Furthermore, we have tried numerous variations, and found that methods and equipment other than those listed led to increased measurement standard deviations!

8   Building WINDOWPANES™

When building the test parts, the exposure is regulated by controlling the laser scan velocity, Vs. The supports are built in the conventional manner using 0.02" layer thickness. Finally, on the last layer, the frame and the panes are generated directly on the free resin surface.

As noted earlier, the values of the cure depth must lie in the range $Dp < Cd < 4Dp$. However, since the whole point of the WINDOWPANE™ procedure is to determine Dp, the method is typically iterative. Fortunately, the procedures converges so rapidly that it is rare when more than two iterations are required.

The perimeter is drawn first, and is strongly solidified. Next, the panes are drawn sequentially, with the entire area of each pane being scanned before proceeding to the next pane. The laser beam diameter should be maintained as close to 0.01" as possible (i.e. Wo about 0.005"). The line spacing hs, is chose to be 0.004", since this value has produced excellent, highly repeatable results. Note that for this case hs / Wo - 0.8, which nicely satisfies laser raster scanning condition I for planar curing, as discussed earlier.

For statistical reasons five complete WINDOWPANE™ diagnostic test parts are required. One should use standard multiple part building techniques to generate all five of them on a single platform. Note that the total time required to build the entire ensemble of five WINDOWPANE™ diagnostic test parts is typically only about 20 minutes.

As we shall see shortly, the resin draining and post curing steps involve longer time periods and are effectively independent of the number of test parts built. For this reason, one does not really save very much time by producing fewer than five parts, and a smaller number of data points will adversely effect the statistical results. Thus, yet again, it is prudent not to alter the procedure.

9   Post Processing

After being built, the test parts are then moved up out of the resin, and maintained in this position for at least five minutes to allow most of the excess resin to drain. Next, they are removed from the platform and placed "wet-side-down" on a piece of the absorbing material, taking great care to avoid getting any liquid resin on the "dry-side". Both ends of the frame are then cut off with a sharp razor blade, so that the panes can now lay flat. After removing the frames from each WINDOWPANE™ part, transfer all five to a clean piece of absorbing material; again taking care to position each of them "wet-side-down". Next, place the five test parts in a temperature controlled, but still cool oven and position a second small piece of absorbing material on top of each. Now, evenly space two five gram weights on top of each "sandwich".

Now, turn on the temperature controlled chamber. A temperature of 80 +/- 5 degrees C, should be sustained for 30 minutes. The purpose of this step is to provide a means for the uncured liquid resin to drain off the part and be absorbed without having an effect upon that portion which is just barely polymerized at the gel point.

The use of any type of resin solvent or physical wiping is ABSOLUTELY UNACCEPTABLE, as either method would almost certainly dissolve or disturb the extremely fragile region on the bottom of each pane. Completely draining all excess resin from the test parts is critical. If this is not done properly, one will obtain incorrect and inconsistent cure depth measurements, and ultimately, erroneous values for Dp and Ec.

When resin drainage in the temperature chamber is complete, place the test parts "dry-side-down" on a clean glass plate to prepare them for post curing. The post curing operation should be performed in a PCA employing appropriate actinic fluorescent lamps, for 60 minutes. Resins used in an SLA-250 would be post cured in a PCA-250, and those intended for an SLA-500 are post cured in a PCA-500.

Even though the parts are very tiny, one hour of post cure is necessary to ensure that the surfaces, which are subject to oxygen inhibition in the air, are thoroughly tack free. Also, the test parts must be sufficiently firm to resist significant deformation during measurement. An hour of post cure has been determined to be appropriate.

10   Physical Measurement

Each double-pane of a WINDOWPANE™ test part is divided into two halves by the centerline of the frame. One measurement is taken in the centre of each individual pane. Since there are two panes generated for each cure depth on a single part, and five WINDOWPANE™ parts per set, this results in 10 measurements of each cure depth. Finally, since there are five different cure depths, a total of 50 measurements must be made per test series, to determine Dp and Ec.

When making a cure depth measurement, first "zero" the micrometer. Then measure the cure depth of an individual pane. We have found the best method involves securing the micrometer in a suitable clamping device, holding the WINDOWPANE™ part with tweezers in one hand and operating the micrometer with the other hand. Try to centre the micrometer tips in the middle of each pane. Then slowly bring the tips together until the ratchet clutch is activated. Because of the clutch, the contact force should be quite repeatable, and at least in principle, should be independent of operator technique. Repeatability of the measurement force is an important aspect of the experimental procedure, and is the reason why a ratchet type digital micrometer is necessary.

When a set of measurements has been completed, the micrometer should be again "zeroed", to insure that the reference has not changed. In the highly unusual event that the zero has shifted, the entire measurement series should be repeated from the point where the last zero was correct.

The values of the measured cure depths are best recorded in an orderly sequence to avoid confusion. We have found that a simple tabular format listing the ten measured values for each of the five nominal cure depths works well. Once all 50 measurements have been obtained, they are then entered, by keyboard, into the "Diagnostic Disk" software soon to be released by 3D Systems. This software will then automatically perform the necessary linear regression analysis of the data.

The data may be considered to be valid provided that it satisfies the following two constraints:

1. The absolute difference between the maximum and minimum measured values for a given cure depth (i.e. the "range" of the experimental data for a single cure depth) must not exceed 0.001".

2. The linear correlation coefficient for the five mean value cure depths, as determined from the entire ensemble of all 50 measurements, must be greater than or equal to 0.990.

If these constraints are both satisfied, the computer program will then complete the processing of the data and output the best linear regression estimates of Dp and Ec. In the event that these data constraints are not satisfied, the program will indicate that a failure of one or more of the data requirements has occurred, and will not output any result. It will then inform the user that a new WINDOWPANE™ data set is required. While this may seem severe, 3D Systems truly does not want users to build parts of poor quality as a consequence of inputting incorrect resin parameters.

Fortunately, the time required to perform the entire WINDOWPANE™ procedure is less than three hours, and if carefully done, excellent results should be achieved in over 90 percent of the attempts. Since the price of accuracy is attention to detail, we did not feel the constraints were onerous.

Finally, when values of Dp and Ec are generated by the Diagnostic Disk program, the user will then have a high confidence that they are indeed trustworthy.

11   WINDOWPANE™ Results

Figure 10 is a plot of the data obtained from a total of 400 individual measurements taken by four different 3D Systems Field Service personnel, each independently using the WINDOWPANE™ technique. The data happens to be for SL resin XB 5081-1. In the interest of brevity, Figure 10 is used to represent a typical example. The actual data base developed at 3D Systems over the past year extends to literally hundreds of WINDOWPANE™ data sets and over ten thousand measurements. A statistical analysis of this data has revealed the following four important results:

1.   The standard deviation of the data is generally very near 0.00015", or about 0.004mm, with the very best results under 0.003mm. This level of measurement precision is about three to four times better than the corresponding values achieved with earlier methods.

2.   The results are very nearly operator independent, provided that care is taken to follow the directions exactly.

3.   Even allowing for +/- three standard deviations, at the 99.7 percent confidence level, the WINDOWPANE™ generated "Working Curves" are typically accurate to within +/- 0.0005", and are very repeatable.

4.   The values of Dp and Ec obtained from the WINDOWPANE™ procedure are sufficiently accurate to enable the use of the   advanced part building methods WEAVE or STAR-WEAVE .

12   Reverse WINDOWPANE™ Procedure

Finally, when the resin parameters Dp and Ec have been generated by the WINDOWPANE™ procedure and output by the Diagnostic Disk software, we strongly recommend that the user should next build the so-called "Reverse WINDOWPANE™" diagnostic test part. This is physically similar to the regular WINDOWPANE™. However, the major conceptual difference is one of intent. The purpose of the WINDOWPANE™ is to determine the values of Dp and Ec for a given resin. With the Reverse WINDOWPANE™, one uses Dp and Ec, with the intention of confirming Cd. This is done by pre-selecting a range of desired cure depths (e.g. 0.009, 0.012, 0.015, 0.018, and 0.021"), and then building the Reverse WINDOWPANE™ diagnostic part to determine if the values of Cd do indeed match the desired values, within 0.0005".

The Reverse WINDOWPANE™ procedure provides an excellent overall check of system performance. If the cure depths are not correct, then the system is probably incorrectly determining either the laser power, or the beam diameter, which will then result in incorrect exposure values and hence erroneous values of

146

cure depth. If after a few tries convergence on accurate Cd values is not achieved, something is probably wrong with the SLA radiometry and a service call is appropriate. Conversely, if the measured values of Cd are within 0.0005" of the desired values, then the system is truly functioning properly.

The Christmas-Tree™ Method

In 1991 3D Systems began to investigate potential diagnostic parts that might also provide accurate means of determining linewidth compensation as well as x and y shrinkage factors, in a simple, rapid, accurate, and repeatable manner. Initially it was assumed that multiple diagnostic parts would be required. Fortunately, after some iteration it became clear that the following important properties could be obtained from a single diagnostic part:

1.   Linewidth Compensation, or LWC.

2.   Shrinkage Compensation Factor in the x direction, or SCF(x).

3.   Shrinkage Compensation Factor in the y direction, or SCF(y).

Figure 11 is a schematic drawing of a top view of this part, known for obvious reasons as CHRISTMAS-TREE™, which is also a trademark of 3D Systems.

The basic concepts behind the CHRISTMAS-TREE™, diagnostic test part are as follows:

1.   Build a series of five simple, geometrically scaled, rectangular slabs all having thickness to width to length ratios of 1:2:10.

2.   Let the range of dimensions extend from 0.200" to 5.000" as shown in Figure 11. In this way we achieve a sizeable span of linear dimensions, while allowing all values to be measured with relatively inexpensive digital callipers (e.g. Mitutoyo "Digimatic" Model 500-351). Also, with this geometry two orthogonal CHRISTMAS-TREE™ parts can be built on a single SLA-250 platform, which is helpful in determining SCF(x) and SCF(y).

3.   Connect the five rectangular slabs together to assure that their orientation with respect to one another is preserved. However, the connection itself should have minimal impact on each slab, to avoid any unnecessary distortions.

4.   Intentionally build all the slabs with zero LWC, SCF(x) and SCF(y). This is done because the whole point of this diagnostic test part is to experimentally measure these quantities rather than assigning arbitrary values.

5. After cleaning in TPM, rinsing in water, drying, removing supports, and postcuring for one hour, measure the length of each slab five times with the digital calliper. Since there are five such slabs, this will involve a total of 25 measurements. Fortunately, each measurement typically takes less than five seconds, so this particular sequence requires only a few minutes.

6. The "base" of the CHRISTMAS-TREE™ test part is quite intentionally shaped in the form of an ascending stair-step, a flat section, and a descending stair-step, as shown in Figure 12. We shall define the width of the outermost step on both the right and left sides as, A, the width of the flat section as, B, and the width of the double step on both the right and left as, C, as shown.

7. Now, measure each of the dimensions A, B, and C, five times on the right and another five times on the left. This will involve another 30 measurements. Thus the total number of measurements on a single part would be 80, or 160 on an orthogonal pair. Even for the case of twin CHRISTMAS-TREES™, the total measurement time should be less than 15 minutes.

8. Input each of the measurements in steps 5 and 6 into the Diagnostic Disk software supplied by 3D Systems. The software will then subtract the appropriate nominal CAD dimension from the measured values. The result will be 50 error values for a single part, or 100 values for twin parts.

9. At this point, the computer program will automatically calculate the mean value of the five errors for each linear dimension, perform a linear regression on the resulting ten mean values, and output the best-fit values of LWC and SCF. If only a single CHRISTMAS-TREE™ has been built and measured, the program will lump the ten mean values together and output a single, composite shrinkage compensation factor.

    However, if twin orthogonal CHRISTMAS-TREES™ were built and measured, the software will sort out the ten separate x and the ten separate y dimensions and determine the best-fit linear regressions for each data set individually. In this case, the software will output the best-fit values for LWC, SCF(x), and Scf(Y).

10. Finally, the software will also determine the best-fit value of LWC from the base measurements described in steps 7 and 8. This is intended as another "cross-check" on the data. If the values of LWC from steps 10 and 11 agree within one mil, the program will output the various quantities noted of LWC from the base measurements described in steps 7 and 8. This is intended as another "cross-check" on the data. If the values of LWC from steps 10 and 11 agree within 0.001", the program will output the various quantities noted above.

Unfortunately, if the values differ by more than 0.001", the software will inform you that a new set of data is needed. Again, this is not intended to be onerous, but rather to significantly increase the user's confidence that the results are trustworthy.

11. Finally, this step describes the ultimate "cross-check" on the self consistency of all the results obtained using the WINDOWPANE™, the Reverse WINDOWPANE™ and the CHRISTMAS-TREE™ diagnostic test parts. 3D Systems strongly recommends that the user rebuild the CHRISTMAS-TREE™ part a second time, using as inputs the best values of Dp, Ec, LWC, SCF(x), and SCF(y) obtained to this point.

If these values are truly correct, then the compensated CHRISTMAS-TREE™ part should, in principle, agree with the nominal CAD dimensions. This is really a wonderful test of the entire system. If the errors on a part of such simple geometry are still large, then it will obviously be difficult to build accurate "real" parts, but at least you will know that something is wrong. Perhaps the system needs geometric calibration? Perhaps there is a problem with the beam profilers or the power measurement? At this point a call to 3D Systems field service would certainly be both justified and appropriate.

However, if the final errors are only a few thousands of an inch, the user will have increased confidence that the system parameters are now properly self-consistent, and that their SLA is, as we noted at the outset, capable of the highest levels of accuracy currently possible with StereoLithography.

To enable the various SL users to generate the WINDOWPANE™, Reverse WINDOWPANE™ and CHRISTMAS-TREE™ diagnostic test parts, they should request build files from 3D Systems, Inc. The files for WINDOWPANE™ parts to be built on the SLA-250 are dependent upon the absolute laser power. Therefore, the operator must select the correct file. This has been done so that the exposure values leading to the required range of cure depths will automatically satisfy all the various constraints noted earlier. In this way, the SLA-250 user need not worry about selecting appropriate scan velocities. For the SLA-500, the software can accommodate any operational laser power level.

Furthermore, the user should also request the new Diagnostic Disk software soon to be released by 3D Systems, Inc. This software will process the data for all three diagnostic test parts, and then automatically perform the full range of calculations leading to Dp, Ec, LWC, SCF(x) and SCF(y).

Finally, once the user has completed the compensated CHRISTMAS-TREE™ part, and has achieved excellent results, we recommend that they are now properly prepared to build the User-Part. When built, cleaned, post cured, and securely packaged for shipment, this part should be forwarded to Mr. Ed Gargiulo, at E.I. du Pont de Nemours & Company, Wilmington, DE 19880-0304. In this way, the user can quantitatively establish exactly how well they are able to build this StereoLithography accuracy test standard on their system with their resin.

References

1. Nguyen, H., "The WINDOWPANE™ Test Part and Procedure", 3D Systems Internal Test Report No. 309, February 8, 1991.

2. Nguyen, H., "An Analysis of the Superposition of Gaussian Laser Beams", 3D Systems Internal Report, November 1991.

3. Richter, J. and Jacobs, P.F., "The Present State of Accuracy in StereoLithography", Conference Proceedings, Second International Conference on Rapid Prototyping, University of Dayton, Dayton, Ohio, pp. 269-294, June 23-26, 1991.

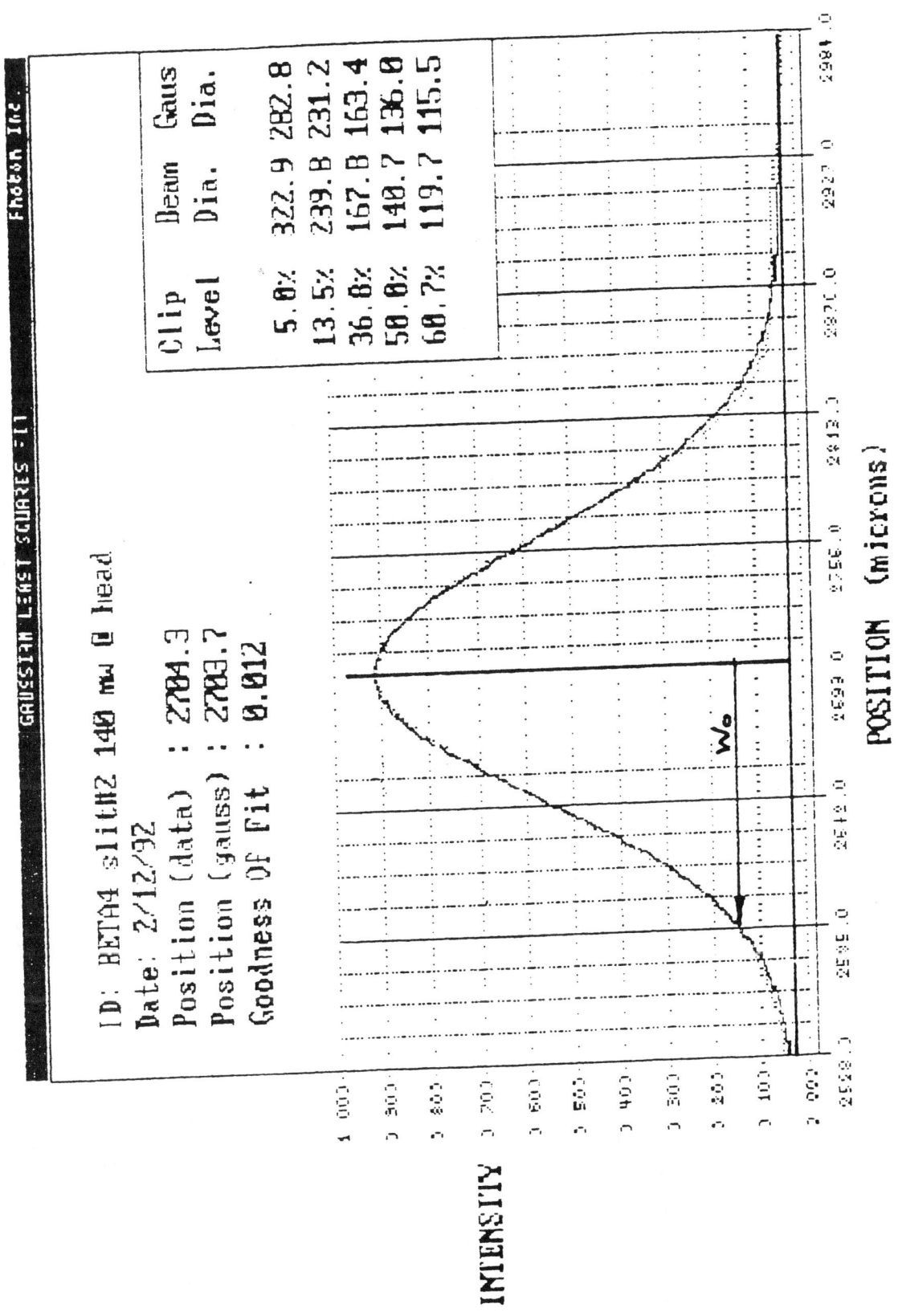

Figure 1. Experimentally measured laser irradiance distribution, relative to a Gaussian

151

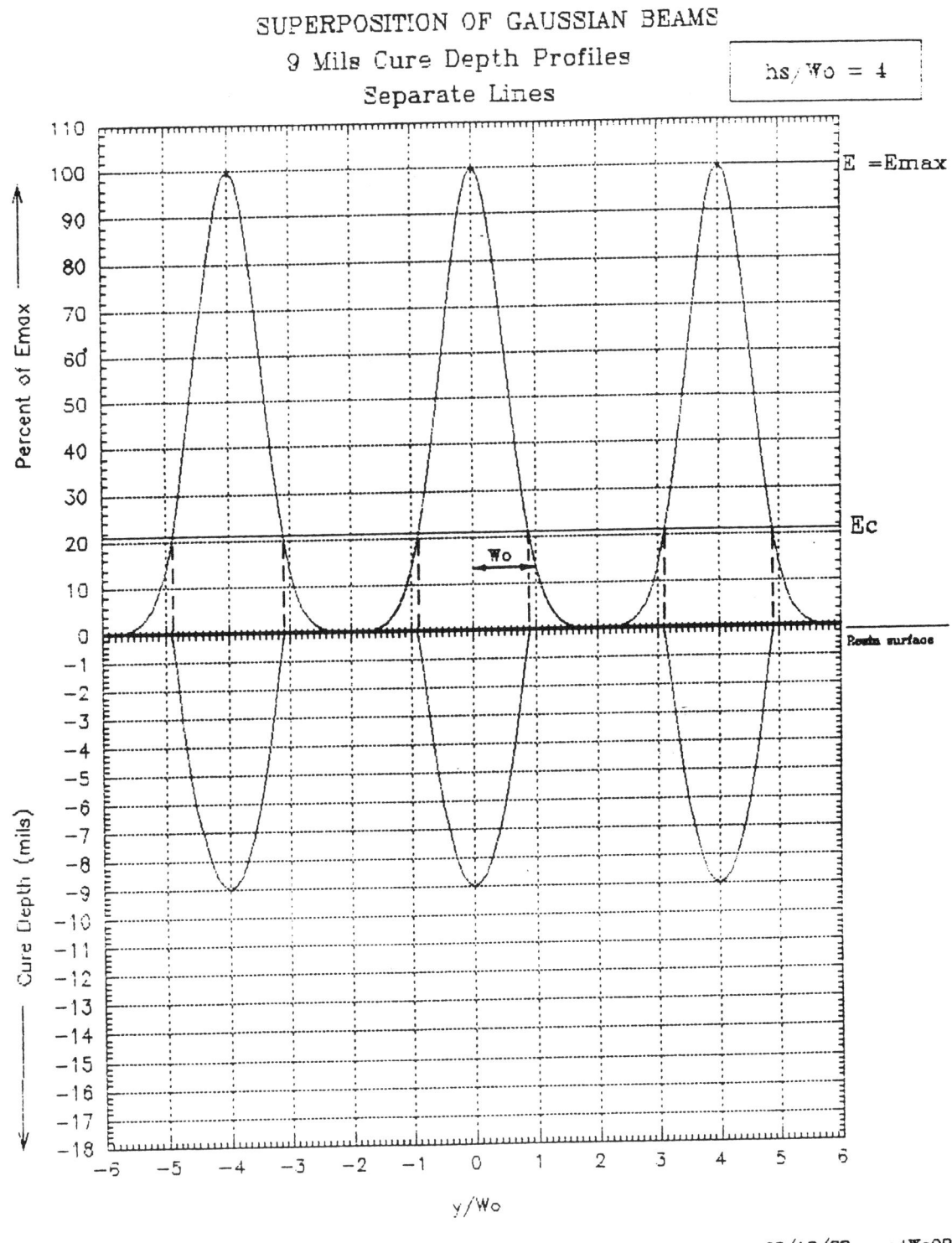

Figure 2.　　　　Super position of Gaussian Beams separate lines, for hs/Wo = 4

152

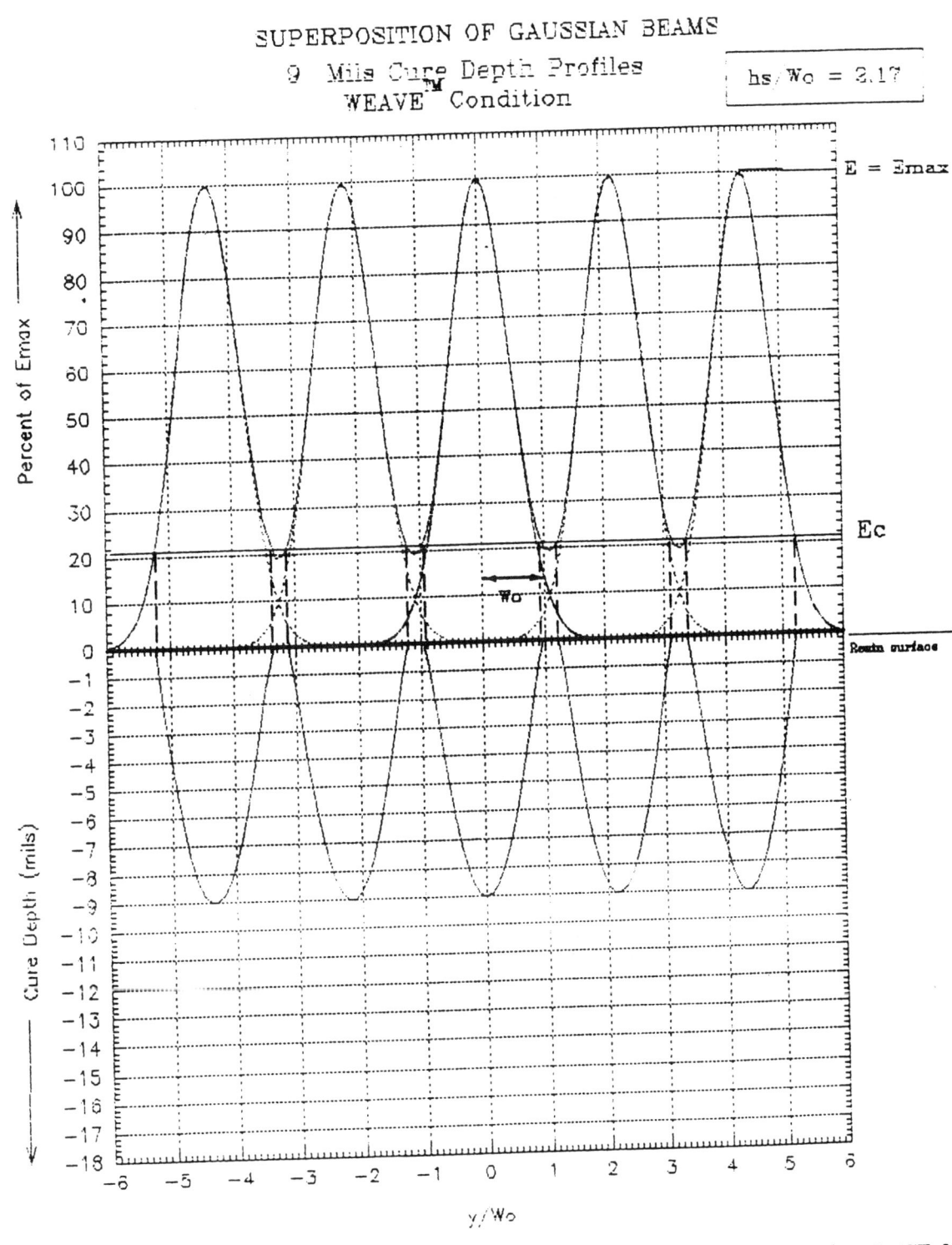

Figure 3. Super position of Gaussian Beams separate lines, WEAVE^{TM} condition, hs/Wo = 2.17

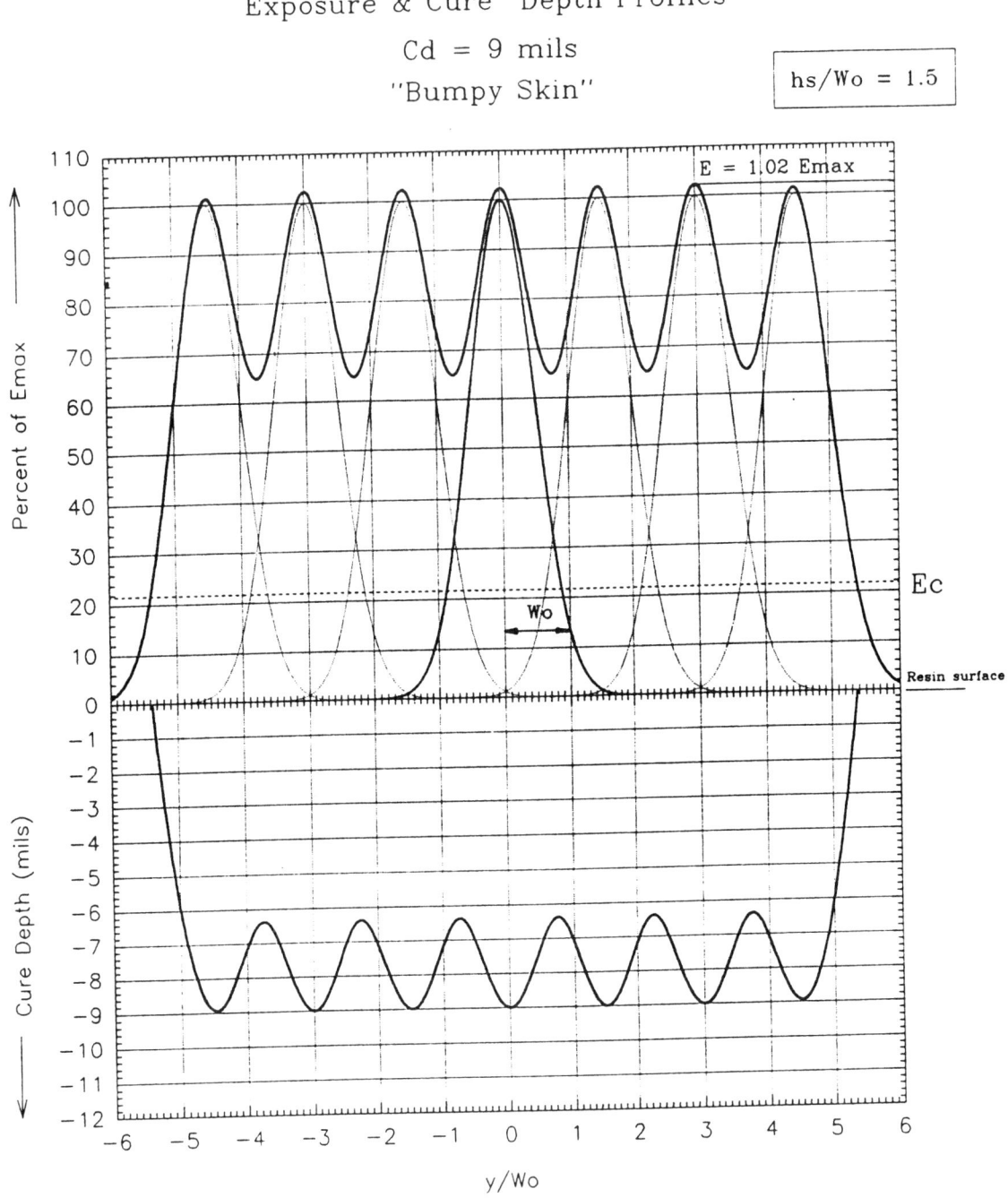

SUPERPOSITION OF GAUSSIAN BEAMS

Exposure & Cure Depth Profiles

Cd = 9 mils

"Bumpy Skin"

hs/Wo = 1.5

Figure 4.   Super position Gaussian Beams Bumpy skin, hs/Wo = 1.5

SUPERPOSITION OF GAUSSIAN BEAMS

Exposure & Cure Depth Profiles

Cd = 9 mils

"Planar Skin For WINDOWPANE^{TM}"   hs/Wo = 0.8

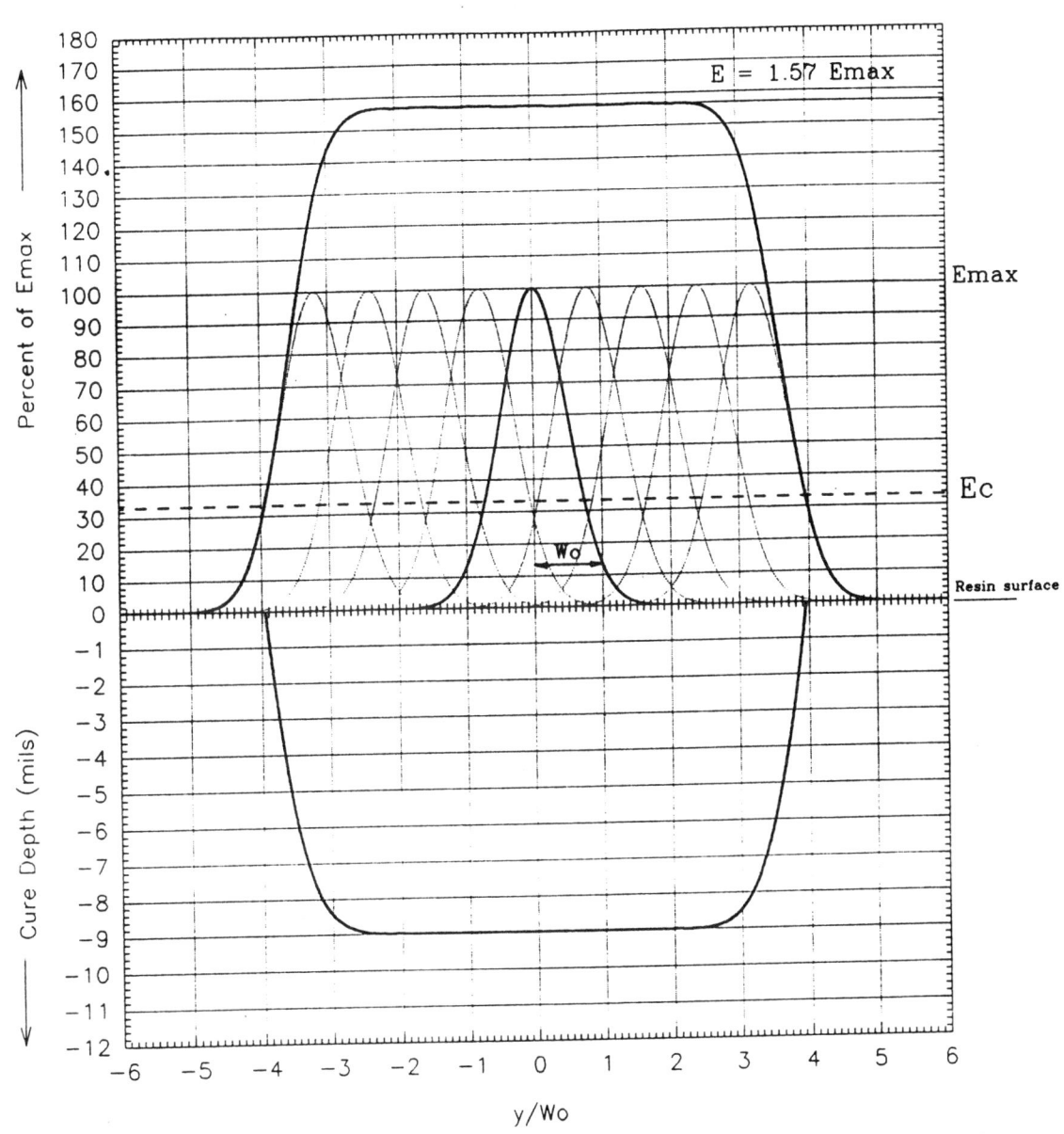

Figure 5. Super position of Gaussian Beams Planar Skin for WINDOWPANE™, hs/Wo = 0.8

Hop Nguyen 05/05/92
jtsup080

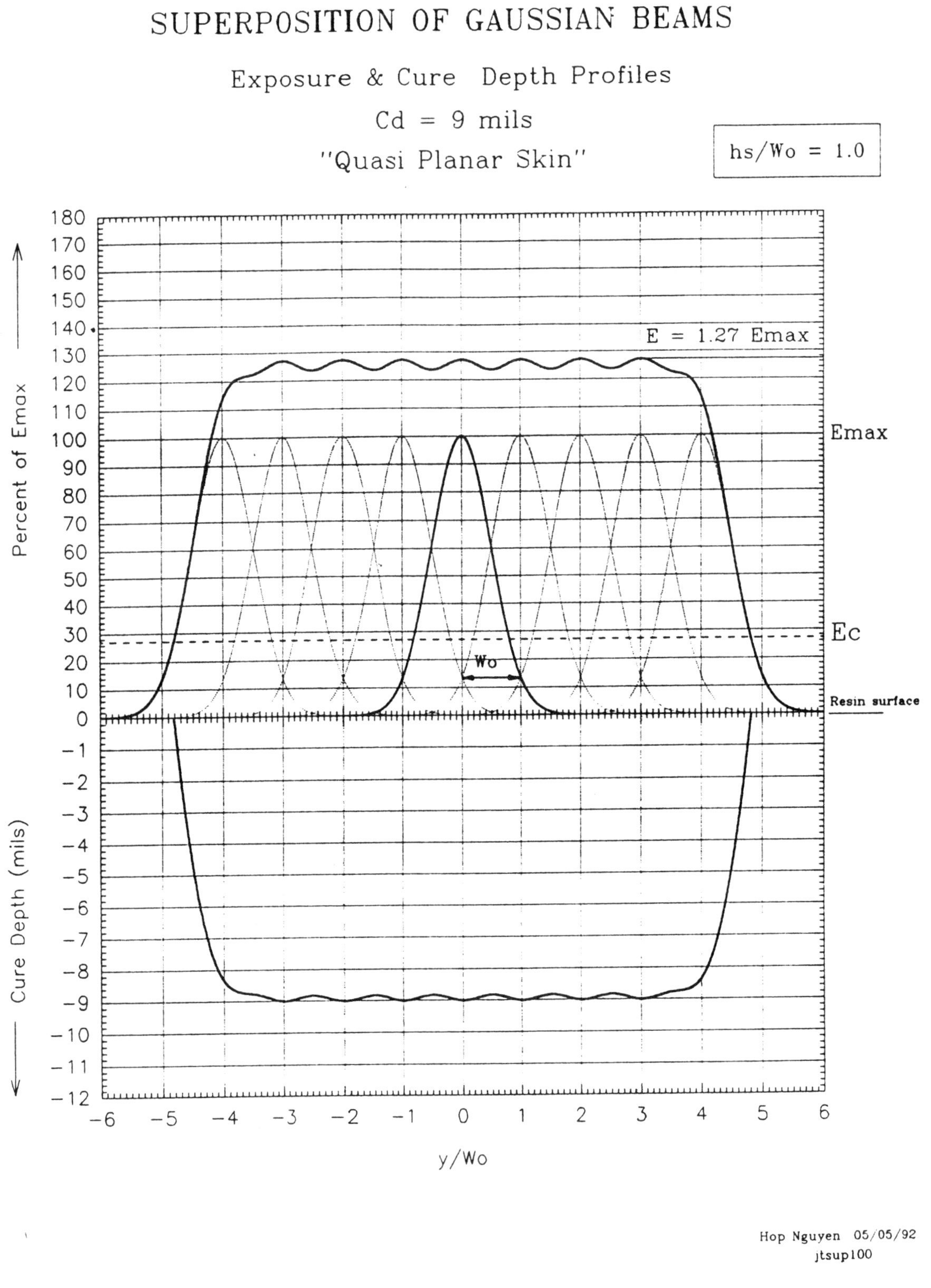

SUPERPOSITION OF GAUSSIAN BEAMS

Exposure & Cure Depth Profiles

Cd = 9 mils

"Quasi Planar Skin"

hs/Wo = 1.0

Figure 6.   Super position of Gaussian Beams Quasi planar skin, hs/Wo = 1.0

Hop Nguyen 05/05/92
jtsup100

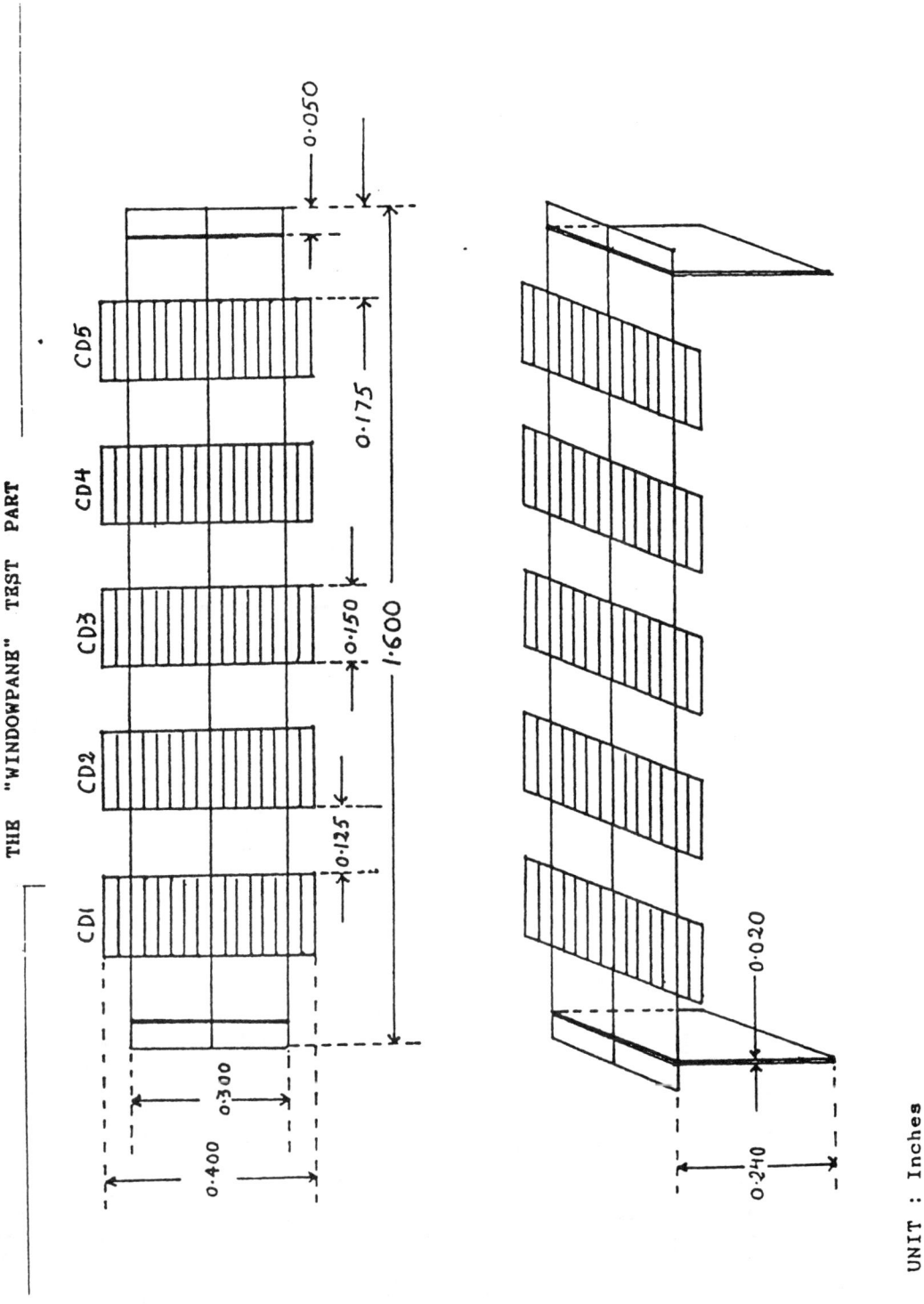

Figure 7. Schematic of the WINDOWPANE™ test part

157

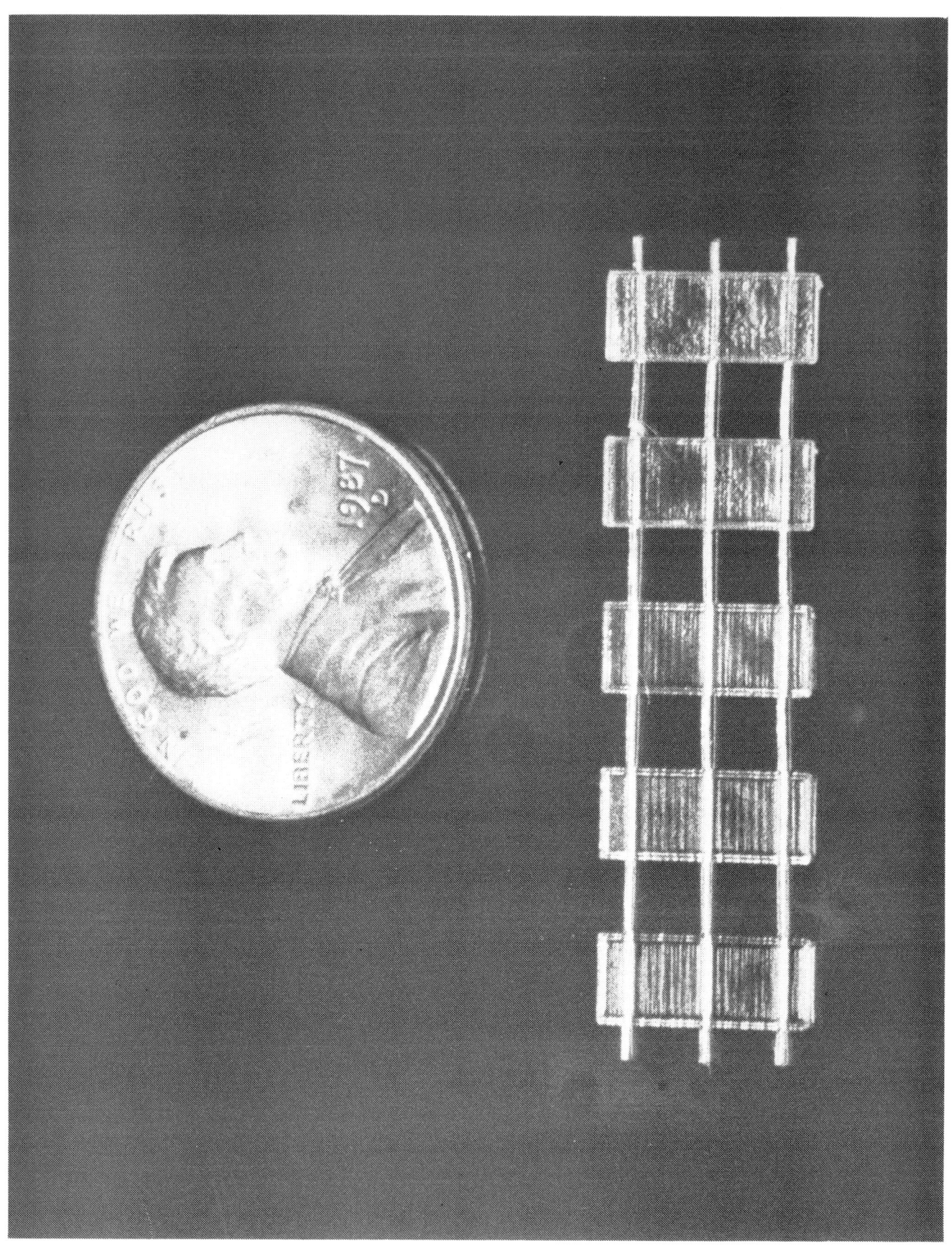

Figure 8. Photograph of an SLA-250 WINDOWPANE™ test part

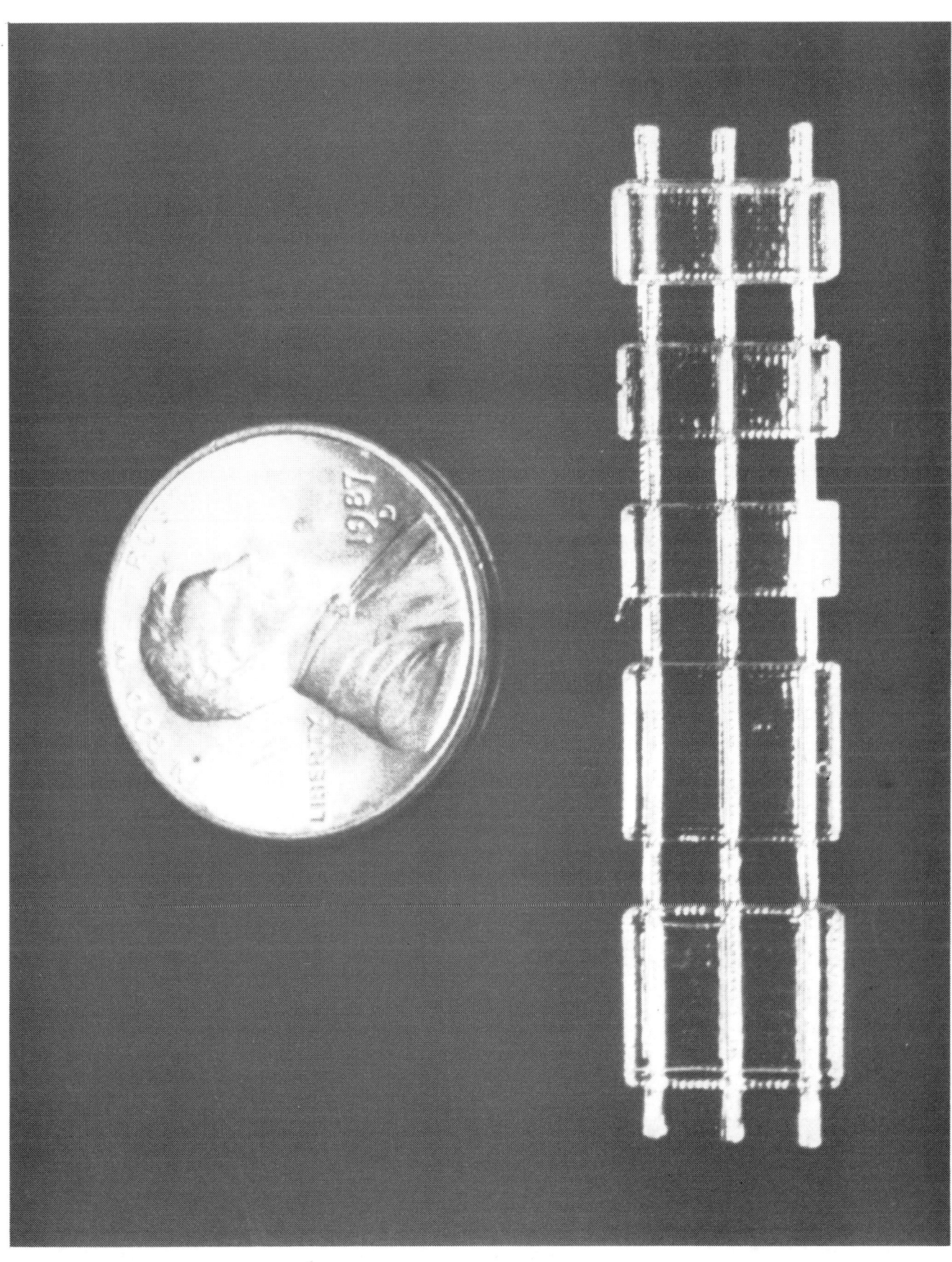

Figure 9. Photograph of an SLA-500 WINDOWPANE™ test part

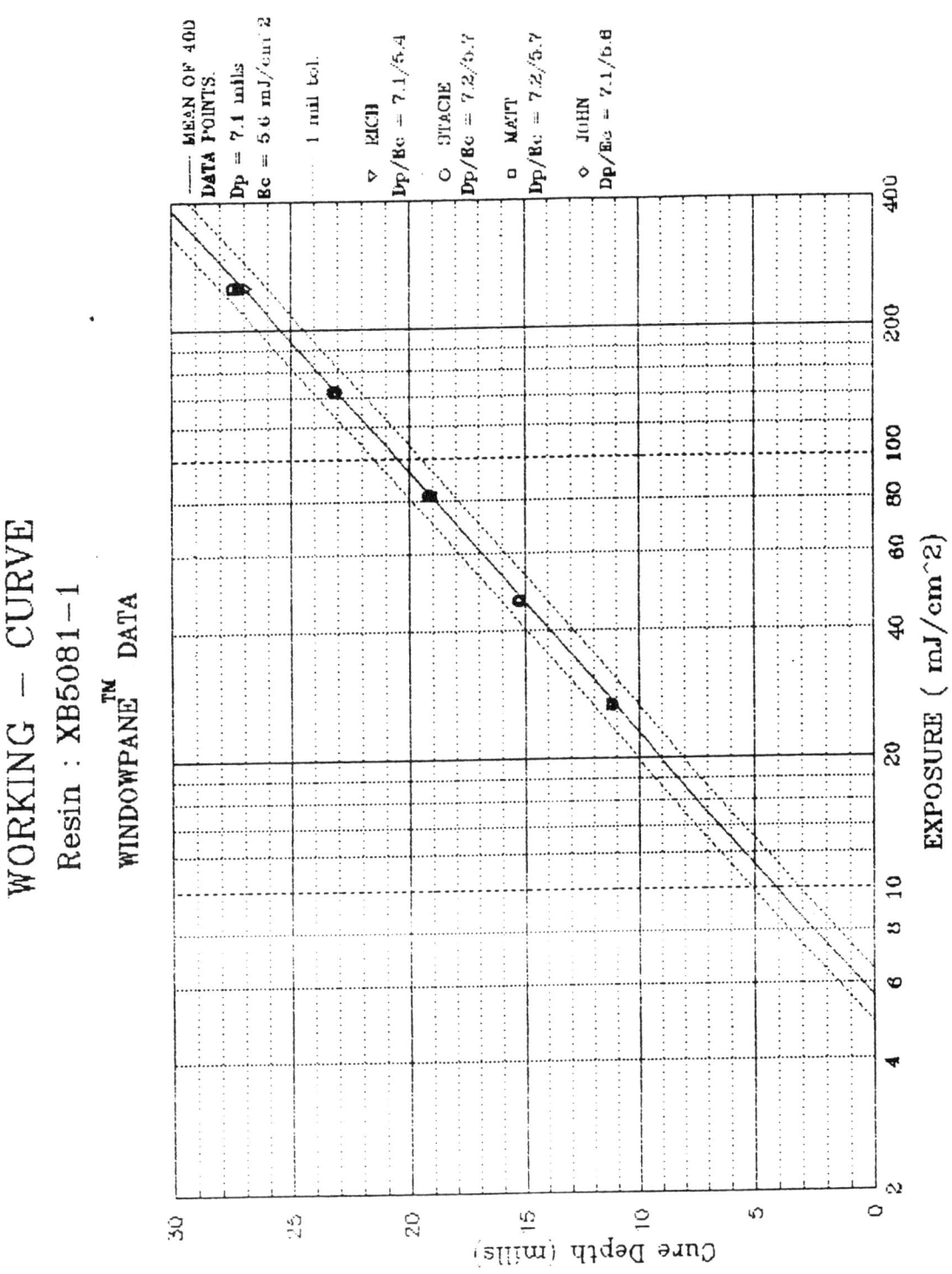

Figure 10.   WINDOWPANE™ generated "Working Curve"

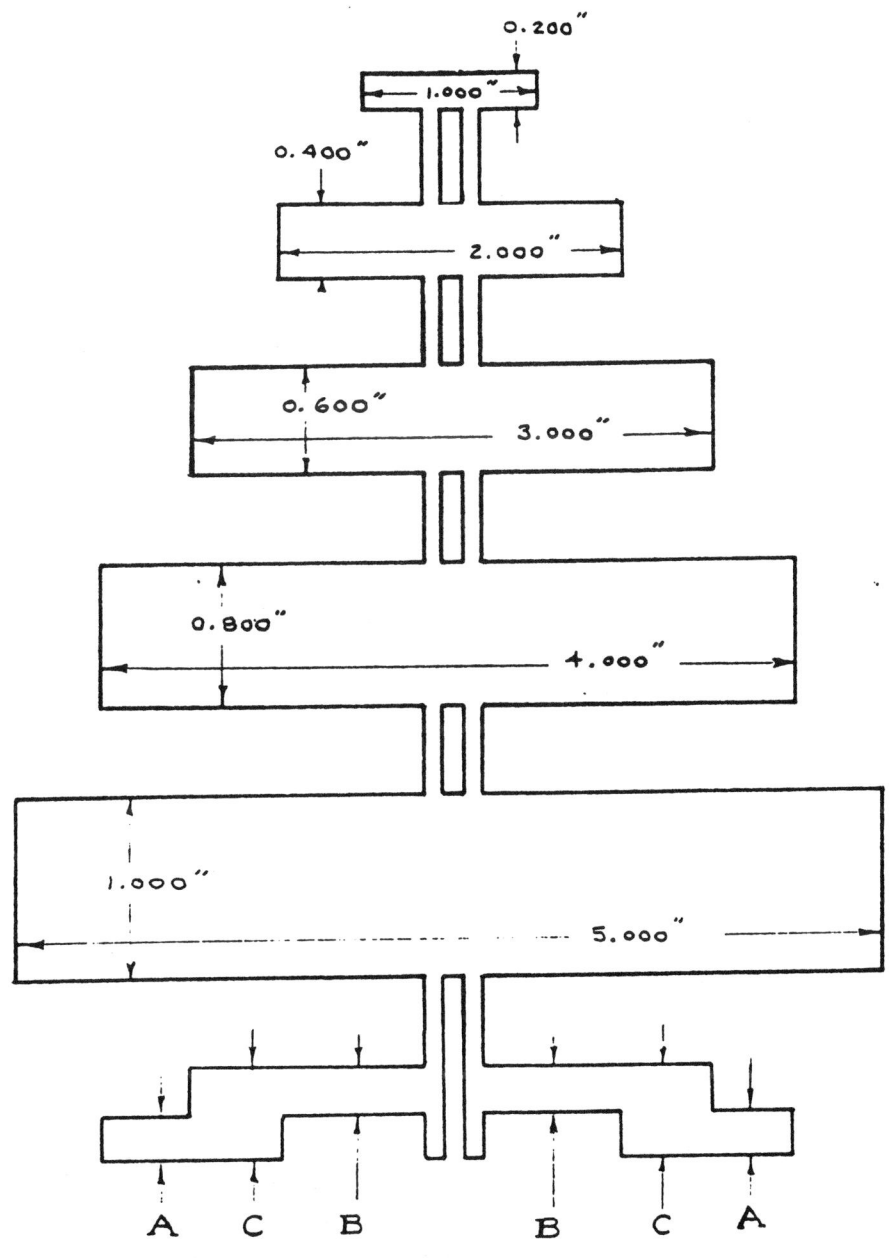

Figure 11.   Schematic of the CHRISTMAS-TREE™ diagnostic test part

161

NEW PHOTOPOLYMER RESINS FOR STEREOLITHOGRAPHY

A. Jacobine, M. Rakas, D. Sutkaitis
Loctite Corporation
705 North Mountain Road
Newington, CT 06111 USA

Abstract

Many current photopolymer resins for stereolithography and other rapid prototyping technologies are based on acrylate ester technology and several contain materials with questionable toxicity such as N-vinyl pyrrolidone [NVP]. The present and future end uses of the resulting stereolithographic parts mandate a search for safer, more responsive materials whose solid properties can be selected with the same criteria now applied to engineering resins.

To this end, we are currently developing stereolithographic resins which contain no NVP; depending on the backbone of the polymer precursor, in situ toughening (as evidenced by yield phenomena) and/or low distortion [curl] are possible. One of these NVP-free resin systems is based upon norbornene-thiol chemistry, rather than acrylate resins. A major advantage of this chemistry is that most polymerization occurs before solidification sets in, resulting in lower stress and thus reduced curl/distortion.

We will present data on photoresponse, mechanical properties (including an explanation of how yield behaviour results in a toughened material) and curl properties, as well as show parts built from these resins. The stereolithography resins investigated will include 2 acrylate-based resins with NVP and two proprietary resins without NVP. Tensile strength, green strength and tensile modulus of these materials are sufficient to allow a number of complex parts to be built with these resins.

1   Introduction

The stereolithographic/rapid prototyping process is unique in that accurate prototype models are produced in a fraction of the time which would be needed to manufacture them via conventional machining techniques. The main components are a computer and associated software, a laser and necessary optics, and a vat of liquid prepolymer which can be polymerized by light to produce a solid polymer. A CAD design is used as the basis for further computations which "slice" the object into many discrete layers. A file is then generated, which in turn guides the laser and optics in order to "draw" the part, layer by layer.

It might seem that the most straightforward component of this process occurs in the vat of prepolymer - a simple chemical reaction versus a complex interplay of software, optics and laser. However, knowledge of the characteristics which the prepolymer must have, and the conditions which the solid or solidifying object is subjected to indicates that a number of competing or antagonistic demands are placed upon the stereolithographic resin. The requirements for the photo-polymerizable material combine rapid photoresponse with good mechanical properties (generally defined as toughness and accuracy) generated by the formation and structure of a network.

The stereolithographic process requires that photopolymerization be accomplished in two stages: in the first stage (part building), partial curing occurs during laser exposure and a "green" part is produced. A green part is simply a laser cured part that has not yet achieved its final state of cure and therefore has not yet achieved its final mechanical properties. In the second stage cure (post-curing), the maximum possible polymer conversion is achieved by low intensity flood exposure of the solid (but green) part to conventional UV lamps.

At this point in the discussion it is important to differentiate polymerization and curing. Polymerization is a chemical process which converts monomer units into polymers. Curing is simply the attainment of "desirable" properties via a polymerization reaction. It is important to note that curing does not imply complete conversion (polymerization) of all reactive groups. It is also important to realize that most reactive compositions are formulated to give optimal or at least desirable properties at less than 100% conversion of reactive groups. This can present problems since additional reaction of functional groups can be expected to occur over time and this will effect the mechanical performance of the object. This type of behaviour has been extensively discussed by Struik in two monographs [1,2] and also by Kloosterboer via a vis acrylate photopolymerization [3].

In order to generate a solid which does not sag under its own weight, the modulus of the material after a partial laser cure must be high enough to allow the solid to support itself. The stereolithographic process requires that after each partially cured layer is produced, it must be submerged in the liquid prepolymer in order to "build" the next layer. For this reason, it is necessary that the resin system used produce a crosslinked network structure since a linear or branched polymer would be dissolved by immersion in its own prepolymer. Other issues which arise upon fully curing the prototype part are also related to the network structure and properties. Depending on the degree of conversion achieved before gelation and the amount of shrinkage which occurs as polymerization continues after gelation, distortion of the prototype part can be extreme or minimized. The stresses produced from dimensional constraints and the liquid-to-solid transition can also result in poor interlayer adhesion, which leads to the delamination of one or more layers.

The stereolithography/rapid prototyping resins investigated for this presentation will include acrylate-based resins, with and without NVP, and developmental proprietary resins without NVP. The proprietary resins are based upon norbornene-thiol chemistry. A major advantage of this chemistry is that most of the polymerization occurs before gelation, resulting in lower stress and thus reduced distortion.

2   Chemical Processes Which Result in a Semi-cured Prototype

Acrylate prepolymers polymerize via a chain-growth, or addition, mechanism. This process is begun when a photoinitiator molecule in the reaction mixture is hit by a photon of light at the appropriate wavelength and two photoinitiator radical fragments are produced. The addition polymerization is propagated when one of the photoinitiator radicals adds to a prepolymer molecule to create a "reactive centre". A chain reaction occurs as many prepolymer units are added in rapid succession to the reactive centre, and the polymer chain grows to high molecular weight very rapidly. A physical analogy would be the addition of pearls onto a string, the monomers add one at a time to the previously reacted monomer. As there are many photoinitiator molecules in the reaction system to generate initiating radicals, a great number of these chains are created simultaneously. For this reason, the photopolymer attains high molecular weight very quickly [4]. In this type of polymerization the reacting composition consists of two components; high molecular weight polymer (often described as the gel fraction) and unreacted monomer (called the sol or soluble fraction).

As the molecular weight of the acrylate increases, mobility of the chains and the radicals decreases. This process is known as vitrification (becoming glass-like). It becomes topologically more difficult to polymerize the remaining acrylate prepolymers, and so incomplete conversion occurs. Although the material is a solid, there remains a large percentage of unreacted acrylate prepolymer within it, and researchers have shown [3] that trapped radicals continue to react slowly over time. This has very important implications for the physical and mechanical characteristics of the fully-cured prototype part. Additional considerations arise when working with a resin which contains a mixture of two or more different acrylate prepolymers (which would produce a photo-copolymer when polymerized). A propagating chain whose last added molecule is type "A" may have a thermodynamic or kinetic preference to add type "A", "B", or type "C" in a mixture. Based on these ratios and the relative amounts of Prepolymer A and monomer and/or prepolymer B and C it is possible to predict and control the sequencing of the A , B, and C units along the polymer chain as well as the total overall composition of the chain. However, with acrylate prepolymers, it has been found that these reactivity ratios change as the polymerization progresses. Therefore, the chemical structure obtained is difficult to predict and may very well be over-influenced by local concentration fluctuations in the monomer mixture; hence its ultimate properties such as modulus, the glass transition temperature Tg, etc. are also difficult to predict, and more importantly influence and control.

Because of these properties inherent in a resin system containing acrylate prepolymers, the ability to design in formulation properties a priori is limited. It is especially important to realize that the performance envelope of acrylate formulations must be determined empirically.

A step growth process is another polymerization mechanism. Generally, two different types of molecules are required, since type "A" cannot polymerize with another "A" molecule nor can type "B" homopolymerize. An "A" and "B" type molecule combine to form a dimer; a dimer then reacts to form a trimer, tetramers, etc. In this polymerization process, molecular weight increases more slowly, although the reaction itself may be quite rapid and at any given time the reaction mixture contains a statistical distribution of oligomers of various molecular weights. As a result, the material is in a liquid state for a far longer time, and stresses due to solidification occur only after vitrification or gelation. If the reaction temperature is above the polymer's glass transition temperature, and the material is able to undergo crosslinking, gelation occurs when all chains are connected to each other, theoretically forming a single molecule.

Many step growth processes form condensation polymers - that is, two molecules react and form a growing chain as well as produce a low molecular weight by-product, such as water or ethanol. In order to attain high conversion and high molecular weights, it is then necessary to distil away the by-product, in order to force the reaction to 100% completion. Obviously, this process would not be suited to stereolithographic resins.

The ideal resin system for stereolithography would be one where the best aspects of both processes were combined in a system which propagated by a rapid free-radical mechanism, yet increased slowly in molecular weight. No low molecular weight by-product would be produced, the reaction itself would be rapid, and because molecular weight would increase relatively slowly, a much greater fraction of material would be reacted before gelation/vitrification occurred. This would minimize solidification and residual stresses in the finished stereolithographic part, and as a result, distortion would be minimized and accuracy increased.

Polymer formation by thiol-ene chemistry has exactly these characteristics. In this type of polymerization a multi-functional thiol (a compound with R-SH functionality) and a multi-functional ene (or olefin) copolymerize. Morgan et al. [5] has pointed out that this type of polymerization possesses characteristics from both type of polymerizations; while addition occurs via free-radical chemistry, "the radical chain length is not directly related to polymer chain length, and the polymer, therefore, grows in a stepwise manner". In addition, under photopolymerization conditions, the thiol and the -ene may only copolymerize - no homopolymerization is possible. This leads to a known, controllable copolymer structure. Lastly, these photopolymerizations are not inhibited by oxygen or the presence of moisture, as are many other UV-curable prepolymers. This type of polymerization process is illustrated in figure 1.

Recently, work in our laboratories has indicated that certain types of strained cyclic internal olefins such as bicyclo[2.2.1]heptenyl derivatives (now to be referred to as **norbornene**) will readily react with thiyl radical. When highly functionalized ($f \geq 2$) norbornene derivatives are reacted with multi-functional thiols such as pentaerythritol tetramercaptopropionate [PETMP, $f = 4$, shown in figure 2], a rapid polymerization takes place. This project is centred around a family of norbornene esters (shown in figure 3) which can be crosslinked with PETMP under ultraviolet (UV) conditions. These resins and the resulting polymers generated are of interest to Loctite because of their proprietary nature and the ability to easily synthesize a wide range of monomers and oligomers with the norbornene functionality, thus gaining the ability to design in properties [6,7]. These features make them very attractive for "next generation" stereolithography resins.

3   Ultimate Properties

3.1   Acrylate-Based Stereolithography Resins

In this section two Loctite commercial resins will be discussed. Loctite 8100 is a mixture of several acrylate resins and also contains NVP. It is intended for applications where the tensile modulus of the fully cured part is required to be over 200,000 psi. Loctite X142837 is also a mixture of several acrylate resins, one of which is isobornyl acrylate [IBA]. It contains no NVP and has a slightly lower modulus, a higher elongation to break, and behaves as a toughened material.

3.1.1 Mechanical Properties of Loctite's Acrylate Resins

Figure 4 shows the stress-strain curve for Loctite 8100. This material, when conventionally cured in a UV Fusion Systems apparatus, has the properties of a stiff material with low elongation to break. The material exhibits an intrinsic yield point briefly before failure occurs at roughly 7% strain. Very little plastic deformation occurs before failure, and consequently, this material cannot be regarded as "toughened". This material is well-suited for applications which require a high degree of stiffness and do not expose the part to a significant amount of handling.

Shear yielding and plastic deformation are observed in Loctite X142837, as shown in figure 5; these results are unexpected, due to the brittle nature of isobornyl acrylate. [Although it may sound confusing, one does obtain **shear** yielding during a **tensile** test. This is because shear deformation is defined to be deformation without a change in volume, regardless of the geometry used.] Generally, yielding and plastic deformation are present only in "toughened" systems, which normally implies a multiphase system. In such a system, the non-continuous phase is produced either by adding a rubbery filler (such as Kraton® particles), by synthesizing very well-controlled block copolymers, such as star block copolymers of polystyrene-b-polyisoprene, or by inducing spinodal decomposition of a blend of two polymers or two monomers. Since none of these technologies were used, and a multiphase system was not expected, dynamic mechanical analysis was used to attempt to understand this phenomenon.

3.1.2 Thermal Properties of Loctite's Acrylate Resins

Films of Loctite X142837 were optically clear, indicating that if two phases were present, either their refractive indices were quite similar or that the domain size of the non-continuous phase was smaller than the wavelength of light. However, tensile results of fully-cured systems seemed to indicate that a multiphase system might be indicated. In such cases, DMA can often clarify the situation. From initial work to determine the Tg of Loctite X142837, it was noticed that a shoulder appeared on the tan δ peak (see figure 6). In order to determine if random or block polymerization were occurring, and to study the presence or absence of the shoulder peak, Tg values were obtained for a range of formulations as a function of wt % IBA.

Because the data obtained did not follow the Flory-Fox relationship, these experiments led to the hypothesis that non-random copolymerization is occurring. The temperature sweeps obtained show that no transition is occurring (no local maxima in tan δ) at or even 10°C below the Tg of homopolymerized IBA (≈ 92°C). It can definitely be concluded from this data that IBA alone is not forming a separate phase in these cured films.

The control film, containing no IBA but otherwise the same composition as x142837, was found to have the same Tg. This appears to indicate that in X142837, IBA is not homogeneously mixing with the molecular components responsible for the transition at 46°C. Although adding more IBA than contained in x142837 does increase the Tg, and adding less decreases it, the values measured are not consistent with each other (that is, roughly doubling the wt% of IBA does not double the increase in Tg). It is as if IBA acts to increase the free volume when small amounts are added, and reduces the free volume present when larger amounts are added. This is unexpected behaviour, due to the high Tg and brittle nature of IBA.

This is to drive home the point that this system is not behaving as it would if it were a one-phase homogeneous film, and that one-phase behaviour would reasonably be expected. The point of these results and this discussion is 1) IBA doesn't appear to phase separate (no tan δ peak at ≈ 92°C); 2) it appears that non-random polymerization is occurring; however, if phase separation exists, it is not due to the formation of domains of pure polymerized IBA.

Loctite 8100, containing NVP along with several other acrylate resins, has a Tg value of approximately 61°C. Its high shear storage modulus (G') value in the rubbery plateau region indicates that this is a very highly crosslinked material, which can be a useful feature when building a part which requires long working time.

3.1.3 Modulus versus Dose

Collection and analysis of data on the build up of tensile modulus with dose was undertaken for a number of reasons, the primary one being to determine the path dependence of the ultimate tensile modulus. That is, if two compositions with roughly the same ultimate modulus can attain that modulus at different rates or increments; this would have implications in stereolithography. Because the part is not fully cured during building, it only receives a fraction of the radiation dose necessary for full cure. If the ultimate modulus is high, but modulus build-up is slow, the part may warp, curl or collapse from its own weight during building and before post-curing occurs.

Modulus versus dose samples were cured using an Oriel "cold" UV flood curing system, which has an optics system that removes infrared light (and thus heat) from the UV light. This results in a true room temperature cure of the resin. Samples were 0.5" w x 0.010"t x 2.0"l; the gage length used was 1.0 inch. Very soft samples were glued into paper tabs at the appropriate gage length; this permitted the uniform use of pneumatic grips. Depending on the softness of a sample, a 2.25-, 22.5- or 50 lb load cell was used to measure the tensile modulus. As before, all tensile testing was performed on an Instron 4505 Universal tester. Figures 8 and 9 show the modulus vs. dose results for the Loctite NVP-free formulation (Loctite X142837) overlaid with those of a competitor's "toughened" resin. (Since both linear and log-log plots can hide a multitude of sins, both plots for each case will be presented). It has been found that when conventionally cured in a UV Fusion System™, these two formulations have a nearly identical modulus. As is easily seen from either plot, Loctite X142837 builds modulus much more quickly.

It is important to remember that Loctite X142837 is an entirely different formulation, not merely Loctite 8100 without NVP. Figures 10 and 11 compare modulus as a function of dose for Loctite 8100 and Loctite X142837. These results seem to suggest that Loctite 8100 builds modulus more quickly; however, a few data points at lower doses are necessary before this can be stated unequivocally.

3.2   Norbornene/PETMP Thin Films

3.2.1 Experimental

All materials tested were cured films of 10-25 thousands of an inch thickness; norbornene resins and thiol were combined in chemically stoichiometric amounts. A UV Fusion System™ was used to "flood" UV-cure the films; all films were cured at a dose of 620 mJ/cm^2. An Instron 4505 Universal testing machine was used to determine tensile properties. A modified ASTM D-882 test method was used, with a crosshead speed of 0.2 in/min; guidelines for width\:thickness

ratios were observed. A Rheometrics RDA II was used to determine the glass transition temperature (Tg) by defining Tg as the temperature at which a maximum in the
tan δ trace occurs.

3.2.2 Mechanical Properties

By creating a family of norbornene monomers, it was expected that mechanical properties could be designed into formulations by proper backbone selection, functionality and by blending two or more norbornene resins together. Data from tensile tests, presented in Table 1, show that a wide range of tensile properties is spanned by formulating one of the resins with PETMP in 1:1 equivalents. A representative stress-strain curve for the ethoxylated bis-phenol A dinorbornene ester [EBPA-DN]/PETMP film is shown in figure 12, and is similar to that of the TMP-TN/PETMP. This curve shows an initial linear elastic region which ends before 0.5% strain and is followed by a nonlinear region where stress is continually increasing; no yielding occurs prior to failure. Figure 13 is a representative stress-strain curve for a hexanediol dinorbornene [HDDN]/PETMP film which used a crosshead speed of 0.2 in/min throughout. At very low levels of strain, a high stress response is immediately generated. An intrinsic yield point is reached almost immediately, and strain softening follows. Around 60-80% strain, strain hardening sets in, and continues until failure. Due to the conditions of the ASTM test and the high elongation to break, some samples were tested using a crosshead speed of 2 in/min above 20% elongation. At this speed, stress did not continue to increase with strain, but instead decreased and then maintained a constant level of stress with increasing strain, indicating that a second yield point in the polymer has been initiated by increasing crosshead speed.

The middle range of mechanical properties that can be formulated is slightly increased by blending together two of the three norbornene esters (see Table 3). The norbornene resins were blended on a weight basis, and were then mixed with a stoichiometric amount of PETMP, the crosslinker. Stress-strain curves show that the unusual features found in HDDN/PETMP films are apparently masked by the presence of EBPA-DN or TMP-TN in the corresponding blended film. Due to the high strain to break in HDDN, one would expect some increase in elongation to break in films where HDDN is a component; however, when added to EBPA-DN or TMP-TN, the elongation to break of these materials is not increased at all.

3.2.3 Thermal Properties

From the data (shown in Table 3), it is seen that EBPA-DN/PETMP films of between 11 and 25 thousands of an inch thickness have essentially the same Tg, while the Tg for 15 and 25 thousands of an inch films of TMP-TN/PETMP differ by approximately 10 degrees. These results suggest that formation of the TMP-TN/PETMP network is more diffusion-limited than the difunctional/tetrafunctional network formation of EBPA-DN/PETMP. While doubling the thickness of a photomer film results in less absorption of light and thus could be responsible for a lesser degree of polymerization (and hence lower Tg), since both sides were irradiated this does not seem to sufficiently explain the dependence of Tg on film thickness for TMP-TN but not EBPA-DN [8].

Only one glass transition is observed for each of the three-component systems studied; this data indicates that the two blended norbornene resins do mix on a molecular level. This is claimed by using the widely-accepted criteria that the presence of a single Tg indicates mixing on a molecular level, while immiscible blends (whose homopolymers have significantly different Tg values) are characterized by more than one glass transition [9].

4   Norbornene/Thiol Resins for Stereolithography

Although a commercial product is not yet available, a team of chemists, chemical engineers and a materials scientist are collaborating at Loctite to formulate a norbornene/thiol resin similar to the ones discussed in the preceding section for the special demands of stereolithographic processing. Work to date has shown that curl parts made from norbornene/thiol materials can exhibit much lower distortion. Curl factors of less than 2.0 have been realized with some formulations; typical acrylate curl factors hover around 10, but can be reduced using non-traditional build styles. Norbornene/thiol resins may be well-suited for SLA use - as well as low curl, their low volatility and the ability to "design in" mechanical properties indicate that these resins may be more "user friendly".

5   Conclusions

Stereolithography requirements demand both a chemical and a material science approach to resin development. The marriage of chemistry and mechanics, for example, is shown in the modulus versus UV dose studies. The utility of this work has been shown, as it can explain why attempting to build the same prototype with two different resins can result in vastly different results, even if both resins have the same ultimate modulus.

Loctite's acrylate-based stereolithographic resins have a range of physical properties, ranging from stiff, with extremely fast modulus build up with UV exposure and low elongation to break, to a toughened material with lower modulus and significantly higher elongation to break.

Loctite is also simultaneously developing "next generation" norbornene-thiol resins for stereolithographic use. These materials appear to offer lower toxicity in some categories, along with lower shrinkage upon curing and thus less distortion. Because this polymerization is governed by step-growth kinetics, and since it is relatively easy to norbornene-endcap a wide range of functionalized oligomers, this chemistry lends itself well to "designed in" properties.

References

1. L. C. E. Struik, "Internal Stresses, Dimensional Instabilities and Molecular Orientations in Plastics,"Wiley, New York, 1990.

2. L. C. E. Struik, "Physical Aging in Amorphous Polymers and Other Materials," Elsevier, Amsterdam, 1978.

3. J. G. Kloosterboer, Adv. Polym. Sci., 84, 1-61, 1988.

4. Odian, George, "Principles of Polymerization," 2nd Edition, Wiley Interscience,1981.

5. C. R. Morgan, F. Magnotta, and A. D. Ketley, J.Polym.Sci\:Polym.Chem.Ed., 15, 627-45, 1977.

6. A. F. Jacobine, D. M. Glaser and S. T. Nakos, in Radiation Curing of Polymeric Materials, ACS Symposium Series 417, American Chemical Society, Washington, D. C., 1990.

7. Walter J. Steinkraus, John Woods, John M. Rooney, Anthony F. Jacobine and David M. Glaser, U.S. Patent 4,808,638 "Thiolene Compositions Based On Bicyclic 'Ene Compounds", February 28,1989, assigned to Loctite Corporation.

8. S. P. Pappas, private communication, April 1990.

9. F. E. Karasz and W. J. MacKnight in Polymer Blends, Vol. 1, D.R. Paul and S. Newman, eds., (Academic Press, New York,1978), pp. 186-243.

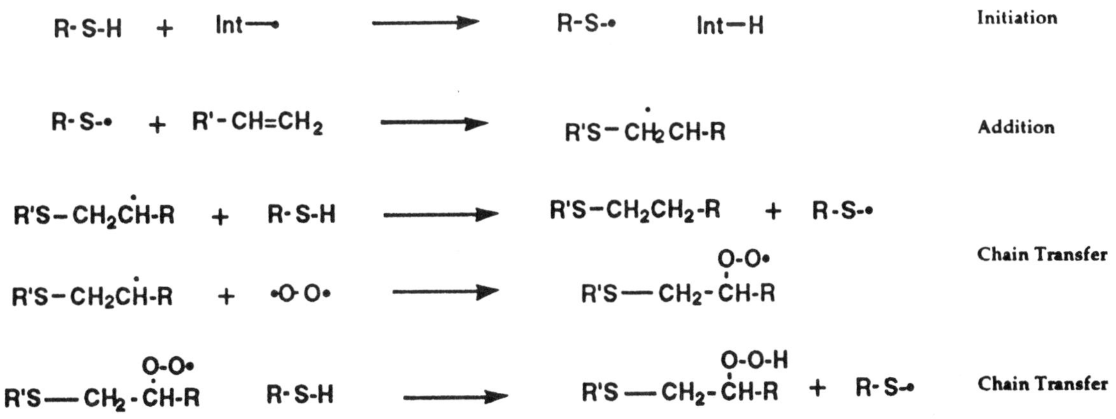

Figure 1   Model Thiol-Ene Polymerization Reaction Scheme

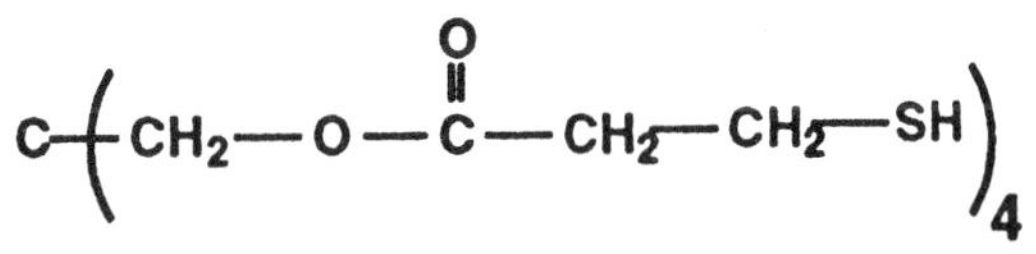

Figure 2   The tetrafunctional crosslinker used,
pentaerythritol tetra-(3-mercaptopropionate) [PETMP].

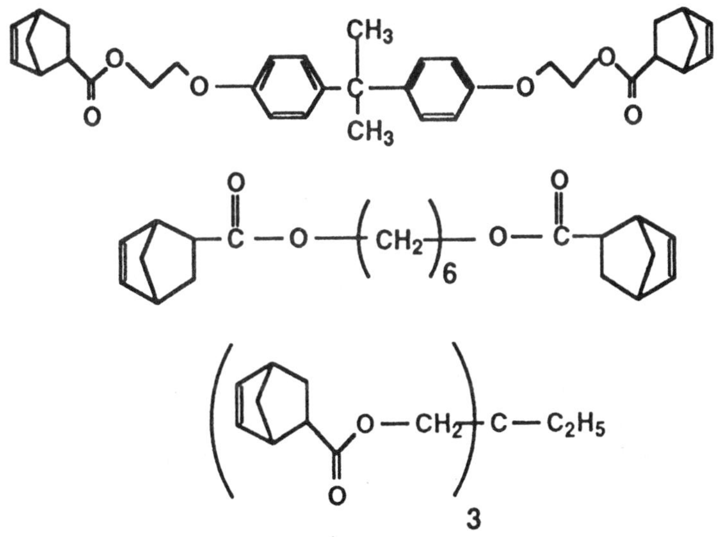

Figure 3   *From top to bottom:* Ethoxylated bis-phenol A dinorbornene [EBPADN];
Hexanediol dinorbornene [HDDN]; and Trimethylolpropane trinorbornene
[TMPTN].

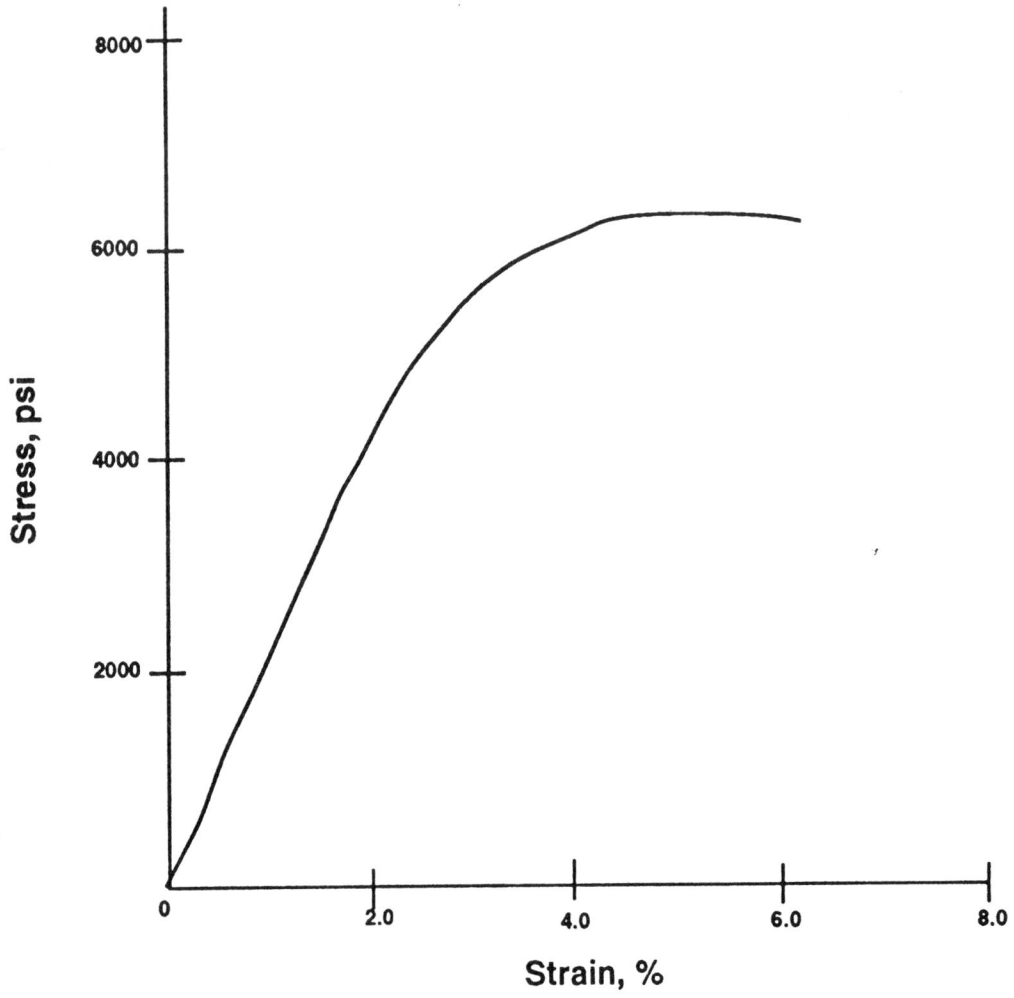

Figure 4   The stress-strain curve for Loctite 8100

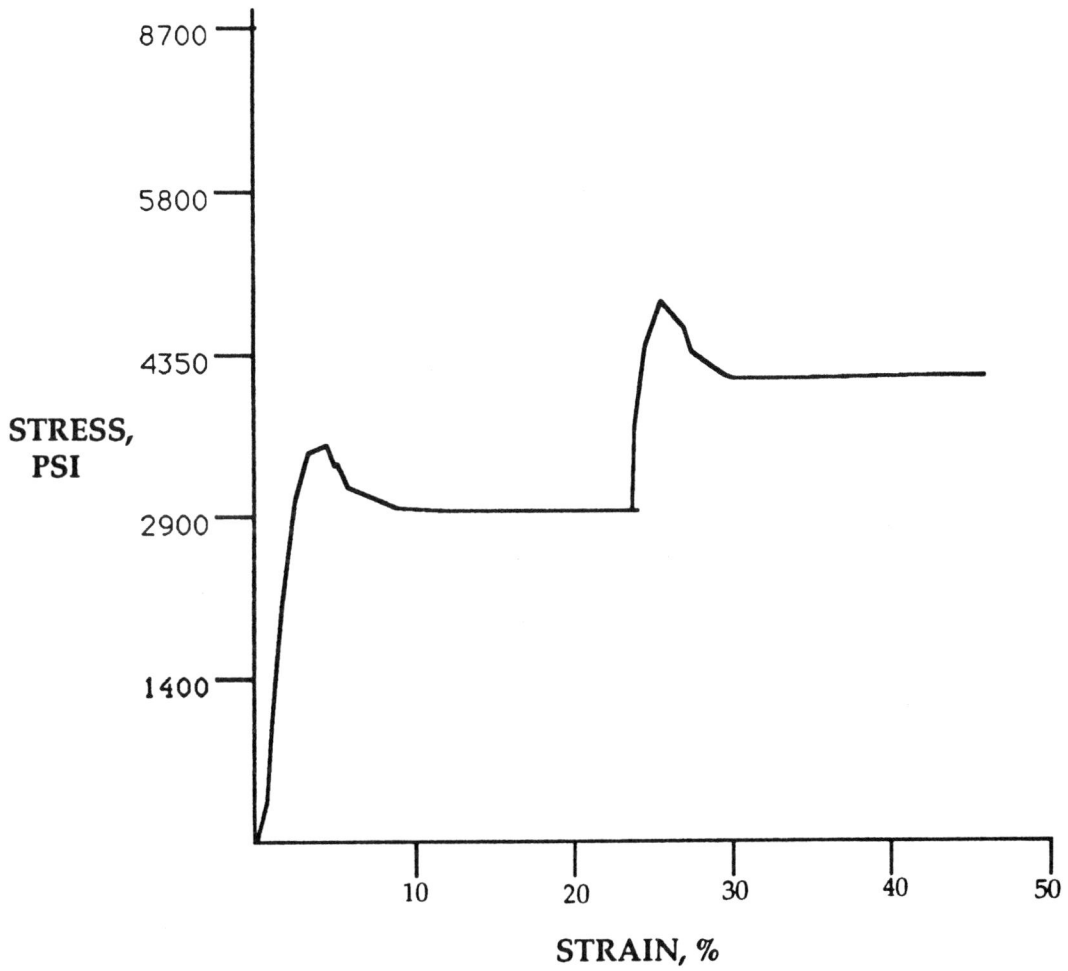

Figure 5   The stress-strain curve of a Loctite NVP-free acrylate resin, X142837

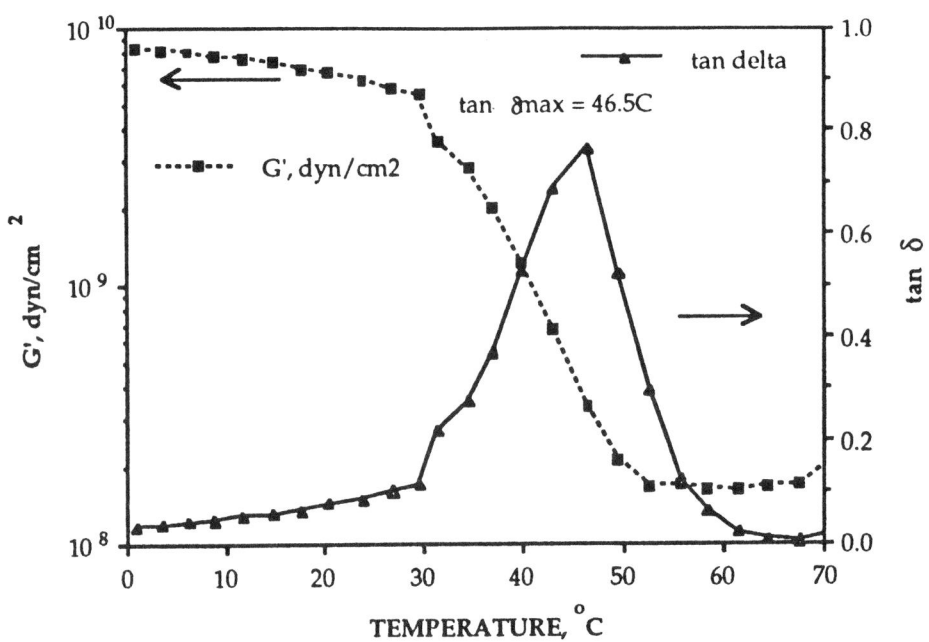

Figure 6   A DMA temperature sweep of a Loctite NVP-free acrylate
stereolithography resin, X142837

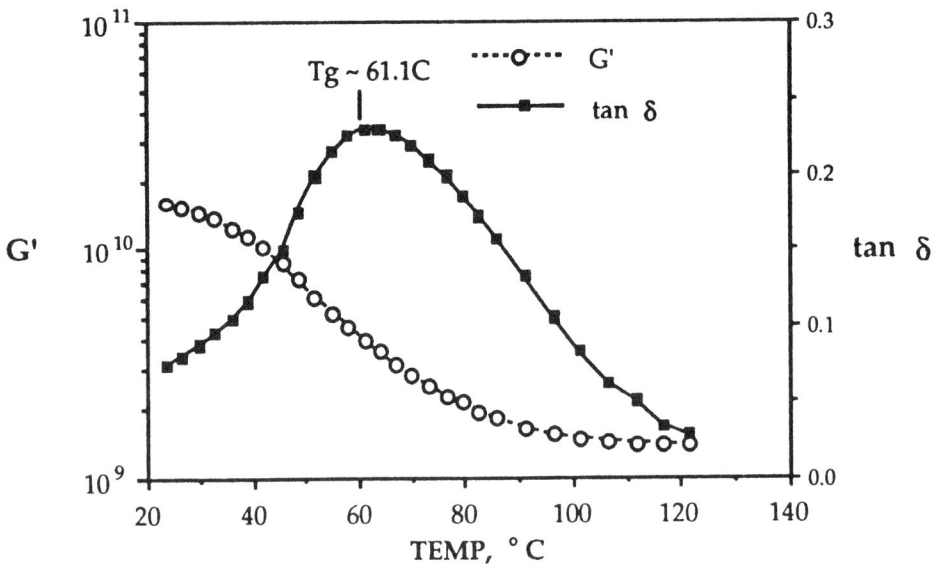

Figure 7   DMA temperature sweep of Loctite 8100

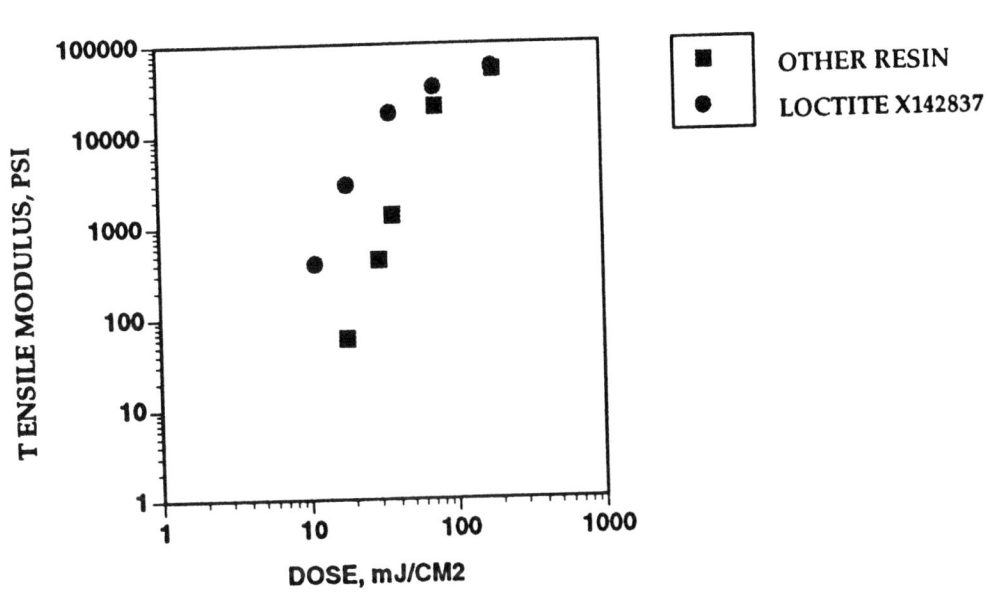

Figure 8   Log-log plot of modulus *versus* dose for X142837 and a competitor's "toughened" stereolithography resin

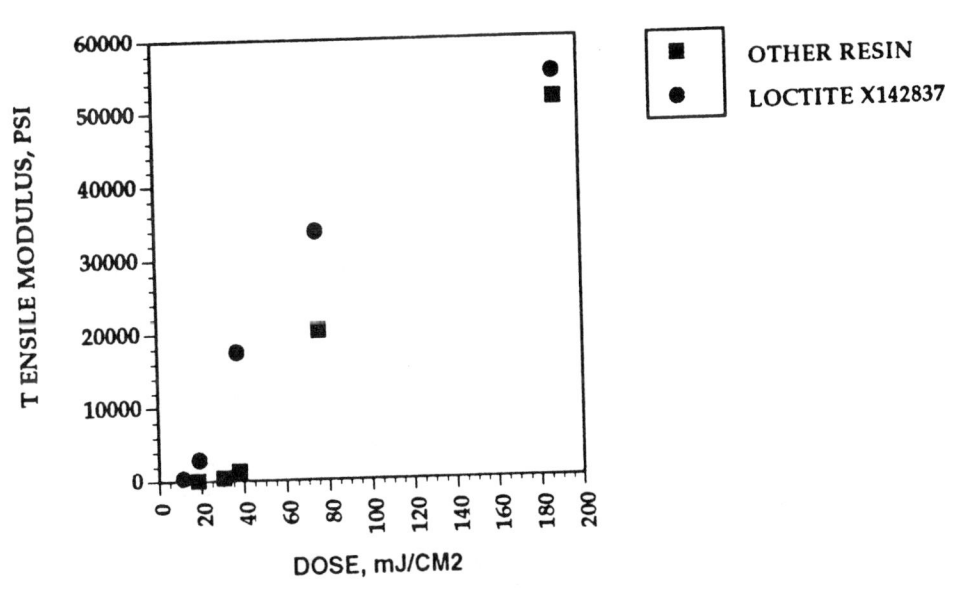

Figure 9   A linear plot of modulus *versus* dose for X142837 and a competitor's "toughened" stereolithography resin

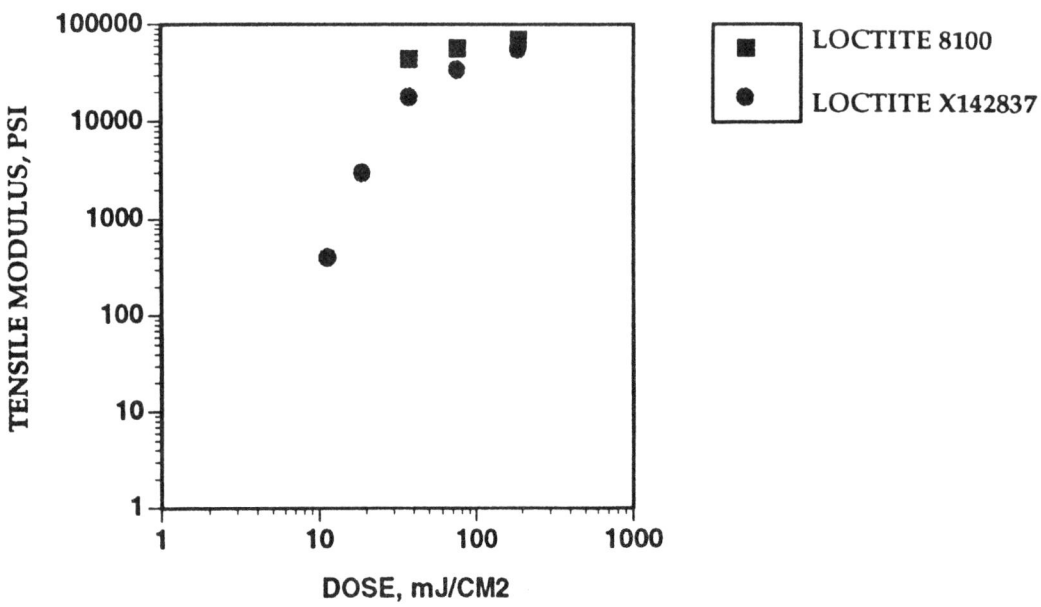

Figure 10   Log-log plot of modulus *versus* dose for X142837 and Loctite 8100
stereolithography resins

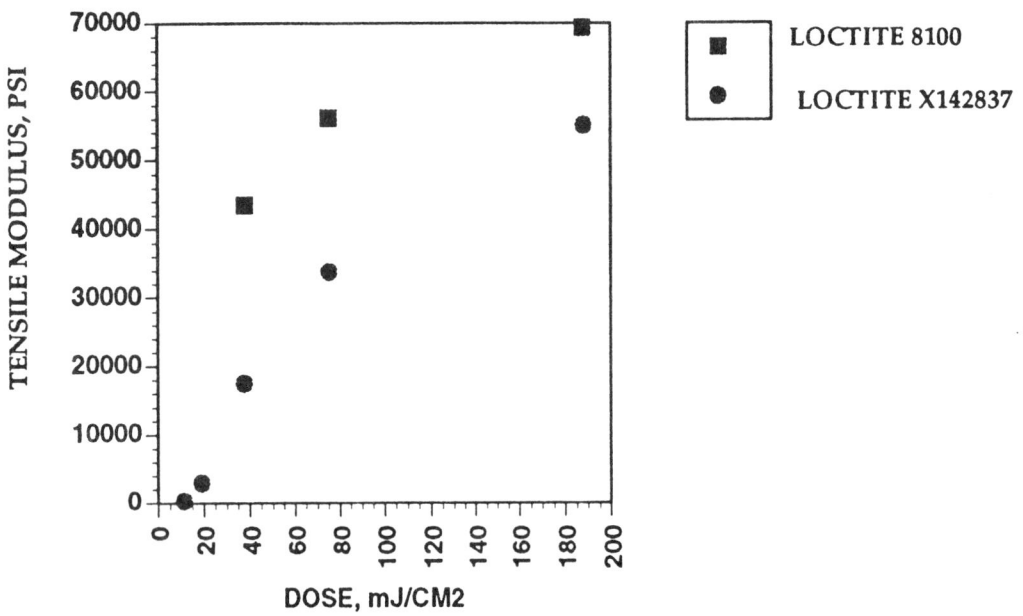

Figure 11   A linear plot of modulus *versus* dose for X142837 and Loctite 8100
stereolithography resins

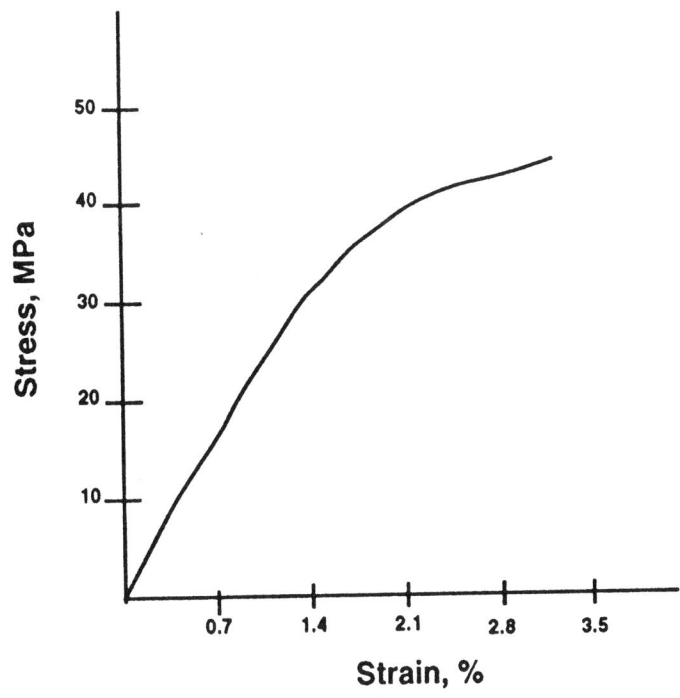

Figure 12   A representative stress-strain curve for the
ethoxylated bis-phenol A dinorbornene ester [EBPADN]/PETMP film

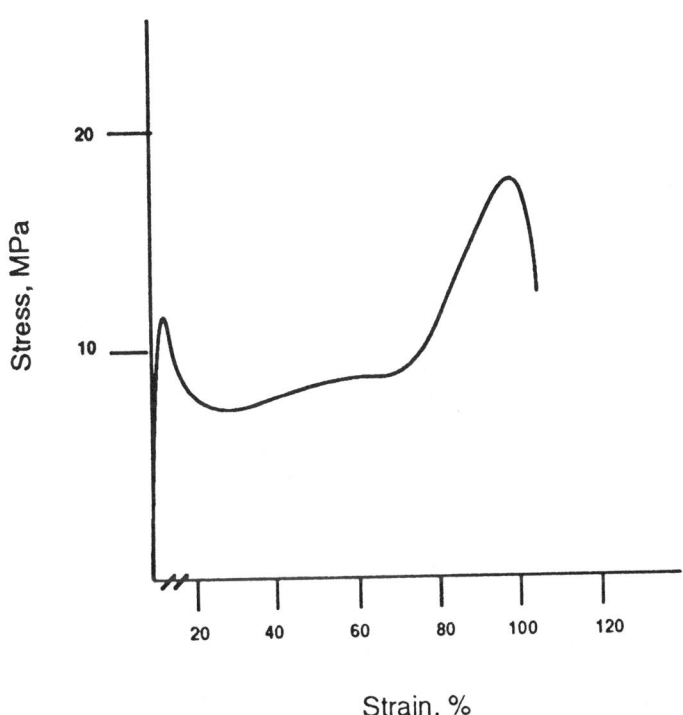

Figure 13   A representative stress-strain curve for the hexanediol
dinorbornene ester [HDDN]/PETMP film

Table 1   Tensile Properties of Films with a Single Norbornene Resin

	HDDN	TMP-TN	EBPA-DN
Tensile Modulus kpsi (GPa)	120 (0.81)	330 (2.3)	280 (1.9)
Stnd Deviation kpsi (GPa)	29 (0.20)	6.9 (0.05)	44 (0.30)
Tensile Strength kpsi (MPa)	2.5 (17)	8.8 (61)	5.9 (40)
Stnd. Deviation kpsi (MPa)	0.22 (1.5)	0.48 (3.3)	0.74 (5.1)
% Elongation to Break	105	4.1	2.9
Stnd. Deviation (%)	12	0.63	0.52

Table 2   Tensile Properties of 50/50 Films of Norbornene Resins and PETMP (1:1 eq)

	EBPA-DN/ TMP-TN	EBPA-DN/ HDDN	TMP-TN/ HDDN
Tensile Modulus, ksi (GPa)	370 (2.6)	285 (2.0)	250 (1.7)
Stnd. Deviation, ksi (GPa)	42 (0.30)	6.8 (0.05)	5.1 (0.04)
Tensile Strength, ksi (MPa)	6.5 (44)	5.6 (39)	6.4 (44)
Stnd. Deviation, ksi (MPa)	2.4 (16)	0.60 (4.1)	0.33 (2.3)
% Elongation to Break	2.2	2.8	3.4
Stnd. Deviation, %	0.90	0.40	0.40

Table 3 Glass transition temperatures (T_g) and experimental conditions for films of norbornene/thiol and two component norbornene/thiol resins

Resin	Thickness, mils (mm)	Initial Strain/ Maximum Strain (%)	Temperature at which a maxima in tan δ occurs (°C)
EBPA-DN	11.8 (0.30)	0.2/0.4	36.4
	13.0 (0.33)	"	38.7
	24.4 (0.62)	"	39.5
TMP-TN	18.2 (0.46)	0.15/0.5	67.8
	27.6 (0.70)	"	55.6
	15.4 (0.39)	"	67.1
	25.2 (0.64)	"	57.6
HDDN	13.4 (0.34)	0.22/0.35	30.1
TMP-TN/ EBPA-DN	16.9 (0.43)	0.4/0.4	52.7
HDDN/ EBPA-DN	14.6 (0.37)	0.3/0.6	35.9
	14.6	"	39.1
TMP-TN/HDDN	16.1 (0.41)	0.2/0.4	46.9
	17.3 (0.44)	"	46.8

STANDARD TEST-FILES FOR BENCHMARKING RP SYSTEMS

Mr R Smith

Sherbrook Automotive Limited
Lichfield, UK

It is less than four years since the first operational RP system was produced, and already there are at least seven differing technologies being implemented, all aimed at producing finished models by directly converting a 3D CAD file into a solid object.

This diversity of technologies makes it even more difficult for prospective customers who wish to either purchase a system, or use a bureau service operating one or other technology to choose between the competing systems and services on offer.

Different machine tools designed to carry out the same task use the same basic technology, and the end user's requirement simplify the choice.

However, in this new, RP industry, with differing technologies to add to the normal differences between the way competing suppliers define and price their equipment and services, some universal definitions of performance are necessary, so that the buyer can more easily judge which system will most suit his or her needs.

Can anyone define and compare the system costs for the different technologies and machines on offer? What is included in the basic price and what is extra? Is provision made for site preparation, installation, training and commissioning? Are service contracts included? Is pre-processing software and work station included? Is post-processing equipment required and included for?

What is meant by processing speed? What is the time for completing one layer? Does any time mentioned specify geometric limitations, or vary depending on the volume of material that must be cured for that slice? Does the time include any pre-processing and post-processing time? Is a multiplier included, as more often than not, the end user requires more than one model of any part.

For most prospective buyers or users of a rapid prototyping system, the most important aspect is the performance of the actual models themselves, as opposed to system performance. It is this aspect that I would like to expand upon.

Potential customers, typically, choose a complex model to evaluate alternative systems. However, these models do not necessarily evaluate and quantify all the criterions that are of importance to the company. The most useful model or range of models would be those specifically designed to allow you to clearly check the success of any RP system in the areas most relevant to the company's needs.

To provide guidance in this area, Cubital have designed a library of 12 objects, each one designed to physically demonstrate at least one feature important to a physical model. This library provides an evaluation kit, offering a universal, empirical tool to benchmark model performance according to industry based standard requirements. This library is in an easy-to-use booklet, that contains drawings and photographs of each model, suggestions on how to measure the model's performance, and suggested models that would be most appropriate for various applications. These are, of course, only suggestions, and each user can evaluate each model in the way that is most suited to his own needs and standards.

To make this library of objects universally accessible, both to prospective system users and to system vendors wishing to demonstrate their system capabilities, these models have been loaded on to diskettes in ASCII STL format files, which are readable by any RP system. Each file name indicates the performance features that can be tested by building the object defined by that file.

All the models are of the same general size, with plain faces, so that a number of models can be built in one block. The size has been chosen so as to be not so large as to be wasteful, nor so small that features are meaningless. You can, of course, vary the scale to suit your own needs and special requirements.

I'd like now to provide a little more information on some of the objects that have been modelled in this library.

Accuracy is one of the most important attributes that a model can have. Some models are actual prototypes of parts, and are required to prove the design both dimensionally and functionally.

Accuracy is a block with well defined internal and external distances in all three dimensions. Errors can occur due to instrumental errors, material instability, warping etc. A rapid prototyping system should be able to maintain accuracy for any geometry, dimension or size.

Blindcav is the model of a block with 3 blind cavities, that is, 1 sided openings in the model.

The cavities in this model vary in their cross-sections, volumes and shapes, and are a challenge for all RP systems since they involve the removal of material from hard to access positions. Initial evaluation can be carried out with the model in a whole condition, and continue by cutting through the tunnel sections. Before cutting or slicing into this or any model, you should check with the system supplier that it would be safe to do so, as some materials, when not fully cured, are hazardous.

Fullcure is a thick solid block of cured resin.

The quality of the curing, the adhesion of layer to layer, and the mechanical properties of the building material can be tested. Again please check that this will not be dangerous, and what precautions should be taken.

Tight gap is a block made up of several simple geometric shapes with very small gaps between them.

When parts of a model have very small gaps between them, there is the danger that the parts will not stay separate, but will fuse together. This model tests the ability of the system to prevent close features from fusing.

Cracktop and manyface are 2 similar looking models that tests the ability of the system software to handle sick files and to handle files with tens of thousands of facets. Errors have been purposely introduced into the cracktop file that are typical of many commercial CAD systems. These faults are missing or inverted facets, missing normals and cracks between facets. The designer's intentions are quite clear, and the diagnosis and correction of faulty files is an important capability of a RP system. Some models have very complex geometry, with numerous curved or circular features, and so require very long files. Any RP system should have the capacity to cater for this requirement.

Interloc is a multi-part mechanism, with small clearances between the parts, which are interlocked together, to form a single assembled mechanism. This model demonstrates mechanical functionality, clearances, freedom between parts, and the elasticity of flexible elements. It allows the user to conceptually evaluate mechanisms without the need for production engineering.

Curling is a block with several horizontal edges and surfaces in which good adhesion and even shrinkage are necessary to obtain the correct geometry. Curling is an unwelcome side affect that can occur with systems that do not fully cure each layer of the model as it is produced, and so needs to finish cure the model separately after it has been completed. Shrinkage is an unwanted by-product which all the competing technologies have to contend with to some degree, some better than others.

Warping is a block which had solid arms protruding in several directions.

Warping is caused by internal stresses due to uneven material shrinkage distorting the dimensional accuracy of the model. For models that are to be used as casting patterns or built up into assemblies, dimensional and positional accuracy are crucial.

Other models in this file are designed to test the following requirements:

Through tunnels, overhangs and thin walls.

We have a limited number of these model libraries here, on our exhibition stand, and you are welcome to examine them. We shall also be able to show you a number of models produced on the Solider system including objects produced from the files in this library.

Each library contains a description and photograph of each model, a list of features and the criteria which each model demonstrates, suggestions on which models would be most useful for the evaluation of various applications and suggestions on how best to evaluate the models produced from these files. There is also a set of diskettes with the ASCII files for the models described in the library. These libraries can be ordered at our stand for the nominal charge of £15 each. This is far less than the actual production cost, low enough to be of no concern to any company, but high enough to deter indiscriminate collection.

STEREOLITHOGRAPHY PROCESS ACCURACY
User Experience

Edward P. Gargiulo

E.I. Du Pont de Nemours and Co.
Wilmington, Delaware, USA

Abstract

This paper presents further results of the SLA User Group (North-American) In-Plane Accuracy benchmark study with more than twenty independent contributors. Data is presented to compare in-plane accuracy capability of various StereoLithography printing styles with other rapid prototyping technologies.

1   Introduction

StereoLithography has continued to grow away from its original form-oriented visualization application toward manufacturing. As users become experienced they seek increased functionality, models with improved fit and function. Accuracy and material properties are being challenged.

The SLA User Group has had a benchmark study in progress since 1990 to identify the sources of SLA process inaccuracy and establish the accuracy capability of the StereoLithography process (1,2). Specific questions relate to the major sources of variability, differences among printing styles, and comparisons to other prototyping technologies. This paper will address these questions based on measurement results from about 85 benchmark parts that have been made by more than 20 SLA Users.

2   Previous Work

The SLA User Group in-plane Benchmark Part, Figure 1, has been documented elsewhere (2) and will only be described here. It is a plate-like part designed to cover the extent of the platform of an SLA-250 and provide a large number of x-y features that can be measured on a coordinate measuring machine. A collection of 154 points are used to evaluate its geometric accuracy.

Figure 2 shows a typical plot of dimensional data. The horizontal axis indicates the CAD dimensions, d, while the vertical axis scales the differences between the CAD and measured dimensions, u, A "least squares" line with a slope, m, and intercept, a, is fit through the data. Two important metrics are taken from this data.

$$RMS\ Error = \sqrt{\frac{1}{N} \sum (u - \bar{u})^2}$$

and

$$Residual\ Error = \sqrt{\frac{1}{N} \sum [u - (md + a)]^2}$$

RMS Error is the proper accuracy metric because it considers the variability about the mean of all the data, but the non-zero slope of the least-squares line indicates a shrinkage that can clearly be corrected by the user when setting up the part. Residual Error is properly a metric of precision, but it removes the variability due to shrinkage and gives a true measure of the achievable accuracy of "accuracy capability".

Table 1 summarizes these and other metrics for a number of benchmark parts all made with the same acrylate material. RMS values (column 1) are seen to vary from 0.018 to 0.050 inches. The large range of the values should not be of concern because the users were specifically asked not to make any compensation (shrink or linewidth) when building these parts. The slope values (column 2) also show a wide variation that is unexplained, but appears to be consistent for individual users. Residual Error values (column 3) are smaller than the RMS values, but variability is large.

When individual part data are separated into two sets corresponding to inside and outside feature dimensions, the effects of linewidth can be identified, Figure 3. The results of such analysis are summarized in columns labelled "inside" and "Outside" on Table 1. As expected, the slopes of the inside and outside feature data sets are similar, but the intercept data, related to a beamwidth compensation, are not consistent. One would expect to find intercepts of the same magnitude but different sign.

Still more information can be extracted from the data if it is further grouped by x and y orientation, Figure 4. From this diagram it is clear that the x and y directions have different shrinkage slopes. This has been found on several parts written by the WEAVE style and is most easily seen when the part is both shrink and beamwidth compensated.

3   A New Basis for Analysis

Previous data analysis has been based on a linear curve fit that minimizes the function

$$\sum (u - md - a)^2 = e$$

189

Figure 3 shows that the inside and outside features may comprise unique statistics and should be treated separately. Furthermore, shrinkage and linewidth compensation can easily be done with the existing StereoLithography software. An analysis scheme can be derived to find these compensation factors while considering outside and inside features.

Given two sets of data, u_i and u_o, representing inside and outside feature dimensions, we can find the shrinkage, m, and half-linewidth, a, that minimizes the function

$$\sum (u_i + a - md_i)^2 + \sum (u_o - a - md_o)^2 = e$$

Following the usual "Least Squares" procedure (3) this is differentiated with respect to the parameters a and m and set equal to zero. Solution of the resulting equations yields the values for the slope and intercept.

$$a = \frac{1}{D}[(\Sigma d_i + \Sigma d_o)(\Sigma u_o + \Sigma u_i) - (\Sigma d_i u_i + \Sigma d_o u_o)(\Sigma d_o - \Sigma d_i)]$$

$$m = \frac{1}{D}[(n_i + n_o)(\Sigma d_i u_i + \Sigma d_o u_o) - (\Sigma d_o - \Sigma d_i)(\Sigma u_o - \Sigma u_i)]$$

where

$$D = (n_i + n_o)(\Sigma d_i^2 + \Sigma d_o^2) - [\Sigma d_o - \Sigma d_i]^2$$

A similar analysis can be performed to include the independent effects of x and y shrinkage.

4   Results

Table II presents a summary of the data for 28 acrylate parts made using the equilateral hatch (also called isohatch or just hatch in this paper). WEAVE™ and STARWEAVE™ printing styles. The uncompensated data are the slope and Residual Error from previous analysis while the fully compensated data are the slope, half-linewidth, and Residual Error from the analysis just described. For each printing style the average and standard error (studentized standard deviation) of the Residual Errors are computed. The differences between the compensated and uncompensated mean Residual Errors are indistinguishable.

This table does allow a comparison of the accuracy capability (shown by the Residual Errors) of the writing styles since all of the parts were made in the same, Ciba-Geigy XB5081, material. The results are summarized below:

Printing Style	Mean Residual	Standard Error
Isohatch	0.0102 in.	0.0040 in.
WEAVE™	0.0081	0.0027
STARWEAVE™	0.0050	0.0011

The Table II data from parts printed with WEAVE styles at layer thickness of both 0.005 and 0.010 inches are shown. These are combined in the above summary because the measurement variability is too large to be assured that the differences between them are real.

The differences among the three printing styles are statistically significant at the 95% confidence level and show that the more recently developed WEAVE and STARWEAVE printing styles do give improved accuracy capability. I have some reservations about the STARWEAVE data because five of the six parts were submitted by the same user and may not be representative of common practice.

Table III shows a summary of data for parts made on SLA-250's and an SLA-500 with different materials and three parts made by alternate rapid prototyping technologies. The SLA-500 data is also from a single user and all four parts were made at the same time in different quadrants of the machine. It suggests that the SLA-500 WEAVE printing style with Ciba-Geigy XB5131 acrylate resin gives results similar to the SLA-250 WEAVE style writing in Ciba-Geigy XB5081 acrylate resin.

Three parts made with the STARWEAVE style in Ciba-Geigy XB5143 resin (a urethane acrylate) have been submitted by three different users. These measurements suggest that this resin may not yet have the accuracy capability of the acrylate resins.

Finally, three parts have been submitted from other rapid prototyping systems. It is not possible to judge the full capabilities of these systems from single parts, but the results are thought to be representative of the state of the art. The CUBITAL part shows an accuracy similar to that of the isohatch printing style, but individual WEAVE style parts have had similar Residual Error values.

The numerically controlled milling machine parts exhibit low residual errors as might be expected. The Perspex (acrylic) part has a Residual Error lower than most of the acrylate STARWEAVE parts, but it could easily be from the same population as the StereoLithography parts. The single aluminium part was measured on four separate days and with different fixturing setups on the coordinate measuring machine. This part is clearly the most accurate one submitted to date and helps us to put StereoLithography accuracy into perspective. The consistent residual error values also show the repeatability of the measurement technique and give confidence that the residual error variability is really related to process variability and not measurement errors.

4.1 Distribution of Error

It is interesting to see that the Residual Errors are improving as the StereoLithography process matures and better printing styles are developed, but there is more to the story. In an earlier SLA User Group Meeting someone suggested that the distribution of errors might give further insight. There are several ways to look at error distributions. Figure 5 shows error distribution charts like those of Figure 2 but the data points have been replaced by mean values and fiduciary bars (at twice the standard error) for each dimension. Each chart records data for several parts built by the same printing style and have been corrected for shrink and linewidth deviations. The open symbols indicate the data from outside dimensions while the closed symbols show inside dimension data. Comparisons among these charts corroborate writing style differences. It is also clear that the error spread is practically the same for small and large dimensions.

Another way to present this same data is in an error histogram or frequency distribution. Figure 6 shows the frequency distribution for isohatch parts. The horizontal axis marks the differences from the desired dimensions on 0.001 "increments over the range from -0.02 to +0.02 inches. The vertical scale marks the number of times a difference in a specific band occurs. Thus the error bar at +0.005 inches shows that difference between the measurement and CAD dimension was between 0.0045 and 0.0055 inches about 101 times. This data is the total for 12 parts that have been fully compensated. As one would expect, the data is clustered about an error of 0.0 with a decreasing number of occurrences as the differences become large.

The histogram approach can be made even more useful with a few more modifications. First, the histogram can be normalized by dividing each bar by the total number of observations so the total of all the values sums to 1.0. Next, the data can be folded about the mean value so the -0.001 inch data is added to the +0.001 inch data, etc. This is useful because we are accustomed to looking at symmetrical tolerance bands. Finally, the level of each bar can be added to the sum of all previous bars (e.g. the value at 0.003" is the sum of the values at 0.0, 0.001, 0.002 and 0.003 inches). The resultant chart is called a cumulative error distribution and the value of each bar shows the probability that the error will not exceed the error level of the bar. For example, the level of the 0.005 inch bar is the probability that the difference will be in the tolerance band ±0.005 inches. Cumulative error distributions for the various building styles are summarized in Figure 7. Observations from these distributions are summarized below:

Probability of Being inside a Tolerance Band

Tolerance Band

Printing Style	0.005 in.	0.010 in.
Isohatch	50%	75
WEAVE	58	82
STARWEAVE	75	95

5   Conclusions

This effort of the User Group has shown that the accuracy capability of StereoLithography has been significantly improved with the introduction of the WEAVE type printing styles. The major sources of error are shrinkage and laser linewidth, both of which can be compensated by the equipment user. Because machines, materials and processes differ slightly, each user must find suitable compensation values based on a developing set of diagnostic parts.

Dimensional errors appear to be evenly distributed over the range of dimensions and follow a normal distribution. This means that the accuracy capability applies equally to both small and large dimensions. The accuracy capability of StereoLithography is dependent on the printing style as follows:

Equilateral Hatch	$\pm$0.020 inch
WEAVE	$\pm$0.016 inch
STARWEAVE	$\pm$0.010 inch

Ninety five percent of all x-y dimensional measurements can be expected to fall within these "tolerance" ranges. It is, of course, possible to hold tighter control of a few critical dimensions with further part iteration and compensation.

The best StereoLithography parts compare favourably with the results of numerical controlled milling, but are not yet as accurate. It is still early to judge the performance of the large capacity SLA-500 and the accuracy influences of urethane acrylate resins being used to improve part durability.

The SLA User Group plans to continue to support this measurement effort to determine the influences of emerging material and machine technology. Parts made by any rapid prototyping technology are welcome and will be measured and included in the database. Two variants of the benchmark part have also been created: one at twice the size for the SLA-500 and a 200 mm part for other desktop manufacturing machines with small working columns.

References

1. Gargiulo, E.P., and Belfiore, D.A. "StereoLithography Process Accuracy: User Experience" Second International Conference on Rapid Prototyping, University of Dayton-RPDL, pp.311-326, 1991.

2. Gargiulo, E.P., and Belfiore, D.A. "Photopolymer Solid Imaging Process Accuracy" PED-Vol.56 Intelligent Design and Manufacturing for Prototyping, pp81-95, ASME 1991.

3. Hoel, P.G. Introductions to Mathematical Statistics, John Wiley & Sons, New York, 1964.

WEAVE and STARWEAVE are trademarks of 3D Systems, Inc.

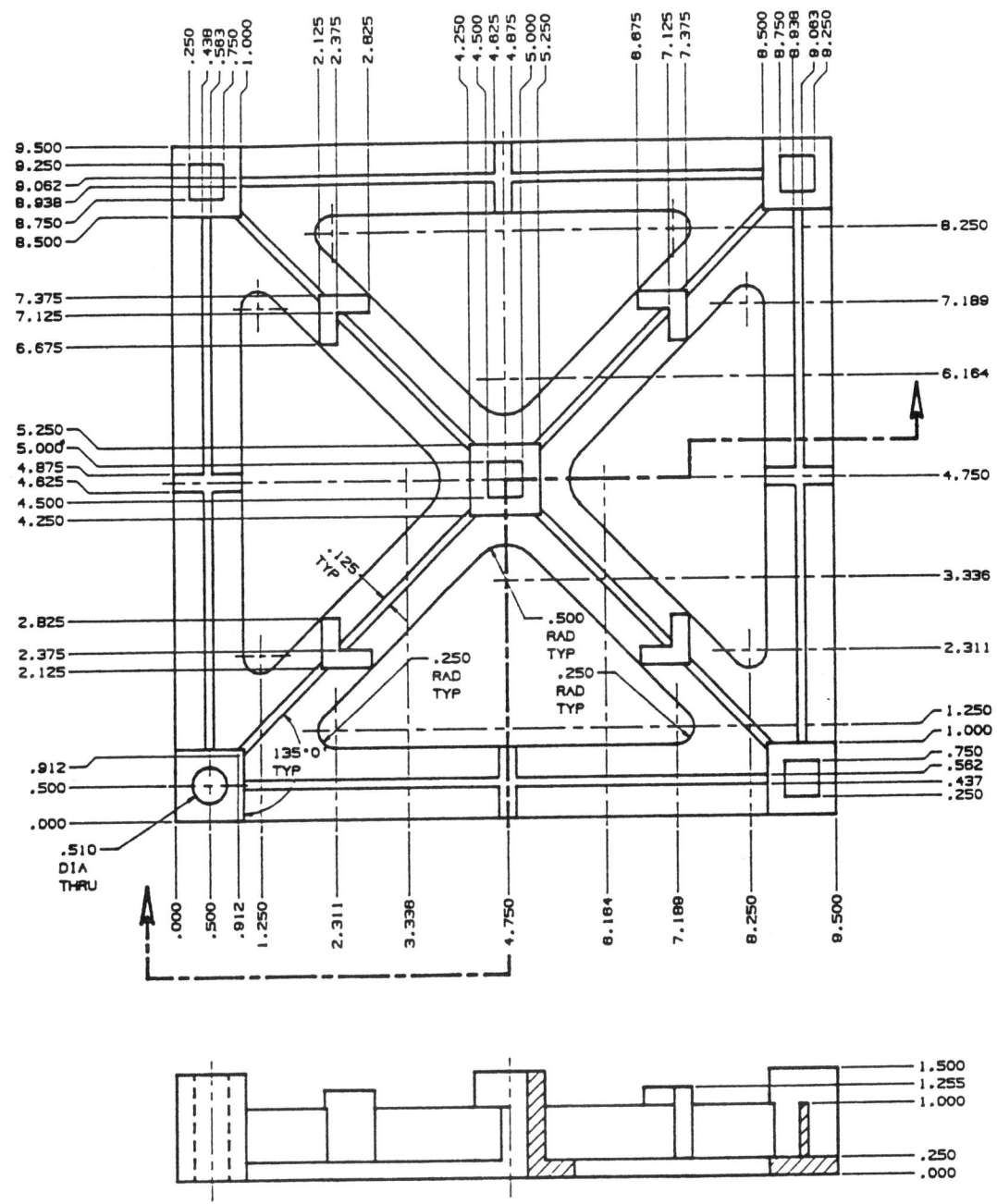

Figure 1   In-Plane Benchmark Part

195

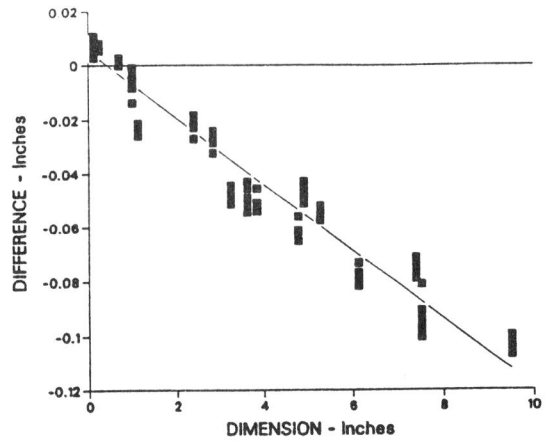

Figure 2   Typical Error Chart

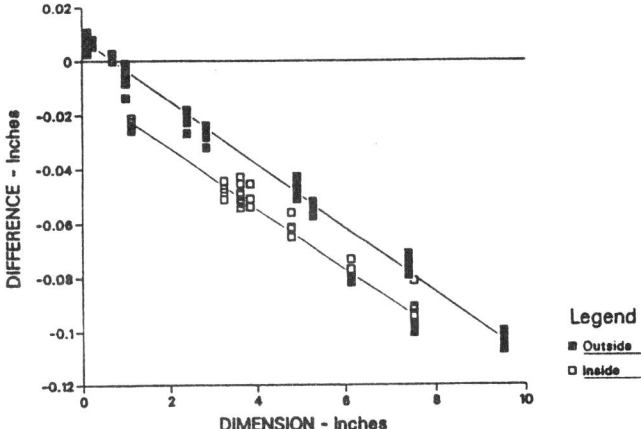

Figure 3   Error Chart: Inside/Outside Data Identified

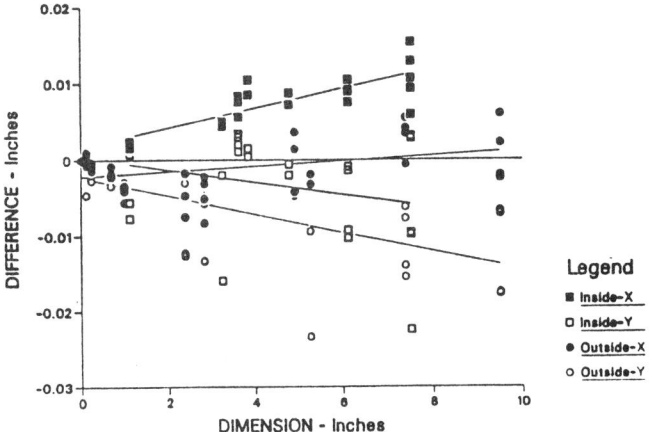

Figure 4   Error Chart: X/Y Data Identified

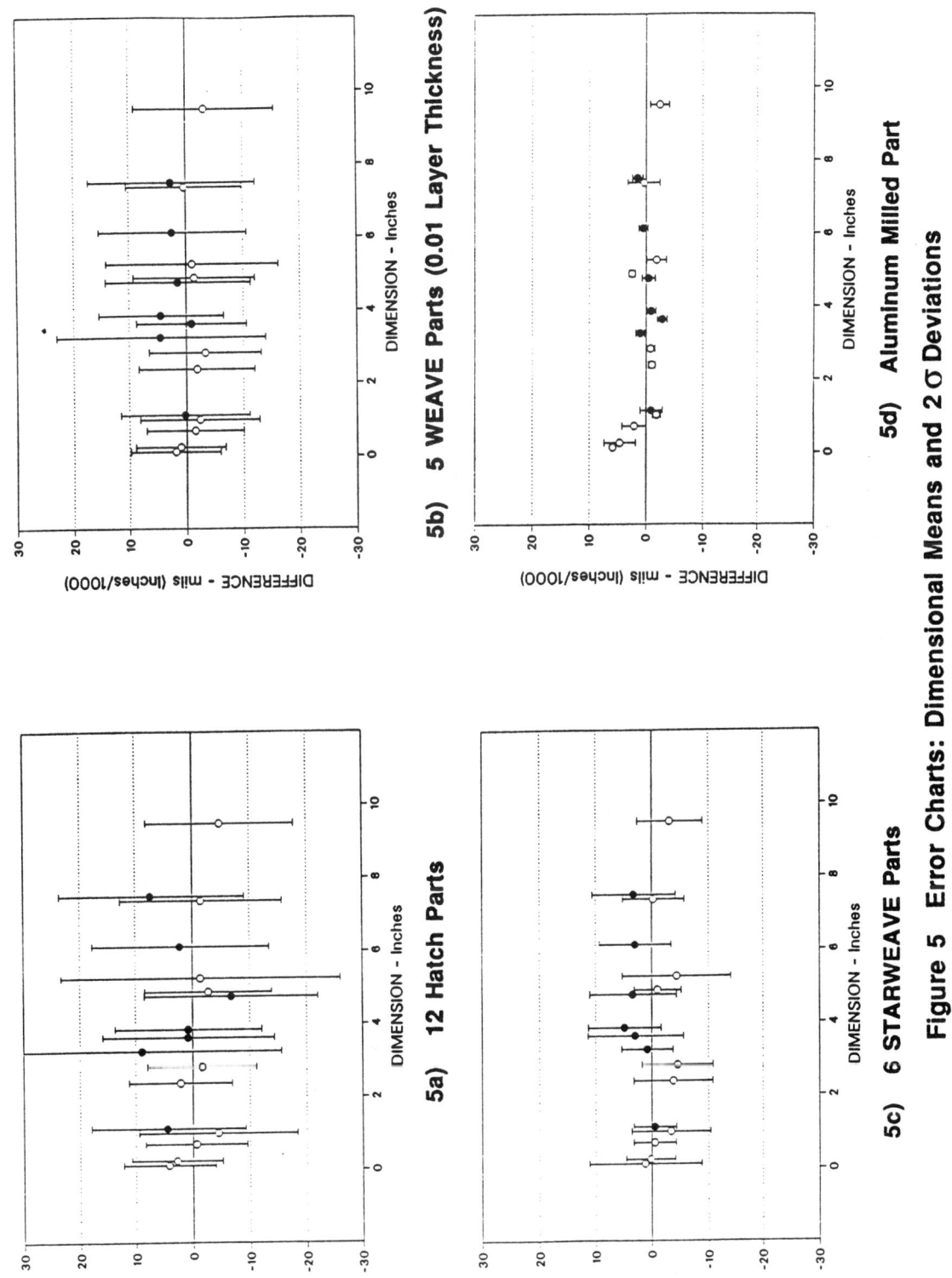

5b) 5 WEAVE Parts (0.01 Layer Thickness)

5d) Aluminum Milled Part

5a) 12 Hatch Parts

5c) 6 STARWEAVE Parts

Figure 5 Error Charts: Dimensional Means and 2σ Deviations

197

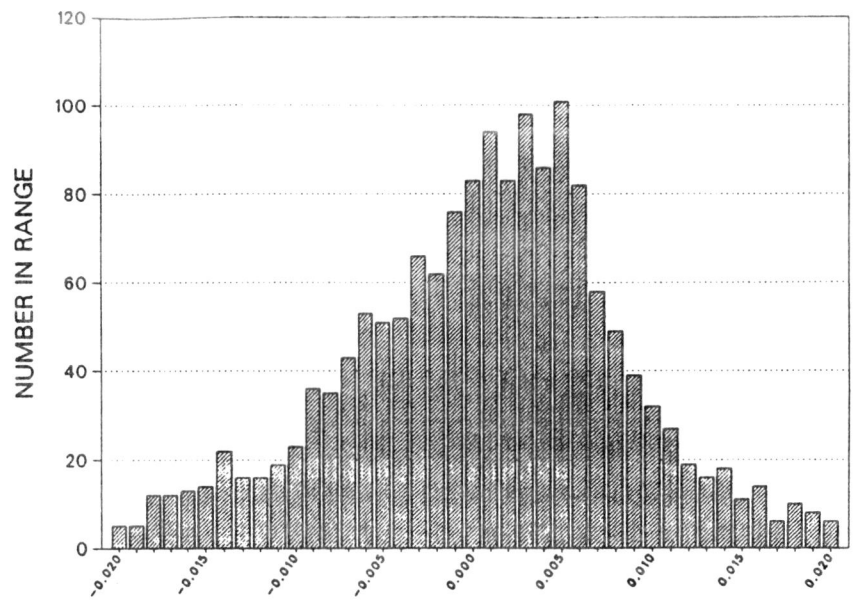

Figure 6   Hatch Style Error Frequency Distribution

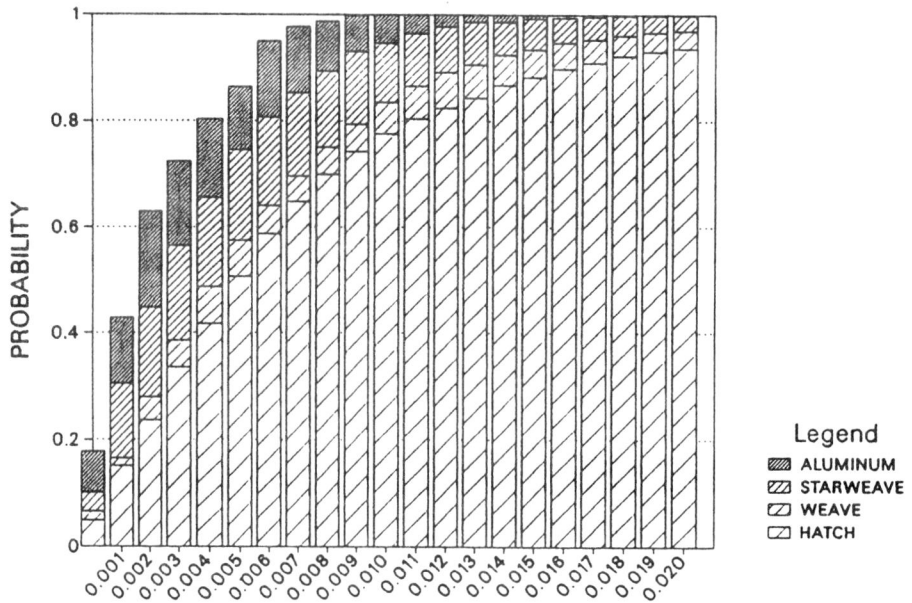

Legend
ALUMINUM
STARWEAVE
WEAVE
HATCH

Figure 7   Cumulative Error Distributions

TABLE 1 - User Part Data Summary
CIBA-GEIGY XB5081 - ACRYLATE RESIN

	RMS	All Data		Outside Dimensions			Inside Dimensions		
	Error mils	Slope %	Residual mils	Slope %	Intcpt mils	Residual mils	Slope %	Intcpt mils	Residual mils

75 mil ISOHATCH STYLE:

REF.	39.3	-1.31	10.4	-1.34	2.6	8.8	-1.25	2.3	13.0
90002	50.2	-1.24	8.0	-1.17	8.6	2.7	-1.12	10.0	4.0
90005	36.4	-1.21	9.7	-1.20	5.2	9.3	-1.14	-0.9	10.3
90006	24.7	-0.83	6.1	-0.85	4.0	6.3	-0.71	-3.1	4.9
90008	24.8	-0.81	7.8	-0.78	6.4	6.5	-0.74	-3.0	8.0
90010	12.9	0.18	11.9	0.15	4.4	11.0	0.27	-0.2	13.6
90012	26.5	-0.88	6.8	-0.90	3.9	6.9	-0.78	-2.8	6.1
90013	16.6	0.23	15.3	0.11	-5.7	11.0	0.21	10.5	14.3
90014	26.7	-0.85	10.1	-0.88	3.7	9.2	-0.78	1.4	11.6
91001	29.7	-0.98	8.3	-0.96	8.1	7.2	-0.83	-7.7	5.2
91020	30.7	-0.85	18.2	-0.90	-3.8	13.8	-0.92	8.4	23.6
91042	29.8	-0.96	10.5	-0.90	9.1	7.7	-0.88	-5.7	9.8

WEAVE STYLES (10 mil Layers):

91003	29.8	-0.99	8.5	-0.95	6.0	6.4	-0.91	-5.2	8.6
91013	5.9	-0.045	5.7	-0.02	-3.9	3.1	0.07	2.7	3.2
91019	21.3	-0.6	11.1	-0.72	-4.3	8.5	-0.61	6.0	9.6
91021	25.1	-0.85	4.1	-0.83	4.2	2.9	-0.79	-3.1	3.7
91034	35.9	-1.20	8.6	-1.16	5.3	5.5	-1.12	-7.1	9.6
91038	35.4	-1.17	10.0	-1.14	4.9	9.8	-1.07	-6.9	8.0
91041	25.6	-0.81	10.2	-0.75	8.6	7.0	-0.69	-8.5	9.2

STD WEAVE (5 mil Layers):

91025	19.1	-0.63	5.8	-0.67	2.0	6.2	-0.49	-3.6	3.3
91035	11.3	-0.26	8.3	-0.25	4.2	6.9	-0.14	-7.5	9.1
91036	21.4	-0.63	11.0	-0.71	0.7	9.4	-0.51	0.7	11.6

STAR-WEAVE

91015	5.9	-0.013	5.9	-0.073	-3.6	3.8	-0.017	1.7	4.9
91017	6.5	0.0003	6.6	-0.04	-2.4	4.9	0.02	1.0	7.7
91031	4.7	0.040	4.5	0.004	-1.6	3.5	0.065	1.5	4.1
91032	3.8	-0.015	3.8	-0.050	-1.1	3.2	0.026	0.3	3.0
91033	4.3	0.0036	4.3	-0.037	-1.1	3.5	0.046	0.6	2.8
91039	4.6	-0.018	4.5	0.0016	3.9	3.3	0.040	-3.5	4.5

TABLE II - User Part Data Summary
Effects of Compensation

	Uncompensated Data		Fully Compensated Data		
	Slope %	Residual mils	Slope %	Width mils	Residual mils
75 mil ISOHATCH STYLE					
REF.	-1.31	10.4	-1.27	4.84	12.0
90002	-1.24	8.0	-1.15	4.53	5.2
90005	-1.21	9.7	-1.14	4.41	10.0
90006	-0.83	6.1	-0.78	2.99	6.6
90008	-0.81	7.8	-0.73	2.87	7.3
90010	0.18	11.9	0.24	-0.92	12.0
90012	-0.88	6.8	-0.84	3.23	7.1
90013	0.23	15.3	0.18	-0.82	14.9
90014	-0.85	10.1	-0.80	3.05	10.7
91001	-0.98	8.3	-0.89	3.49	7.3
91020	-0.85	18.2	-0.89	3.31	19.3
91042	-0.96	<u>10.5</u>	-0.85	3.37	<u>9.4</u>
MEAN		**10.3**			**10.2**
STD.ERR.		**3.5**			**4.0**
WEAVE STYLES (10 mil Layers):					
91003	-0.99	8.5	-0.92	3.6	7.5
91013	-0.045	5.7	0.000	-0.08	5.7
91019	-0.62	11.1	-0.67	2.46	12.5
91021	-0.85	4.1	-0.81	3.13	3.5
91034	-1.20	8.6	-1.15	4.49	7.3
91038	-1.17	10.0	-1.13	4.37	9.3
91041	-0.81	<u>10.2</u>	-0.71	2.84	<u>9.0</u>
MEAN		**8.3**			**7.8**
STD.ERR		**2 .5**			**2.9**
STD WEAVE (5 mil Layers):					
91025	-0.63	5.8	-0.61	2.32	6.5
91035	-0.26	8.3	-0.22	0.90	8.1
91036	-0.63	<u>11.0</u>	-0.62	2.32	<u>11.9</u>
MEAN		**8.4**			**8.9**
STD.ERR.		**2.6**			**2.8**
ALL WEAVE PARTS:					
MEAN		**8.3**			**8.1**
STD.ERR		**2.4**			**2.7**
STAR-WEAVE					
*91015	-0.013	5.9	-0.0006	0.15	6.0
*91017	0.0003	6.6	-0.030	0.07	6.6
*91031	0.040	4.5	0.030	0.16	4.4
*91032	-0.015	3.8	-0.029	0.08	3.8
*91033	0.0036	4.3	-0.007	-0.00	4.3
91039	-0.018	<u>4.5</u>	0.028	-0.07	<u>4.6</u>
MEAN		**4.9**			**5.0**
STD.ERR.		**1.1**			**1.1**

TABLE III - User Part Data Summary
Miscellaneous Parts

| | Uncompensated Data | | Fully Compensated Data | | |
	Slope %	Residual mils	Slope %	Width mils	Residual mils
WEAVE					
XB5143					
91016	0.011	11.8	0.047	-0.29	11.7
91026	-0.87	7.9	-0.84	3.19	8.9
91040	-0.40	8.1	-0.37	1.43	8.1
	MEAN	9.3			9.6
	STD.ERR.	2.2			1.9
SLA-500 WEAVE					
XB5131					
*91027	-0.82	10.2	-0.74	2.92	9.1
*91028	-0.81	5.7	-0.83	3.14	7.1
*91029	-0.17	9.0	-0.090	0.44	8.8
*91030	-0.10	7.6	-0.12	0.42	7.7
	MEAN	8.1			8.2
	STD.ERR	1.9			0.9
CUBITAL					
91X01	-0.063	9.8			
NC MILLING					
PERSPEX					
91X02	-0.10	4.5			
ALUMINUM					
91X03	-0.03	3.0			
91X04	-0.04	3.1			
91X05	-0.04	3.1			
91X06	-0.04	3.0			

CAD Data for Rapid Prototyping (Harnessing the Power of Solid Modelling)

Geoff Sutcliffe

SDRC, Stevenage,
UK.

1   Preface

The goals of Improved Product Quality in reduced timescales and at reduced cost is being achieved by those companies who are able to assimilate, within a re-structured design process, technologies that give early insight to proposed product designs.

Rapid Prototyping is just such a technology but one whose requirement for high integrity 3D product representation has a direct impact on the type of CAD system used. The current level of development of Solid Modelling system gives rise to the opportunity of radically changing the traditional way of designing.

2   Introduction

In the early days of Solid Modelling systems all but a few observers were impressed by the notion of representing solid 3D objects within the "mind" of the computer. The primitive nature of these early systems and the cumbersome way in which they were driven combined with their hunger for resource meant that they were far from ready for use in the production design environment.

Today industry is recognising that solid modelling is not only a practical interactive tool capable of being used by designers but is a viable alternative to traditional methods of holding "product descriptions" hence terms like "product definition databases" and "single product models" are being banded around by many CAD CAM companies keen to stay up with the trend.

The high pace of technological progress in CPU and Graphics power, that has contributed to the viability of these systems will continue and is essential if the requirement of a full product description, including data on costing, performance, manufacturing and process data is to be carried with the model without performance penalties.

3   The need for ease of change and design insight

The current generation of solid modellers are able to offer more than just capturing of a proposed design but provide the freedom of exploring options. Systems that offer parametric modelling capability, within limits, allow changes to be made that reflect through the complete design, however if the rules that describe inter relationships within the model need to be changed, it can require some basic re modelling of the part.

A more powerful technology that compliments parametrics and extends beyond dimension driven changes is Variational Geometry, here the rules can be changed after the event and the part will reflect the new status of the design. It is technologies like these that really impact the usefulness of solid modelling as a design tool. Design is inevitably an evolution of an idea so change is essential, the earlier a change occurs the easier and cheaper it is to make and the more impact it has on the product and its resulting costs.

The issue of making design changes early is a key element in the argument for Concurrent Engineering. Knowing what changes to make requires product understanding early on in the design.

A key enabling technology in achieving this is product simulation or analysis, giving design insight into the performance and behavioural characteristics of proposed designs ensuring a far greater understanding before commitment. Analysis covers a wide spectrum from Finite Element methods for structural analysis, dynamics, fluid flow through to mechanism analysis, NC machining verification and injection mould simulation, the list continues to grow. Traditionally these tools are used to verify designs rather than fundamentlaly influence the design.

4   Where computer simulation can't go!

For all the power of computer graphics for visualisation, assembly interference checking and simulations there is one vital piece of information that cannot be given and that is the feel of it, at least not until Virtual Reality has progressed a little further! For some products this is a key parameter in its acceptability.

Here Rapid Prototyping is perhaps one of the most significant technologies that harnesses the power of solid modelling producing within hours a physical model of the part conceived on the computer. A part that not only can be held but can sometimes be used for prototype testing or at least be used as a former for producing prototypes with the required material properties.

The benefit of being able to present physical design alternatives for hand held products to clients and customers, can actually cut out the long cycle of product development on a design that fails to meet customer requirements. So it is here in the use of geometric product descriptions not only for the design analysis function and ultimately to manufacturing but for the production of physical prototypes that offers, dare I say it, the most tangeable benefits of harnessing the power of solid modelling.

With many companies offering commercial systems for Rapid Prototyping and Bureau services opening, the way seems clear for rapid growth, however like Solid Modelling in the early years different technologies are vying for position.

Stereolithography being the first commercial systems has developed rapidly into a stable reliable technology. Other systems evolving new approaches, in some cases to avoid patent issues, are promoting specific benefits.

There are now today many serious industrial users of Rapid Prototyping some justifying the acquisition of the technolgoy directly others using bureau services, but all have benefited from reductions both in cost and timescale for the production of prototypes.

For all systems the starting point is a computer model, the form most widely recognised by RP systems is the STL format which while not being a "precise" model (i.e. it is faceted,) requires a high degree of integrity. That is the model needs to be a complete 3D representation and unambiguous.

This therefore limits the source of data to either 3D surface modelling systems or 3D Solid Modelling systems. The latter reducing the risk of models where the surfaces look OK but in fact the topology of surface normals may be inverted resulting in the RP systems trying to create parts of the model inside out!

The fact that most RP systems use a faceted model is not a major limitation on accuracy as the facets can be refined to what ever limits of accuracy required. Some systems are capable of working with precise models but here it must be noted that the laminar nature of the modelling process will produce a stepped (or rasterised) surface independently of profile shape.

2D and 3D wireframe systems are of no direct use to an RP system, naturally the data can be used as the starting point for creation of a full 3D model but in these circumstances the cost of developing the model must be seen as an additional cost and time factor to the RP process.

It becomes apparent that where Rapid Prototyping is going to be used Solid Modelling brings additional benefits to the design process.

It is this downstream use of Solid Modelling data that is thrusting it into the fore as a key technology for complete product definitions as used within Concurrent Engineering.

5   Solid Modelling a core technology of Concurrent Engineering

There are many disciplines such as Manufacturing Engineering, Marketing, Field Service, that require not only access to the design data but have input during the design cycle. This means that the solid model is required to evolve under control and with ease of change. This Solid Model database and the application that creates and controls it becomes the engine that drives the design process.

The availability of Rapid Prototyping serves as an excellent example of how technology is speeding up the feedback that would result in changes to the design, once the first prototype is produced the information gained will no doubt result in modification. If these can be reflected in the computer model easily and quickly then a new STL file can be output and a revised prototype produced within hours!

The ripple effect of even the most minor change to a model can be significant and therefore technologies such as Variational Geometry are invaluable to ensure that the design intent is not violated, additionally to manage this speed of data revision, Data Management is required to ensure that all issues such as authorisation, notification revision control etc are carried out.

Most companies today are beginning to be aware of the true value of computer models however the use of behavioural prediction is still in the main used to verify a design rather than guide the design process. There is a strong parallel here with Rapid Prototyping because of the speed with which RP models can be produced early straight from the concept solid models, the feedback drives the design. The same can be true for all forms of computer simulation, if performed on concept solid models the "proof of concept" analysis can direct the design directly affecting quality, material and cost of manufacturing, at a point where the cost if change is minimised. As is well understood Concurrent Engineering is a methodology requiring a revised approach to design often requiring restructuring of a companies organisation.To support the resulting new processes within an organisation there are three essential technologies. Solid Modelling to provide the engine for product definition and design evaluation, Product Simulation to guide the design decisions for as many aspects of performance and manufacturability as deemed important and Data Management to control Data, Product and Process.Solid Modelling has come of age and the growth in its implementation illustrates that companies are beginning to harness its power. Its use in Rapid Prototyping is a highly visible and valuable illustration of this.

RAPID WIND TUNNEL PROTOTYPE USING STEREOLITHOGRAPHY AND EQUIVALENT TECHNOLOGIES

Ron Jamieson
Grafton software Applications
U.K.

Abstract

Stereolithography (SLA) is the name given to a process whereby a laser beam of ultra violet light is guided into a bath of u-v light sensitive liquid acrylic. Where the light strikes, a process of photopolymerisation solidifies the liquid to a given depth. In this manner a solidified 'slice' of a 3D object can be produced. Successive slices can be cured until a 3D object is 'grown'.

This paper discusses the initial investigation into the feasibility of using SLA as a valid production process for wind tunnel models. The need for good quality Computer Aided Design (CAD) models is discussed and reference will be made to the rules imposed on CAD modelling together with an overview of how improvements can be made.

The purpose of this work was to examine the new technology of Rapid Prototyping (RP) and its impact on time, accuracy and cost when used for the production of wind tunnel models. In this study a 1/14.4 scale model of a proposed wingtip was used as a prototype. The work involved four separate stages:

Stage 1:- Transfer of CAD model data
Stage 2:- Production of an STL file
Stage 3:- Production of an acrylic model
Stage 4:- Production of aluminium and steel castings.

1   Transfer of CAD model data

An IGES file was supplied by B.Ae Filton which described the surface geometry of a winglet. This was read by the Unigraphics (UG) IGES translator using default settings. It was found that simple 'ruled' surfaces produced a fault resulting in their omission from the UG file. However, the more complex 'sculptured' surfaces which described the aerofoil geometry came through with no apparent problems. A second tape was sent and read with the same results. After discussion with B.Ae. it was decided to continue with the data already read since all of the important data had transferred and the 'ruled' surfaces which were in any case planar could be easily generated in UG. This was achieved using a drawing supplied by B.Ae. and ensuring that the edge curves of the existing surfaces where used as boundary curves for the new surfaces. Ruled surfaces were also used to close off any surface gaps such as that formed by the wing trailing edges. Stage I was then complete (see Fig 1.).

2   Production of an STL file

The Stereolithographic Apparatus (SLA) requires a file which describes the outer profile of a given model in terms of faceted triangles (tessellation), this is achieved by listing the cartesian coordinates of the corner points in a set order. This file is referred to as an STL file and is the interface between the CAD system and most of the RP systems. The technology is well documented; see reference list, and this report will concentrate solely on the rules imposed on CAD interfaces for the production of STL files. At this stage what is important is the quality of the SLA interface algorithm offered by a particular CAD vendor. In this study

Unigraphics which can handle both surface and solid models, offers a well documented easy to use interface.

The UG SLA interface requires that a couple of parameters are set which will determine the accuracy of the model. These are:

a) Triangular tolerance
b) Adjacency tolerance.

Triangular tolerance determines how close the facets approximate the surface while Adjacency tolerance allows the system to determine if two surfaces are attached (note! adjacency tolerance is not required when using solid models). In addition and to ensure that the SLA rule which requires that all models reside in positive cartesian space and that the Z axis is vertical, the UG SLA interface checks for these conditions and advises on them.

2.1 Problems Encountered

The model was placed in positive space, the default settings for triangular and adjacency were accepted and the SLA algorithm was run. The early attempts all failed because:

a) The model was not completely closed;
b) The adjacency tolerance was violated;
c) More than two surfaces shared a common edge.

2.2 Solution

Closing the model was simply a matter of examining the model while zooming, rotating and testing for existing surfaces. Gaps such as that along the trailing edge which might not matter when generating N.C. tool path, had to be closed for SLA interface.

While zooming it became apparent that many of the surfaces had distorted edges and did not actually meet.

This explained why the adjacency tolerance was violated. Discussions with B.Ae.led to the conclusion that as the Anvil 4000 CAD system used by B.Ae. is single precision, the distortions probably take place during the IGES translation. The solution was to rebuild adjacent surfaces so that they used a common edge spline; adjacency was then assured.

The new surfaces were created on separate layers and subsequently tested for accuracy against the 'old' surface using the surface to surface deviation algorithm supplied in the UG system. In this manner accuracies of the order of .02mm were maintained.

The third fault; which is a surface model limitation, was caused by breaching the rule which states that no more than two surfaces can share a common edge with another surface. The top wing surface broke this rule and the solution was to break down the long fillet surface into two parts. This rule needs to be borne in mind when designing future parts for RP systems since re-work can take time and accuracy can be lost.

211

2.3   Settings

The model now successfully ran and all that remained was to select a sufficiently accurate triangular tolerance to ensure that a practical limit of 30,000 facets was not exceeded. On advice from 3D systems the model was split into four components each of which could use 30,000 facets and thereby offering increased accuracy. This was done with the tolerances set at:

    Triangular tolerance   = .05mm
    Adjacency tolerance   = .05mm

The output file size suggested that the wing stump file contained 31,000 facets using the above settings.
The output files were simply appended using a DOS routine at 3D systems. Experiments with the adjacency tolerance showed that while this did not affect the file size i.e. number of facets, it could confuse the system regarding which surface was adjacent to which.

2.4   Supports

Production of parts using the 3D systems version of RP require supports underneath the part and on any overhanging parts which protrude more than about 3mm (see Fig 2). The supports are generated in a thin honeycombed fashion which are easy to remove after production.
As shown in Fig. 2, the winglet was produced with the tip surface vertical. This was to ensure that no deviation due to bending under its own weight was induced during manufacture. A support could have been used but this would have resulted in some 'finishing' which would affect the aerofoil surface. The support under the winglet was generated using the underside surfaces and creating a pillar.

3   Production of an acrylic model

Four parts and one support STL file were delivered to 3D systems. These were read into the SLA system and examined on a high quality graphics workstation. The parts assembled and the slicing and weaving algorithms all ran smoothly. Two winglet parts were produced in .25mm slices which took approximately 40 hours. This was due to the length of the support, the volume of the parts and the action of the process.
Fig 3 shows one winglet still attached to its support and the baseplate. The layer deposition is clearly visible prior to curing as is the faceted effect on the wing stub. After production, the parts are about 98% solid and stable. The curing oven cures the remaining 'entrapped' resin before the part is ready for finishing. Finishing involves removal of excess polymer, removal of supports and light sanding. The process can take a few hours and is a necessary part of this type of RP technology.

In addition the curing oven offers an unwanted source of deformation as observed along the winglet trailing edge where the section is thin. Since curing involves both heat and soak time it must be concluded that a form of stress relieving has taken place.

The parts as cured were quite robust, one was taken by for conformity analysis while the second was retained for use in Stage 4.

4 Production of aluminium and steel castings.

Although the acrylic models are rigid and the latest materials are tough, they were not considered suitable for direct use in the low speed wind tunnel. The acrylic model was used as a master for both high and low speed wind tunnel testing.

The lost wax method of casting seemed to offer a rapid and convenient way of obtaining metal winglets with hopefully the RP acrylic substituting for wax. Unfortunately whereas wax melts readily when purged with steam, acrylic requires a higher temperature and expands by about 1% before melting. This has resulted in moulds breaking and the attempts are well documented in Ref. 2. For this study then, we were left with the following procedure:

a) Use the RP model to manufacture a rubber mould;
b) Use the rubber mould to produce an epoxy resin master;
c) Use the epoxy master to produce an epoxy mould;
d) Use the epoxy mould to inject wax;
e) Dip wax in ceramic slurry;
f) Burn out wax;
g) Cast winglet.

Steps b) and c) were precautionary since the casting company; Sterling Metals, had no previous experience of handling acrylic models produced by RP and preferred instead to produce an epoxy master which they were used to dealing with. The epoxy master and moulds were made by a commercially available system.

Casting was achieved using both the low pressure and gravity die casting methods. The low pressure casting burst its runners during the pour and was scrapped. The cast parts included one .025mm oversize aluminium example. This was achieved by use of a gasket on the mould joints producing an oversized wax master. Two aluminium and two steel winglets were cast and taken for dimensional analysis at B.Ae. Filton. See Fig.4.

References

1. Proceedings of the Second International Conference on Rapid Prototyping, June, 1991, Dayton, Ohio, USA.

2. W.E.Cromwell,"Prototype Casting by Stereolithography', Allied-Signal Aerospace Co.

3. Emmanuel Sachs, Michael Cima and James Cornie,"Three Dimensional Printing: Ceramic Shells and Cores for Casting and other applications", Massachusetts Institute of Technology.

Participating Companies Included:

A) 3D Systems,Inc.,Limited, Unit 7, The Progression
Centre, Mark Row, Hemel Hempstead, Herts, HP2 7DW.

B) McDonnell Douglas, Information Systems Limited,
Merion House, Guildford Road, Woking.

C) Sterling International Technology Limited,
Gipsy Lane, Nuneaton, Warwicks.

D) British Aerospace Commercial Aircraft, Wind Tunnel
Department, Filton.

E) D.Ae.S. College of Aeronautics, Cranfield
Institute of Technology.

This paper is an extract from the proceedings of the forthcoming ICAS 92 conference to be held in Beijing China. Copyright is assigned to ICAS.

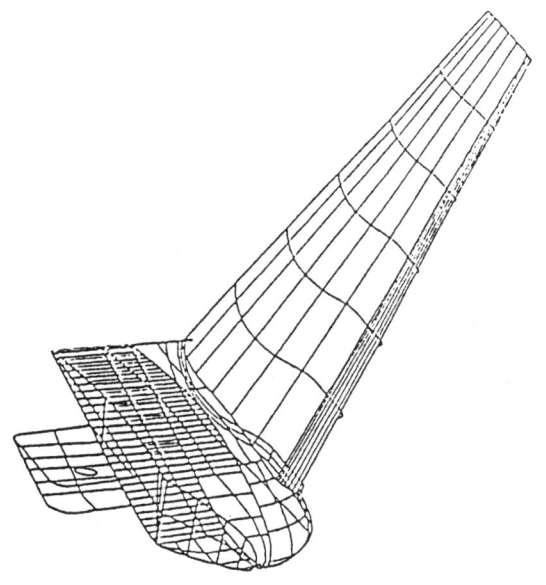

Figure 1

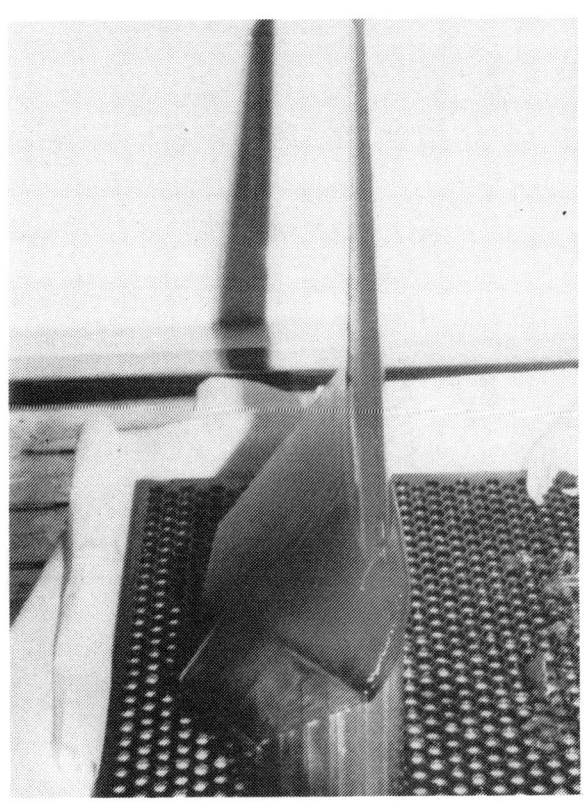

Figure 2

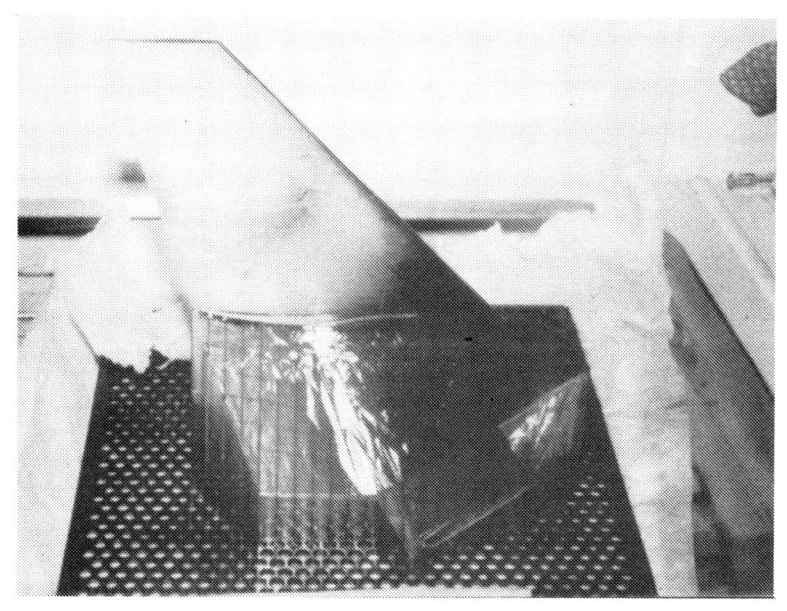

Figure 3

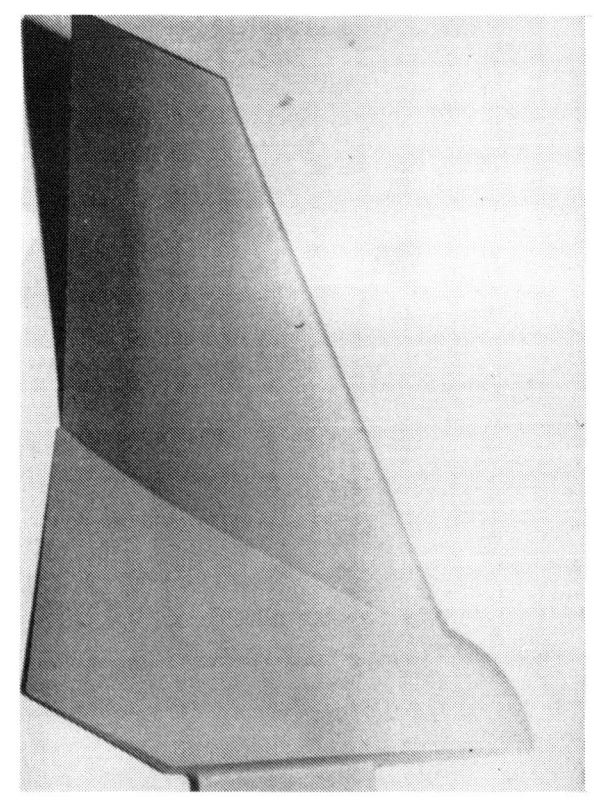

Figure 4

WET POWDER POURING AND RAPID PROTOTYPING

A. Ruder, H.P. Buchkremer, D. Stöver

KFA - Forschungszentrum Jülich - IAW
D-5170, Jülich, Germany

1   Abstract

This paper presents results from a preliminary study aiming at the possible implementation of the Wet Powder Pouring (WPP) process in the accelerated production of functional parts in the shape (i) of Rapidly Prototyped (RP) patterns. A mould for WPP was produced by embedding a RP polymeric pattern in a silicon rubber paste. Following curing of the silicon rubber, the RP pattern is then removed from the mould which is subsequently filled by pouring into it the WPP mixture (ii).

A rigid "green-body" in the shape and size of the RP pattern, received after drying the mixture, was removed from the mould and introduced into a furnace where debinding and sintering were carried out in a single continuous run.

The WPP production cycle (iii) of a net-shape from S. Steel 316, Stellite 6 and UDIMET 700, a Nickel base superalloy, of 50mm of diameter and 9mm maximal height RP pattern was completed in about 30h. The final products retain the shape and surface quality of the original RP pattern.

These results indicate a possible, positive, application of the WPP process in the post-shaping of RP patterns.

2   Introduction

RP comprises, in general the transformation of computer designed images into three dimensional rigid bodies (patterns) by a selective and controlled processing of energy sensitive material(s). Since the RP pattern-materials are suitable only for a narrow range of engineering applications, the final engineering part has to be produced from compatible materials processed mainly by what may be called "lost pattern casting" (which is similar to the traditional "lost wax casting"). A more detailed description of the different types of RP and its current applications is given elsewhere (Ashley, 1991; Dickens, 1992).

WPP suggests a different processing route in the shaping of the final engineering parts from a RP pattern. The WPP is a Powder Metallurgy (PM) process in which a wet flowing powder-carrier-binder mixture is poured into a mould, the volatile carrier is then removed by evaporation and the binder precipitates onto the particles, forming a net of connecting bridges which hold the powder particles in the shape and size of the designed "green-body" (copying the shape and size of the RP pattern). Since the process utilizes relatively small volume fractions of binder, ca. 5vol.%, a short time is needed for carrier and later binder removal (debinding). A full debinding and sintering cycle, carried out in the same furnace, can be completed in less than 10 hours (Ruder et. at., 1991; Ruder et. al., 1991).

(i)   the term "shape" is used since during WPP processing changes in dimensions, mainly due to sintering densification, take place; a compensation factor has to be introduced in the pre-design.

(ii)   in the present study only spherical metallic powders were used in the powder-carrier-binder mixtures.

(iii)   including: mould production, mixture preparation, pouring of mixture, drying, debinding and sintering.

3   Experimental Procedures

The main steps in the WPP production of a part from a RP pattern (iv) are given in the schematic flow chart in Fig. 1 and include the following details:

3.1   Mould Production

The pattern was embedded in two different types, soft or hard, of commercial silicon rubber pastes. After the rubber was fully cured, at 60°C for 2h, the pattern was removed leaving a mirror imprint of its shape in the silicon rubber mould. Since the pattern has a relatively simple geometry, moulds were produced as single, monolithic units. Photographs of the pattern and the respective moulds are shown in Fig. 2.

3.2   The Production of "Green-bodies"

"Green-bodies" were produced by pouring an agitated powder-carrier-binder mixture into a vibrating mould and subsequently by evaporating the volatile carrier. The evaporation was carried-out in a glove-box at sub-atmospheric pressure of about 50mm H_2O, at room temperature, and was completed in 15h. After evaporation, the dry binder holds the powder particles in the shape of the original pattern and the formed rigid "green-body" can be removed from the mould for further processing.

Three different metallic powders (v) and therefore three different mixtures, as given in Table I, were tested during the evaluation study.

3.3   Debinding and Sintering

This step is carried out by a continuous run in the same furnace, normally under vacuum or a protective atmosphere. Since small volume fractions of binder were used, high heating rates have been employed during the debinding and sintering stages.

Heating rates of up to 5°C/min were employed at temperatures between room temperature (RT) to 400°C, and 10°C/min from 400°C up to the sintering-temperature (ST).

Typical debinding and sintering steps of the above alloys included the following time/temperature cycle:

1)	heating from RT to 350°C;	0.5-1.0h
2)	holding at 350°C;	2.0.3.0h
3)	heating from 350°C to ST(vi);	1.5-3.0h
4)	holding at ST;	<u>1.0-2.5h</u>
	total "energy time":	5.0-9.5h

(iv)   the RP pattern is a 4mm thick relief of a trade-mark logo protruding from a Φ 50 x 50mm disk and has been supplied by Dr Dickens - Department of Manufacturing Engineering and Operations Management, University of Nottingham, UK.

(v)   arbitrary choice, not addressing specific material selection.

(vi)   the alloys in the present study were sintered at 1200-1300°C.

4   Examination

Only few simple methods were employed to examine the "green" and sintered parts received in the present preliminary study, including:

-    visual examination to detect possible large surface defects and/or outstanding deformations in "green" and sintered parts,

-    shape and size retention and reproducibility of the sintered parts was evaluated by measuring, at least two parts from each material and the RP pattern, the main diameter at four positions and the height of the protruding logo from the facing at nine specific points,

-    density measurements (Archimedes in water) of the sintered parts,

-    Scanning Electron Microscopy (SEM) of the "green" and sintered outer surfaces.

5   Results and Discussion

From the three start materials, 19 parts were produced and the following results are given according to the above examination sequence:

5.1   Visual

In two UDIMET 700 parts, cracks were observed after the drying (carrier removal) stage and the parts were rejected.

In one S. Steel 316 part, a crack was observed after sintering - rejected.
One S. Steel 316 part was heavily deformed during sintering - rejected.
One Stellite 6 part was damaged during removal from the mould - rejected.

Crack(s) formation during the drying stage is probably due to too fast drying, where powder particles that have not completed sedimentation, after pouring, are surrounded by a liquid which shows an increasing viscosity on one hand, but is not strong enough to sustain the proceeding dimensional changes on the other.

Crack(s) and deformation observed after sintering result probably from:

-    crack growth from an already existing crack in the "green-body",
-    differential shrinkage (due to inhomogeneous particle distribution, unisotropic friction between the part and the substrate, local temperature gradients),
-    gravitational forces affecting the dimensional stability of the part during transition from "green" to sintered body.

The other parts, upon visual inspection, looked "sound" in the "green" and in the sintered conditions. In Fig. 3 a photograph of typical sound "green" and sintered parts is given.

5.2 Dimensions

The results of the measurements are given as processed data in Table II. Beside the calculated normal Standard Deviation (SD), the additional maximal differences in diameter and in height, ΔD and ΔH respectively, give an extended idea about size retention.

Since it was found that the maximal differences, ΔD and ΔH, in the sintered parts can not be correlated to specific and repeating points in the pattern therefore, the differences in the sintered parts can be related mainly to the WPP processing. Inhomogeneous particle distribution within the "green-body" can promote differential shrinkage during sintering resulting in non uniform and random distribution in the dimensions. Temperature gradients during sintering can also affect local densification rates resulting, together with the above, in relatively high ΔD and ΔH values.

Sinterability characteristics of each of the processed materials results in final mean-value dimensions corresponding to the particular material.

5.3 Density

The measured densities of the sintered parts is given relative to the theoretical density (TD) of each material:

S. Steel 316:   88-90% TD
UDIMET 700:   90-93% TD
Stellite 6:   95-97% TD

5.4 Surface

In general, the surface quality(vii) is transformed from the RP pattern to the sintered parts. Typical "green" and sintered surfaces as shown in the low magnification (about 3x of Fig. 3) photographs in Fig. 4 reproduce the criss-cross lines of the RP lithography. The filling and build-up of the fine surface features and the edges of the successive layers by the powder particles in a "green-body" can be respectively observed in Fig. 5.

Although sintering enhances smoothing of the outer surfaces, the micro-morphology is preserved as shown in Fig. 6 taken from a part made from Stellite 6 sintered to near full density.

The formation of only a few micropores, observed on the surfaces, can be minimized by a better control of powder pouring and by adapting suitable mould (pattern) design for WPP processing.

(vii)   indicating features observed by visual or microscopical inspection

6 Summary

- Metallic parts in the shape of a RP pattern were produced in a very short time, 30h, by employing the WPP.

- The sintered metallic parts have good surface quality and reasonably depict the shape of the original pattern.

- Implementing WPP into RP suggests a different, simple and economical processing route in the production of engineering, net-shape parts.

Acknowledgement

The authors wish respectively to thank Dr. P. M. Dickens and Dr. P. M. Standring, both from the Faculty of Engineering, University of Nottingham - UK, for their direct and indirect contributions to this study.

For performing part of the experimental and part of the graphical work, the authors wish respectively to thank Ms S. Schwartz and Ms H. Moitroux.

References

1. Ashley, S. (1991) Rapid Prototyping Systems. Mechanical Engineering, April, pp 34-43.
2. Dickens, P. M. (1992) Rapid Prototyping. Caddesk, May, 1992 pp 34-37.
3. Ruder, A., Buchkremer, H. P., Hecker, R., Stöver, D. (1991) Wet Powder Pouring. Proc. of the Second ASM Paris Conf., Paris (F) 11-13 Sep. 1991, ASM European Office-Brussels (B). (to be published).
4. Ruder, A., Buchkremer, H. P., Hecker, R., Stöver, D. (1991) Wet Powder Pouring - An Accelerated PM Process, Proc. of the Int. Conf. on PM AERO '91, Lausanne (CH), 4-6 Nov. 1991, MPR Publishing Services-Shrewsbury (UK). (to be published).

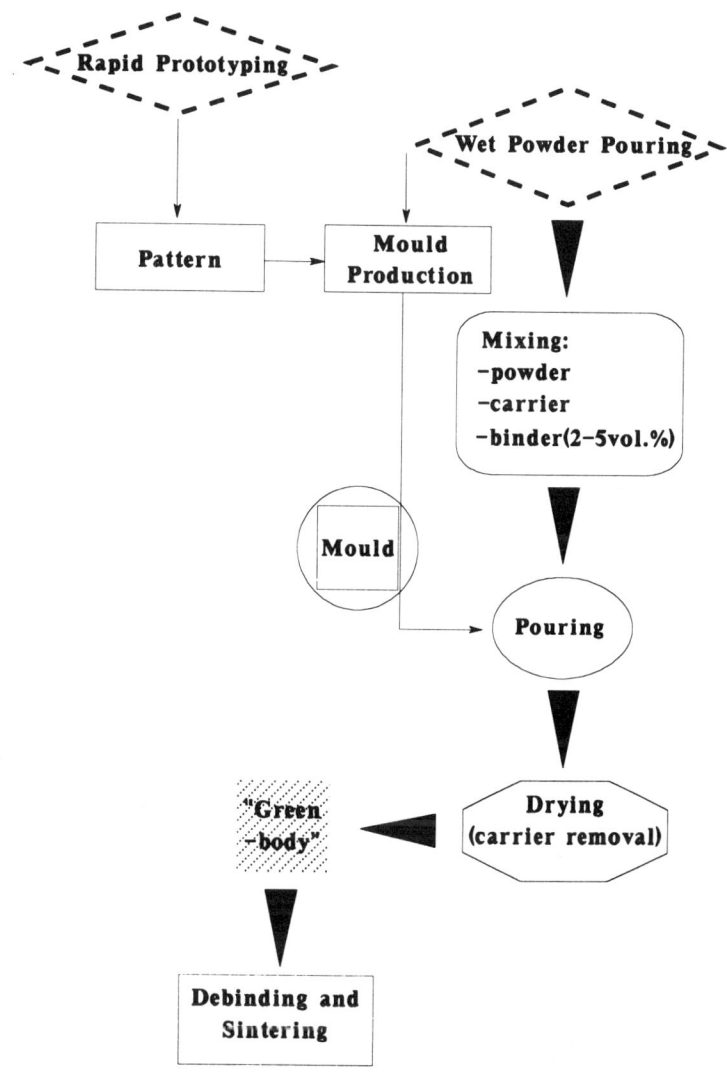

Figure 1.   Schematic flow chart showing the main steps in the production of functional, net or near net-shape, parts from Rapid Prototyping patterns via the Wet Powder Pouring process.

Figure 2. A photograph of the Rapidly Prototyped mounted pattern and two of the silicon rubber moulds, produced from the respective pattern, which were used in the WPP process. The RP pattern is on the left.

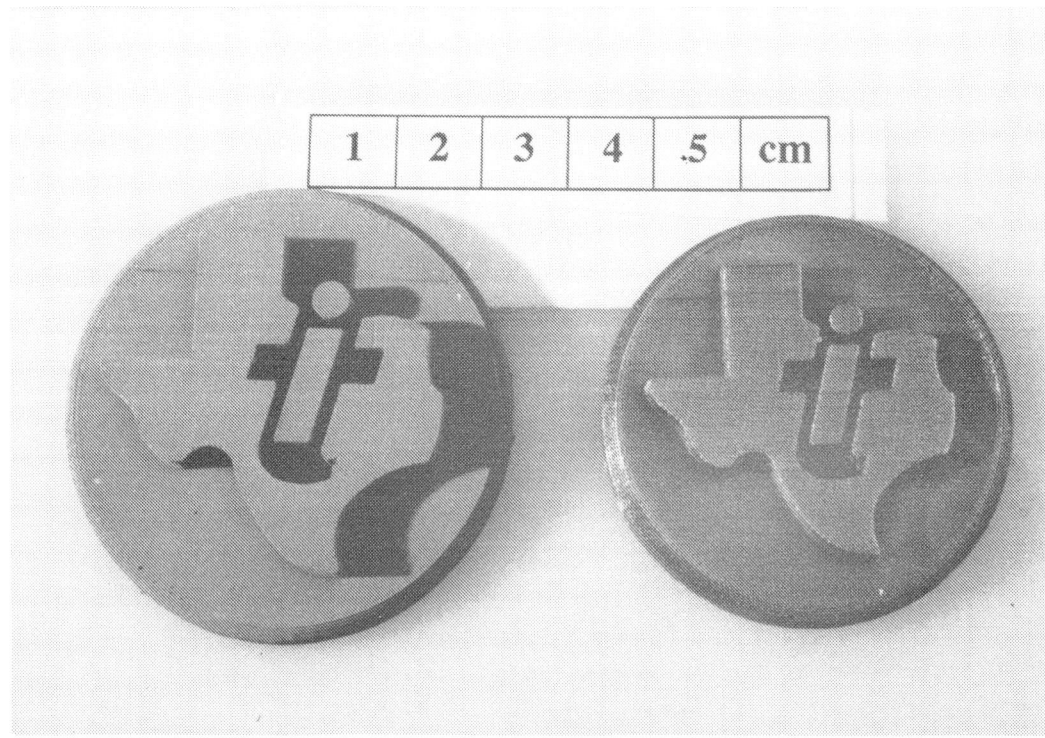

Figure 3. A photograph showing typical "green" and sintered parts. The "green-body" is on the left. The smaller dimensions of the sintered part on the right are due to densification processes taking place during sintering.

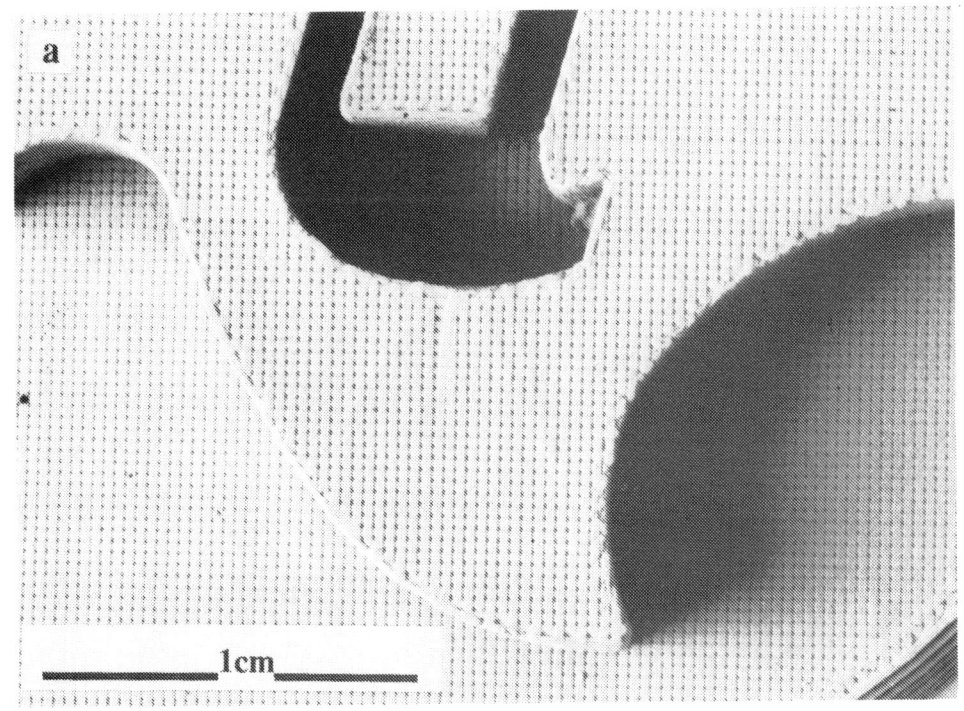

a. the "green-body"

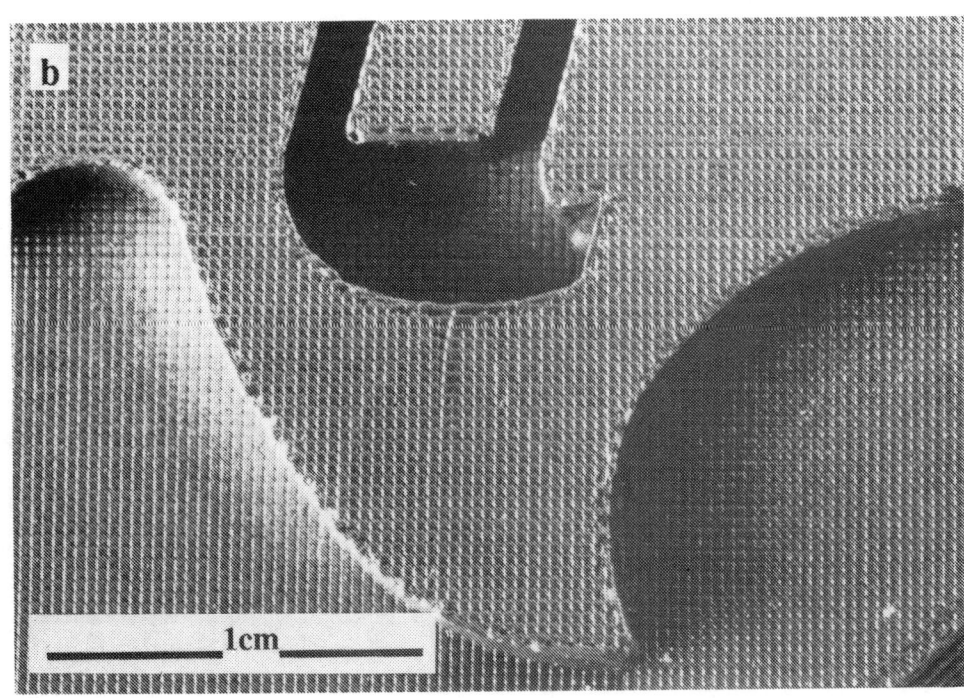

b. The sintered part.

Figure 4. The criss-cross morphology seen in the two photographs was taken from the outer surfaces of:

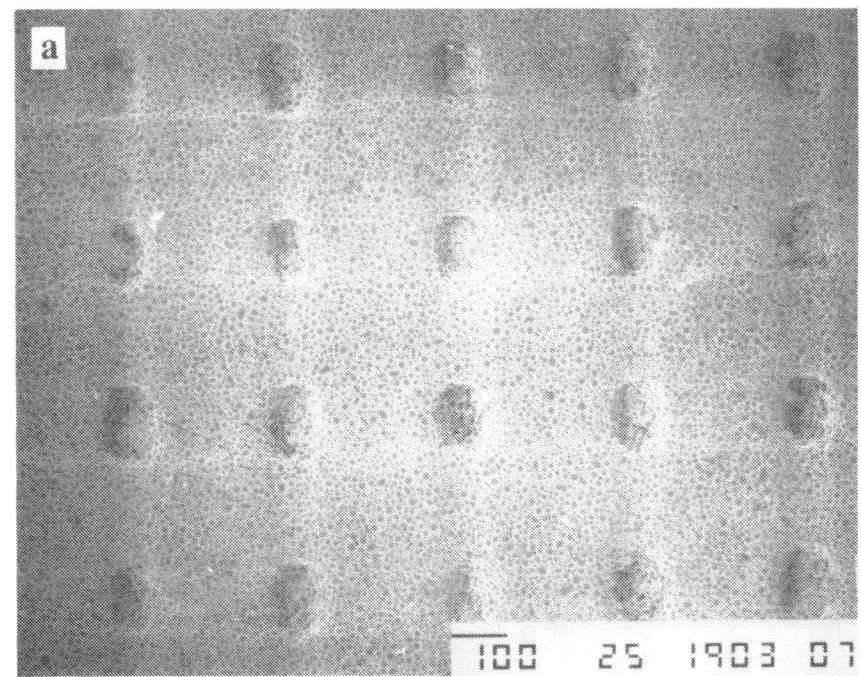

a. the arrangement of powder particles forming the criss-cross surface morphology,

b.   the edges of the successive layers forming the protruding logo.

Figure 5.   SEM micrographs taken from a "green-body" showing:

Figure 6.   SEM (back scattering mode) micrographs taken from the same spot on the surface of a sintered Stellite 6 part. Because of the back scattering mode, only the "criss" from the original RP lithography can be clearly seen. Since the part has been sintered to near full density, no interparticle porosity has been observed. The magnification increases from a to c.

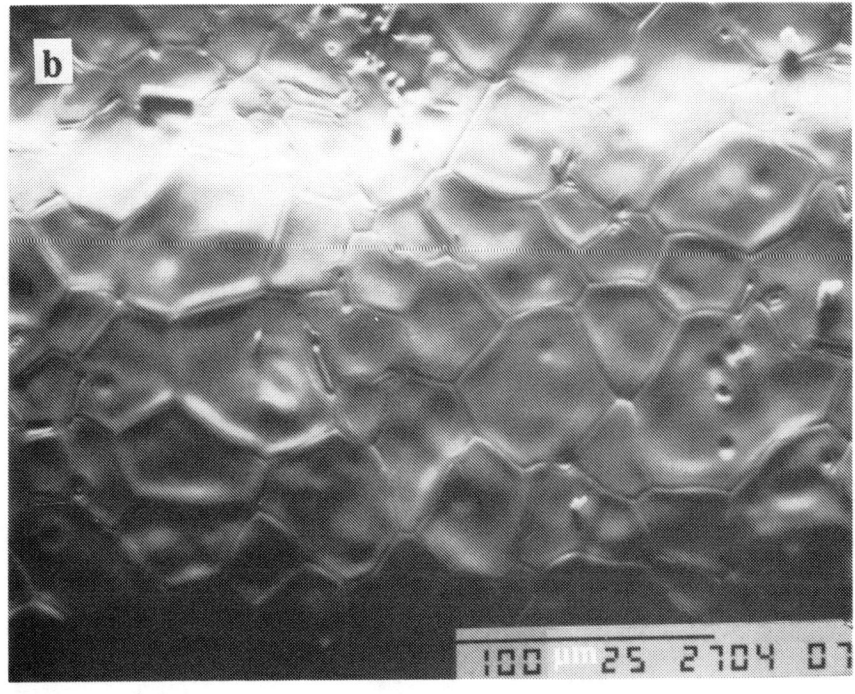

Figure 6b

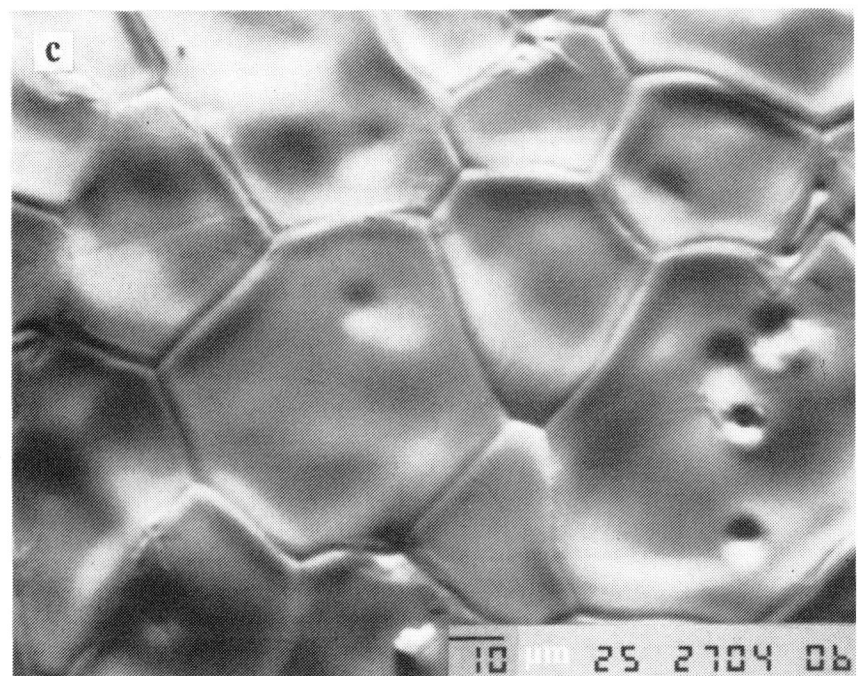

Figure 6c

Material	Particle size [μm]	Binder cont.[v%]
S. Steel 316	-22	4-5
UDIMET 700	-150	3-4
Stellite 6	-160	3-4

Table I: Powders and binder content used in the present study.
The binder content is relative to the volume of the "green-body".

Material	Mean Dia. $\pm$SD & max. (ΔD), [mm]	Mean Height$\pm$SD & max.(ΔH), [mm]
S. Steel 316	45.00 $\pm$ 0.05 (0.15)	3.32 $\pm$ 0.05 (0.19)
UDIMET 700	45.24 $\pm$ 0.13 (0.38)	3.29 $\pm$ 0.04 (0.07)
Stellite 6	43.72 $\pm$ 0.05 (0.15)	3.21 $\pm$ 0.10 (0.31)
RP Pattern	50.65 $\pm$ 0.09 (0.23)	3.73 $\pm$ 0.04 (0.12)

Table II: Measured and processed dimensions taken from sintered parts and from the RP pattern.

Rapid Design : Pre-Requisite for Rapid Prototyping

Graham Charlesworth

Parametric Technology,
Nottingham,
UK.

1   Introduction

The demands of today's product design environment require that solid modelling systems provide much more than a full three-dimensional representation of mechanical parts and assemblies. The key to success in today's highly competitive marketplace is managing change rapidly, efficiently, and late in the design cycle. A new concept in feature-based parametric solid modelling has emerged that uses an intuitive language of features and dimension driven parameters to create models optimized for "what-if" analyses.   This approach develops a highly flexible definition of mechanical parts that can be used to generate limitless variations of geometry instantly.   The benefits to industry are substantial, resulting in faster product time to market and shorter lead times.

Solid modellers are among the most powerful computer-based design tools available.   The solid modelling approach is the only one to completely and unambiguously represent the 3D geometry of parts and assembles, in contract with older more traditional wire frame and surface-based systems.   For this reason, solid modellers are the only type of design tool capable of fully supporting today's widely diverse range of engineering applications, from analysis to manufacturing. However, product design is a complex iterative process involving constant change. And in order for a solid modeller to succeed in contributing to the bottom line, it must not only support all aspects of the design-to-manufacturing process but also be able to effectively manage changes to the design.

The challenge facing today's solid modellers is thus twofold.   On the one hand, solid modellers must provide highly precise representation of the models within the design.   The parts and assemblies must furnish information to a wide range of tightly integrated engineering applications that produce detailed engineering drawings, analysis information, manufacturing NC files, etc.   On the other hand, solid modellers must also be flexible enough to incorporate changes to a design late in the cycle and automatically update all impacted applications. Without the ability to perform what-if analyses, the geometric modelling power of solid modellers is largely lost in the everyday engineering world.

2   How Well Can A System Manage Change?

Most solid modellers on the market today are unable to manage engineering changes effectively, because they represent data more the way a typewritten document does than a flexible spreadsheet. At the core of many traditional solid modellers lies a geometry database, predominantly in the form of a constructive solid geometry (CSG) tree or boundary representation (B-rep) surface model. In either case the geometric model is the result of a series of mathematical operations.   It is the end product rather than a set of intuitive features or instructions that could have been specified by the user to create such a model. As a result, these solid modellers are good at extracting detailed information from the static geometry database but cannot generate a whole new instance of the model geometry based on a new set of features from the user.

There is a new concept known as feature-based parametric solid modelling, though, that is capable of incorporating changes effectively and generating new instances of geometry. Feature-based parametric solid modelling combines the principles of the spreadsheet with a dynamic solids-based geometric database. The distinction between this approach and traditional CAD/CAM systems lies in the way in which models are created and the way information is stored. First, feature-based parametric systems create models through specifying sets of intuitive features. These features (holes, slots, fillets, drafts, shells, etc.) form a language closely linked to the terminology used by designers. Second these feature fully define the 3D model and are therefore stored at the heart of the system as a type of "geometry engine" that may be used by the modeller to generate different instances of the 3D model.

One problem facing traditional solid modellers is that they cannot be converted into feature-based parametric systems without sacrificing compatibility with an existing customer base. This is because traditional systems do not store any form of the intuitive feature set used to initially define the model. Instead, they store only the static "end product" geometric representation.

3   Managing Change Effectively

In order for a solid modeller to perform what-if functions similar to a spreadsheet, there are a number of fundamental attributes that the system must possess. The following is a description of the five key attributes as they relate to what feature-based parametric solid modellers should provide.

3.1   Full Associativity

Solid modellers must be able to reference all applications back to single data structure, so that when an engineer makes changes to a drawing, there is no need to remember to manually make these changes to all other related applications. A change made somewhere should automatically be made everywhere. Furthermore, communication between applications should not require translators like IGES. Translators prevent the rapid exchange of information between applications in two directions. And two-way associativity is a vital element in allowing both drawings and models to be changed directly.

3.2   Intuitive and Easy to Use

Solid modellers must communicate via the language of design and manufacturing engineers, because it is the engineers who specify changes in the design in terms only they understand. Solid modelling systems should use a language of features that are defined by groups of parameters or dimensions. These parameters define how the elements of a feature relate back to the model, and they are the means by which features are changed. Features are specified in a sequence whose order must be modifiable. Examples of commonly used features include holes, slots, and fillets, but many others may exist, including feature operations like mirroring, shelling, surface drafting, and bending.

If a solid modeller uses features, it is important that they possess extreme flexibility. Features must not be predefined, or "canned". For example, a hole feature should be able to assume any shape, extend through any number of entities, and be dimensioned in any possible way to any part of the model. Systems that require the user to pre-define and store a features shape or allowable method of dimensioning place severe limitations on the user. In order to make large-scale changes to a model that employs this type of feature, the user must often define and store a new set of features and then swap the old features for the new.

3.3   Fast Regeneration and Fast Redefinition

Managing change effectively requires that the solid modeller's geometry engine be capable of performing fast regenerations of the model. Fast regeneration means that when a user changes a feature that was defined earlier in the design process, the system can "back-up" to that feature instantly to obtain a representation of the model at the time the feature was created. The modeller can then make the changes and regenerate a new instance of the model's geometry. In addition to providing this capability, a solid modelling system must also let the user suppress or "turn off" individual and groups of features in order to simplify working on a complex model or evaluate the impact of some features while others are temporarily "turned off". Along with providing feature suppression, the system must also enable features to be resumed or brought back into the model at the stage when they were defined.

3.4   A Wide Range of Dimensioning Schemes.

No solid modeller should limit the way the designer defines the important or driving dimensions on a model. The driving dimension on a model must exactly reflect the design intent in order for the system to rapidly incorporate changes that occur later in the design cycle. Some solid modellers, however, limit the way dimensions may be defined because there are typically hidden obstacles, or constraints, that interfere with the original design intent.

An illustration of this can be made with a rectangular hole feature in a simple block. Many solid modellers require that the user first dimension the profile of the rectangular hole with respect to itself, and then place the hole with locating dimensions on the part. This approach imposes limits on the allowable types of dimensioning schemes, in that the user cannot obtain the dimensioning scheme. Each element of the rectangular hole feature is individually dimensioned with respect to the part, (i.e., the feature is defined in the context of the part and makes no sense standing alone without reference to the part).

The reason some solid modellers limit the allowable range of dimensioning schemes is that in some modellers, the term "feature" will actually refer to the definition and storage of groups of Boolean operations between primitive solid shapes. Before such a system can subtract, add, or intersect one solid primitive from another, it must know its shape and size and be able to place it with respect to the model.

Thus, the driving dimensions behind the resulting geometry are the dimensions of the primitive forms and the set of dimensions used to position the primitives on the part. This in turn forces the user to think of these "features" as Boolean operations, which is all they really are in this type of modeller.

In addition to providing a wide range of dimensioning schemes, solid modellers must also group features (UDF's). The advantages of user-defined features are numerous and include speeding up the creation of repetitive multi-feature features and customisation to a users's own environment.

3.5   Efficiency - The Family of Parts Concept

Finally, a solid modeller will automatically be efficient if it possesses the four attributes just presented. The reason is that models created by a next-generation feature-based system can be stored simply by storing the feature list or recipe to create the model, rather than the full 3D geometric representation. It is not uncommon for the storage requirements of a modelling system to be an order of magnitude less than for a traditional solid modeller. Solid modelling systems should also provide the option of storing a full double-precision file of the model geometry.

Furthermore, the feature-based parametric approach lets whole families of components and assemblies be stored with practically no additional space requirements that are needed to store one generic representation. These families of parts are small tables containing the variable parameters, features, and dimensions referred to in a generic model. Solid modelling systems should use this approach to read entries from family tables, plug new values in, and generate new instances of geometry.

For example, a sheet metal component that was designed on a next-generation feature-based parametric solid modeller. The single part was composed of features such as wall, bends, punches, and notches. Once completed, an "unbend" feature was added to partially unbend the part and automatically take bend allowance into consideration. Next, a family table of this part was defined, and an element called "flat 1" was added to the table specifying the inclusion of all features.

With the instance defined, the designer was able to then suppress the "unbend" feature on the part, resulting in two parts with the storage requirement of one. Both the flat instance and the fully bent part would be included in the drawing and stored. Changes made to the bent part in the drawing would automatically update the flat instance.

The concept of families of parts and assemblies in feature-based parametric systems introduces the potential to support libraries of standardized components. These libraries may be stored efficiently, and members may be called up whenever needed.

Not only does the next-generation feature-based parametric solid modeller increase productivity and decrease time to market, it also provides a valuable tool for conceptual design, since it can quickly incorporate a change. The following is an illustration of how a powerful solid modelling system can respond to substantial changes and generate a new instance of geometry instantly. The key to the substantial changes in this example is that they are brought about by changing only one dimension value on the model. This dimension corresponds to the placement of the handle on the drill body and all of the features that support the handle. The change can be made by modifying this dimension value in either the drawing or the part model. Because the system is two-way associative, all other applications are updated automatically. Since all of the changes are brought about by changing a single parameter, this example is known as the "One Number Test".

The complex geometry of this power drill was defined by a number of notable and powerful features. First, the complex geometry of the handle was created so that it could be moved via a single dimension change with respect to the upper drill body. Next, the model was cut and shelled automatically by specifying the removal from a surface. Ribs were defined to extend into the drill housing until they met the shelled out walls, and numerous drafted surfaces, fillets and cuts were made. Because the handle was created prior to the shelling, the designer could make changes easily, and the system would regenerate the shell and subsequent features automatically, regardless of the drill's shape.

4   Summary

Because product design is a complex iterative process involving constant changes at every stage of a product's development, the most important attribute of a solid modeller is its ability to manage change effectively. Not only must the modeller provide a full 3D representation of the design it must also be able to rapidly generate many variations to the model in response to design and manufacturing needs.

By taking advantage of a feature-based approach, designers can create libraries and families of parts efficiently by avoiding the redundant storage of information. By providing tools that effectively manager change in the engineering workplace, this feature-based parametric modeller can provide substantial contributions to the bottom line through increased productivity and shorter product time to market.

THE NEED FOR SPEED

**Tim Plunkett, Director
of Formation, Rapid Prototyping Bureau
Unit A3, Spinnaker House, Hempsted, Gloucester.**

1   Abstract

Time to market is now recognised as having a direct impact on the profitability of a new product. Principles such as concurrent engineering have been born to help reduce development times, integrate multi disciplinary teams and provide better final designs. Unlike concurrent engineering, prototyping has been around for years, to provide the first few parts of a new design. However as timescales reduce and risk levels rise the demands on prototypes increase. They are needed faster, to be more accurate and more representative of the final component. This is where Rapid Prototyping comes in with representative, accurate parts available in hours or days.

2   Introduction

'Time is money,' an adage that is as old as the hills and is still as pertinent now as it has ever been. Large sums of money were invested in developing and building clippers to bring tea back from India in the 1870's. Premium rates were available for the cargo of the first ships home.

In a similar way today the financial rewards for being first into the market can be substantial. However very few companies can quantify the lost profits if they are late. The inability to quantify the sums involved have and do, represent a constraint on the uptake of Rapid Prototyping.

In todays environment it is the financial justification that decides whether or not a project will proceed. Thus whilst 'market lead' remains unvalued in the equation false results will be achieved. Only when companies are prepared to quantify this parameter will the financial equation demonstrate the overwhelming evidence for Rapid Prototyping(RP).

Putting aside any kind of justification, those companies that have jumped in and produced parts using Rapid Prototyping systems inevitably came back for more. Typically once the engineers have had experience of the engineering benefits the components bring they drive the further introduction into the company.

3   Bureau Operation

When operating a Rapid Prototyping (RP) Bureau the speed of turnround is very important. Each customer believes he is the only customer and is predominantly interested in how quickly the parts can be available. Frequently there is a negative lead time due to earlier programme slippages. Whilst the process is fast it must be accepted that there are certain limitations.

One such limitation is data transfer. The three dimensional computer model that forms the input to the system either has to be modelled from scratch or the data imported from the customer.

Another limitation is build time, clearly if a part is going to take 24

238

hours to produce using StereoLithography then by the time pre and post processing is included a 48 hour delivery is going to be difficult to achieve.

The following sections address some of the opportunities that are available and the processes that can now be invoked to get to a realistic prototype rather than an acrylic model.

4   Computer Aided Design (CAD)

A growing number of companies utilise CAD in the design phase of a project. Developments continue not just in the code and fuctionability but in the ability to use the same data to perform other functions. RP is one such function, where the time already invested in producing the database can be partly amortised into the time required to produce a prototype. The key element is now, how to transfer the data around. Where identical CAD systems are in use problems seldom arise, however where dissimilar CAD Systems are in use the outlook is not necessarily so optimistic.

Neutral formats have been around for years but are supported by different packages to different degrees. Thus an IGES file from package 1 may be gibberish to the IGES translator or CAD package 2.

If a solid modelling system is being used then short of stripping off the surface and exporting this through a neutral format no means of data exchange exists to cope with dissimilar systems.

Then there are .STL files. These form the gateway to most RP systems. A recognised format that stands between CAD systems and systems such as StereoLithography. As more companies use RP so the number that can output the STL format files grows. This is a major advantage as not only does it reduce risk in the data translation (less than 5% of .STL files prove unusable) but it saves time. It is far quicker to create the STL file on the host system and export rather than export/import another format and then create a .STL file. As the essence of the whole process is speed this should not be understated.

5   First Off

The unusual attribute of RP Systems is the speed with which CAD data can be translated into the first physical part. Frequently this is just the start as other materials are ultimately required. However the other processes used are impotent without that first off master patten.

There are limitations to any process and applicability must always be viewed in the light of the application. It is very unusual to find a single solution to everyones problems, this is no different. However if this technology is combined with many of the existing crafts then the results can be dramatic. Most problems can be overcome and satisfactory solutions defined. In over one year of trading Formation has only declined one job as being unsuitable (on economic grounds) and propose an alternative solution that was not at our disposal for another.

It is not my intention to go over how StereoLithography works as this is adequately covered elsewhere, more to concentrate on what can be done with the master model once it has been created.

6 StereoLithography Models

The advent of new resins that can be used with RP Systems, is making possible the direct use of acrylic models for testing form, fit and function.

Many components produced are ultimately to be injection moulded. These frequently have snap fits to hold components together. Last year these could not be functionally produced, now they do not represent a problem. Some components that have been made carry a specific warning that if assembled they will not separate due to the clip design.

Where styling concepts are being reviewed 'form' is the difference between success and failure. Small changes to the design can not only reduce manufacturing costs but also improve product appeal. A physical model can be signed off with a significantly higher level of confidence than a drawing or even a rendered image and without introducing a hold up in a project schedule.

Clearly highly stressed parts, high temperature parts and many others are unsuitable for testing if the base material is an acrylic. However most work can be done at ambient and with the resin available pump components have been produced and run. Similarly vending machines have many moving parts whilst not having a stringent environmental requirement. These parts can be assembled and fully tested prior to release of production tooling.

7 Metal Castings

For some parts the only way to achieve a representative prototype is to produce a metal casting. This can be achieved either by sand casting or investment casting.

The sand casting route is relatively simple. The StereoLithography part is used as a patten either directly or as a fast track to a resin tooling. The complexity of the part affects overall times and the number of cores etc that will be required. However the same principle can be used to create outside profiles and the necessary coring. The end result is a component in the required material and with representative grain flow that can be available in two weeks.

If the component is to be investment cast then there are two options depending upon the component complexity. The master can be used to create on epoxy tool from which wax copies can be taken and invested. The material limitations are only governed by what the foundry can cast. Complexity is important because as the epoxy tool sophistication rises so does the manufacturing time until in the limit conventional tooling might as well be produced. The process does allow for many waxes to be produced from a single StereoLithography master. Small development batches of investment castings also become viable as the high cost of conventional tooling is not incurred.

Alternatively it is possible to produce investment castings directly from SteroLithography masters. The disadvantages are that it is a one for one process and it takes longer. However complexity is not an issue. Formation has good links with Shellcast, a Canadian foundry who is able to offer this service, and has produced many components in this way in circa four weeks.

8   Plastic Prototypes

Polyurethane (PU) is the most commonly used plastic for prototyping. There is a large range of grades than can cover most applications and many environments. PU can be moulded either from silicone mounds, generated from a StereoLithography master or from resin moulds. Size is seldom a limitation and rapidly changing cross sections can also be encompassed. For most parts injection moulding is going to be the production option hence the parts are designed with drafts and suitable split lines in mind.

Where the final material is absolutely necessary in the prototype then mould tools can be created from the StereoLithography master using techniques such as metal spraying. With this process a thin layer of low melting point alloy is sprayed onto the master before being backed with epoxy. Any cooling pipes, ejectors, etc are also incorporated at this stage. Tools produced this way certainly do not have the life of production tools, however the requirement is usually for 100 or less components and as such this is not a problem. Tools made this way can be available within a week depending on complexity and injection machine characteristics.

9   Conclusion

Business today requires everything faster. RP is now a fully fledged technique for speeding up the availability of prototype parts. Just as CAD has developed, so has RP so that truly representative parts can now be produced.

Working practices like concurrent or simultaneous engineering, Total Quality Management (TQM), Quality Function Development (QFD) and Taguchi all help to produce better designs.

However they do bring the decision points in a development programme forward and impose a right first time ethic. Rapid Prototyping is an engineering tool to assist with these changes in working practice, a means of improving communication and reducing risk. The overriding attribute however is speed, no longer does a project need to wait for prototypes.

Comparison
of
Rapid Prototype Systems

Geoff Lart

ProtoMod Limited

1   Resume of Common Features

All Rapid Prototyping systems attempt the transformation of a computer representation of an object to a physical representation, with a minimum of manual intervention. The applications of such a process are still only being realised, and in conjunction with secondary processes to reproduce copies from a master may offer new routes to viable production.

The most common input format to all these systems is known as the STL file, which represents the outside surface of an object as a number of triangles.

The most common source of this STL file is a CAE database describing a Solid or Surface model. This description of the model is presented to the Rapid Prototype system, where it will eventually be cut into a number of horizontal slices, in software. Each of these thin layers is then built, and attached to those already built to provide a complete model.

Most of the systems then require some degree of post processing but the importance of this to the quality of the finished model varies.

2   Brief description of some Rapid Prototype Systems

2.1   Stereolithography - 3D Systems - California.

3D Systems were the first to commercialise the process, and now have over 300 machines around the world. Theirs is a fundamentally simple process, made to produce excellent results by careful development and careful process control. A simplified diagram of their system is shown in Figure 1.
A vat of liquid polymer contains an elevator tray which starts just (>0.1mm) below the surface of the liquid. Above the vat are two galvanometer controlled mirrors which direct a fine laser beam on to the surface of the vat. Where ever the laser strikes the surface of the liquid, the liquid solidifies; almost instantaneously, to a well defined depth, and only within the diameter of the laser. The laser is directed onto the surface of the liquid in a manner which completely solidifies a single layer of the required model. When a layer is finished the elevator (and model so far) are lowered into the liquid, more liquid floods on the top that layer and the process is repeated. Thus each layer is built up, until the whole model is finished and completely submerged. It is raised and removed.

2.2   Stereos - EOS - Germany.

The EOS system is very similar in operation to the 3D Systems' equipment described above. Around 3 or 4 have been sold in Europe.

2.3   SOUP-Solid Object UV-Laser Plotter-Mitsubishi-Japan.

This system again relies on a UV laser to solidify a liquid in a vat. The main difference is that the laser is guided by an XY plotter mechanism, and transmitted by fibre optic cable. One has been sold to Mercedes, and another is at the importer's site in Germany. Several systems are in use in Japan.

2.4 SCS-Solid Creation System-Sony & Japan Synthetic Rubber - Japan.

Another system using a similar approach to that of 3D Systems. There seem to have been some sales in Japan, but no effort to sell in other areas. They have described a system of up to 1m vat size.

2.5 Laser Modelling - Quadrax - Rhode Island.

In Feb. 1992, after a legal battle with 3D Systems in the USA, Quadrax ceased to manufacture Laser Modelling Equipment, and various aspects of their technology now belong to 3D Systems. The system was similar to 3D Systems, but used a more powerful, visible light laser, variable beam diameter at the resin surface, and a different recoating process. Mentioned here just for completeness.

2.6 Selective Laser Sintering - DTM Corp - Texas.

In some ways similar to the scanning laser / photopolymer systems described above, DTM spread a thin layer of finely ground powder onto a working piston. The laser energy is directed onto the powder from above, via a scanning system where it causes the powder to sinter to become a solid. The working piston is lowered, a new layer is spread, and the scanning repeated. Materials include wax, nylon, polycarbonate, and ABS.

2.7 Solider - Cubital - Israel.

This system again uses UV sensitive liquid, but the manner of selectively exposing it to light energy is different. A thin layer of liquid is spread, and exposed to a light source through a mask. Excess liquid is removed, and a number of processes performed to support the model during construction. This sequence of; spreading resin, preparing the mask, exposing, and processing the cured resin continues until the model is finished. The system is best suited to producing large numbers of models. Four or five machines in each of Europe and the USA.

2.8 Laminated Object Manufacturing - Helisys - California.

A completely different approach is used by the LOM system. A sheet of paper (generally) is laid down on a working table. The outside profile of the layer to be built is cut using a laser directed by an XY plotter. The laser only cuts to the depth of a single layer. A second layer of paper is laid down on top of the first and a heated roller passes over the two squeezing and bonding them together. These processes are repeated until the whole model has been built.

2.9 Fused Deposition Modelling - Stratasys - Minneapolis.

An XY plotter device carries an extrusion head. Material is extruded onto a work platform, in only the areas within the bounds of the model. When one layer is complete the table is lowered by one layer thickness, and the extrusion process can begin again.

3 Some Strengths and Weaknesses of these Systems

Attempts have been made to classify these Systems by material or process, but this is not necessary, and comparisons can be made between individual solutions to similar problems.

Some areas in which all these systems can be compared are: Data input, Wasted material and Need for supports.

Having said that, one group that can be considered in direct competition are the scanning laser systems of 3D Systems, EOS, and Mitsubishi; all are available in Europe, all offer similar vat sizes, and all require some sort of support structures. This group will be addressed first.

3.1 Laser Polymer systems

Some areas to compare these systems are: Ability to change the vat, Control of beam focusing on liquid, Scan Speed and Build Strategy.

3.1.1 Ability to Change the vat. (3D Systems and EOS)

One advantage of not being first into the market is that you can take a good look at your competition's products and improve on them. So EOS have a refined system for changing the vat, without draining the resin. All the resin wetted parts; elevator, and levelling system, are changed with the vat, making it a relatively quick and straight forward operation. In addition to this a range of smaller vats can be used, allowing a bureau to offer small models in a specialist material. A similar system for the SLA 250 cannot be far away.

3.1.2 Control of Beam Focusing on Liquid.

With a laser/photopolymer system the beam must be focused onto the resin surface. As the point to be cured moves away from the centre of the vat, two effects occur; the distance between the scanning mirror and the resin surface changes causing the beam to become de-focused, and the shape of the beam on the resin surface changes from ideally circular to elliptical. This is shown in Figure 2. This leads to a loss of specific energy at the intended point of curing. The three systems to be considered use 3 different approaches to overcome this geometric problem.

(i)   3D Systems.

3D Systems use the simple approach of making the distance between the mirrors, and the resin surface long in relation to the vat size. The SLA 500 uses a large flat mirror above the vat to achieve this with the galvanometers low down to the side of the vat. De-focusing is reduced to insignificant levels, and the extent to which the beam is no longer circular is also reduced, but not eliminated.
The advantages of this approach are that; it involves no extra moving parts and can not go wrong, and it provides a faster beam speed for the same mirror

speed. One potential disadvantage is that errors in mirror positioning are magnified, but this is not a problem because the mirrors can be positioned so accurately that other errors become more important, mainly resin shrinkage during cure.

(ii)   EOS

EOS use shorter throw optics for their 400mm and 600mm vat sizes. To correct de-focusing a third galvanometer and lens is used to continually refocus the beam onto the surface of the resin.
This cannot address the problem of the beam becoming elliptical.

(iii)   Mitsubishi

On Mitsubishi's larger systems both problems are avoided altogether by using an XY plotter device instead of scanning mirrors. The beam is always perpendicular to the resin surface and is always correctly focused.

3.1.3   Scanning Speed.

Two factors affect scanning speed: Laser Power and Mechanical Limits.

(i)   Laser Power.

The specific energy of the laser at the resin surface is controlled by the speed of the beam over the surface. The maximum speed is dictated by the maximum power that the laser can produce, although this may be tempered by build parameters.

(ii)   Mechanical Limits.

In the case of some of the Mitsubishi systems the maximum beam speed is not set by the available laser power, but by the ability of the XY positioning device to respond.

3.1.4   Build Strategy

When the resin turns from a liquid to solid, it shrinks. This can be the cause of model deformation during or after the build process.
In an attempt to reduce the effect of this shrinkage 3D Systems have a sophisticated build strategy known as WEAVE, which allows the resin to do most of its shrinking without causing any deformation.
Although the theory and practice of WEAVE is documented, it is uncertain if any of the other systems offer a similar facility yet.

3.2   Data Input

All these systems can accept STL files as input, some systems can accept various other forms as well.

3.2.1 STL File Format.

The STL file approximates the outside surface of the model with a number of triangles. This coupled with the fact that coordinates are stored by value rather than by reference makes STL files quite bulky. This problem can be overcome by the use of common compression algorithms which allow STL files of up to 5M bytes (about 16 000 triangles) to be stored on a 3 1/2" diskette.
In an ideal world the use of facets to represent the outside surface would not be apparent, with sufficiently fine facetting a smooth surface would result.

However the use of such fine facetting has two effects: Slow boolean operations and Facet normal problems.

(i)   Slow Boolean Operations.

When two solids are intersected certain types of Solid Modeller must intersect all the relevant facets. The greater the number of facets, the longer this will take.

(ii)   Facet Normal Problems.

As facets become smaller, it becomes more difficult for the solid modeller to decide which is the inside and which is the outside of a facet. In the limit a facet may become a straight line.
Although STL translators are available for most CAE systems and the quality of STL files is improving, it may still be necessary to enlist the help of a specialist to smooth the transfer of data from CAE System to RP system.

The STL file was specified some years ago, when available computer power was limited by comparison to today. So although it is well defined and can be made to work, some other formats are available now.

3.2.2   Other data formats in use include;

SDRC universal format,	Cubital, Sony.
NC codes	Stratasys.
CATIA model files.	EOS.
CFL	Cubital's own format.

The CFL format is also facetted, but in this case, the facets may be multi sided with multiple holes in. In addition the coordinates of the vertices are stored by reference, rather than by value, which saves space and preserves the connectivity of the model.
An STL file can be generated from a CFL file, and vice versa. The CFL also allows for the description of an object as a series of contours or "Frames", but this is not widely used.
Once the data is secured on the RP hardware, all systems have proprietary products for viewing, moving, mending, and providing supports where necessary.

These products each have there own strengths and weaknesses, and are only really relevant to the system operator.

Some systems slice the model in batch before build time, while others slice the model in real time as the model is built.

All these details may be of technical interest, but are largely irrelevant to the engineer who wants a model in his or her hands as soon as possible. The effect of a 6 hour batch slice can easily be dwarfed by a bank holiday weekend or a faulty diskette.

3.3   Waste Material

Another area of interest is the amount of waste material generated during the build process.

Supports will not be considered as waste material for the purposes of this discussion, because their volume is generally small in comparison to the model.

There are two reasons why waste is important: Cost and Environmental.

(i)   Cost.

Material used has to be paid for, and the waste is of no use to the customer.

(ii)   Environmental.

Increasingly important in some markets is the environmental consequence of disposing of waste photopolymer.

3.3.1   Waste Material by System Type.

(i)   Scanning Lasers Systems.

All these systems have a similar wastage which will be low, related to the area of the model, and the number of nooks and crannies that resin can remain in after draining. Simple grid like support structures may be particularly bad in this respect.

All the resin cured, is useful model (or supports) that the designer wants. The resin that remains in the vat can be reused for future models.

(ii)   Solider System - Cubital.

Cubital appear to have a potentially more serious problem with waste.
A full layer of resin is spread at each slice, and that which is not cured is removed by a suction device It is what happens to this collected waste that presents the problem.
Cubital buy it back from their users in order to purify it, and prepare it for reuse. If this recycling process is successful then waste will be minimal. However if

significant quantities of this resin cannot be recycled for any reason, this will be a major cost, which must in the end be reflected in the cost of models.

A further loss of resin occurs at the milling stage. When liquid resin is spread, it is spread in layers thicker than the final model will be built in, in order to ensure a flat surface after the milling operation. Typical values are; for a final layer thickness of 150 microns, 170 microns of resin will be spread and cured. This represents a waste of 13% of the model volume.

A small amount of resin remains in the "Corner" between the vertical face of cured resin, and the surrounding wax. This will be cured by the second exposure. This volume of waste is small and probably similar to the amount which remains on a model from a scanning laser system.
The wax used by the Cubital system can be considered in two areas;

(a)   Wax removed by milling.

The amount of wax removed during the milling process will be related to the thickness of wax applied, which is slightly greater than the layer thickness. This wax will be mixed with cured resin fragments, and will probably be discarded.

(b)   Support Wax.

The larger volume of wax to be reclaimed will be that which surrounds the model to support it. This can be reclaimed at the washing stage, although it's not known how efficient this is.

(iii)   Helisys

The waste produced by the LOM system is simple to quantify. It is the volume of the bounding box which is not useful model. It is inert and can be treated as waste paper. Although it will larger by volume than most of the other systems the material is cheap, and waste will be of minor cost.

(iv)   Stratasys

If support structure is not considered waste, then Fused Deposition Modeling need not produce any waste. The material is inert.

(v)   DTM

With careful control of the powder this system need have virtually no waste.

Waste - Conclusion

When Cubital have procedures in place to efficiently recycle resin and wax the cost of waste for all these systems is insignificant in comparison to the cost of the capital needed to buy them, and the cost of the personnel needed to support them.

3.4 Need for supports.

Much has been said about the need for supports on 3D Systems' SLA. Models built on all the scanning laser systems invariably need supports, and it can be a time consuming job to create these manually. However at least one system is available which will automatically generate a support structure.

A model which is incorrectly supported may not build properly, bowing is a particular problem which may occur with inadequate supports.

The nature of some other systems means that the part is inherently supported as it is built. Cubital, Helisys and DTM fall into this category. Stratasys have a requirement for supports specific to their system.

4 Comparative Exercise.

In order to try and distinguish between these systems a small solid model bench mark has been created. The STL file describing this part was sent to a number of systems and models received from 7 of them. The model is shown in Figure 3.

This model does not test a lot of important factors concerning Rapid Prototype systems, including large scale accuracy, and warping, but it has made a start in the distinguishing those systems that can reproduce fine detail, and various other factors of performance.

5 Presentation of Results.

All this consideration of contributing factors is all very well, but what most people are interested in are models at the end of the day.

Slides will be shown presenting some results from this model.

Acknowledgements

This work would have been impossible without the cooperation of the manufacturers of the RP systems which are discussed here.

3D Systems	UK and USA.
Stratasys	USA.
Cubital	Switzerland, Germany, and Israel.
DTM	USA.
Mitsubishi	UK, Germany, and Japan.
Sony	UK, Japan.
Quadrax	USA.
Helisys	USA.

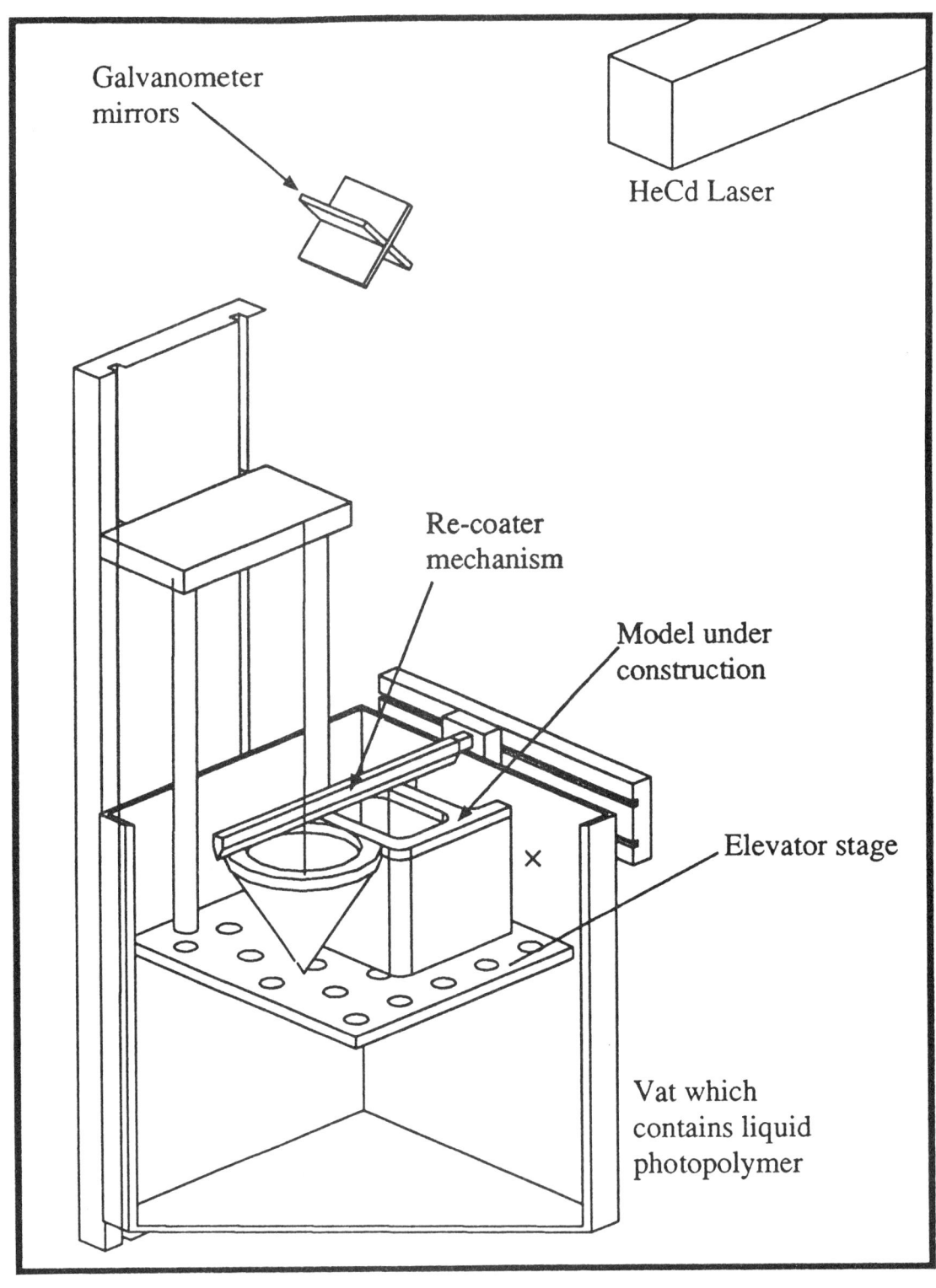

Galvanometer
mirrors

HeCd Laser

Re-coater
mechanism

Model under
construction

Elevator stage

Vat which
contains liquid
photopolymer

Figure 1.　　　　Simplified diagram of 3D Systems SLA 250.

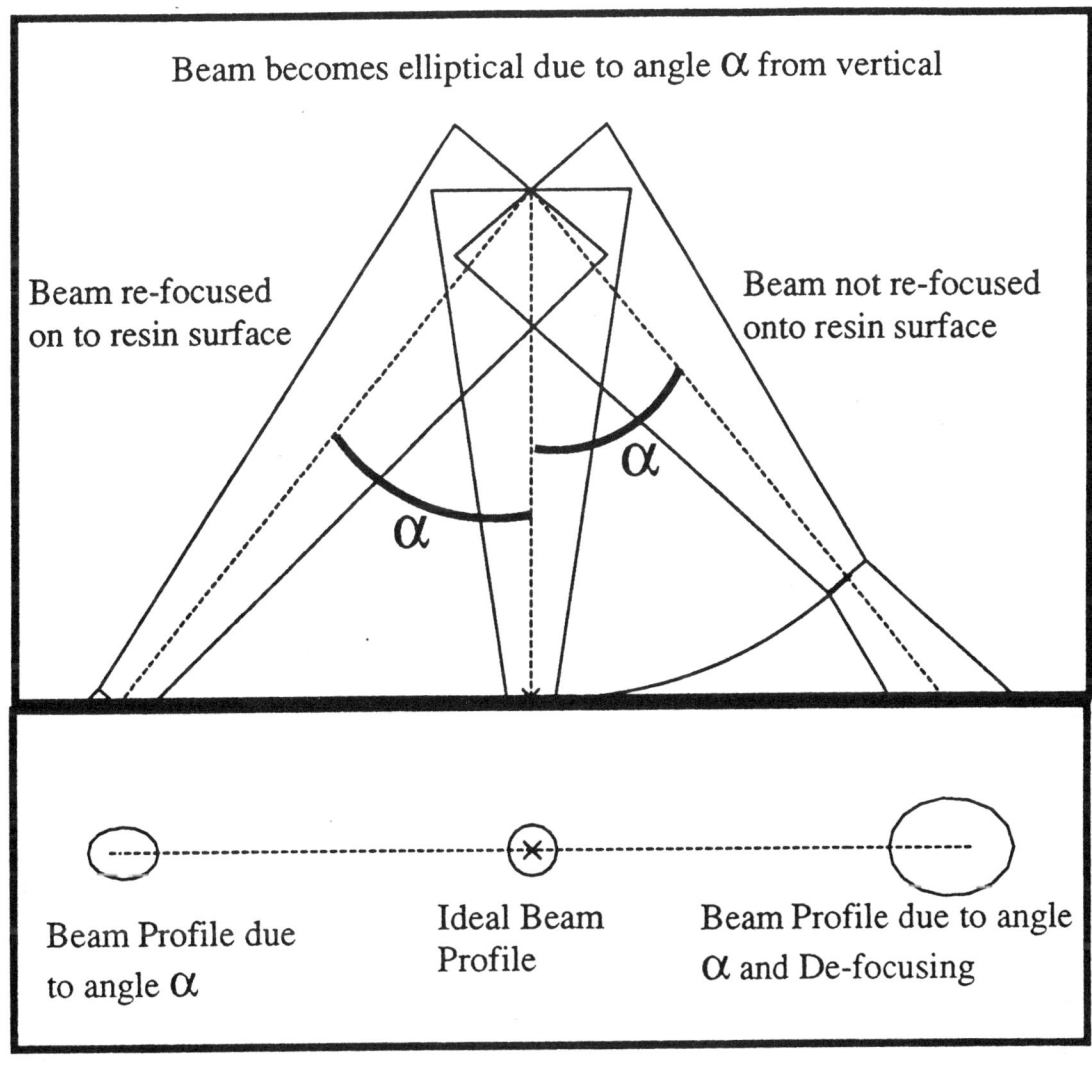

Figure 2.   Beam profile due to deviation from vertical and de-focussing.

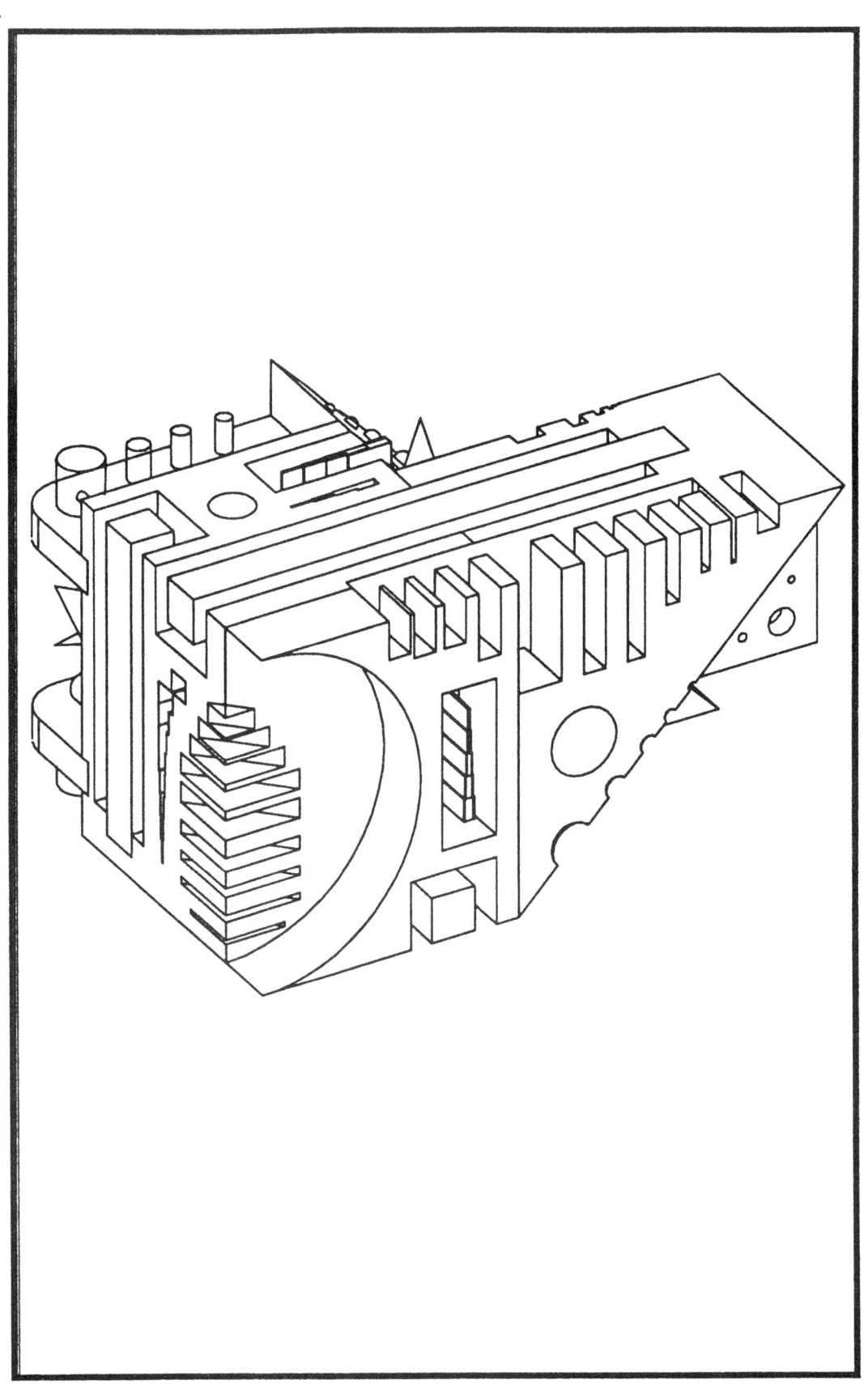

Figure 3.   General view of model used in comparative exercise.

RAPID SHEET METAL PRODUCTION BY THE

ELECTROCHEMICAL MACHINING PROCESS

Ian Leonard
Leonides, 62 Thorns Road, Bolton, BL1 6PD, UK

Alan Duffield
Amchem Ltd, 28 Roman Way, Coleshill, Birmingham B46 1HQ, UK

Preface

The Electro-Chemical Machining Process (E.C.M) has been adapted to produce accurate complex shaped components from thin sheet metal.

Plane cathodic electrodes separated electrolytically from the processed sheet by perforated plastic membranes, allow rapid but selective dissolution of the metal when subjected to a high current density pulsed D.C. supply.

Typically peripheries in 1mm thick stainless steel can be cut through in approximately 2 minutes, while 0.1 mm is pierced in less than 20 seconds. The process is particularly suitable for those metallic alloys which are too hard or work harden by conventional pressing, punching or machining or are too exotic to be eroded by the photo-chemical etching route. They include tool and spring steels, nickel alloys, Nimonics®, Hastelloys®, titanium, zirconium and amorphous glassy metal foils and tapes.

The E.C.M. processor utilises plastic film membranes which can be cut by low powered yag lasers (or use photographic resist films) directly linked to a simple P.C. based CAD system

This new technique, which is now patented, is ideal for prototype and/or small batch quantities of sheet metal components for aircraft, gas turbine, motor racing or chemical plants.

1   Introduction

Electro-Chemical Machining Process

The basic principles of E.C.M. (Ref 1,2,3) are well known, being effectively the reverse of electro plating but the process, has not by and large, fulfilled the high expectations of the 1970's when P.E.R.A., T.I. Group and other machine tool producers throughout the world, actively investigated its potential for many metal machining operations, such as gear hobbing, broaching, die sinking and under cutting.

Twenty years later E.C.M. has found only a few successful niches, some so specialised that they weren't even contemplated in the original work. Major applications are the shaping and forming of advanced gas turbine blades. TransTec in cooperation with several major gas turbine manufacturers have pioneered the deep drilling of very small blade cooling holes, in that many E.C.M. multi hole "drillers" are now operating around the world. (Ref. 4)

However, E.C.M. has generally proved to be a complex process to control, requiring expensive high pressure corrosion proof pumps (>25 bar), filters, electrolyte cooling and corrosion protection and large D.C. power supplies, besides high tooling costs and associated effluent disposal problems.

Most E.C.M. processes use electrolytes such as sodium nitrate or chloride for profile shaping and acids-nitric or sulphuric (20% W/V) for fine hole drilling. Essentially E.C.M. has been considered as a continuous machining process, with controlled metal removal rates and surface shaping and profiling as the prime objectives.

2   Sheet Metal E.C.M.

This report describes for the first time an innovative patented (Ref. 5, 6, 7) and low cost ECM process which causes very rapid removal of selective areas of plane sheet metal, so that through penetration is achieved simultaneously from both sides. Thus a thin line periphery of a complex sheet metal component can be produced, with both accuracy and repeatability.

Test have proven that normal ECM current densities of 50 - 100 Amps/cm^2 at 20 to 40 volts D.C., penetrate 1.0mm, stainless steel sheet in approximately 2 minutes, whilst 0.1mm foil etches through in less than 15 seconds. Of significance no specialised tooling is necessary. The sheet metal (anode) being held between a pair of cooled flat electrodes (cathode) made of stainless steel or titanium.

Selective etching is achieved by interposing between the sheet surface and electrodes perforated insulating membranes. This can be a resist layer as is commonly used for the photochemical acid etching process, but much more accurate results, without undercut are achieved by using a thick self supporting membrane, such as 1.6mm p.c.b board or 1mm acrylic or pvc plastic sheet. This acts like a concave lens to focus the metal dissolution, without the membrane having to be adhered to the metal.

This process is in fact a progression from the well established chemical milling used in the aircraft industry on aluminium alloys, but without the need for aggressive acid etching solutions which corrode away the metal in a difficult to control regime.

By applying the necessary energy for anodic dissolution with an electro potential in a non-aggressive electrolyte, very controllable, yet rapid metal removal rates can be achieved. This process therefore greatly expands the number of exotic alloyed materials, which hitherto could not easily be machined mechanically or chemically, because of their high strengths and intrinsic corrosion resistance. Sheet metals, tubes and even extrusions of this very wide range of chemical and heat resistant alloys can now be considered - the Nimonic® and Hastelloys®, titanium and zirconium alloys and the new amorphous glass metal foils and tapes (especially the magnetic) are all suitable.

3   Process Techniques

The sheet metal E.C.M. is achieved in fairly simple equipment compared to conventional modern E.C.M. which require stainless steel containers and high pressure circuitry pipes and pumps. The electrolyte is always at low pressure contained in plastic tanks with plastic recirculatory pumps. The processed metal sheet is submerged between a pair of cooled flat plate electrodes, spaced apart 10 to 20 times the sheet thickness. A pulsed and intermittent electrolyte flow is directed on both sides of the metal sheet, simply to remove debris. The time of processing is so short that there is no opportunity for the electrolyte to approach boiling.

The power supply is also quite conventional and low cost, thyristor controlled DC units, similar to that used in MIG/TIG welding with the ability for variable intermittent pulsing.

The current/time profile is amenable to automatic control because the point of co-penetration of the sheet is very sharply defined, there being an area change of several magnitudes in only a few seconds.

The sheet is protected on both sides by either resist layers or plastic membranes in which the shapes to be dissolved are replicated by low powered laser or photo processing.

Of importance, is that each side of the sheet can have very different machined patterns, holes and profiles, which can produce fold lines, hole countersinks, cooling fins or throughcut areas. Two examples of such sheet components are shown in Figure 1.

4 Process Parameters and Applications

Because it is now practical to electro chemically machine a wide range of different metals and alloys, a number of specific electrolytes need to be employed. Their ideal characteristic being to ensure that all the elements in any particular alloy go into solution, so avoiding debris or gels. These alternatives are listed in Table 1 as a guide.

Material	Electrolyte	Electrolyte Type
High Tungsten, Molybdenum Alloy	Sodium Hydroxide (30%)	Alkali
Low Alloy Steel, Copper Alloys, Brasses, Aluminium Alloys, Pure Nickel	Sodium Nitrate Sodium Chloride (20 - 30%)	Neutral
Nickel, Cobalt, Chrome Alloys, Stainless Steels	Nitric Acid (20%) Sulphuric Acid (20%)	Acid
Titanium, Zirconium Alloys	Hydrochloric Acid (10 %)	Acid

Table 1.   Suitable Electrolytes for Various Alloys

By this E.C.M. process, it is possible to produce quite complex three dimensional components which can be stabilised by tab folding, riveting, spot welding or even vacuum brazing. A typical example with all these features is shown in Figure 2.

The process can be readily adapted to machine other shaped sheet metal forms, i.e. tubes or extrusions by using concentric electrodes. This would enable both internal and external features to be achieved such as splines, screw threads, cooling fins and countersunk holes.

As the speed of machining is a matter of seconds or at most a few minutes, depending solely on metal thickness, it is clear that sheet metal E.C.M. processing is ideal for very rapid prototyping, where several different components might be needed in succession. For example, in motor racing, quite slight alterations are needed urgently to mounting brackets or pedals to suit an individual driver or track conditions. These could be produced in the pits whilst the racing car is making test laps and be modified accordingly.

In medical operations there is very often an urgent and practical need to provide a specific prosthesis in stainless steel or titanium actually during the course of an emergency (in Trauma) operation. This process can provide a complete precisely shaped component, to the surgeon's actual dimensions, electro polished, passivated and autoclaved sterile within 30 minutes.

The ability to use a P.C. based CAD system via a 50 watt yag laser to cut thin plastic membranes on a simple X-Y CAD plotter can ensure a real direct-action link between design "back to the drawing board" modifications and development testing which is so short and that prototype times can be effectively reduced. This need is only too apparent in today's engineering, and especially the aircraft and gas turbine industries, where costs are so high because the sheet metal production methods currently employed are quite inappropriate for the small production quantities inherent to aircraft, both civil and military.

To conclude, this is a new sheet metal process that really needs funding to evaluate its potential.

References:

1. De Barr, A.D. and Oliver, D.A. (1968) - Electrochemical Machining, Macdonald and Co, England.

2. Benedict, G.F. (1988) - Non Traditional Machining Processes, Dekker, New York.

3. McGeough, J.A. (1988) - Advanced Methods Of Machining, Chapman and Hall, London.

4. Ahmed, M.S. and Duffield A. (1990) - The Drilling Of Small Deep Holes By Acid E.C.M., Society Of Manufacturing Engineers Technical Paper MR90-243.

5. Leonard, I. (1990) - Patent PCT/GB90/01622 "Producing Prostheses" by E.C.M.

6. Leonard, I. and Ross, R. (1991) - Patent PCT/GB91/01851 "Prostheses And Methods And Apparatus For Making Same".

7. Leonard, I. (1992) - Patent Application No: 9101734.3 "Continuous E.C.M."

NOTE: References in the text to Nimonics® and Hastelloys® are the registered trade mark of the International Nickel Co and Haynes International Ltd.

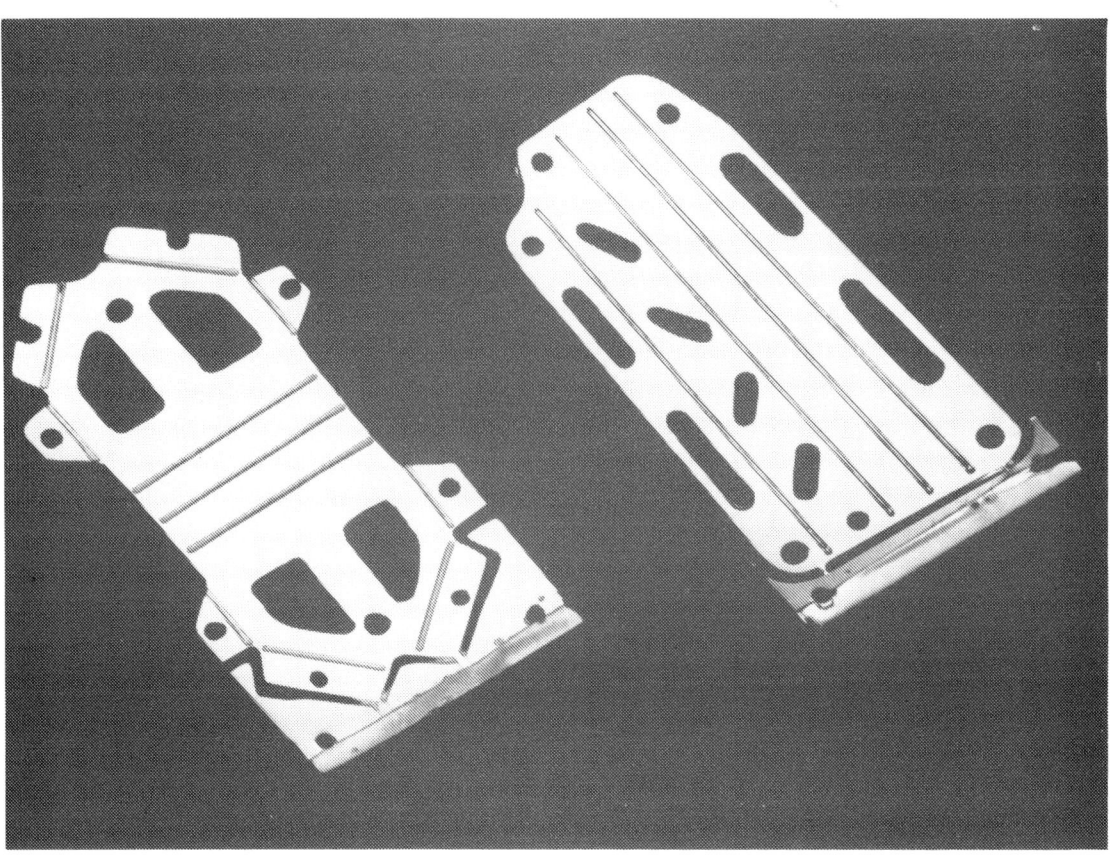

Figure 1. Single Sheet Prostheses made by 2 Minutes of E.C.M.
(1mm stainless steel)

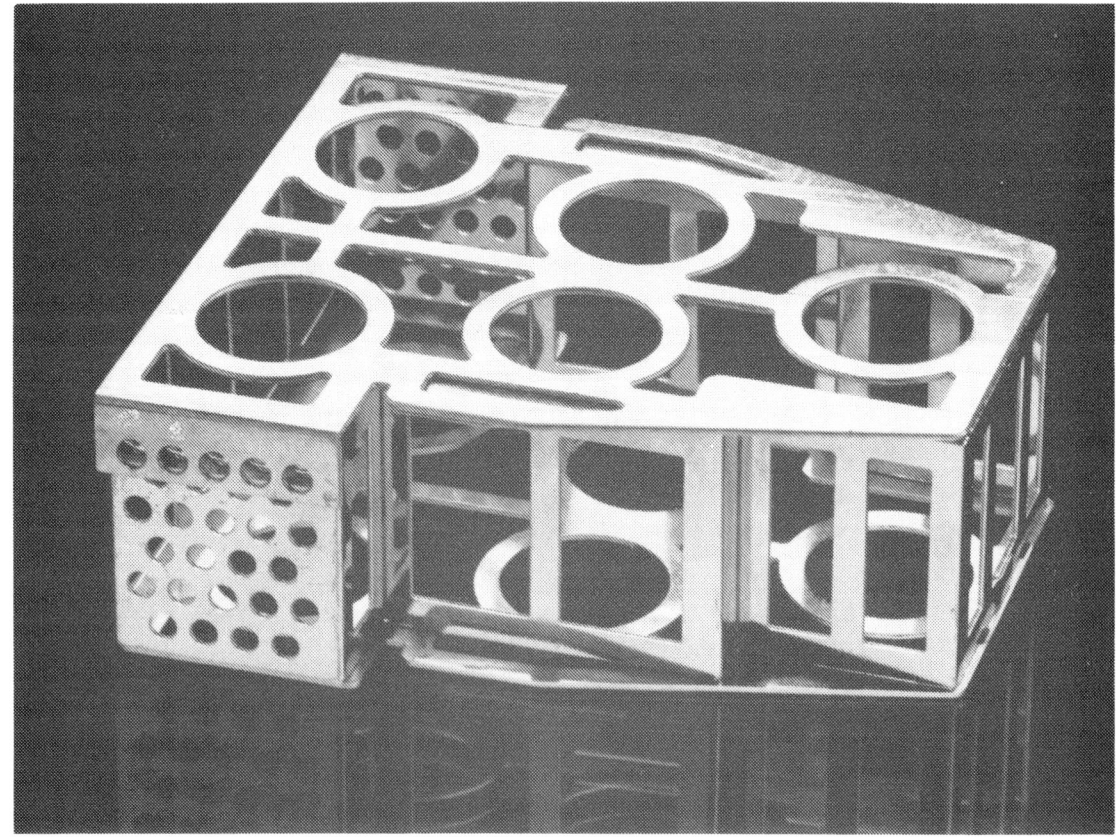

Figure 2. Centrifuge Basket Folded from E.C.M. Machined Sheet.
(0.5mm stainless steel)

RAPID PROTOTYPE CASTING

Mr Martin Koch

Industrial Engineering Department
California Polytechnic State University
San Luis Obispo, CA 93407

1   Abstract

Traditional methods for producing prototypes in the foundry industry are frequently very expensive and time-consuming resulting in a limited number of possible design iterations. This limitation is referred to as the "Tooling Bottleneck". The process is further complicated by the varying shrink and gating requirements of the
different cast materials. Rapid prototyping techniques are being applied to this bottleneck in both the production of prototypes and the subsequent foundry tooling. This paper presents a review of the use of rapid prototyping within foundry processes.

2   Introduction

The Foundry Industry (Foundry) is the world's sixth largest and one of its most ancient. Its products are everywhere and its processes are diverse. It is not an industry that is likely to disappear soon but it is one that is in great need of modernization. As with many industries one of its most pressing problems is that of how to reduce the time and cost of the product development cycle. This is especially true because of the supporting role that Foundry provides to the other manufacturing industries. As these industries evolve to shorter development cycles so must Foundry or its products will be replaced by other options. The key to this reduction in cycle time lies with solving the "Tooling Bottleneck" of pattern production. It is here that Rapid Prototyping (RP) can mature by integrating its capabilities with existing Foundry methods and it is a promising option for the solution of this fundamental problem. By participating in this solution the RP world can move forward from its current stage of providing expensive prototypes for the 'high-end' design market to the routine working stage of being a keystone in the day to day manufacturing cycle.

The "Tooling Bottleneck" problem offers a unique opportunity for RP. This is because the main strength of RP is its ability to make patterns, and the main need of Foundry is for such patterns, where the current/traditional pattern making process is so expensive and time consuming that the transition to a RP based system can be financed by the savings of doing so even while RP is still in its expensive development stage. Foundry is overwhelmingly pattern dependent in both its product development cycle and manufacturing phase. Regardless of the casting method the industry has as its central process the utilization of a physical pattern to produce molds into which to cast metal. This is true for both the design and manufacturing cycles. The purpose of this paper is to understand the nature of this bottleneck and how RP can be used to mitigate it.

The focus here will not be on the usable methods to make casting from the different existing RP systems (although these will be touched upon briefly), but rather upon the needs of Foundry for RP and how these systems can augment and benefit its existing processes. It is the belief of this author that the near-term opportunities within the foundry industry for RP lie not with the replacement of existing production molding methods by the direct output of RP systems, but rather with the integration of RP systems into the rapid and cost effective development of tooling for existing methods. The focus in this paper will be upon the Investment Casting process. Investment Casting (IC) is the fastest growing segment of the industry, its aerospace and electronics segments have been working with RP systems and the problems of producing wax injection molds parallel those of both the die-injection and permanent mold processes. When RP can effectively participate in this process then it will have left the esoteric and expensive portion of the industry and truly come of age. Additionally, I will focus upon two types or periods of pattern needs: original design and manufacturing. We will begin with a description of the industry's current methods.

2   Current Methods

Investment Casting (IC) is expendable pattern casting. Here a physical pattern is produced, traditionally in wax. The pattern is produced by injecting the pattern wax into a mold (normally of aluminum) at a temperature where the wax is a paste (typically about 71°C) and at a pressure around 300 psi. This is normally done by semi-skilled labor with a cycle time of a few minutes. It is a quick and inexpensive process which uses low cost materials and has a high output rate and, in some instances is automated. It is very difficult for RP systems to compete directly with this efficient pattern production method. If internal features are necessary, as is frequently the case, a 'soluble core' is made first via another injection mold using a higher melting temperature wax. This core is then set into the pattern mold and the pattern wax is injected around it. Once formed the combined wax piece is placed into a solution which dissolves out the soluble core wax resulting in a hollow pattern that can have complicated and smooth internal features. Both the core waxes and the pattern waxes can be worked to remove any undesirable features resulting from their molding. One thing that should be kept in mind with IC is that the pattern does not need to be produced as one piece. It can be composed of several subassemblies that can be glued or otherwise joined. This aspect lends itself towards the production of complex pieces that can not be made via any other methods of machining or casting. These wax patterns are then attached to wax 'gating' systems, (in multiples, if small enough) to form a 'tree'. This tree is then dipped in a ceramic slurry and dusted with refractory to form a stucco type skin surrounding the wax. The dipping and dusting process is repeated over a period of time to form a multi-layer shell. When ready the shell is then 'de-waxed' in a steam autoclave to remove the bulk of the wax and then 'burned-out' in a furnace to completely remove the wax residue and pre-heat the shell for casting. The hot shell is then filled with the metal of choice. This type of casting provides the widest range of surface finishes, it can produce the most intricate and precise castings and in some cases it is the only method that can be used with good effect with some metals. For example titanium is frequently investment cast and does not lend itself well to sand casting.

3   Current Prototyping Methods

The current method for prototyping is to go ahead and make the wax injection tool. If the prototype is accepted then this tool is used for production. It is this method that is the "Tooling Bottleneck" in IC. Tool production is a lengthy and expensive process that limits design iteration cycles. It is with this prototyping need that RP has begun to play a role. RP systems have been used with good results in IC. The key to producing prototypes here is to concentrate on the expendable pattern requirement. There are two alternatives for doing this. The first is to use the output of the RP system directly as the expendable pattern. The second alternative is to use the RP piece in the process of making a wax injection tool/mold.

3.1   Direct casting a RP piece as an expendable pattern.

This has been tried with the stereolithography pieces, the LOM Paper pieces and the waxes from fused deposition (Stratasys) and SLS (DTM). With any of these systems the roughness of the layered surfaces have to be smoothed on either the patterns or the castings in order to be able to compare favorably with traditionally-made pieces. The capabilities of RP systems to produce hollow patterns can bypass the soluble core process when the smoothness of internal features is not critical.

3.2   Stereolithography, photo-resin processes.

The problem with the direct utilization of the resin pieces of the stereolithography process, lie with the mismatch between the resin and the traditional pattern waxes. These waxes normally melt at about 71 °C. The resins do not melt but rather sublimate at approximately 390 °C. Therefore, when the invested shell is flash de-waxed in the autoclave at 93 °C the resin merely expands and cracks the thin shell. Therefore the resins can not be used as direct replacements for pattern waxes without process modification. There are however, several solutions that have been successfully applied. One of these, is to build not a solid resin piece but rather an open matrix that is then hand-filled with wax. This eliminates the vast majority of the resin and mitigates the expansion problem. Another solution is to use the solid flask method of investment casting where the thin layered shell is replaced by a more monolithic massive mold. This method gives rise to other problems concerning expansion and venting of the mold cavity. A third method, especially with titanium casting, involves the coating of the solid resin piece with a layer of wax followed by the shell investing process (perhaps with shell reinforced modification). The resulting larger pattern is sometimes acceptable because the titanium casting would normally have to be chemically milled in order to remove the surface beta phase. A final method that I haven't seen but might be feasible would be to build the part as a shell or skin leaving the center as uncured liquid or an open support matrix. Drain holes could be designed in or drilled later and a vacuum applied to remove the fluid. This could result in a basically hollow structure that could collapse upon itself during the burnout cycle.

3.3 SLS, Fused Deposition, LOM

In the area of the direct investment casting of the output from the SLS and Fused deposition pieces, these methods can be used with great effectiveness when the pattern material is investment wax itself. Foundries do not agree as to which waxes to use and often are proprietary and secretive in their waxes. Since both Stratasys and DTM can both work from customer supplied materials this is not a problem for the unique "high-end" portion of the market. The paper patterns of the LOM process also are reported to work well with the investment casting process. The paper can be burned out, with little expansion and ash residue.

3.4 Machining investment castable wax.

Another alternative for rapidly producing prototypes for IC involves the less esoteric system of machining prototype waxes. We have used this method very effectively. Traditional 'proof of tape' cnc wax is inadequate for IC because of its incompatibility with the normal IC shell process. This type of wax is normally mostly a polymer that melts at about 180°C and stays very viscous. As such when tried by IC foundries this material would expand instead of melt, destroying the ceramic shell molds. However, newer wax formulations have addressed this issue resulting in a very flexible and inexpensive prototyping media that can be used in existing casting methods. This material can be easily cast into different sized machining blanks; it is simply reusable by remelting the chips, and as a wax it is fast to machine and safe to work with. Sub-assemblies can be machined separately and then glued together to make complicated patterns. One interesting method is to use a standard fiber reinforced soluble wax, which machines very nicely, to produce a core wax representing the pattern's internal geometries; machinable pattern wax is then injected around this soluble core and machined to the external geometries. The core wax is then dissolved off leaving a pattern with both complicated internal and external features that you couldn't machine otherwise. The result is a very flexible and powerful IC prototyping system that is inexpensive, quick, and smoothly integrated with existing casting capabilities. We have used this to reduce prototyping costs significantly in some cases.

RP system can and have produced complex pieces for use as direct investment casting patterns. This capability can serve the industry well for high-end prototyping but does not address its day to day needs. For the near term RP systems cannot compete with the current injection methods for producing production patterns. To produce a set of RP patterns a foundry can have a set of injection tools produced, with the advantage that if the prototype works then the production tooling is already in hand. Interestingly enough when you present the possibilities of the current RP systems to an investment caster, he will focus on the comparison of the output rate and cost of the those systems with the current wax injection method and reject their viability. It usually takes a little time and work to get him to see the possibilities of quickly and cheaply making the tooling via RP. To penetrate the larger IC market RP systems bureaus should be focusing upon the production of the more complicated, multicomponent injection tools.

4   RP for Injection Tooling

The second alternative for using RP systems for making expendable patterns is that of using the RP piece to make a mold for wax injection. It is in this area where the greatest opportunity for RP within IC exists. This can be done via replication from a RP master positive. There are several methods for doing this but the key here is to build the RP master with the necessary parting planes and gating systems in place. Frequently what is now done is to build the RP master as a complete unit and then to depend upon the pattern maker to define and construct the parting surfaces. This is normally done by hand and involves burying the positive in a clay or plaster up to the parting line. Replication epoxies or rubbers are then cast against this mounted master to form a mold segment. The process is repeated for each mold segment and for each mold set. The result is the production of unique mold sets via a labor intensive method. It is far better to build the master with the replication method firmly in mind, allowing smooth integration with existing methods. In this way you can easily cast multiple mold sets of the same geometries. Additionally, the spray metal method can be used effectively to produce injection tools from mounted RP masters.

Another method that has been tried is that of injecting wax against the RP master to form a wax mold segment. This wax is then investment cast to produce the injection die. This injection die can be of aluminum, steel or even cast iron. This raises the possibility of producing permanent molds via an RP based IC process. The possibility of using RP to effectively make inexpensive permanent and die molds has perhaps the greatest potential in the Foundry industry as they are very expensive to produce.

5   Conclusions

The IC Foundry industry offers immense possibilities for the successful application of RP systems because of its great dependency upon physical patterns for both its prototyping and production phases. RP systems have been successfully applied to the task of making expendable patterns but the key to penetrating this industry is to concentrate upon solving the problems of the production of wax injection tooling. We have not touched upon the tooling needs of the other segments of the industry but these are also full of promise for the rapid prototyper.

References

-   Menon, U., Koch, M. Rapid Prototyping for Foundry Tool Making
    in Solid Freeform Fabrication Symposium (1991) Proceedings,
    (eds. Marcus, Beaman et al) pp. 95-101

THE APPLICATIONS AND BENEFITS OF
RAPID PROTOTYPING AT
TEXAS INSTRUMENTS INCORPORATED

Paul Blake

Texas Instruments Incorporated
Lewisville, Texas

1   Abstract

Texas Instruments Incorporated has successfully integrated StereoLithography rapid-prototyping technology into the mechanical, product, and manufacturing engineering design processes of the Defense Systems and Electronics Group. Use of rapid prototyping technology has resulted in improved design quality, has reduced product development cost and cycle time, and has aided the concurrent engineering methodology. The initial intent of rapid prototyping to provide concept models has been broadened by the development of additional engineering and manufacturing applications. These additional applications have significantly contributed to its acceptance and overall success. This paper reviews the brief history of rapid prototyping at Texas Instruments, outlines several engineering and manufacturing applications and provides an example program case study.

2   Introduction

Rapid prototyping is a significant addition to the technological improvements used by the engineering community to design and produce functional products. Its impact to improve design productivity is analogous to the introduction of CAD/CAM systems in the 1970's. Since rapid prototyping's introduction into the marketplace five years ago, numerous benefits have manifested themselves in all engineering disciplines. These benefits include improved design quality, reduced product development costs and cycle time, increased engineering and manufacturing productivity, and facilitation of concurrent engineering.

This paper outlines Texas Instruments (TI's) overall experience with rapid prototyping (RP) technology, specifically Stereolithography (SLA), its engineering and manufacturing applications, benefits received, and additional advanced applications developed within the investment casting industry. Applications and one case study are provided to outline typical benefits and cost and cycle time savings realized when SLA RP technology is used in the product development lifecycle.

3   Use of Rapid Prototyping within Texas Instruments

TI currently utilizes rapid prototyping equipment produced by 3D Systems, specifically the SLA-250™ and SLA-500™. Four SLA-250s are used at three different locations (Lewisville, McKinney, and Temple, Texas). These sites represent the Defense Systems and Electronics Group (DSEG) and Data Systems Divisions of TI. The SLA-500 is grouped with two of the SLA-250s at the Lewisville Texas facility. Three of the SLA-250s have been in use since 1989. The forth SLA-250 was added in 1990. The SLA-500 was acquired in 1991 to increase the overall capacity and ability to produce larger parts from 10 in. x 10 in. x 10 in. (25.4 cm x 25.4 cm x 25.4 cm) on the SLA-250 to 20 in. x 20 in. x 24 in. (50.8 cm x 50.8 cm x 60.9 cm) on the SLA-500.

268

Solid-model computer data bases are used as the inputs to the different rapid prototyping facilities. No 2-D or 3-D wireframe data bases are used because of the incomplete nature of their data sets. Surface wireframe data bases, if constructed correctly, are used. Data inputs are received via communication links and local area networks from the various engineering development sites across the United States.

Since the initial installation of the three SLA-250s, over 4,500 parts have been produced of approximately 1,250 unique designs. The parts have been used for various purposes, including models for: concept form, fit, and function checks, assembly fit checks, engineering analysis, design optimization, methods and tooling studies, wire and cable routing optimization, human factors studies, and marketing concept communication. Secondary applications have been developed, including the substitution of the wax pattern with an SLA part in the investment casting process and the development of temporary tooling for potting molds. These applications are used throughout the product design cycle. The majority of the parts produced at TI are in the detailed and assembly part design phases. Figure 1 outlines the overall product development phases and shows which applications are typically used within each phase.

Each of these applications has provided substantial benefit to the engineering and manufacturing community. Specifically, these benefits include enhanced visualization capability, improved design integrity and quality, lower development costs, and shorter cycle times for concept model production and preproduction investment castings. These benefits will be discussed in detail in the applications and case study sections.

4   Applications and Benefits

Numerous engineering applications exist for rapid prototyping parts. Other industry specific applications have also been developed. Examples include plastic injection mold tooling, spray metal tooling, and plating. Four engineering and manufacturing rapid prototyping applications used at TI are discussed in this section. They include prototype models, wax pattern substitution for investment castings, potting mold tooling, and concept communication models.

4.1   Prototype Models

The fundamental application of rapid prototyping is to produce prototype models for design engineers. The current SLA prototype turnaround cycle, defined as time from database receipt to part fabrication completion, is between two and ten days. This is a dramatic decrease over conventional methods which typically take months. Therefore, earlier in the design cycle the engineering team may visually, dimensionally, and functionally inspect and review part and assembly designs. This capability allows the design engineer to iterate new ideas into the design. Also, subsequent design and assembly problems are eliminated that would not have been found until later in the design cycle. Figure 2 shows the overall design cycle and how the typical problem found loop may be reduced by utilizing computer modeling and rapid prototyping. This results in two specific benefits: design improvement and product development cycle time reduction.

Rapid prototyping is not the only method used to visualize and produce a prototype model. Various methods have been used in the past to different degrees of success. They include paper dolls, computer models, and machining from stock. Table 1 compares these methods according to cost, cycle time, part accuracy, visualization capability, part strength, and assembly capability. Clearly, the rapid prototype part provides the cheapest functional part in the shortest time. This benefit alone has provided the engineering community with the ability to produce a computer solid or surface model and have a functional prototype back in their hands within days instead of weeks to months at a significantly reduced cost.

Before TI began using rapid prototyping, typical prototype models were built using conventional machining methods. An example part that demonstrates typical cost and cycle time savings is illustrated in Figure 3. The pictured housing assembly consists of two parts and was initially fabricated from wrought aluminum. Each part cost $3,000 and was completed in four weeks. A second iteration was needed to accommodate design requirement changes. This time, the SLA RP technology was chosen to build the prototype parts. The parts were built for $175 each in four days (actual machine run time was 18 hours). This represents a 20X cost reduction and a 7X decrease in cycle time. The second set of prototype parts allowed the design engineer to verify that the incorporated changes were correct and ready for manufacturing release. A total of $5,500 and three weeks were saved!

A second example is provided in Figure 4. It shows a series of electronic chassis built in nine months. The first four parts (from left to right) were used as design evaluation models, from the initial geometry concept to the detailed feature design. The final two chassis are investment casting model iterations. (See investment casting application.) Each model was fabricated in approximately five days. Actual machine build time was approximately eighteen hours. This turnaround time shows a five-week savings over conventional machining methods.

These models have been used for such specific applications as customer, management, and engineering reviews, as well as human factor studies. The prototype model also provided the engineer a tool to concisely communicate functional design intent with the customer. For example, the proposed placement of a particular knob did not follow the customer's specified design guidelines. However, the design engineer believed that the proposed placement was within the customer's functional requirements and provided a superior design. With the SLA model present, the proposed design was approved in one meeting with the customer. Without the model, the ability to visualize and functionally test the concept would have been limited to 2D drawings. The decision would have been delayed for additional study, causing lost cycle time and additional cost.

Another prototype model application is the ability to verify piece part assembly and methodology. The chassis in Figure 4 houses approximately 25 subassemblies, which break down into over 250 different parts. The engineer assembled the piece parts together, then determined part clearances, interferences, assembly methodology, and flex circuit routing and lengths. Nine different part interferences were found and corrected in the design phase of the program. This early detection avoided material scrap, part rework, and engineering change notices in the manufacturing and assembly phases of the program. Just as important, the engineer determined that numerous assembly clearances did meet the assembly requirements.

4.2   Investment Casting

A significant and immediate impact on the cost and cycle time associated with the investment casting process has been achieved with SLA RP technology. The SLA part is used as a substitute for the wax pattern part in the investment casting process. This eliminates the need for low-production-run wax pattern tooling. The TI Defense Systems Electronics Group product development and production cycles apply particularly well to this cost saving process. Typical initial delivery requirements are for low production quantities of below twenty systems. This low quantity makes the investment casting process less effective because of the high costs and long lead times for wax pattern tooling. Thus, castings are typically not integrated into the system until the full-scale production phase is implemented.

The two types of investment casting processes are solid mold (sometimes known as "flask" casting) and shell casting. They differ only in the method used to form the ceramic mold. Currently, the most successful procedure is to use the SLA part as a wax pattern substitute in the solid mold process. In the shell process, the SLA part expands more than the traditional wax pattern as it is heated to melt it from the mold. This increased expansion causes the SLA part pattern to crack the weaker mold in the shell process, but not in the metal-reinforced mold of the solid-mold process. (It should be noted that newer resins and additional processes are becoming available that will eliminate this problem with the shell-mold.)

Four specific benefits have resulted from the development of this process. First, cycle time has been reduced by 50 percent from between four and six months to between six and eight weeks (including SLA part generation). Second, the tooling costs are postponed until full-scale production. (Typical tooling costs range from $5,000 to $40,000.) Third, when tooling is generated for full-scale production, the initial part design has been completed. The need to change the tooling while in fabrication to accommodate part design changes is eliminated. This results in an overall saving of typically 30 to 40 percent of the original cost of the tool. Fourth, the system may be qualified to meet the customer's structural requirements as cast parts, not machined parts. Therefore, as the program progresses into full-scale production, the structural qualification of the system has already been completed using cast parts.

Over 400 castings have been produced using this process. Figure 5 is an example of a casting made from an SLA part pattern. The initial requirement for the part shown in Figure 5 was to produce 12 castings. However, the wax tooling was delayed and over 100 parts were subsequently produced over a period of four months. This process, even though intended for low-scale production, allowed the program to maintain delivery schedule until production tooling became available. The parts shown in Figure 6 (electronic chassis discussed in the prototype applications section) and Figure 7 are other examples of the types of part geometry that have been cast.

4.3   Potting Mold Tooling

Several applications were not anticipated in the initial phases of rapid prototyping implementation in Texas Instruments. As design engineers have become more acquainted with its capabilities additional applications have been developed. Temporary tooling for potting molds is one such application.

Figure 8 shows a flex circuit, an SLA potting mold, and an example piece made from the mold. In this example, the flex circuit would break because of the twisting and bending motions as it was assembled and disassembled. A strain relief was designed to reduce the stress and keep the cable from breaking during assembly. Before the strain relief could be implemented into production, the part design and the potting material had to be tested to ensure that they met the specified requirements.

The engineer decided to use a SLA part as temporary mold tooling to produce test parts. The testing was done in two phases. Several SLA models of the potting mold were produced in the initial phase. Parts made from the mold demonstrated that the selected material was satisfactory, but that the design geometry could not provide sufficient strain relief. Therefore, the design was iterated and a new SLA model was produced. The second design proved that the geometry did meet the strain relief requirements. When testing was completed, the mold geometry was provided to the supplier for production integration.

Overall, the program was able to design, produce temporary tooling, determine the correct material, and test the design functionality within a two week cycle. This was accomplished without formal drawings, hard tooling, or vendor manufacturing cycles. Cost savings are estimated to be over $40,000 in engineering and technician labor, tooling materials, and scrap elimination. Also, two months in cycle time was saved.

4.4   Concept Communication Models

SLA RP parts have also facilitated the ability to generate customer communication concept models for a decreased cost over conventional methods. The models are used for proposals as well as to show system concept and design progress to various vendors, supplies, and customers. Figure 9 shows a system that has been built, painted, and had additional hardware assembled to represent the proposed system. Customer feedback has been very supportive of the model. The model is repeatedly used in meetings to facilitate clear communication when discussing part geometry, systems interface, functional requirements, etc.

4.5   Other Applications and Benefits

Other engineering and manufacturing applications are currently in use and under development. Air-flow analysis and optimization, radar cross-section analysis, vendor quotes, and ergonomic studies are four such applications. Each application has unique benefits for each particular engineer, program, and industry. Future developments and improvements include stress analysis techniques, shell-mold casting processes, and materials to produce a part in the correct end-state material.

5   Case Study

SLA RP technology has been used on numerous active programs within the past three years. Program application and use depends upon program requirements. The following case study shows details of one program's SLA RP applications, cost savings, and cycle time improvements.

A program was studied that extensively used the SLA RP technology for various applications. Initial program requirements dictated that more than twelve unique parts be designed, analyzed, and manufactured (quantity of sixteen pieces per part) within a six-month cycle. Part size ranged from 3 inches to 36 inches, shape from medium to very complex, and functionality from simple covers to complex bulkheads. These requirements provided a significant challenge to the project design and manufacturing engineers.

The engineers decided to extensively use SLA parts in all phases of the program. Specific applications included piece part and assembly models for engineering evaluations for part fit checks, tooling and wire routing definition, and customer reviews. Also, to meet the manufacturing cycle time and cost requirements, three alternative approaches were studied. These approaches included the traditional methods of machining from wrought stock, investment castings from wax patterns, and investment casting in the solid-mold process using the SLA parts as the wax substitute. Using the SLA parts in the investment casting process was chosen for eight of the parts. The eight parts selected were the large and complex housing and bulkheads. The remaining parts were manufactured by traditional machining methods.

The SLA-part investment casting process met the program requirements while providing a shorter production cycle at a reduced cost. Figure 10 compares the cycle time, cost, and additional available design time of the three manufacturing processes studied to fabricate the eight parts. The SLA pattern investment casting process resulted in cost savings of over $335,000 and two months cycle time over machining from wrought stock. In comparison to the investment castings process a savings of over $115,000 and three months in cycle time was realized.

In addition to the overall manufacturing benefits, several engineering benefits were realized. Each part was produced for prototype evaluation in its cast and machined configurations. The following are examples of the benefits and lessons learned.

1) Prototype parts were used for part and assembly design verification. Approximately one of every four required design iterations resulted from problems that the prototype models clearly demonstrated. These ranged from part interference to cable connector misalignment. If the prototype parts had not been built the detection of the design problems would not have been found until each part was manufactured two to four months later in the design cycle. Also, additional time and materials would have been used resulting in a significant cost and cycle time increase.

2) The engineer was able to iterate the design up to eight weeks later in the design cycle without negatively impacting other manufacturing lead time and cost requirements. (See Figure 10) This was beneficial because three parts underwent several design changes within that period, which would have substantially increased the overall cost of tool production or machining.

3) The ability to use the investment casting process allowed the design engineer to apply design-for-assembly principles, combining smaller parts into one part on four occasions. An estimated sixteen parts would have been required if all parts were machined from stock.

4) A complete assembly of parts was used to assist in the cable routings and length optimization. Typically, this process is done using engineering judgement, drawings, and computer data bases. Optimization does not occur until each part is produced and the actual assembly is fabricated. The rapid prototype assembly enabled the engineers to optimize cable lengths and routings in the initial design phase. An estimated 30 to 40 engineering change notices were avoided and three month of cycle time were saved.

5) The structural analysis requalification cost of the system was eliminated. Before the SLA RP casting process was implemented, machined parts were typically used. Upon completion, the system would undergo structural qualification through a series of tests. As the program progresses into full-scale development, cast parts would replace the machined parts. This replacement of parts would require new system-structural-analysis qualification tests. Because cast parts were used from the initial phases of the program, the requalification costs of integrating castings into the system was avoided. This situation resulted in over $20,000 in savings.

6) The initial test gating castings were used as tooling proof parts for secondary machining operations. One step of the casting process is to establish a correct gate and runner system. Typically, the casting foundry requires four test SLA patterns to establish the gating requirements before acceptable castings are produced. Of the four test SLA patterns used patterns used at the foundry, one

274

test casting was returned to the engineer. This part was used as a tooling proof part for the subsequent machining operations, resulting in reduced machining cycle time and less scrap in the initial production lot.

The program used SLA RP technology to resolve engineering and manufacturing problems and to meet cycle time production and cost requirements. It is very difficult to quantify cost and cycle time avoidance savings because of the problems associated with estimating what might have taken place. However, it has been conservatively estimated that over $450,000 has been saved or avoided in overall costs! Finally, the program was able to fulfill very aggressive scheduling and delivery requirements. Program personnel have stated that the benefits of rapid prototyping have been a key factor to the meeting customer requirements and to the overall success of the program!

6   Conclusion

The different applications and the case study presented clearly demonstrate the benefits and savings of rapid prototyping technology. Texas Instruments uses these applications on a daily basis to continuously improve design quality, increase engineering productivity, and reduce development and production costs and cycle times. This continued improvement is a key to survival in today's competitive market environment. Rapid prototyping technology's future is bright as it continues to mature into the 1990's. One day rapid prototyping will become rapid production as part designs and tooling will be fabricated in the desired end-state material. Texas Instruments will continue to utilize and develop rapid prototyping technology and applications to remain competitive in today's and tomorrow's marketplace.

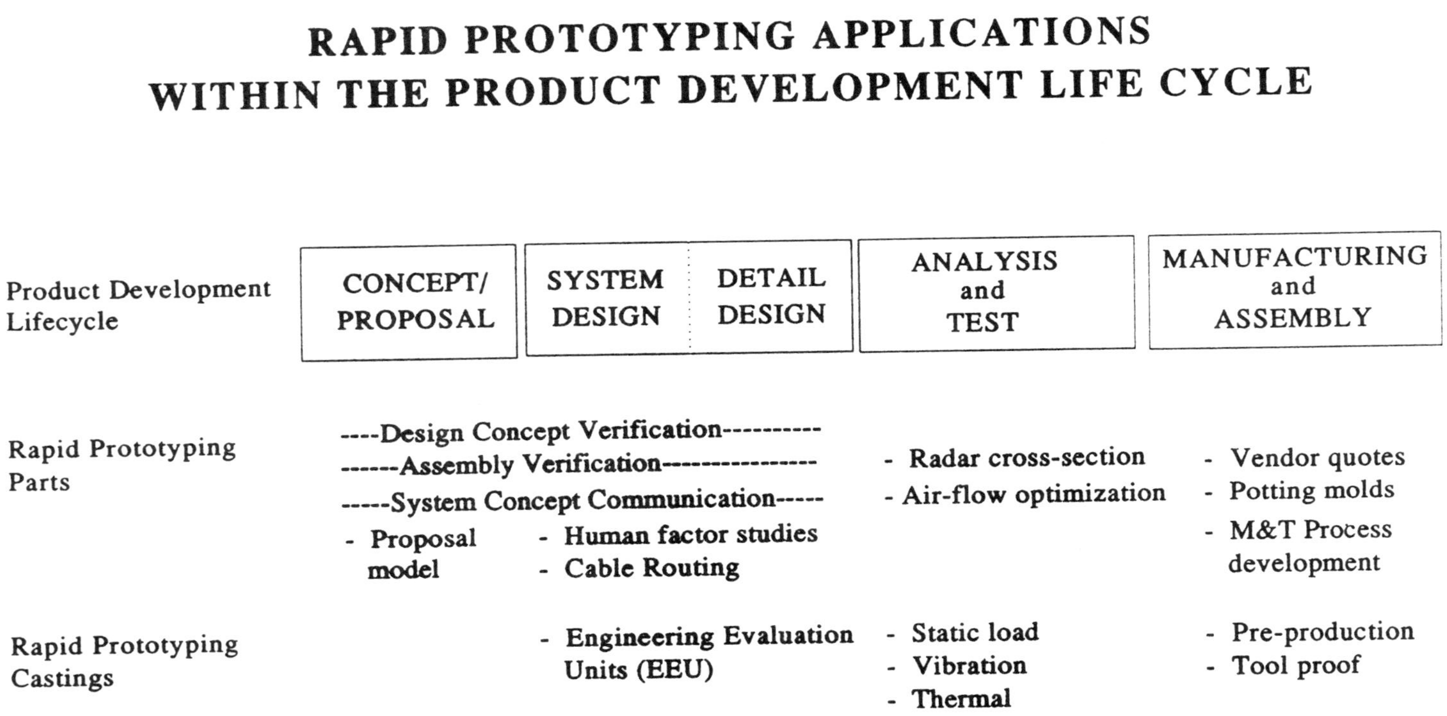

RAPID PROTOTYPING APPLICATIONS
WITHIN THE PRODUCT DEVELOPMENT LIFE CYCLE

Product Development Lifecycle	CONCEPT/ PROPOSAL	SYSTEM DESIGN	DETAIL DESIGN	ANALYSIS and TEST	MANUFACTURING and ASSEMBLY

Rapid Prototyping Parts

----Design Concept Verification----------
------Assembly Verification----------
------System Concept Communication------
- Proposal model
- Human factor studies
- Cable Routing

- Radar cross-section
- Air-flow optimization

- Vendor quotes
- Potting molds
- M&T Process development

Rapid Prototyping Castings

- Engineering Evaluation Units (EEU)

- Static load
- Vibration
- Thermal

- Pre-production
- Tool proof

Figure 1   Rapid prototyping applications in the product development life cycle

276

Mechanical Part and System
Product Development Life Cycle

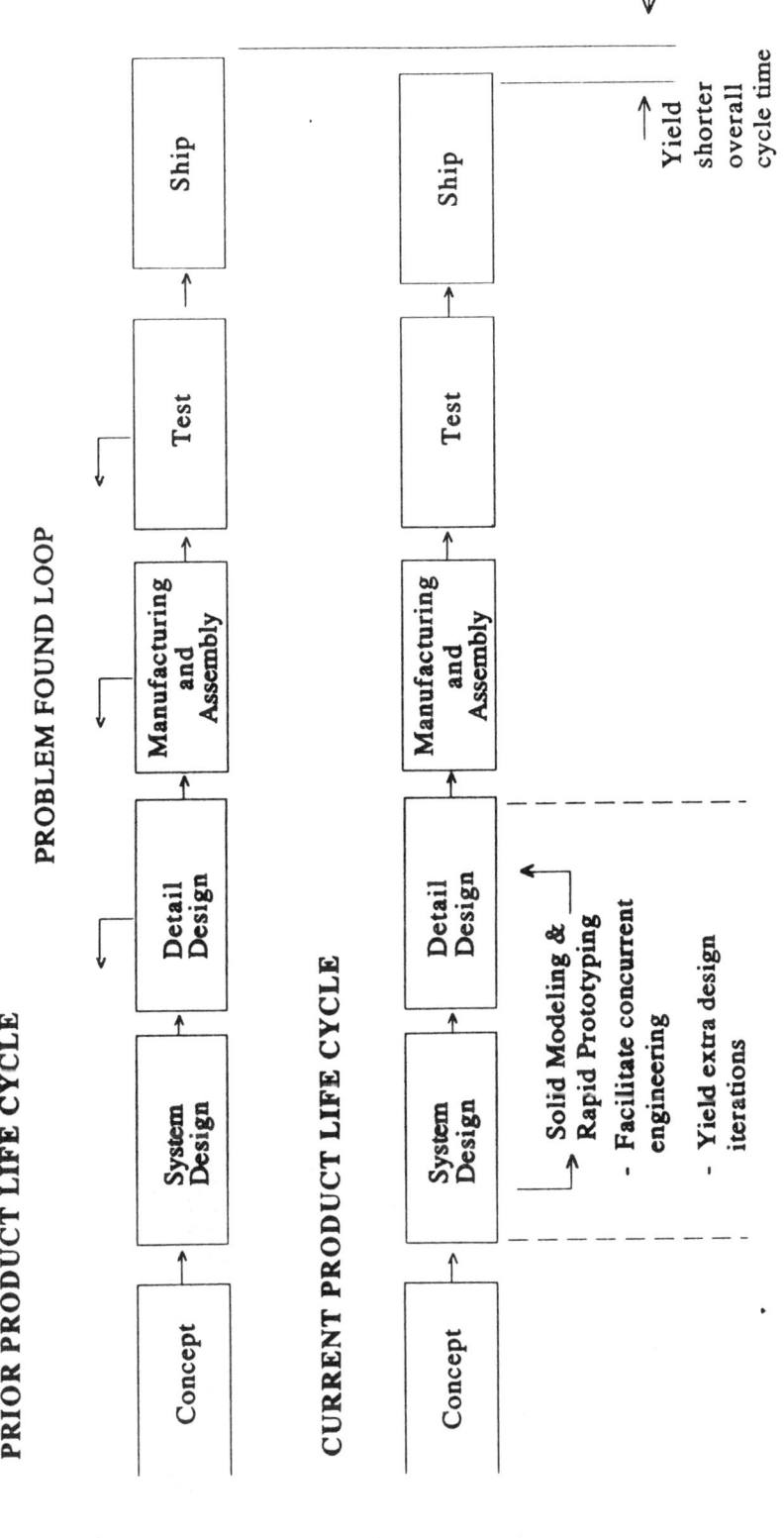

Figure 2   Problem-found loop in the product design cycle

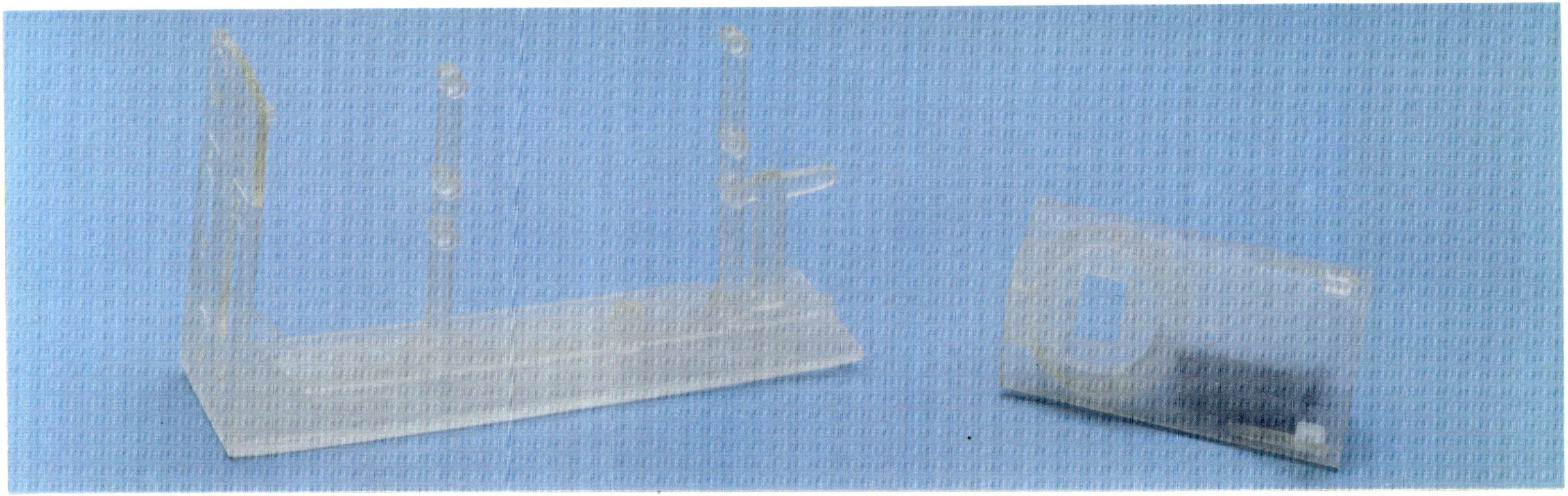

Figure 3   SLA RP Prototype part example

Figure 4   Example of part design over nine months

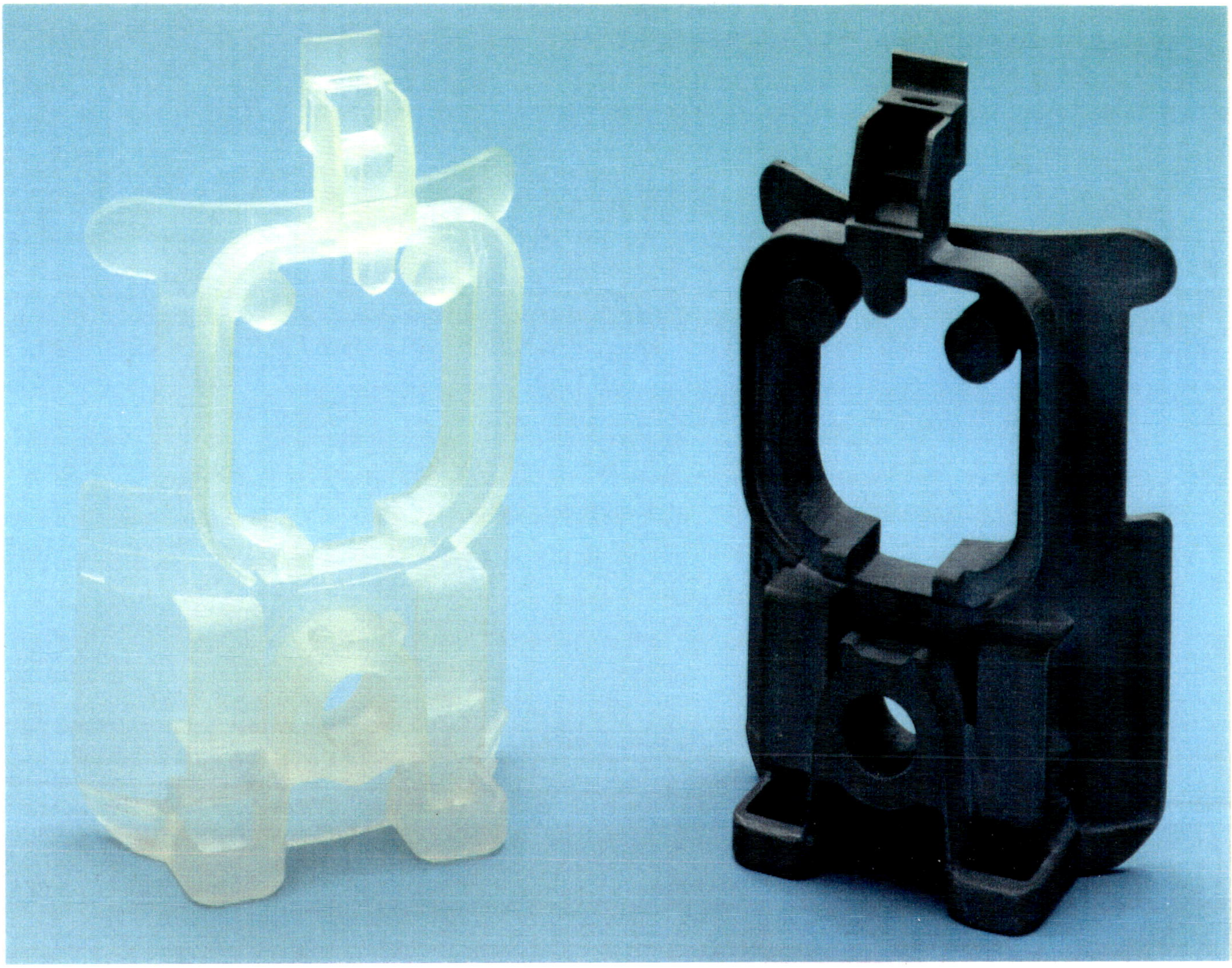

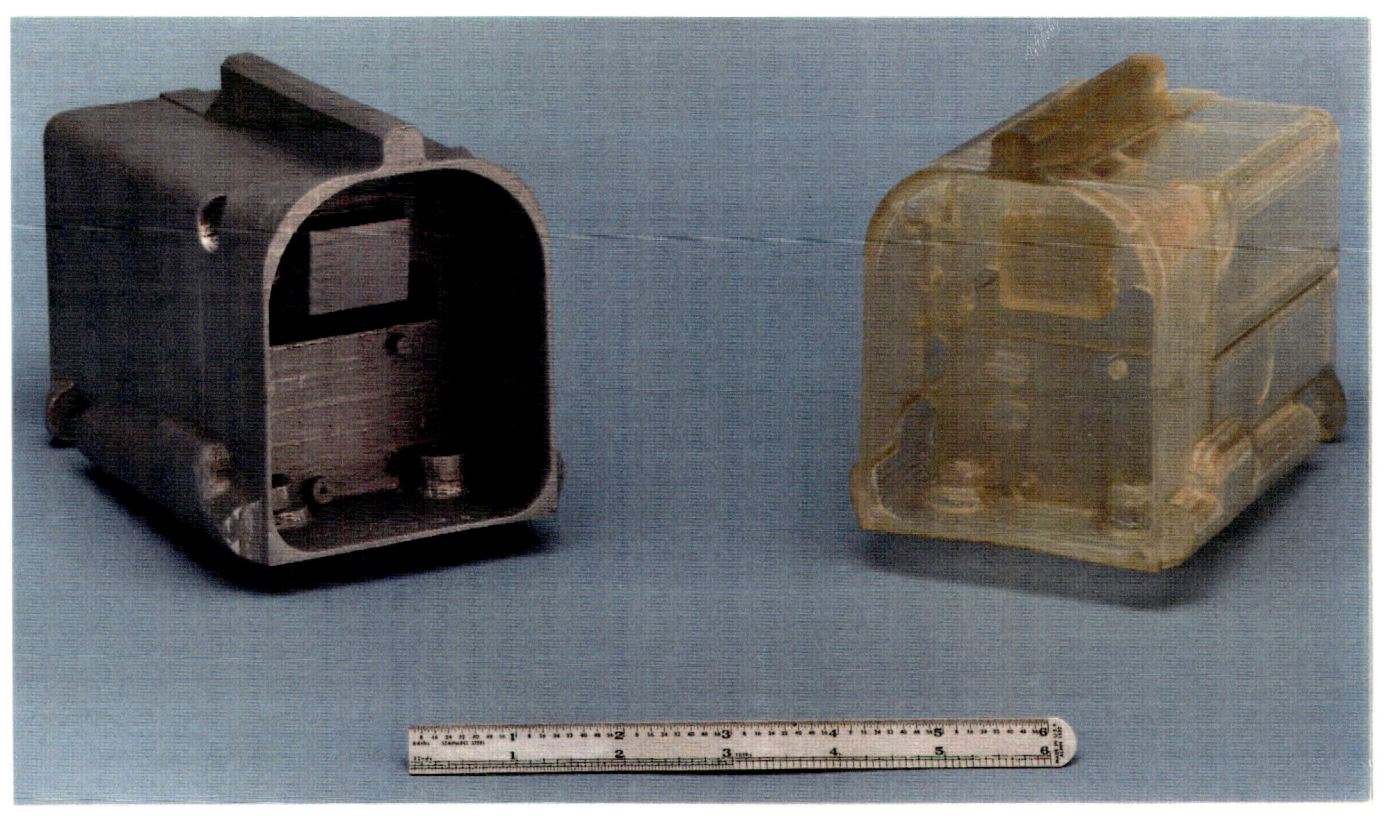

Figure 5   SLA Pattern and investment casting

Figure 6   SLA Pattern and investment casting

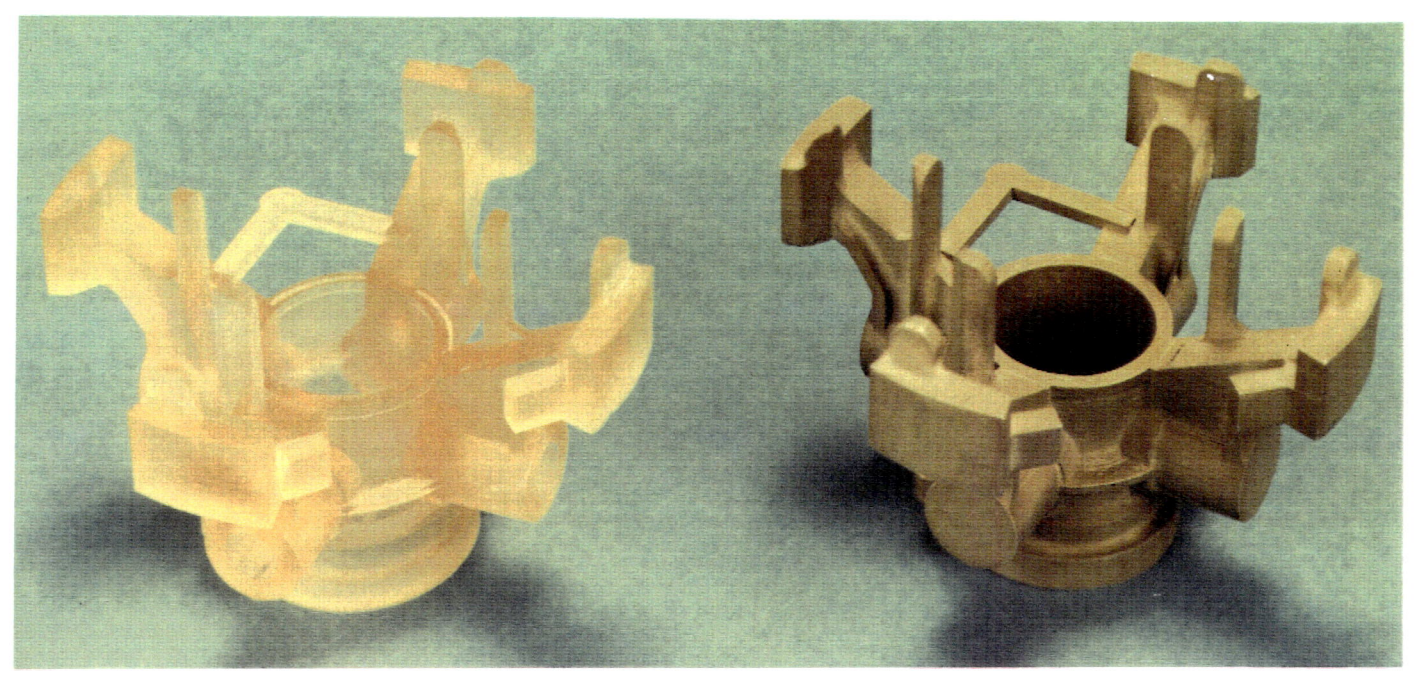

Figure 7   SLA Pattern and investment casting

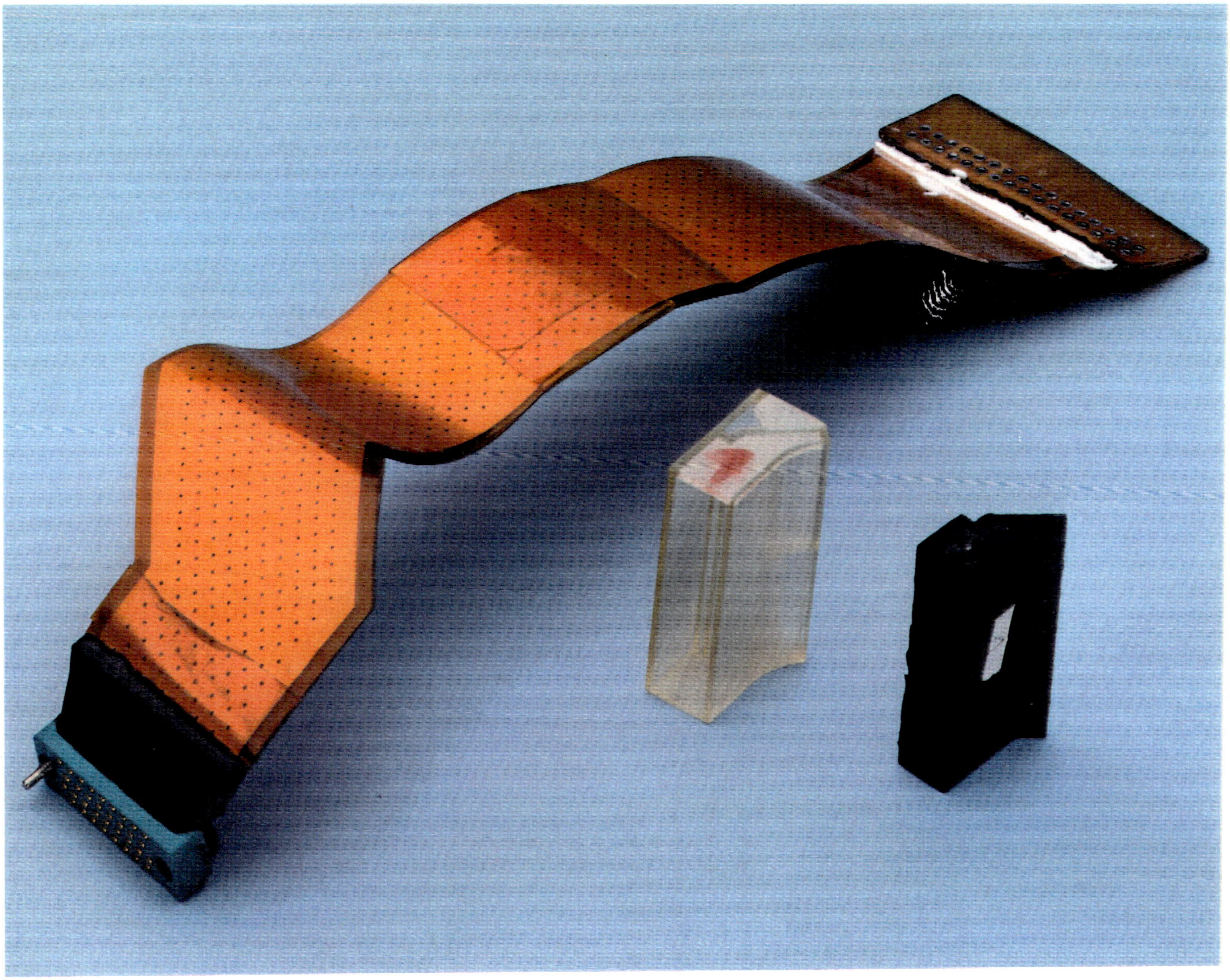

Figure 8   Temporary tooling application

Figure 9   Concept communication model application

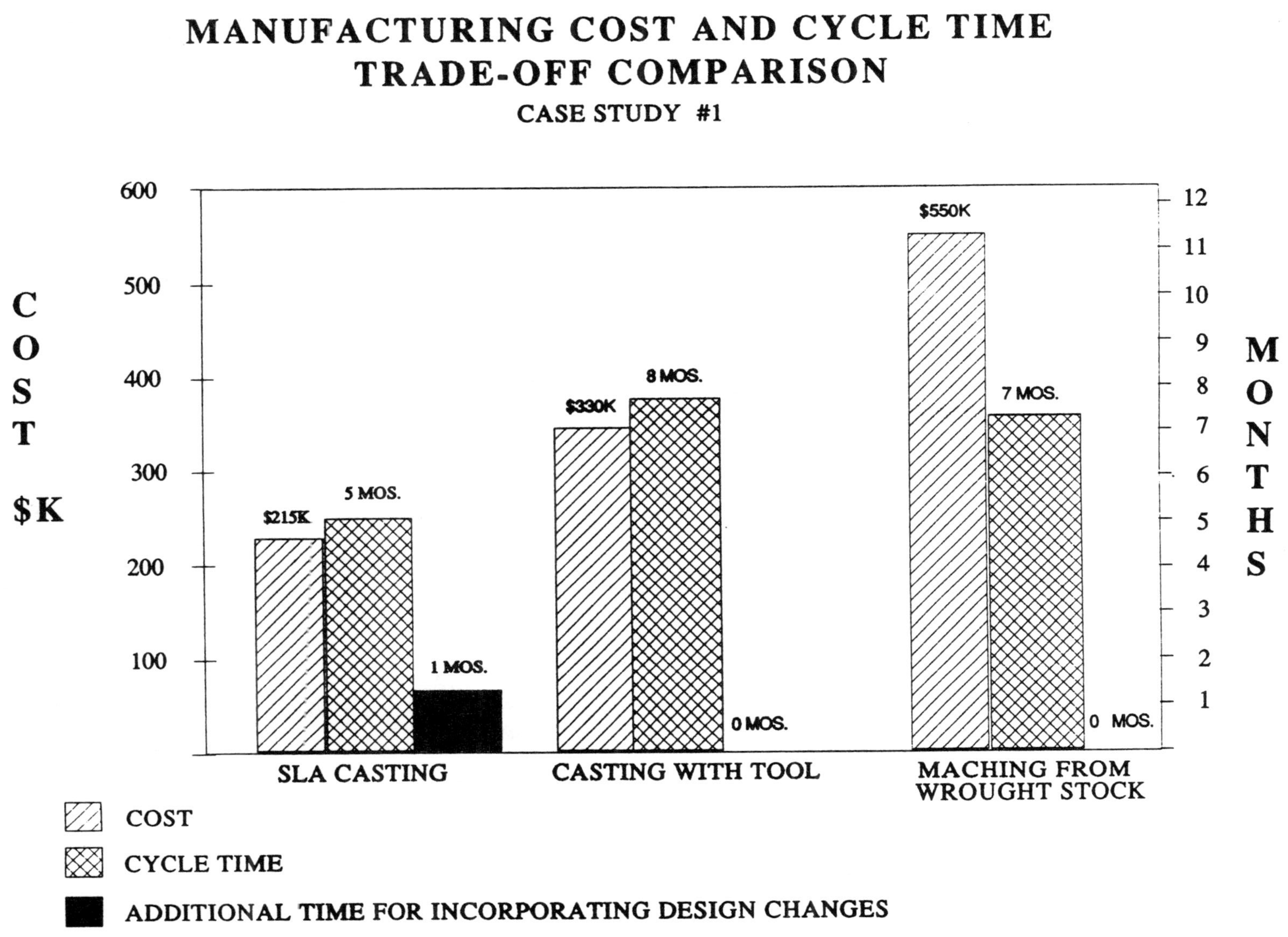

Figure 10 Cost and cycle time comparison

ENGINEERING PROTOTYPE MODEL & PART COMPARISON

	Cost	Cycle Time	Accuracy	Visualization	Part Strength	Assembly Capability
Wireframe[1]	Low	Days	Very Poor	Poor	N/A	Poor
Paper Doll	Low-Med[2]	Days-Weeks[2]	Very Good	Poor/Good	Poor	Poor
Solid Model[1]	Low-Med[2]	Days-Weeks[2]	Excellent	Good	N/A	Good
Rapid Prototype Part	Low	Days[3]	Very Good	Excellent	Good[4]	Very Good
Rapid Prototype Casting	Low-Med	Weeks[5]	Very Good	Excellent	Excellent	Very Good
Machined part from wrought stock	High	Weeks-Months[6]	Excellent	Excellent	Excellent	Excellent

1 COMPUTER GENERATED MODELS VERSUS PHYSICAL PROTOTYPES
2 LENGTH DEPENDS UPON DESIGN COMPLEXITY
3 TYPICALLY 2 TO 10 DAYS (PART CONFIGURATION DEPENDENT)
4 RESIN DEPENDENT; RESINS ARE IMPROVING
5 TYPICALLY 4 WEEKS (PART CONFIGURATION DEPENDENT)
6 TYPICALLY 4 TO 6 WEEKS (PART CONFIGURATION DEPENDENT)

Table 1   Prototype part comparison

288

STEREOLITHOGRAPHY TO TOOLING IN THE AUTOMOTIVE INDUSTRY

David Ian Wimpenny
Rover Advanced Technology Centre
University of Warwick

Graham Tromans
Stereolithography Department
Model Development - Forward Programmes
Rover Canley

John Upton
Stereolithography Department
Model Development - Forward Programmes
Rover Canley

Preface

A Stereolithography (SLA) facility has been operational in Rover (Canley) for the last twelve months. To date, the technique has been used to provide models for designer, to aid visualisation (fitment and aesthetics). However, the potential to develop the use of SLA technology was recognised early on.

As a natural development SLA models were installed in vehicles in an attempt to assess component performance. Unfortunately the current models are not ideally suited to this role due to their inherent brittleness and low temperature resistance.

As a result Rover has collaborated with the Advanced Technology Centre, at the University of Warwick, to develop techniques for producing tooling from SLA models to manufacture more suitable prototypes.

A facility for vacuum casting prototype components in silicone moulds has already been established and is operating successfully within the SLA department at Rover. Further developments have enabled the production of complex cored prototypes, in a wide variety of resins.

This paper describes the potential applications of SLA technology within the automotive industry, from prototype models to production tooling. Examples of the developments made to date are given.

1   Introduction

Twelve months ago a stereolithography facility was established at Rover,Canley,based around a 3D Systems inc,SLA-500 (see Figure 1). The initial role for the unit was to satisfy the demand for models of components for new vehicles. Over this last year, however, the full potential of this technology has become apparent, with applications from modelling through to production.

Applications include:-
1. Visualisation
2. Fitment
3. Flow analysis
4. Design analysis
4. Mechanical operation and light function testing
5. Full component performance verification
6. Tool development and manufacturing improvement
7. Low and medium volume production

2   Direct use of Stereolithography Models

The SLA process enables the conversion of CAD drawings to three dimensional models in a matter of hours, rather than days or weeks. Complex components which would be difficult to model using traditional modelling methods represent little problem for SLA (see Figure 2). The generation of models directly from the CAD data ensures that the most recent design revision is being utilised and that the influence of human skill is reduced.

The main application areas for SLA models are:-

2.1 Visualisation

A soon as an initial design is produced, all the separate engineering functions who need to have an input in to the way the component is designed, manufactured and assembled can sit around a table with the model. A model is a powerful visual tool, ensuring misinterpretation of two dimensional drawings is avoided. In particular changes to the design for ease of manufacturing or assembly can be made at a very early stage. External part suppliers can gain a rapid appreciation of the component required and thus calculate a more reliable price and delivery.

2.2 Fitment

Fitting parts to cars to check they can be assembled and do not foul neighbouring components should be undertaken as early as possible. Unfortunately the lack of reliable models often delayed this essential check, sometimes with disastrous results. The speed and reliability of SLA models enables a dramatic improvement to be made in this area.

3 Casting resin models in RTV Silicone moulds

Once an SLA model is fitted to a vehicle there is a natural desire to see if the model can be used to show whether the part functions correctly. Unfortunately SLA models are not ideally suited for the loading and temperature regime this often entails.

Limitation of SLA models:-

1. Limited mechanical property range
2. Very brittle
3. Poor elevated temperature resistance

The limitations of SLA models were anticipated by Rover, in addition to purchasing the SLA-500 machine, the SLA facility was also equipped with an MCP Vacuum Casting System (see Figure 3).

Silicone moulds are cast around SLA parts and these are used to cast models in more durable resins (usually polyurethane resins). The vacuum casting facility is used to produce both the silicone moulds and the resin parts (see Figure 4).

Vacuum casting has a number of benefits:-

a) No air entrapment
b) Clean environment (no contaminating debris)
c) Low humidity
d) Semi-automated process (consistent results)
e) Reduced health and safety problems

The moulds and resin parts are produced without any trapped air and the influence of varying atmospheric humidity is eliminated (particularly important for polyurethane resins). The process is semi-automated, thus reducing the influence of human error and more consistent components are produced. This is particularly important as the resin systems used are very fast curing to increase the production rate. With a pot life measured in seconds, vacuum casting is the only way consistent results can be ensured. The enclosing of the casting process significantly reduces the health and safety risk and maintains the integrity of the working environment.

3.1 Matching the appearance and 'feel' of models to the production part

Where closer aesthetic matching of models to the production component is required then SLA models can be filled and sanded to produce a smooth surface finish, comparable with that of the production part (see Figure 5). Moreover, a wide variety of resins can be cast to match the 'feel' and mechanical performance of the intended component. Indeed, where the ultimate choice of material for the part is still under review the effect of varying the properties of the material can be assessed by casting parts in different resins. Rover have experience of producing prototype models which mimic materials from rigid thermoplastics to flexible elastomers (see Figure 6).

3.2 Flow Analysis

The ease with which SLA can produce complex hollow geometry has enabled models to be made which would have been impossible to produce by conventional modelling methods (see Figure 7).

In addition to allowing visualisation of these components, the SLA models can be used for gas or fluid flow analysis. Indeed, the ability to produce transparent models allows analysis of flow by means and to a level of pinpoint accuracy, otherwise impossible. Unfortunately, many of the applications where fluid/gas flow is involved are located in the hostile under-bonnet environment. The low temperature resistance of the current SLA resin (Cibatool-XB5131) allows only short-term elevated temperature testing to take place. To obtain information from room temperature tests requires the use of fluids with a viscosity which matches that of the real working fluid at the elevated operating temperatures. In addition to the time and detailed data required to formulate these fluids, the information from the tests cannot be used to predict certain fluid flow phenomena, such as cavitation for example.

Though the introduction of more durable SLA resin systems will reduce this problem, Rover has also been developing prototyping methods to enable the production of complex hollow parts in a wide variety of materials.

Techniques based on both fusible and soluble core technology have been investigated and developed. These cores combined with the standard silicone moulds allow high temperature resin parts to be cast (see Figure 8). In addition to producing components in high temperature resins, metal parts have also been manufactured.

Lost core techniques are currently under development to enable models of cylinderheads to be produced in resin for flow analysis. In the case of a cylinderhead it may prove simpler to use SLA models of the water, gas and oilways (ie. the negative of the component) rather than a model of the cylinderhead.

3.3 Design Analysis

Component performance prediction by design analysis is a vital part of the development process and an area where SLA can play a vital role. The performance of many components is only verified by testing prototype parts, a stage which comes late in the development phase, leaving little time for amendments to be made to the design.

An alternative approach which has been developed at Rover Gaydon is to use SLA models (both directly and indirectly) to perform empirical design analysis tests such a photoelastic analysis and SPATE (stress pattern analysis by thermal emission).

Photoelastic analysis relies upon the birefringence of certain materials (transparent plastics in the main) which means that their optical properties are changed when load is applied.

The optical change of models under load can be measured and used to calculate the stress in the proposed production part. Though SLA resins are birefringent, SLA models cannot be used directly for photoelastic analysis as significant levels of stress are locked in to the parts during manufacture. Instead models are cast in a suitable material (usually epoxy resin) using a silicone mould. Improvements in SLA resins and build patterns may enable the direct use of SLA models for photoelastic testing in the future.

The direct use of SLA models is possible with SPATE analysis. SPATE works by detecting minute temperature changes in structures submitted to cyclic loading. By cyclically loading SLA models it is possible to measure these small temperature changes on the surface of the models and thereby calculate the stress in the proposed part. A correlation between tests conducted on SLA models and actual components has been established (See Figure 9).

Both photoelastic and SPATE techniques can show high stress points in a component allowing design modification to be made very early on. This approach can be faster than FE techniques and provides representative models which can be loaded exactly as the intended component.

3.4 Optical components

The complexity of modern automotive light cluster units make them ideal candidates for production by SLA techniques. In addition to passive visualisation and fitment, the ability to produce parts which can function optically is desirable. The production of optical quality components in different coloured transparent resins is possible by vacuum casting, as parts with no air inclusions are produced. Optical quality lighting components have been cast in resin at Rover using silicone moulds, cloned from current production parts (see Figure 10). Unfortunately is has not been possible to obtain similar parts using SLA models as patterns for silicone moulds, as even the smallest surface blemish will significantly undermine the optical integrity. Improvements in the surface finish of SLA models, combined with better finishing techniques (perhaps plating), offer the best hope of reaching this goal in the future.

3.5   Large components

The current size limitation of SLA models has not presented a major problem for Rover. The vast majority of automotive components (as with most engineering parts) can be accommodated within the 500mm (approximately) cube available for the SLA-500 machine. Indeed the efficient use of the machine when producing small components has presented more of a problem. Where large components are required, scaling the models (for example half size) can suffice in some cases (see Figure 11).

When this has not been appropriate, models have been produced in separate sections and then adhered together. To aid assembly, location features can be incorporated into the sections (see Figure 12).

As a result of the size limitation of the vacuum casting facility, where resin castings of large parts have been required these have also been produced in sections and adhered or fastened together. Indeed parts have been modified to provide suitable flanges for joining. To enable large components to be moulded in one piece the use of resin injection moulding (RIM) technology, with rigid moulds is being investigated.

4   Prototype production and tooling

Prototype parts must be considered as distinct from models. To produce prototype components, which are suitable for full performance validation, parts must be produced which compare closely with the intended production component, this usually means the same material and production process. To enable the full range of performance tests (fatigue, static strength and stiffness and environmental test) up to one hundred prototype parts may be required.

Prototype production is not just important for component performance testing, an essential aspect of prototype production is tool development and manufacturing trials. For plastic automotive parts the production methods are generally injection moulding, blow moulding and vacuum forming, with a small percentage of compression moulded items. For metallic components metal pressings constitute a large proportion of parts, cast , machined and forged items complete the picture.

The use of RTV silicone tooling is limited to low pressure, low volume and low temperature production processes. Silicone moulds distort under pressure, even their own weight or the weight of the cast resin. Because of the generally poor surface on SLA parts, wear or damage to silicone moulds can be very high, allowing the production of only 10-20 parts. Thus prototype (soft) tooling methods are under development to enable up to one hundred representative prototype parts to be produced using the various manufacturing techniques. SLA models are being adopted as the master pattern to enable this tooling to be manufactured.

5 Low/Medium Volume Production

The current trend in the automotive industry is away from a small range of mass produced vehicles to a wider range of vehicles, produced in lower volumes. These vehicles can be targeted at a particular 'niche' in the market, providing customers with products that more closely match their needs.

Unfortunately, the lower production volumes (ranging perhaps from 3,000 to 50,000 PA.) mean that the current high volume production technology is inappropriate. In particular, tooling with a life of over 1 million components is too costly to amortise over low/medium volume production quantities. Moreover the long lead-time to manufacture production tools delays the vehicle launch date and thus erodes the market lead.

Soft tooling techniques that can satisfy the required production quantities at a lower cost and much shorter lead-times than traditional tooling methods, will be a key technology in automotive industry of the future. Rover recognised the vital importance of lower volume tooling techniques and a research group was established at the Advanced Technology Centre (ATC) to develop this technology.

A serious flaw in the viability of soft tooling methods is their inherent reliance on a master pattern. The existence or accuracy of this master pattern could not always be relied upon, thus calling in to question the whole principle of soft tooling. If it proved necessary to machine the master pattern then cutter paths had to be generated, leaving soft tooling with little advantage over machining the tool conventionally. The emerging technology of SLA thus provided the vital method for producing a pattern quickly and cheaply.

5.1 SLA to Tooling Development Programme

The SLA facility at Rover (Canley) was established primarily to produce models however, the potential for developing the process was recognised early on. One particular area of interest was the use of SLA to produce tooling from prototype up to medium volume production. It was therefore natural that a collaborative project was formed between the Rover SLA department and the soft tooling Group at the ATC to explore the potential further.

5.1.1 Facilities in Rover Stereolithography Department

To enable the production of models in a wide variety of resins, within one department, the following equipment was installed:-

a) 3D Systems inc, SLA-500
b) Sparc Station 52P, Silicon Graphics computer 25G
c) MCP Vacuum casting system (MCP-004MC Vacuum casting unit and MCP-H400 Vacuum heating unit)
d) UV ovens (post-curing apparatus)
e) Shotblasting unit

5.1.2 Facilities at the Advanced Technology Centre

The Advanced Technology Centre is ideally equipped to undertake research in to both plastic and metal forming tooling (see Figure 13 & 14).

The production equipment includes:-

a)   200 tonne - Dual injection Battenfeld injection moulding machine
b)   100 tonne - compression moulding machine
c)   RIM press and resin injection machine
d)   Vacuum forming machine (1m x 1m platen size)
e)   Compression moulding lab test machine
f)   Metal casting facility
g)   Soft tooling manufacturing facility including metal spray and resin/glass spray equipment

Test equipment to support the tool development programme includes:-

h)   Coordinate measuring machine
i)   Wear test equipment
j)   Tensile, compressive, flexural and torsional test equipment
k)   Ultrasonic NDT equipment
l)   Dedicated component test rigs

5.2 Accuracy of SLA Models

Errors in the dimensional accuracy of SLA models are often neither apparent, nor important, when they are used for visualisation. Even for fitment trials, flexibility in the model usually enables the part to be assembled successfully. However, when producing tooling any error in the model will be reproduced in the tool, with serious consequences for any components subsequently manufactured.

In theory the linear accuracy of components produced by SLA has improved significantly in recent years, figures of 0.005" (0.127mm) have been quoted (Jacobs & Richter 1991). There is little doubt that with equipment correctly set-up these figures are attainable on simple, flat components. Indeed, the accuracy of 3D SLA equipment is checked routinely using a flat test specimen, commonly referred to as a christmas tree.

However in tests conducted at the ATC, the dimensions of real, three dimensional, SLA parts have been found to differ significantly from the CAD model. Deviations approaching 1mm have been measured in a 100mm long component (water elbow). These tests indicate that the error does not arise from the initial creation of the model, in the SLA bath, but in subsequent handling and post-curing. In particular the handling of the model in the 'green' state to remove the supports can lead to distortion. Care must also be exercised during post-curing to avoid heat build up (too rapid cure), this is known to produce warping. Providing alternative support to models once the SLA supports have been removed is vital otherwise parts will be post-cured in a distorted position.

Improvements to the handling, support removal, post-curing routine have been implemented which have lead to a dramatic reduction in the distortion of the particular component studied, from 1mm to 0.25mm. Unfortunately this is not a universal solution, the level of error depends upon the particular component and the skill of operator. Techniques for handling, removal of supports and subsequent post-curing must be improved and if possible automated, as a matter of urgency.

The long term dimensional stability of SLA models is also currently under investigation. If this cannot be relied upon then 'fresh' SLA models will be used to produce resin master moulds or new SLA models produced when required.

Until a reliable method of producing accurate models is developed, SLA models will be checked with a coordinate measuring machine, prior to their use as master patterns for tool manufacture.

5.3   Surface Finish

An inherent problem with SLA models to date, has been their relatively poor surface finish, caused by the increment of the model in the bath. This is particularly noticeable on inclined surfaces in the horizontal plane and on cylindrical features with horizontal axes.

The majority of soft tooling techniques accurately reproduce the surface finish of the pattern. In principle it should be easier to improve the surface quality of the model than improve the finish of the soft tool, which tend to be hard and wear resistant.

Techniques have been developed to improve the surface finish of SLA models, primarily to enable visual matching of models to finished components. These methods are laborious and their success depends on the skill of the craftsman.

A technique employed at Rover is to paint the surface of the model with UV curable resin, the same type as used for the model, which is then cured locally using a portable UV light source. The resin is built up until the model is smooth. The surface is then 'cut back' with abrasive paper until the peaks of the SLA model just become visible. In theory, undertaken correctly, this method should just fill the steps in the surface, without significantly undermining component accuracy. Tests are currently in progress to assess the repeatability of the method.

5.4   Soft Tooling - Technology of Interest

5.4.1   Metal faced tooling:

Electrodeposited or metal spray shell, backed with metal filled resin or low melting point alloys, using SLA model as the pattern.

5.4.2   Electrodischarge machining (EDM) electrodes:

Hausermann abrading process or metal spray/electrodeposited shell, backed with resin or metal, using SLA models as the pattern.

5.4.3 Investment casting from SLA models:

Direct use of SLA models as lost cores for investment casting using the honeycomb method. Indirect use of SLA models to produce tooling for soluble or fusible core materials.

5.4.4 Lost cores for plastic forming:

Use of SLA models as patterns to produce tooling for fusible and soluble cores for injection moulding and RIM.

5.4.5 SLA models for sand casting:

Use of SLA models directly as patterns or indirectly to cast resin patterns for sand casting.

5.4.6 Press tooling from SLA models:

The use of resin faced (polyurethane resin or slate filled epoxy resin) press tooling is established technology within Rover, for the production of prototype pressed steel/aluminium components. This technology is under development to enable the production of larger numbers of components. SLA models, suitably finished, could be employed as patterns against which the resin tools are cast. In the short term this approach could be used for small pressed components. For larger panels plaster masters are currently used, but with improvement in the SLA technique, including an increase in the maximum component size and better surface finish, body panels from SLA models may become a reality.

5.5 Development of SLA models for tooling

Where tooling becomes the ultimate aim behind the production of SLA models there will need to be a shift away from using the standard model of intended component, to models designed with tooling in mind. These could incorporate tapers, shrinkage allowance, split-lines, runners and risers and features to ensure alignment of tool sections. This move, together with tool development during prototyping, will ensure that manufacturing is considered very early in the development process.

6   Summary

The demand for new technology from SLA users and the eagerness of SLA equipment suppliers to develop the process means that SLA is a rapidly moving field with new resins, build patterns and completely new systems under development. SLA has implications for manufacturing industry from design to prototype and production, as graphically illustrated in the automotive industry.

The potential uses for SLA would appear endless, indeed they will be only be limited by our imagination to apply this technology.

References

Jacobs, P.F. Richter, J. Advances in stereolithography accuracy, 3D Systems Inc. August 1991.

Bibliography

Bak, D.J. Quick path to prototype tooling. Design News. June 25, 1990.

Baum, R. Speed in the art of fashioning models. The Engineer. 23/30 April 1992.

Jacobs, P.F. Richter, J. Advances in stereolithography accuracy, 3D Systems Inc. August 1991.

Napier, S. (Ed) Ciba-Geigy Resin Aspects, Edition 26, 1991, Publ.No 38165/e 910430/230.

Weiss, L.E et al. A rapid tool manufacturing system based on stereolithography and thermal spraying. ASME Manufacturing Review, September 1989.

Acknowledgements

The authors wish to thank Geoff Calvert, Principal Engineer, Experimental Stress Analysis, Kevin Allin, Senior Engineer, Test Technology and Clive Buckberry, Principal Engineer, Applied Optics, Rover Gaydon for their technical assistance with respect to the use of SLA models for Design and Flow analysis. The authors would also like to thank Valeo Limited for their cooperation in obtaining photographs of the SLA heater unit and motor housing.

Figure 1 Stereolithography facility at Rover, Canley

Figure 2 SLA model of a heater unit motor cover

Figure 3 Vacuum casting unit at Rover Canley

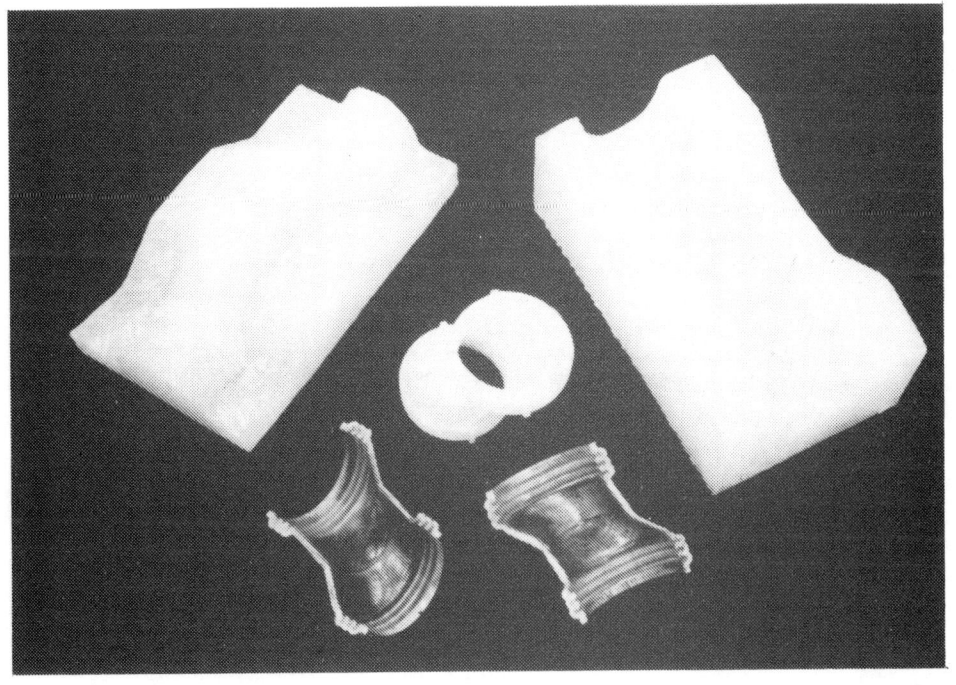

Figure 4 SLA model, silicone mould and cast resin model

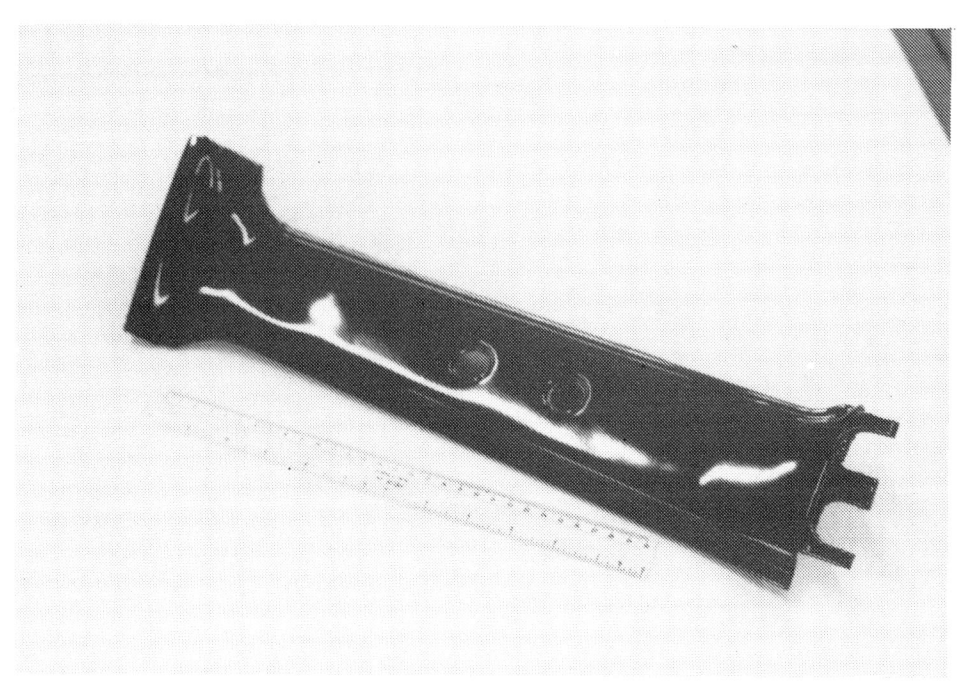

Figure 5   SLA model of 'B' post finisher, showing highly polished finish achieved by surface treatment

Figure 6   Flexible pipe, cast from silicone mould and the original SLA model

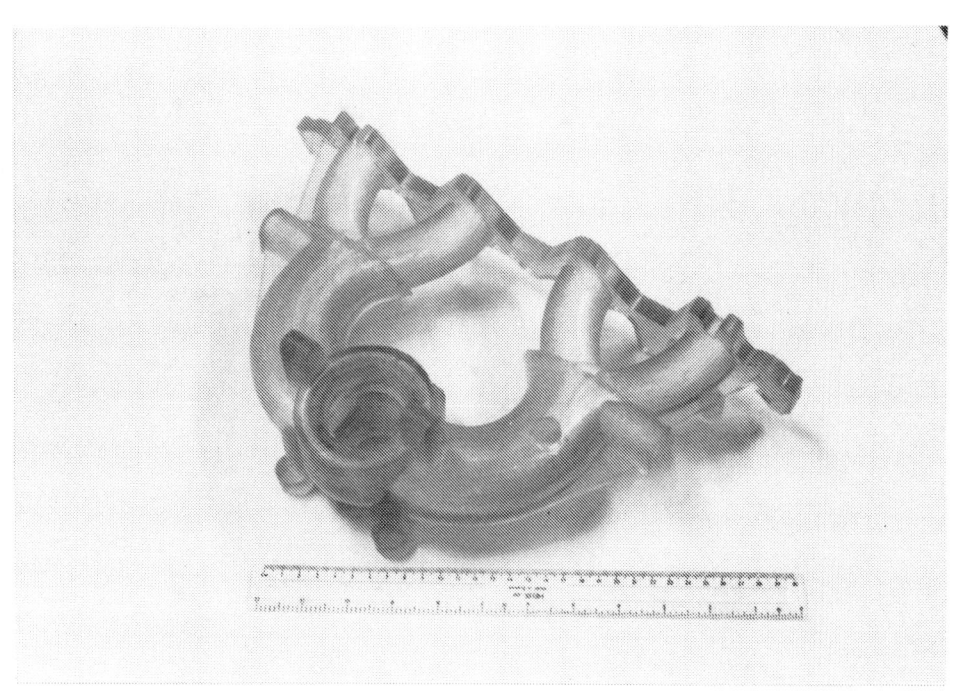

Figure 7 SLA model of an automotive inlet manifold

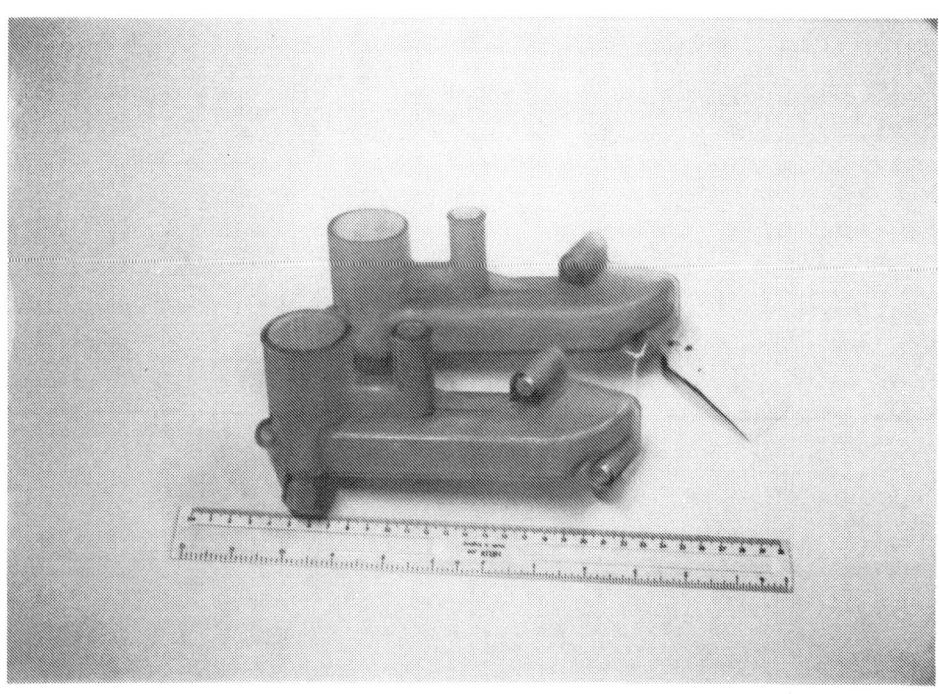

Figure 8 Water elbow for flow analysis, cast in high temperature resin (top) and original SLA model

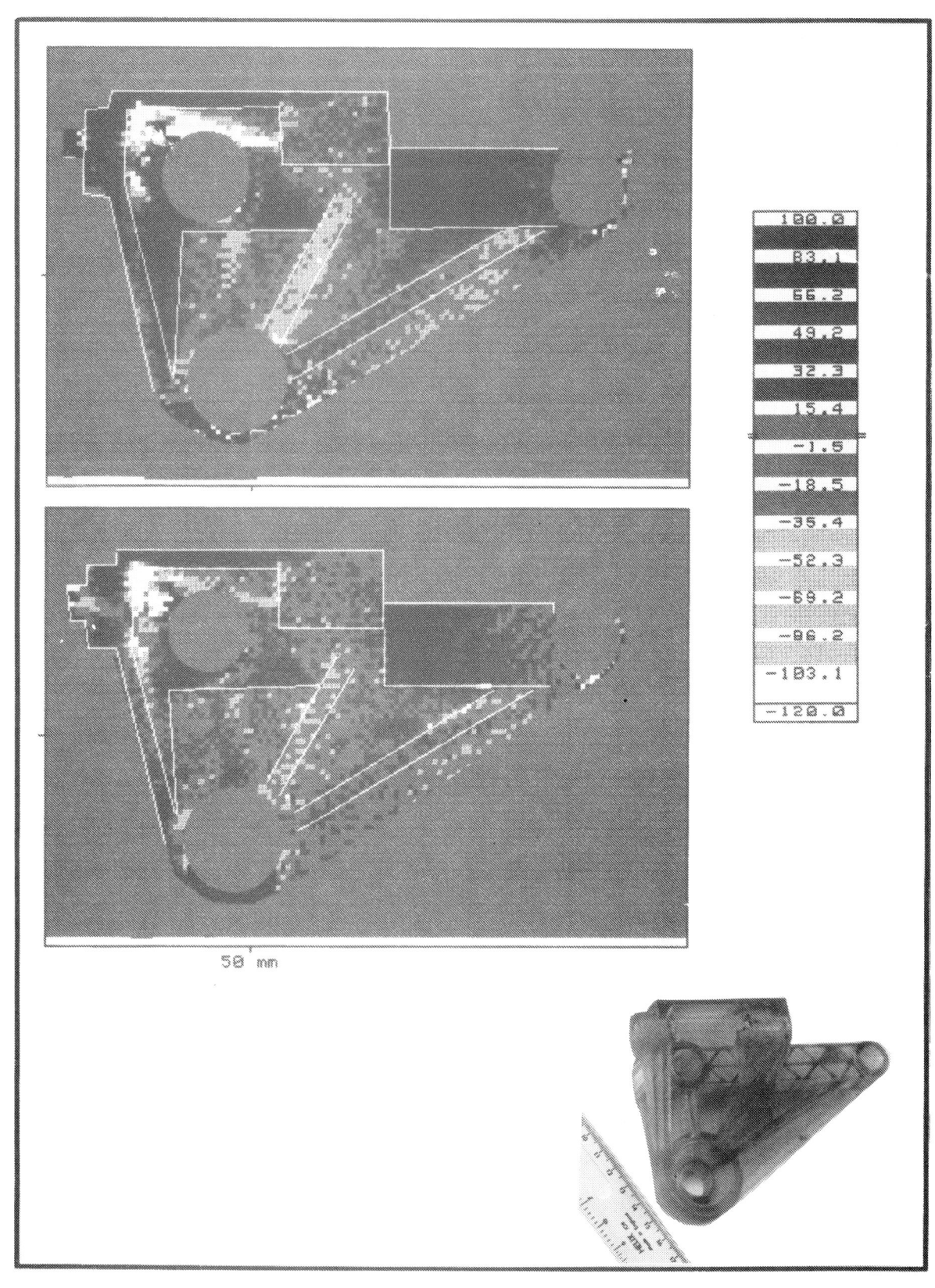

Figure 9 SPATE analysis of an SLA model (top) and actual component showing a correlation in the stress pattern. The component analysed is an alternator bracket (SLA model is shown inset).

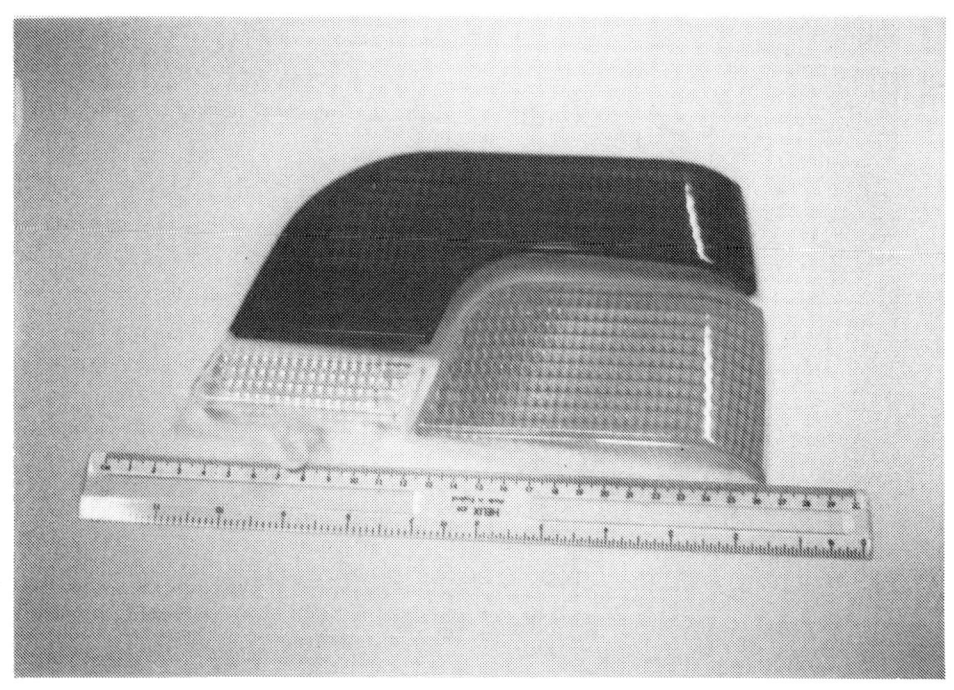

Figure 10 Light cluster lenses, vacuum cast from silicone mould

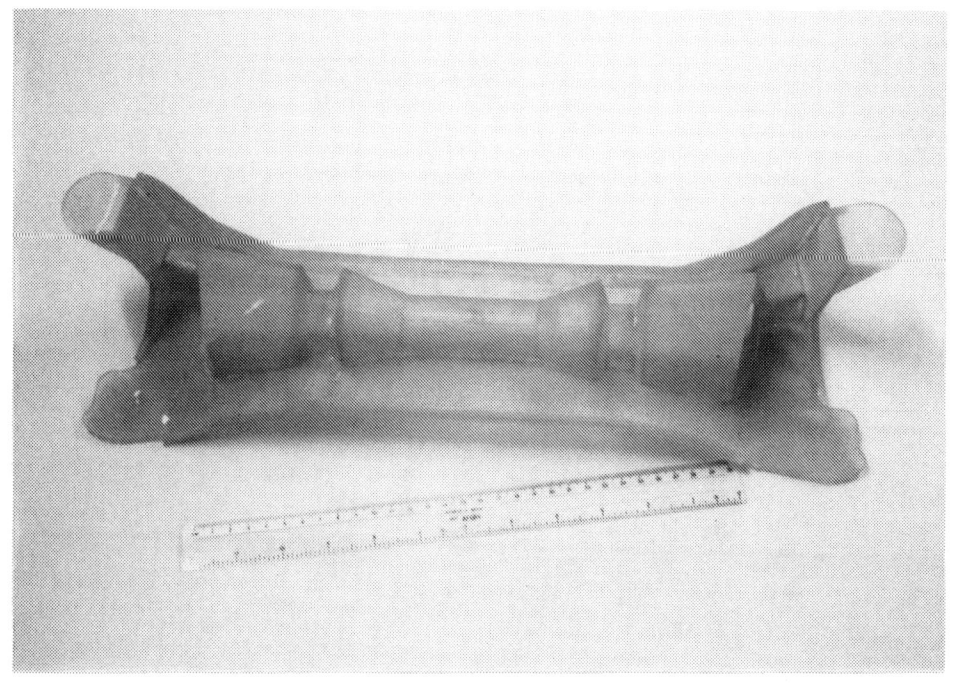

Figure 11 Half scale model of an automotive subframe

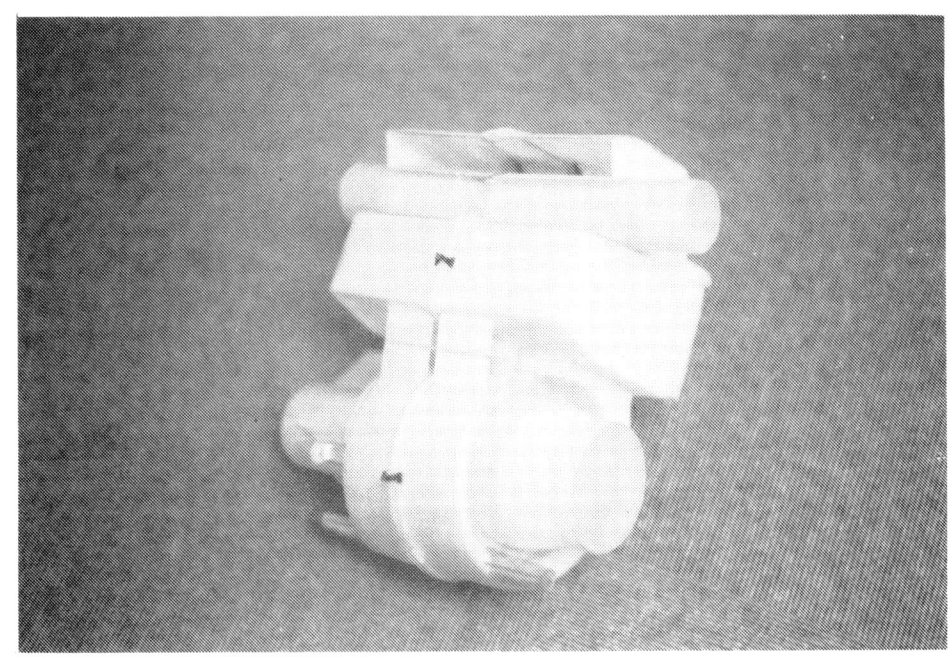

Figure 12 SLA model of a heater unit assembled from several individual sections

Figure 13 100 tonne compression moulding press

Figure 14 200 tonne injection moulding machine (top left)
RIM press and injection unit (bottom right)

STEREOLITHOGRAPHY TOOLING

Dr P M Dickens and Mr P Smith

University of Nottingham
Nottingham, UK

1 Introduction

Manufacturers are striving to reduce the lead time from concept to product launch and so the areas of Design, Prototype production, Testing, Tooling manufacture and Manufacturing efficiency are constantly under review.

Rapid Prototyping is therefore very useful in this process, because it is not just a group of new model making techniques but also a new industrial philosophy. In the majority of industry, designers have become used to waiting weeks or months for their designs to be changed into prototypes which can then be checked and tested, manufacturing engineers also wait considerable periods for tooling to be produced before they can start full scale manufacture.

With the advent of Rapid Prototyping designers can now have a prototype in a few days instead of waiting weeks or months. These models are used for checking the aesthetics of a design and to check form and fit. Some functional testing of these models is possible where there are no severe mechanical stresses and where the working temperatures are low. The major limitation with Rapid Prototyping at the moment is the limited number of materials available with the different systems and the generally poor mechanical properties of these. However, more materials are being introduced, and the choice of Stereolithography resins for example has grown so that now we have resins which provide snap fit parts or elastomeric type parts.

This change in expectation of the waiting time is now becoming more widespread amongst manufacturing engineers and so there is a demand to reduce the time from concept design to manufacture down to a few weeks. This has been possible for many years in some areas with the use of 'soft' tooling, using sprayed metal tooling, resin tooling, plaster cast moulds etc. Although 'soft' tooling can produce many thousands of parts using injection moulding, provided the moulds are plated and treated with respect, it is not suitable for more severe processes such as forging.

It is therefore necessary to investigate how Rapid Prototyping can be used to produce hard tooling.

2 Rapid Prototype Tooling

Apart from the more traditional methods of tooling manufacture (1) there are a number of existing techniques being used to produce 'Hard' tooling with Rapid Prototype models.

The Hausermann Abrading process, developed by Addison of Illinois in the USA, moulds a mixture of resin and 220 grit silicon carbide over a model and then this abrasive negative is used to abrasively machine a graphite electrode which can then be used for Electrical Discharge Machining (EDM) (2).

The 3M Tartan Tooling process can produce moulds for plastics production using sintered powders. An epoxy negative is cast around a model and then a mixture of tool steel, copper and tin powders is moulded within this negative. After sintering the powder mould, it can be used directly in production. The copper and tin powders probably alloy to give a bronze/tool steel matrix (3).

Now that it is possible to produce complicated models very quickly, the technique of producing EDM electrodes by moulding a graphite/resin mixture around a model may be worthy of further investigation, despite the high electrode wear.

The above techniques still require considerable time to produce either the electrode for EDM or the tooling itself. As electrode manufacture can account for up to 50% of the cost of Electrical Discharge Machining (4) it was decided to investigate the possibility of copper plating Stereolithography parts to manufacture electrodes.

3   Stereolithography Electrodes

Toolmakers have successfully produced EDM electrodes by copper plating plastic products and The Danish Technological institute (DTI) are also known to be attempting to use Stereolithography electrodes (5).

There are a number of methods available to coat a plastic part with metal such as sputtering, which is often used to provide a very thin coating of gold on no-metallic objects for analyses in a Scanning Electron Microscope. However, this process does not provide a metal layer which would be thick enough to manufacture an electrode and it is difficult to coat parts which may have features shadowing each other.

It is possible to metal spray a coating but it is virtually impossible to obtain a uniform thickness with this process, specially on complicated surfaces.

Electroless plating (6) appeared to be the most promising method of providing the copper layer as this gives a uniform thickness which can have a high gloss finish.

If greater thickness of copper was required it was decided that the electroless copper plated part would then be electroplated.

3.1   Electrode Preparation

A Stereolithography part manufactured by Texas Instruments was chosen as it was small and shallow but contained fine surface features. At the time the particular resin type was not known. This part was mounted onto a copper tube using a commercial epoxy resin and then electroless plated with a 5 micron thick layer of copper (See Figure 1) by an outside company.

An AGIE Electrical Discharge Machine was set up to erode a disk of Special K tool steel (BS 4659 BD3; AISI D3; WKSTOFF 2080) (7) using the following settings.

Voltage	100 volts
Amperage	5.6 amps
Time on (spark)	130 micro seconds
Time off (spark)	130 micro seconds

These settings were chosen to give minimum wear on the electrode but at these values the process was unstable and provided little erosion.

The settings were then changed to:-

Voltage	200 volts
Amperage	10.8 amps
Time on (spark)	240 micro seconds
Time off (spark)	240 micro seconds

These settings produced erosion of the tool steel as can be seen in Figure 2 but after a short while the process again became unstable and on investigation the surface of the copper was seen to have started to break up (See Figure 3).

After arrival of the resin details it soon became apparent why the surface had deteriorated. The resin used was Desolite SLR 805 produced by DSM Desotech Inc.
This resin is generally used for investment casting as it starts to soften at 45 degrees centigrade and then degas to aid the burn out procedure from the ceramic shell (8).

The temperatures produced by the sparks during the erosion process are greatly in excess of this and so heat the dielectric between the electrode and the workpiece. It is therefore quite easy for dielectric temperatures in excess of 45 degrees centigrade to be reached.

Further Stereolithography parts were obtained in Ciba Geigy 5081-1 which has a Glass Transition Temperature of 130-150 degrees centigrade (9) and electroless copper plated as before. The electrode was again set up this time with an aluminium disc to give lower electrode wear with the following settings:-

Voltage	100 volts
Amperage	8.3 amps
Time on (spark)	180 micro seconds
Time off (spark)	180 micro seconds

This part did not erode with these settings and it was suspected that the electrical conductivity around the coating was not sufficient. The settings were then changed to give a much higher current:-

Voltage	100 volts
Amperage	37.1 amps
Time on (spark)	42 micro seconds
Time off (spark)	75 micro seconds

This higher current did give erosion of the aluminium but also led to damage of the electrode as can be seen in Figure 4. Subsequent measurement of the copper layer showed it to be only 1 or 2 microns thick.

It was then decided to increase the thickness of the copper layer, adding more material by electroplating which increased the copper thickness to 20 microns.

The electrode was again set up using the settings:-

Voltage	100 volts
Amperage	8.3 amps
Time on (spark)	180 micro seconds
Time off (spark)	130 micro seconds

As there was a plating defect at one corner of the logo the electrode was offset. This electrode was able to machine the aluminium blank at the standard cutting speed for a copper electrode. Unfortunately, some bubbles had occurred beneath the copper during the plating process and one of these led to a defect which prevented the electrode from continuing to full depth. The smooth finish was achieved by reducing the current to 2.4 amps (See Figure 5).

4   Conclusions

This work has shown that it is possible to copper plate Stereolithography parts and then use them as electrodes for Electrical Discharge Machining. Similar machining times can be obtained to those achieved when using a solid copper electrode. However, the process of electroless plating followed by electroplating is time consuming and so is not particularly suitable for the philosophy of Rapid Prototype tooling. A simpler process is required for producing a thin copper layer of 10 - 20 microns on Stereolithography parts and so this will be pursued in the near future at Nottingham.

References

1. Milton, R., 1989, "Contract Shop Expands EDM's Role", Modern Machine Shop.

2. Anon, April 1992, "Complex Moulds Abraded", Metalworking Production, p78.

3. Terchek, R.L., April 1990, "Composite Mold Materials Muscle Into IM Applications", Plastics Engineering, pp55-57.

4. Juggi, H., 1985, "EDM Electrodes : Copper, Tungsten - or Both", Modern Machine Shop.

5. Meiritz, B.,Brite-EuRam project No. BREU-0157, started June 1990. Danish Technological Institute, Production technology, Teknologiparken, DK-8000 Aarhus C, Denmark.

6. W Canning PLC, Surface Finishing Technology, The Canning Handbook.

7. George H. Cook & Co. Ltd., Corporation Street, Sheffield, Company Data Sheet on Special K - Cold Work Tool Steel.

8. DSM Desotech Inc. Data Sheet on SLR 805, November 1, 1990.

9. 3D Systems Inc. Data Sheet on Stereolithography Resins, 7/91.

Figure 1   Electroless plated TI Logo in Desolite SLR 805.

Figure 2   Tool steel blank showing eroded area.

Figure 3   Electroless plated TI Logo showing the copper plate breaking up.

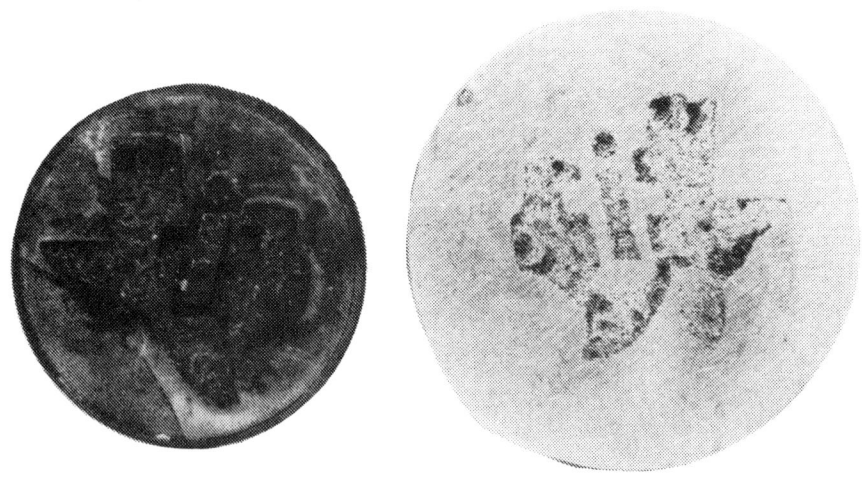

Figure 4   Electroless plated TI Logo in Ciba-Geigy 5081-1 and aluminium blank.

316

Figure 5   Electroplated TI Logo in Ciba-Geigy 5081-1 and eroded blank.